THE POLITICS

OF INSANITY

HUGO N. GERSTL

THE POLITICS
OF INSANITY

HUGO N. GERSTL

SAMUEL WACHTMAN'S SONS | DEKEL PUBLISHING HOUSE

THE POLITICS OF INSANITY

HUGO N. GERSTL

Copyright © 2016

Dekel Publishing House
www.dekelpublishing.com

North American rights by
Samuel Wachtman's Sons, Inc.
978-1-941905-04-3

Editor: Pnina Ophir

Cover image
Bald eagle portrait © Stephen Mcsweeny / Dreamstime.com

Design and typesetting by

For information contact:

Dekel Publishing House
P.O. Box 45094, Tel Aviv
6145002, ISRAEL
Tel: +972 3506-3235
Fax: +972 3506-7332
Email: info@dekelpublishing.com

Samuel Wachtman's Sons, Inc.
2460 Garden Road, Suite C
Monterey, CA 93940, U.S.A.
Tel: 831 649-0669
Fax: 831 649-8007
Email: samuelwachtman@gmail.com

The hatred stirred up by politics
does what hatred always does:
It breeds hatred in return.

Truth seldom flourishes in
an atmosphere of politics or emotion.

By the same author:

Fiction

The Wrecking Crew

Arcade

Assassin

Legacy

Against All Odds

Billy Jenkins

Amazing Grace

Scribe

Misfire

Standoff

Nonfiction

The Politics of Insanity -2016

The Politics of Hate - 2012

How to Cut Your Legal Bills In Half

The Pets Welcome™ Series

TABLE OF CONTENTS

FOREWORD

CAN WE EVER HAVE
A _UNITED_ STATES OF AMERICA AGAIN?

In 2012, in *The Politics of Hate*, I lamented the fracture of the old political system where Democrats, Republicans, and even the occasional third party candidate had worked together to make representative democracy work in America. In 1994, Newt Gingrich's so-called "Contract With America," set out to systematically destroy the old talk-it-out world of compromise which had ensured that civility would lead to forward movement, the passage of necessary laws, and a positive, constructive society.

From that time forward, the entire world of politics in America endured a "sea change" – a terribly unfortunate one, which pervades politics to this day. Now it has become each [party] [politician] [special interest] for itself. "Compromise" has become a symbol of weakness, of defeatism. It is "un-American." If you hold firm beliefs, you fight to push through those beliefs, even at the expense of propelling the country into gridlock.

In 2008, we elected the first Black president in our history. Through two terms, his opponents systematically tried to destroy him, not because he didn't have good ideas, but because in the rarified halls of vested power, without using the "N" word, they would make sure (nod, nod, wink, wink) that this Uppity N*gg*r went back to where he belonged. The Grand Old Party, the Republicans, were hijacked by the "Tea Party" in 2012. By 2016, things have morphed into utter insanity. Moderation and responsible conservatism has gone the way of the Dodo bird. It's become an infringement on our "right" to believe in and to act on every conceivable crackpot idea and to force it down the throats of our unwilling compatriots.

President Obama's increasingly meaningless statement, "We are not 'red states' or 'blue states,' we are the United States of America," rings more hollow with each passing day.

By December 21, 2015, the shortest day of the year, America had descended to a nadir in politics when billionaire industrialist and reality TV superstar Donald Trump, whom then-Democratic Presidential Candidate Martin O'Malley described as an "anti-immigration carnival barker," commented on the Democratic Party debate of a few nights earlier. When candidate Hillary Clinton was delayed in returning to the stage because she had to wait in line to go to the ladies' room to relieve herself. Trump, ever the model of civility and class, said,

> "You know why she didn't get back to the stage on time? I'll tell you … it was *disgusting*, absolutely *disgusting,* so disgusting I don't even want to talk about it. Of course she's the same Hillary Clinton that got *shlonged** by Obama in the last election."

> (**Schlonged* is an obscene reference to the male gender symbol, crudely related to "prick" and this statement was an obvious put-down to Clinton's equality for both sexes platform, hinting that had she gone to men's restroom and simply sat in a stall and done what she had to do, she would have been back on stage earlier, but the

fact that she insisted on using a toilet reserved for women was somehow proof that she considered herself above condescending to use the men's room).

What is even more obscene is that as we head into the final stage of the 2016 Presidential elections, Mister Trump, the Republican candidate who defeated all 17 Republican presidential candidates by a comfortable margin, is running neck and neck with Hillary Clinton, the Democratic nominee. This is the same Donald Trump, whose statements of dubious "wisdom" include:

- Deny *any* Muslim admission to the United States. Later, he amended that statement by saying, "Temporarily, until our representatives can figure out how to solve this situation."

- Throw out all illegal Mexican immigrants. Drive them down to the border, dump them on the Mexican side, and build a wall around the southern perimeter of the United States – and make Mexico pay for it!

- In referring to a female rival Republican presidential candidate he asked a crowd, "Tell me, would you really want to call that the face of your President?"

- "I love Blacks. I have always done well in the Black community. Some of my best friends are Blacks."

- In October 2015, he stated, "I'm a Presbyterian." In November 2015, he stated, "I'm a Presbyterian." In December 2015, when it appeared that Fundamentalist Evangelical Christians were forging ahead in the polls, he said, "I'm an Evangelical Christian."

- Trump challenged Barack Obama to prove that he was born in the United States – and continued to maintain that the birth certificate showing that the President had been born in Hawaii could easily have been forged until September, in a one sentence note, with not the slightest hint of apology, Trump said, "President Obama was born in the United States."

And yet, with each increasingly offensive and incendiary statement "the Donald" makes, his polling numbers among his core constituents surge. "Mainstream" Republican Party leaders cringed in shock. "Someone that outlandish could *never* win in America." Much the same was said about Hitler in 1932.

* * *

The separation of Church and State, originally meant not to keep the *Church* safe from the *State*, but to keep the *State* safe from the *Church,* has become more tenuous than ever. Protestant Christian Fundamentalists believe in absolute terms that America is first and foremost a *Christian* nation, more than that, a *Fundamentalist Christian* nation. And what the hell are we doing with a (N*g*er) President whose name is Barack *Hussein* Obama? Religion has pushed its way to the forefront in the schools, in rock concerts *and in politics,* provided it's White Anglo-Saxon Protestant Christianity.

* * *

With the rise of the Islamic State of Iraq and the Levant (ISIL), equally often called the Islamic State of Iraq and Syria (ISIS), the United States of America, nearly 325,000,000 strong, has gone berserk. Many of our compatriots believe that Armageddon is moments away because 18 people were killed in San Bernardino, California by two "terrorists" who were "inspired" by ISIS (meaning they were never really members of that group, but they "could have been" ISIS sympathizers).

Others wonder, with 325,000,000 people in the U.S., how come we seem to have chosen two of the worst candidates imaginable?

* * *

On February 13, 2016, another fracture of democracy-destroying proportions took place. There has been hell to pay and that will continue until well after the elections. The United States Supreme Court, the third and perhaps most powerful arm of American government (the others being the Legislative and Executive Branches), has been staunchly conservative for the past forty years. Today the balance in the High Court is razor thin, ideologically four to four. The conservative element of the Court consisted of Chief Justice John Roberts (61, Roman Catholic, Caucasian, appointed by George S. Bush, Republican); Clarence Thomas (67, Roman Catholic, African-American, appointed by George H.W. Bush, Republican); Samuel Alito (65, Roman Catholic, Caucasian, appointed by George W. Bush), and, until February 13, 2016, Antonin Scalia (79, Roman Catholic, Caucasian, appointed by Ronald Reagan, Republican), unquestionably the *primer inter pares* of the conservative contingent.

The liberal wing presently consists of Ruth Bader Ginsburg (82, Jewish, Caucasian, appointed by Bill Clinton); Stephen Breyer (78, Jewish, appointed by Bill Clinton); Sonia Sotomayor (61, Roman Catholic, Latino, appointed by Barack Obama, Democrat); and Elena Kagan (55, Jewish, Caucasian, appointed by Barack Obama).

The "conscience of the Court" and by far the most influential Justice and tiebreaker, Anthony Kennedy (79, Roman Catholic, Caucasian) was appointed by Ronald Reagan. Significantly, Kennedy was appointed during Reagan's final year in office, when the Republican icon was a "lame duck" president, just as Barack Obama was called a "lame duck" president in 2016.

What a difference a generation makes! Justice Kennedy's nomination came after Reagan's failed nominations of Robert Bork, who was nominated in July 1987, but rejected by the Senate on October 23; and Douglas Ginsburg, who withdrew his name from consideration after admitting to marijuana. Kennedy was subjected to an unprecedentedly thorough investigation of his background, which he easily passed by a bipartisan vote. Justice Kennedy has been the moderate and the swing vote in virtually every 5-4 decision in the past decade.

But today's rules have changed, much to the disgrace of American democracy.

The day after Scalia's death in 2016, the Republicans, who controlled the Senate, announced that they would approve *no one* as long as Obama was president. In fact, they bragged that any nomination would not even get out of Committee. Riding a wave of their increasingly Reactionary base, Republicans had wrested control of the Senate in 2014.

The appointment and confirmation of Justices to the Supreme Court of the United States involves several steps set forth by the United States Constitution, which have been further refined and developed by decades of tradition. Candidates are nominated by the President of the United States and must face a series of hearings in which both the nominee and other witnesses make statements and answer questions before the Senate Judiciary Committee, which can vote to send the nomination to the full United States Senate. Confirmation by the Senate allows the President to formally appoint the candidate to the court.

Before 1981, the approval process of Justices was usually rapid. From the Truman through Nixon administrations, Justices were typically approved within one month after their nomination. From the Reagan administration to the present, however, the process has taken much longer. The average number of days from nomination to final Senate vote since 1975 has been 70 days. The politicization of the process has come into sharp focus today.

Confirmation requires a majority vote of the Senate. The Senate consists of 100 senators, two from each state. As of October 2016, the Republicans, with 54 senators, control the Senate and thus the confirmation process. In the 2016 elections, there are 34 Senate seats up for grabs. Of these, 10 are hotly contested, too close to call.

In a "double down" political ploy, current President Obama nominated Merrick Garland, 63 and Jewish, to fill the empty seat which arose after Scalia's death. This presents an "impossible" conundrum for reticent Republican Senators: Garland is a highly respected *moderate* judge, widely respected as the Chief Judge of the United States Court of Appeals for the Federal Circuit, second only to the United States Supreme Court in power and prestige.

Under the United States Constitution, President Obama did exactly what he was supposed to do. He was elected as President for a full four-year term, *not* for a 3¼ -year term. President Reagan, whom the Republican Party appears to have worshipped since 1980, nominated Justice Kennedy during his last year in office. Justice Merrick was approved by a bipartisan vote in the Senate during his confirmation to the Court of Appeals. The Republicans became obstructionists to the very Constitution in which they wrapped themselves. This creates a potential disaster for the Republicans which they choose to ignore – they don't see it and they don't *want* to see it:

1. The Democrats will go all out to demonstrate that the Republicans are complete Constitutional hypocrites.

2. There is a likelihood that the Democrats will oust the Republican Senatorial candidates engaged in the most hotly contested contests, thus regaining control of the Senate; and

3. When and if that occurs, and if the Democrats elect Hillary Clinton as President of the United States, she will most likely nominate someone much younger and far more liberal than Merrick Garland. A Democratic President for the next 4-8 years would most likely have at least two more appointments, given Ginsburg's age and ill-health and Breyer's age, and then the Supreme Court would have a truly liberal majority for the next twenty-five years!

So the Republican Party, which in its present incarnation seems to have been taken prisoner by the right wing extremists of that Party, has dramatically increased the stakes to the extent that they may be facing their worst drubbing since Barry Goldwater lost the election in 1964, and might even relegate the once-proud, responsible Conservative "Grand Old Party" to a perennial "opposition" political movement.

* * *

Politicians seem to think no farther than getting themselves elected or re-elected. The communications *mavens* sold a lot more advertising when Donald Trump sucked all the air out of the room, so that when any other Republican primary Presidential candidate spoke responsible, commonsense ideas that could be embraced by all of us, they seemed to fade into the woodwork. In media parlance, "Money talks, bullsh*t walks."

It was true when I wrote *The Politics of Hate* in 2012, and it is as true today: whether your initials are NBC, CBS, ABC, CNN, MSNBC, or FOX, that the media moguls want nothing more than to secure million dollar media deals. After all, their media empires thrive on sheer power and unlimited money from advertising revenues built on the backs of those who spend their hard-earned money on Budweiser, Chevrolets, and Exxon-Mobil, Insurance Companies, and, most of all, pharmaceutical houses peddling everything from erectile dysfunction-erasing aphrodisiacs (Cialis, Viagra- $11-to-$25 a pill if you buy it in the U.S., 43 cents if you buy the exact same formula outside the U.S. and get it shipped in via the U.S. Postal Service), to nostrums guaranteed to cure various forms of cancer, diabetes, heart problems, and hepatitis-C.

The lure of $100,000 in lecture fees is a powerful aphrodisiac. The lure of power, the adulation, the cheers are an even greater aphrodisiac. Politicians, fearmongers, "talking heads," and captains of industry revel in their fame, their glory, and their self-styled wisdom, when the country is in greater debt than any nation in history, and we are slipping faster and faster into becoming a third world nation each year.

If the public starts putting two and two together and the answer comes out "four," you won't be able to dazzle them with your brilliance or baffle them with your bulls**t anymore. But so far, the "average" American can still be led to believe that 2+2 equals whatever number the spin masters want to make it. Attach "cold war" epithet names to sound fiscal and social policies. Speak louder than the other guy and roll in stinkier dirt, even if you're using more of the same old scare tactics, tactics which have already propelled our country into being the largest, most muscular laughing stock in the world.

What is even worse, more than 40% of Americans continue to buy into the politics of insanity without stopping for even a moment to consider exactly what these political hatemongers are offering in exchange for turning one faction out and securing the benefits of power for themselves. Memories are short. Fear is bewitching. Its sound bites are shorter and it sells far more easily than hope.

But it would be simplistic and naïve to blame either of the two major parties for trying to unseat the other party. What happened in 2014 was what has so often happened in our political history. The Democrats swept in on a wave of "Change You Can Believe In!" in 2008. *They had the votes necessary to swiftly and decisively pass a series of programs which could greatly have benefited our nation.* After all, they had effectively campaigned on a platform that Republicans had stonewalled, blockaded, and ruined our economy.

Instead of delivering a *fait accompli* and then promoting it to the public by showing *specifically how their program would benefit us all,* the Democrats became embroiled in what Democrats are historically so successful at doing: splintering, backbiting, cannibalizing their own, and *finally, after the populace was disgusted and confused, and after the Republicans had had all the time they needed to publicize how the Democrats were back to their old "tax and spend" ways,* the Democratically-controlled Congress passed a watered-down healthcare bill (which Republicans immediately derided as "ObamaCare") which no one understood. The Republican minority convinced the American people that the Democrats were "out of touch with mainstream America," and that we should "turn out this do-nothing Congress."

And that's exactly what happened! The Democrats once again shot themselves in their collective feet. They got thrown out *and they deserved to get thrown out*!

But until he ultimately lost the primary election to Hillary Clinton in May 2016, there was one voice in the wilderness. A virtually unknown 74-year-old Jewish Socialist from New York

City, one of only two United States Senators who was registered as neither Democrat nor Republican, but "Independent," who spoke with such a strongly stereotyped Brooklynese accent that you could "cut it with a knife," was delivering a serious message that resonated with younger Americans. "It's time to break the stranglehold of ½ of 1% of the billionaire population, which controls the financial fortunes of the rest of us." While it seemed that Bernie Sanders and his message was doomed to oblivion in the general election, and more people than not said, "It can't be done," a few people, then a few more, then millions more started to *think*.

But there were *wild* voices as well. Scary voices. Voices that seemed to command an even larger audience. Voices whose populist message, "We're mad as hell and we're not going to take it anymore!" convinced a hefty portion of our citizenry, fundamentalist Christians, disaffected, largely undereducated, under-employed , *angry* people from every fringe of the political spectrum, that they could change the fabric of Washington, the evil "insiders," by voting for those voices that appealed to our worst nature.

Whether the message came from the fringe "left," like Bernie Sanders, or the fringe "right" like Ted Cruz, the common thread was one of disgust with the status quo and a demand for change. But while the insanity of the current political season has sold more advertising than the media ever dreamed possible, and while it has, perhaps, been far more entertaining and has made the self-described most powerful nation on earth either a laughingstock among nations or, worse, a nation whose values seem to have descended into craziness, the truth of the matter is that the true strength of the United States lies not only in its diversity but in the historical fact that we are, at core, a *centrist* society, a stable ship of state which does not list too far to the right or to the left; and no matter how shrill the voices of fear, hate, and even hope, there will *not* be a revolution of the fringes and change will neither come swiftly nor dramatically.

While the Democrats have suffered a rude, hard, perhaps well-deserved slap in the face, the dancing-in-the-streets celebration of the Republicans is premature. No one ever won a campaign by overestimating the intelligence of the American voting public. The way the President and Congress are now aligned, no dramatic changes occurred during the 2014-2016 Congressional session. It's gridlock once again. The Republicans did not pass *their* program – whatever that undisclosed program was – and as the Presidential election nears, three things have become increasingly obvious:

1. The economy *is* demonstrably better, not because one party or the other is in power, but simply because the economy has always been cyclical.

2. The Republicans have, for the first time in memory, failed to "hang together." They splintered among their own, while each primary contender *re*-invented himself in a far more conservative image.

3. Veer too far to the right or too far to the left, and you will easily capture the vocal *minority.* But vocal or not, it will still be a *minority* and in order to get elected in a two-person race, you have to win *more than* 50% of the electorate.

As former President Bill Clinton candidly pointed out, "It's the economy, stupid."

Regardless of political infighting or outfighting, what we are doing is akin to two fleas fighting over which one owns the dog. We seem not to realize that we have run out of time and money; that we no longer have the luxury of political gamesmanship and needless, stupid bickering. There is more hatred in the world today than there was four years ago. More people, less resources, and what most scientists see as a critical worldwide problem, global warming, which is decried by the most conservative factions as "fiction." There's a new worldwide terrorist phenomenon – ISIS or ISIL, depending on what day of the week it is and what politician is talking.

The media pundits who so powerfully directed public opinion four years ago have now started to question their own wisdom in light of the Trump phenomenon and the Bernie Sanders Revolution. As of September 20, 2016, 51% of Democrats say they trust the media, 30% of so-called Independents trust the media, and only 14% of Republicans trust the media. Many years ago, I saw the movie *On the Beach*, based on the Neville Shute novel. In that movie, man's desire to dominate other men resulted in a nuclear holocaust that ultimately destroyed the entire world. Just before the end of the movie, the camera panned onto a group of do-gooders carrying signs that read, "There's still time, Brother!" At the very end of the movie, there were no more beings alive. The wind blew and the camera paused on a single sign with the words, "There's still time, Brother!" Given the political climate today, one must ask, "Is there still time? Is there still any sanity left?

INTRODUCTION

It has always seemed strange to me that when men or women run for public office, they always use the term *Fight*. "I will *fight* to lower your taxes!" "I will *fight* the other fellow's corrupt ways!" "I will make sure you have a *fighter* for you in [Congress / City Hall / the office of city dog catcher] whatever."

More than fifty years ago, I became a trial lawyer. The term *fight* surfaced more often than not. I somehow amassed a reputation as being a "pit bull," a "junkyard dog," and other, more colorful if less flattering names. It was a reputation I felt really wasn't *me*, but if that kind of reputation brought in business, I could live with it.

As the years passed, I started to wonder and I started to ask questions. Why was it necessary for a politician to say he or she would *fight*? Fight for *what*? Exactly what would a *fight* accomplish that working together – reasoning, compromising, and coming to agreement – would not accomplish easier, better, more efficiently, and cheaper? That was the premise of my book *How To Cut Your Legal Bills in Half*, which promoted mediation instead of ever-costlier court fights.

Think, for a moment: *Exactly what does a fight accomplish?* People get their emotions up. They feel they cannot compromise or they'll lose face, that they'll somehow be *less than* the other fellow. If one's opponent says, "Yes," then that person says "No" as a knee-jerk reaction, not because you will get anything done, but because you'll make sure the other guy doesn't get anything done *either. You* will have the dubious satisfaction of knowing you've blocked something your opponent wanted even if, in your calm, rational mind, you knew that the other fellow's proposal would move things forward; not admitting that if you compromised on this point, the other fellow might compromise on something *you* wanted and something could get done.

If you think I'm wrong, look at what's happened in the United States in the past two decades: gridlock, stagnation, inaction, and, finally, and, at one point, an economic recession the likes of which we hadn't seen since the Great Depression.

The Democrats, who came into the Obama years with a filibuster-proof majority, immediately started squabbling and fighting so they couldn't even pass legislation that should have been a "no brainer." Republicans raised their traditional "politics of fear" bogeyman to the ever shriller chastisements that the Democrats had totally gutted a perfectly sane medical system, embarrassed us in the international arena, and humiliated our reputation in every field; that Barack Obama was the worst President the United States had ever endured, and the only thing worse was Hillary Clinton's tenure as Secretary of State. "She ought not to be running for President, she ought to be in Federal prison!"

Unfortunately, those who revel in bah-humbugging the other party's proposed programs with outmoded epithets and claims of "Wait 'til we get into office. Have we got a program for you!" have not come forward with *one single positive idea about what they're going to do or how they're going to do it. Not one except,* "We're going to build a giant wall, a beautiful wall, between Mexico and the United States to keep the Mexicans out and we're going to make *Mexico* pay for it!" or "We're going to China to trade in accordance with *our* rules or we will stop trading with them and *that* will show them we mean business!"

This is truly ***The Politics of INSANITY.***

It doesn't have to be that way. If we all stopped fighting and stonewalling and blaming and dumping garbage on the other fellow, and learned to work *together* for the good of us *all*, just think what we could accomplish. *Trillions of dollars* spent on foreign wars, when all it takes is *one single terrorist* to escape the safety nets and come into the United States, could have been saved and spent on *roads, schools, healthcare, social programs, growing food, and paying off our debt – things that we need, not things that would make us temporarily feel more macho.*

You think cooperation won't work? Try telling that to the Chinese, who've *made* it work. Or to the Indians, whose economy continues to get better each year. Or to the French, who, according to the World Health Organization, have the world's best and most affordable system of delivering universal healthcare. All of these societies, who have learned to *cooperate and work together* rather than *fight*, are moving *up* on the indexes by which we measure quality of life, while we in the United States, who we believe to be the greatest, strongest, richest, most moral country on the face of the planet ("Yes, indeed, Our God is better than their god!") are, for some absolutely inexplicable reason, moving *down. Why? What are we doing wrong?*

* * *

Don't get me wrong. There's a time and a place for everything, including all-out competition. The Olympic Games are such a venue. High school football games are an appropriate place for such an outpouring of emotion. Even overpriced professional sports draw more spectators year after year as our overfed, under-exercised, increasingly obese men, women, and children live vicariously through sports heroes that are paid millions of dollars a year, while teachers, whose influence on tomorrow is surely more positive and tangible, struggle and work 100-hour weeks to bring home a modest income.

In the sports arena, there are rules which make the competition fair, controlled, and honorable. In football, "unsportsmanlike conduct" warrants a 15-yard penalty. Pass interference is punished by an automatic first down. In soccer, which is a very secondary sport in the United States, even though it's the most popular sport in the rest of the world, a deliberate act will get you a "red card." Not only are you ejected from the game, but your team has to play the remainder of the game with one less player than the other side.

It is only in the political arena where even the most dishonorable actions are acceptable, where lies are as plentiful and cheap as tap water, and where reputation-killing defamation is sloughed off as "politics as usual."

When was the last time you heard someone running for office say, "Vote *for* me because *I did* ..." rather than "Vote *against* the other fellow" or "Don't vote for so-and-so because *he* (or *she*) is ... [take your choice of negative images]." Does that really seem right to you? Shouldn't we be voting *for* an idea, a person, a proposal that makes sense rather than *against* someone because of completely unproved allegations thrown against someone's reputation?

Under Bill Clinton's presidency, our budget was balanced (indeed, we had a surplus), we were at peace, people were employed, and life was pretty damned good. Can you say that about our lives today? Simple question: Was the United States better off in 1999 than it is today? Was life better for *you*, easier for *you* 16 years ago than it is today?

"But," you say, "Bill Clinton was an immoral philanderer. How *dare* he do what he did with an aide and *lie* about it to the American people? He *deserved to be impeached and removed from office!*"

Oh, really? From 9 to 5, Bill Clinton did as good a job as anyone has ever done in the White House. While I don't justify his after-hours frolics, he was a damned good president. So was FDR, so was Eisenhower, and so was John F. Kennedy. Would anyone care to delve into *their* after-hours bedroom antics? Perhaps all the hypocritical moralists on both sides of the aisle might like to do a little research. Even better, perhaps the American bury-their-head-in-the-sand sheep, who follow honey-worded hypocrites might even want to open their eyes, their ears, and their *minds* by doing a little research themselves, instead of meekly accepting what the officeholder wannabe *du jour* wants them to hear.

A mind is a terrible thing to waste! *Yet that's just what 95% of us are doing. We are being led around by those who have not even a small percentage of the brains God gave us, who have the morals of a goat, and who are capable of talking "prettier" and spouting venomous attacks in such an attractive manner that we follow them blindly over the cliff.*

While it's so easy to trample on a dream or a good idea by saying, "That's so stupid it will never work," exactly *what have we got to lose by trying it out?* If it fails, we're in exactly in the same place we are now. And if it succeeds? What then?

WAKE UP, AMERICA!

PART ONE

HOW THE U.S. ELECTION

SYSTEM WORKS

1

HOW THE U.S. ELECTS ITS LEGISLATURE AND ITS CHIEF EXECUTIVE OFFICER, THE PRESIDENT; AND HOW THE SUPREME COURT JUSTICES ARE APPOINTED.

A. CONGRESS – THE LEGISLATIVE BRANCH

First, let's make sure we get this straight … despite the "urban legend" that the United States is the world's greatest *democracy*, it has never been, and never was intended to be, a democracy in the true sense of the word. If it was, there would simply be one person, one vote, and majority rules. 325,000,000 people would meet and vote in a *very* large room. But that's not the way it works. We have a representative government. In the *legislative* branch of our government, the population of the United States is made up of a Congress consisting of two houses. The upper house, the

29

Senate, consists of 100 *Senators*, two from each state, regardless of the population of the state, and the lower house, the House of Representatives, has 435 *Representatives*, which are based on the population of each state.

The United States of America consists of fifty states, each of which has its own Chief Executive, called the Governor, its Legislative Body which can be called by many names, and its own Judiciary. Some states are huge but have small populations. Alaska, for example, occupies 663,268 square miles but has a population of only 738,432. Rhode Island, by contrast, has an area of 1214 square miles and a population of 1,056,298. California (163,696 square miles) is the most populous state in the nation with a whopping 39,144,818 inhabitants, whereas Wyoming (97,000 square miles) is home to a miniscule 544,270 residents. The United States has a total population of 325,000,000, which means that approximately 1 out of every 8 people living in the United States resides in California. In a completely democratic society, Californians would have 72 votes for every vote coming assigned to Wyoming.

In the earliest days of our Republic, the least populous states felt they would have almost no power in Congress, and that states with more inhabitants would completely dominate the ability to make laws which would govern our country. On the other hand, the more heavily populated states felt that if each state had an equal number of Congressional members, the tail would wag the dog and the majority would be held hostage by the smaller states.

The solution was really quite elegant. The upper house, the Senate, would be based on absolute equality of representation among the states: California would have two Senators and Wyoming would have two Senators. The lower house, the House of Representatives, would be population-driven. For example, today California has 53 Representatives in the lower house and

Wyoming has 1 Representative. Since most laws require the approval of *both* houses, the balance has worked quite well.

This is all well and good for Congress, even though with its current atmosphere of gridlock, very little seems to get done.

B. ELECTION OF THE PRESIDENT – CHIEF OF THE EXECUTIVE BRANCH

The election of the President of the United States, the Chief of the <u>Executive</u> branch of government, is not by direct vote. The President is elected by a majority of a body called the <u>Electoral College</u>.

The Electoral College is a *process*, not a place. The process consists of the selection of electors, the meeting of the electors where they vote for President and Vice President, and the counting of the electoral votes by Congress. The Electoral College consists of 538 electors. *270 electoral votes are required to elect the President.* A state's entitled allotment of electors equals the number of members in its Congressional delegation: one for each member in the House of Representatives plus two for that state's Senators. For example, California has 53 Representatives and 2 Senators. It has 55 electoral votes. Wyoming, with 1 Representative and 2 Senators gets 3 electoral votes. The District of Columbia is allocated 3 electors.

Each candidate running for President in a given state has his or her own group of electors. The electors are generally chosen by the candidate's political party.

The presidential election is held every four years on the Tuesday after the first Monday in November. When a voter votes for a candidate, he or she is actually voting for the candidate's *electors*. Most, but not all, states have a "winner-take-all" system that awards all electors to the winning presidential candidate. Only Maine and Nebraska have a variation of "proportional representation."

After the presidential election, the state's governor prepares a "Certificate of Ascertainment" listing all of the candidates who ran for President in that state along with the names of their respective electors. The Certificate of Ascertainment also declares the winning presidential candidate in that state and shows which electors will represent the state at the meeting of the electors in December of the election year.

The meeting of the electors takes place on the first Monday after the second Wednesday in December after the presidential election. The electors meet in their respective states, where they cast their votes for President and Vice President on separate ballots. The state's electors' votes are recorded on a "Certificate of Vote," which is sent to the Congress and the National Archives as part of the official records of the presidential election.

Each state's electoral votes are counted in a joint session of Congress on the 6th of January in the year following the meeting of the electors. Members of the House and Senate meet in the House chamber to conduct the official tally of electoral votes. The Vice President, as President of the Senate, presides over the count and announces the results of the vote. The President of the Senate then declares which persons have been elected President and Vice President of the United States. The President-Elect takes the oath of office and is sworn in as President of the United States on January 20th in the year following the Presidential election.

But even before the Electoral College comes into play, each of the two major parties (and the lesser parties as well) has a *convention* where that party selects its *candidate* to run for President in the *general election*.

And that is what the Presidential primary season is all about.

C. APPOINTMENT OF SUPREME COURT JUSTICES

There are nine seats on the United States Supreme Court. Although the presiding Justice is called the Chief Justice, he or she has the same vote as every other Justice. Justices are not elected. They are appointed by the sitting President, subject to approval by a majority of the Senate. The appointment of each Justice is for life. As shown above, the present division in judicial temperament is 4 liberals, 3 conservatives (with Scalia's death and a vacancy), and 1 conservative-leaning moderate swing vote. If the Republicans win the Presidential election and maintain control of the Senate, they will undoubtedly appoint a conservative Justice to replace Antonin Scalia. If the Democrats win the Presidential election and regain control of the Senate, they will equally undoubtedly appoint a liberal justice.

Most critical, however, it is anticipated that in addition to the presently vacant seat which developed because of Scalia's death, at least 2 justices, both liberals, will retire and be replaced within the next 4-8 years.

D. THE PARTY COVENTION

A United States presidential nominating convention is a political convention held every four years by most of the political parties who will be fielding nominees in the upcoming U.S.

presidential election. The formal purpose of such a convention is to select the party's nominee for President, as well as to adopt a statement of party principles and goals known as the *platform,* and adopt the rules for the party's activities, including the presidential nominating process for the next election cycle. Due to changes in election laws, the primary and caucus calendar, and the manner in which political campaigns are run, conventions since the later half of the 20th century have virtually abdicated their original roles, and today are rarely more than ceremonial affairs.

Generally, usage of "presidential campaign nominating convention" refers to the two major parties' quadrennial events: the Democratic National Convention and the Republican National Convention. Some minor parties also select their nominees by convention. From the point of view of the parties, the convention cycle begins with the *Call to Convention,* usually issued about 18 months in advance. The Call is an invitation from the national party to the state and territory parties to convene to select a presidential nominee. It also sets out the number of delegates to be awarded to each, as well as the rules for the nomination process. The conventions are usually scheduled for four days of business. There is no rule dictating the order, but since 1956 the incumbent party has held its convention second. Since 1952, all major party conventions have been held in the months of July, August or early September.

In 1916, the Republican Convention was held in Cleveland, Ohio from July 18-21. The Democratic Convention took place in Philadelphia, Pennsylvania the following week. Each party sets its own rules for the participation and format of the convention.

The convention is typically held in a major city selected by the national party organization 18–24 months before the election is to be held. As the two major conventions have grown into large, publicized affairs with significant economic impact, cities today compete vigorously to be awarded host responsibilities, citing their meeting venues, lodging facilities, and entertainment as well as offering economic incentives.

During the day, party activists hold meetings and rallies, and work on the platform. Voting and important convention-wide addresses usually take place in the evening hours. In recent conventions, routine business such as examining the credentials of delegations, ratifying rules and procedures, election of convention officers, and adoption of the platform usually take up the business of the first two days of the convention. Balloting was usually held on the third day, with the nomination and acceptance made on the last day, but even some of these traditions have fallen away in 21st century conventions. The only constant is that the convention ends with the nominee's acceptance speech.

Each convention produces a statement of principles known as its *platform*, containing goals and proposals known as *planks*. Relatively little of a party platform is even proposed as public policy. Much of the language is generic, while other sections are narrowly written to appeal to factions or interest groups within the party. Unlike electoral manifestos in many European countries, the platform is not binding on either the party or the candidate.

Because it is ideological rather than pragmatic, however, the platform is sometimes itself politicized. For example, defenders of abortion rights lobbied heavily to remove the Human Life Amendment plank from the 1996 Republican National Convention platform, a move fiercely resisted by conservatives despite the fact that no such amendment had ever come up for debate.

Since the 1970s, voting has for the most part been perfunctory; the selection of the major parties' nominees have rarely been in doubt, so a single ballot has always been sufficient. Each delegation announces its vote tallies, usually accompanied with some boosterism of their state or territory. The delegation may pass, nominally to re-tally their delegates' preferences, but often to allow a different delegation to give the leading candidate the honor of casting the majority-making vote.

Before the presidential nomination season actually begins, there is often speculation about whether a single front runner would emerge. If there is no single candidate receiving a majority of delegates at the end of the primary season, a scenario called a *brokered convention* would result, where a candidate would be selected either at or near the convention, through political horse-trading and lesser candidates compelling their delegates to vote for one of the front runners. The closest to a brokered convention in recent years was at the 1976 Republican National Convention, when neither Gerald Ford nor Ronald Reagan received enough votes in the primary to lock up the nomination. Since then, candidates have received enough momentum to reach a majority through pledged and bound delegates before the date of the convention.

More recently, a customary practice has been for the losing candidates in the primary season to release their delegates and exhort them to vote for the winning nominee as a sign of party unity. Thus, the vote tallied on the floor is unanimous or nearly so. Some delegates may nevertheless choose to vote for their candidate.

The voting method at the conventions is a "rolling roll call of the states" (which includes territories). The states are called in alphabetical order (Alabama is first; Wyoming is last). The state's spokesperson can either choose to announce its delegate count or pass. Once all states have either declared or passed, those states which passed are called upon again to announce their delegate count.

The organizers of the convention may designate one of these speeches as the keynote address, one which above all others is stated to underscore the convention's themes or political goals.

The 2004 Democratic National Convention featured Senator Barack Obama, whose speech brought the future President national recognition for the first time.

The final day of the convention usually features the formal acceptance speeches from the nominees for President and Vice President.

E. STRATEGIES TO WIN THE PRESIDENCY

A candidate needs 270 electoral votes to be elected President. In the four most recent elections the popular vote and the Electoral College vote were as follows:

Year	Democrats	Republicans	
2000	48.3% - 266	47.8% - **271**	**- Bush**
2004	48.1% - 251	50.6% - **286**	**- Bush**
2008	53.8% - **365**	46.2% - 173	**- Obama**
2012	51.9% - **332**	48.1% - 206	**- Obama**

This shows that the actual popular vote is not necessarily tied to the Electoral College vote. The Electoral College vote, which is state-by-state, is the only vote that counts.

Using the last several presidential elections as indicators, 18 states are Democratic safeholds and 23 states are almost certain to vote Republican. However, while the Republicans control more states by number, the Democrats appear to predominate in electoral votes. The 2012 vote was as follows. 9 states, "tossup states" are the most critical in all recent elections. Those marked with an asterisk (*) voted Democrat in 2012.

2012 ELECTION

Democrats	Republicans	Tossup States
California – 55 electoral votes	Texas – 38	*Ohio - 18
New York – 29	Georgia – 16	*Pennsylvania – 20
Illinois – 20	Tennessee – 11	*Virginia - 13
Michigan – 16	Arizona – 11	*Florida - 29
New Jersey – 14	Indiana – 11	North Carolina-15
Washington – 12	Missouri – 10	*Wisconsin - 10
Massachusetts – 11	Alabama - 9	*Colorado - 9
Maryland – 10	South Carolina – 9	*Nevada - 6
Minnesota – 10	Kentucky -8	* Iowa - 6
Oregon – 7	Louisiana - 8	
Connecticut – 7	Oklahoma - 7	
New Mexico – 5	Utah - 6	
Maine - 4	Kansas - 6	
Rhode Island – 4	Arkansas - 6	
Hawaii - 4	Mississippi - 6	
Vermont – 3	Nebraska - 5	
Delaware – 3	Idaho – 4	
District of Columbia – 3	West Virginia -5	
	Alaska - 3	
	Montana - 3	
	Wyoming - 3	
	North Dakota – 3	
	South Dakota - 3	
217	**191**	**126**

In order to get to 270, the Democrats need 53 more electoral votes and the Republicans need 79 more electoral votes. The Republicans have never won a modern presidential election without winning Ohio.

In the 2016 presidential election, the Democrats need to capture Ohio, Pennsylvania, and North Carolina or Florida, Pennsylvania, and one other tossup state.

That is why the most advertising dollars will be spent, the greatest number of volunteers will be used, and the most vigorous efforts to fight over votes will occur in Florida, Pennsylvania, Ohio, North Carolina, Virginia, and Wisconsin. Unquestionably, Hillary Clinton's selection of Tim Kaine, former Governor and now Senator from Virginia, which abuts Pennsylvania, to be her Vice Presidential running mate was a shrewd, calculated move to appeal to voters in these critical tossup states.

California, New York, and Illinois between them have 104 electoral votes – nearly 40% of 270 votes needed to elect the President. Yet the money spent on advertising in these three states is miniscule because they are so firmly entrenched as Democratic states that the Democrats don't really need to spend a lot of money, and it would be a waste of precious funds for Republicans to spend extra money in these states.

But tossup states are called that because they are the most hotly contested and thus they are the key to every presidential election.

On July 30, 2016, Alexander Burns and Maggie Haberman, writing in the *New York Times* underscored the important of the tossup states as follows:

"Donald J. Trump, confronting a daunting electoral map and a significant financial disadvantage, is preparing to fall back from an expansive national campaign and concentrate the bulk of his time and money on just three or four states that his campaign believes he must sweep in order to win the presidency.

"Even as Mr. Trump has ticked up in national polls in recent weeks, senior Republicans say his path to the 270 Electoral College votes needed for election has remained narrow — and may have grown even more precarious. It now looks exceedingly difficult for him to assemble even the barest Electoral College majority without beating Hillary Clinton in a trifecta of the biggest swing states: Florida, Ohio and Pennsylvania.

"President Obama won all three states in 2008 and 2012, and no Republican has won Pennsylvania in nearly three decades.

"With a divisive campaign message that has alienated many women and Hispanics, Mr. Trump appears to have pushed several traditional swing states out of his own reach. According to strategists on both sides of the race, polling indicates that Mrs. Clinton has a solid upper hand in Colorado and Virginia, the home state of Senator Tim Kaine, her running mate. Both states voted twice for George W. Bush, who assiduously courted Hispanic voters and suburban moderates.

"In addition, Trump allies have grown concerned about North Carolina, a Republican-leaning state that has large communities of black voters and college-educated whites — two audiences with which Mr. Trump is deeply unpopular.

"While Mr. Trump is not ready to give up entirely on any of the major battlegrounds, advisers have become increasingly convinced that his most plausible route to the presidency, and perhaps his only realistic victory scenario, involves capturing all three of the biggest contested electoral prizes on the map, and keeping North Carolina in the Republican column.

"Mr. Trump and his running mate, Gov. Mike Pence of Indiana, are expected to campaign intensively across those four must-win states, with Mr. Trump trumpeting a set of blunt slogans through mass media and Mr. Pence focused on shoring up support from conservatives and right-of-center whites.

"There is no imminent plan, Trump advisers say, to match Mrs. Clinton's spending on television ads. Instead, they intend to aim Mr. Trump like a battering ram at a small number of targets, to keep delivering his provocative message on trade, terrorism and immigration.

"The primary 'super PAC' backing Mr. Trump, Rebuilding America Now, is taking an identical approach: It has reserved airtime only in Ohio, Florida and Pennsylvania. The main outside group supporting Mrs. Clinton, Priorities USA Action, is advertising in those three states and half a dozen more.

"John Brabender, a Republican strategist who has worked extensively in Pennsylvania and the Midwest, said Mr. Trump had a real but tenuous path to victory, involving a smaller map of swing states than typical for a presidential nominee. Mr. Brabender said Mr. Trump would certainly have to seize Pennsylvania, which has not voted Republican since 1988.

"'Does Trump have to run the table of the top three targets? Absolutely,' Mr. Brabender said. 'The fact that we have to worry about winning Pennsylvania to win the presidency tells you it's a difficult task.'

"Mr. Trump's inability to broaden the Republican electoral map has heartened supporters of Mrs. Clinton, even as Democrats in general have been dismayed by Mr. Trump's tenacity in national polls. In the aftermath of the Republican convention, Mr. Trump appeared to enjoy a modest bounce, pulling even or slightly ahead of Mrs. Clinton in several national surveys conducted before the Democratic convention.

"Gov. Terry McAuliffe of Virginia, a longtime political ally of the Clintons, said that Mrs. Clinton could effectively throttle the Trump campaign by winning Virginia, where he is confident of her standing, and one other swing state. He named Florida as the most inviting option.

"'If you put a combination together of Florida and Virginia, it's virtually impossible for Republicans to win the presidency,' Mr. McAuliffe said. 'Electoral College-wise, we are in a very strong position today.'

"Each of the key states presents a mix of larger cities and less populated agricultural and former industrial areas, where Mr. Trump has most often gained traction. Mr. Trump's message of clawing back lost jobs has resonated most in distressed manufacturing regions.

"But with the exception of Pennsylvania, where joblessness is slightly higher, the unemployment rate in each swing state hovers near the national average of 4.9 percent or lower.

"Democrats caution that they view Mr. Trump as a wild-card candidate with unpredictable pockets of support, potentially capable of warping the political landscape even late in the election season.

"For now, though, Mr. Trump is grappling with a magnified version of the dilemma that threatens to stymie Republicans every four years. Democrats have won a consistent set of 18 states in every presidential election since 1992, giving them a base of 242 Electoral College votes even before counting some of the biggest swing states. As a result, the last two Republican nominees, Mitt Romney and John McCain, would have needed to capture nearly all the contested states on the map in order to win.

"At an earlier point in the campaign, Mr. Trump had hoped to leverage his support from working-class whites and independent voters to put some overwhelmingly Democratic states in play, including New York and Massachusetts. Paul Manafort, Mr. Trump's campaign chairman, said this month that Mr. Trump intended to compete in strongly Democratic states like New Jersey and Oregon. In an email on Thursday, Mr. Manafort said the political landscape offered Mr. Trump numerous paths to victory.

'We have many different ways, much more than Romney had,' Mr. Manafort said.

In private, Trump advisers say the campaign now takes a colder and more clinical view of the electoral map. Mr. Trump, Republicans believe, may have even fewer ways to count to 270 than Mr. Romney and Mr. McCain had, because of his debilitating unpopularity with women and nonwhite voters.

"Mr. Trump continues to fight at a severe financial and organizational disadvantage against Mrs. Clinton, leaving him without the funds to campaign effectively across all of the states Mr. Romney contested. At the end of June, Mr. Trump had less than half as much cash in reserve as Mrs. Clinton, $20 million to her $44 million. In several major swing states, Mr. Trump's campaign has not yet approved final budgets for his state-level operations, according to Republicans in communication with his campaign, leaving Republicans on the state and national levels uncertain about his ability to mount major advertising and get-out-the-vote operations.

"And in some of the most crucial states, Mr. Trump continues to face resistance within his own party: In Ohio, he has feuded openly with the popular Republican governor, John Kasich, a former primary opponent who has refused to endorse his campaign. In Florida, some of the most influential Hispanic Republicans in the southern part of the state have withheld their support, hobbling his candidacy there.

"The map is not entirely forbidding for Mr. Trump: Both Republicans and Democrats see him as holding an edge in Iowa, a heavily white state with six electoral votes that President Obama won twice. And some top Trump aides remain hopeful that the larger terrain of the election will shift in his direction.

"Trump advisers have argued to national Republicans that they are well positioned to compete in Michigan, a Rust Belt state that no Republican presidential candidate has won since 1988. Should Mr. Trump overtake Mrs. Clinton there, it would allow him a bit more room for error in one of the other cornerstone states.

"Strategists for Mrs. Clinton largely dismiss that possibility, pointing out that Mr. McCain and Mr. Romney also hoped to compete in both Michigan and Wisconsin, only to see the states slip away well before Election Day. Joel Benenson, the chief strategist for Mrs. Clinton's campaign, said Mr. Trump had not yet made inroads in any nontraditional swing states. 'There isn't any state that they're making us play defense in, that we wouldn't already compete vigorously in anyway,' Mr. Benenson said.

"Still, Mr. Pence campaigned on Thursday in the Detroit suburbs, in what amounted to an early prospecting expedition for the Trump campaign into Democratic territory. The Indiana governor intends to spend most of his time in the Rust Belt, including Ohio and Pennsylvania. Mr. Pence, who is popular on the right, is also expected to play defense for Mr. Trump in a few conservative states, like Georgia and Arizona, where Mrs. Clinton may be competitive. A former radio host, Mr. Pence will be a ubiquitous presence on conservative talk shows, to ensure that the Republican base stays loyal to its unorthodox nominee.

"Robin Hayes, the chairman of the North Carolina Republican Party, said he anticipated that Mr. Pence, an evangelical Christian, would visit the state often to speak about 'North Carolina Judeo-Christian values.' Mr. Hayes, a former member of Congress and a friend of Mr. Pence's, said it was essential for Mr. Trump to defend Republicans' grip on North Carolina in order to win nationally. 'There's no substitute for winning, and it is a critically important state,' Mr. Hayes said. 'It's going to be an absolutely bruising kind of campaign.'"

PART TWO

THE PRIMARIES

2

WHAT ARE PRIMARIES?
HOW DO THEY WORK?

We have previously mentioned the way in which a President is elected. But how does one get to be a party's candidate for the Presidency? Although the smaller parties have differing ways of selecting their Presidential candidate, we will focus on the two major parties, the Democratic Party and the Republican Party.

Each of these parties has the same basic manner of selection. Primary elections or caucuses (depending on the State) are held in all 50 states plus U.S. Territories. These usually occur 4-6 months prior to that Party's convention. Voters in the states elect delegates who will cast their vote for specific candidates, subject to certain rules set by each Party.

An overview of how this worked in 2016 with respect to each major Party was as follows:

DEMOCRATIC PRIMARIES

The 2016 Democratic Party presidential primaries and caucuses were a series of electoral contests organized by the Democratic Party to select the delegates to the Democratic National Convention held July 25–28, 2016 and to determine the Party's nominee for President in the general election. The primary elections occurred between February 1 and June 14, 2016. Under the Rules of the Democratic Party, an extra 714 unpledged delegates, called "superdelegates," were appointed by the Party independent of the primaries' electoral process. Superdelegates consist of "Distinguished Party Leaders," Governors, Senators, Representatives, and Members of the Democratic National Committee.

The Democratic Party presidential primaries and caucuses are indirect elections in which voters elect delegates to the 2016 Democratic National Convention; these delegates in turn directly elect the Democratic Party's presidential nominee. In some states, the party may disregard voters' selection of delegates or selected delegates may vote for any candidate at the state or national convention. In other states, state laws and party rules require the party to select delegates according to votes, and delegates must vote for a particular candidate. There were 4,051 pledged delegates and 714 superdelegates in the 2016 cycle. Under the party's delegate selection rules, the number of pledged delegates allocated to each of the 50 U.S. states and Washington, D.C. is determined using a formula based on three main factors:

The proportion of votes each state gave to the Democratic candidate in the last three presidential elections (2004, 2008, and 2012).

The number of electoral votes each state has in the United States Electoral College.

The stage of the primary season when they held their contest. States and territories that held their contests later are given bonus seats.

A candidate had to win 2,383 delegates at the national convention, in order to win the 2016 Democratic presidential nomination.

Six major candidates entered the race starting April 12, 2015, when Hillary Clinton formally announced her second bid for the presidency. She was followed by Vermont Senator Bernie Sanders, former Governor of Maryland Martin O'Malley, former Governor of Rhode Island Lincoln Chafee, former Virginia Senator Jim Webb, and Harvard Law Professor Lawrence Lessig. Prior to the Iowa caucuses on February 1, Webb and Chafee withdrew after consistently polling below 2%. Lessig withdrew after the rules of a debate were changed such that he would no longer qualify to participate.

Clinton won Iowa by the closest margin in the history of the state's Democratic caucus. O'Malley suspended his campaign after a distant third-place finish, leaving Clinton and Sanders the only two candidates. The electoral battle turned out to be more competitive than expected, with Sanders winning the New Hampshire primary while Clinton scored victories in the Nevada caucuses and South Carolina primary. On four different Super Tuesdays, Clinton secured numerous important wins in each of the nine largest states including California, New York, Florida, and Texas, while Sanders scored various victories in between.

On June 6, 2016, the Associated Press and NBC News stated that Clinton had become the presumptive nominee after reaching the required number of delegates, including both pledged and unpledged superdelegates, to secure the nomination. On June 7, Clinton officially secured a majority of pledged delegates after winning in the California and New Jersey primaries. President Barack Obama, Vice President Joe Biden and Senator Elizabeth Warren formally endorsed Clinton on June 9, 2016. Sanders confirmed on June 24 that he would vote for Clinton over Donald Trump in the general election and, on July 12, 2016, formally endorsed Clinton in Portsmouth, New Hampshire, marking the start of an alliance. On July 26, 2016, the Democratic National Convention officially nominated Hillary Clinton for President and Senator Tim Kaine of Virginia for Vice President.

REPUBLICAN PRIMARIES

The 2016 Republican Party presidential primaries and caucuses were a series of electoral contests taking place between February 1 and June 7, 2016. These elections were designed to select the 2,472 delegates to send to the Republican National Convention, who would select the Republican Party's nominee for President. 1,237 votes were necessary to select the Presidential nominee. The Republican nominee was Donald Trump.

Seventeen major candidates entered the race starting on March 23, 2015, when Senator Ted Cruz of Texas was the first to formally announce his candidacy. Thereafter, former Governor Jeb Bush of Florida, retired neurosurgeon Ben Carson of Maryland, Governor Chris Christie of New Jersey, businesswoman Carly Fiorina of California, former Governor Jim Gilmore of Virginia, Senator Lindsey Graham of South Carolina, former Governor Mike Huckabee of Arkansas, former Governor Bobby Jindal of Louisiana, Governor John Kasich of Ohio, former Governor George Pataki of New York, Senator Rand Paul of Kentucky, former Governor Rick Perry of Texas, Senator Marco Rubio of Florida, former Senator Rick Santorum of Pennsylvania, businessman Donald Trump of New York and Governor Scott Walker of Wisconsin entered the race. This was the largest presidential primary field for any political party in American history.

The first candidate to declare his candidacy was Texas Senator Ted Cruz, who was popular among grassroots conservatives due to his association with the Tea Party movement. The grassroots conservatives were represented by Cruz and Carson, the Christian right by Huckabee and Santorum and the moderates or establishment were represented by Bush and Christie. Some candidates were seen as appealing to both conservatives and moderates, such as Kasich, Jindal, Walker, Rubio and Paul. Two notable candidates from the previous primaries in 2012 returned for a second consecutive run in 2016: Santorum and Perry. Lastly, there were candidates with minimal to no political experience, Carson, Trump and Fiorina, who touted their lack of political experience as a positive while others criticize it as making them unqualified for the office. The field was the most diverse presidential field in American history. This included two Latinos (Cruz and Rubio), a woman (Fiorina), an Indian-American (Jindal) and an African-American (Carson). Five were the sons of immigrants: Cruz (Cuban father), Jindal (Indian parents), Rubio (Cuban parents), Santorum (Italian father) and Trump (Scottish mother).

Widely viewed as a very open contest with no clear front-runner, potential candidates fluctuated in the polls for an extended period from late 2012 to the end of 2015. By the time the primary season started in early 2016, three candidates had clearly emerged ahead of the rest of the field: Marco Rubio, Ted Cruz, and Donald Trump. Trump maintained wide poll leads throughout 2015 and into 2016, primarily due to his brash and unapologetic style of speaking and campaigning, emphasizing a disregard for political correctness, as well as populist and nativist policies, earning him the support of working-class voters and voters without college educations, among other demographics. However, this same brash attitude and polarizing policy stances generated numerous controversies in the media, and many of the other candidates sought to become the "anti-Trump" candidate by condemning his rhetoric and more radical policies. This gave rise to Senators Cruz and Rubio, who both emphasized their youth in comparison to most other candidates, as well as possible appeals to Hispanic voters, despite both being at different ends of the Republican political spectrum; Cruz was backed by his origins in the Tea Party movement and support among Evangelicals, while Rubio was seen by many as having broad appeal to both the conservative grassroots and the moderate "establishment" factions of the GOP, while also risking criticism from both sides. Ohio governor John Kasich, a moderate Republican, remained in the race for an extended period of time, despite widely being viewed as having little to no chance to win the nomination.

Prior to the Iowa caucuses on February 1, Perry, Walker, Jindal, Graham and Pataki withdrew due to low polling numbers. Despite leading many polls in Iowa, Trump came in second to Cruz, after which Huckabee, Paul and Santorum withdrew due to poor performances at the ballot box. Following a sizable victory for Trump in the New Hampshire primary, Christie, Fiorina and Gilmore abandoned the race. Bush withdrew after scoring fourth place to Trump, Rubio and Cruz in South Carolina. On March 1, 2016, Rubio won his first contest in Minnesota, Cruz won Alaska, Oklahoma and his home state of Texas, while Trump won seven states. Failing to gain traction, Carson suspended his campaign a few days later. On March 15, 2016, Kasich won his first contest in Ohio. Trump won five primaries including Florida. Rubio suspended his campaign after losing his home state, but he retained a large share of his delegates for the national convention.

As the primary season entered the spring, the mostly-consolidated field resulted in a closing of the gap between Trump and Cruz, with Trump sweeping the South, the Northeast, and parts of the Midwest, while Cruz performed strongly in the West and scored a surprise victory in Maine. Kasich, unable to win any other states besides Ohio, remained far behind in a distant third. After Cruz's upset win in Wisconsin, speculation began to arise that the convention would be a brokered one in which the establishment would choose Kasich or someone else, since both Trump and Cruz were not viewed favorably by the establishment.

As April came to a close and Trump won a resounding victory in his home state of New York, both Cruz and Kasich were mathematically eliminated from possibly becoming the nominee. Both men then formed an alliance to block Trump from winning the nomination, ahead of the "Acela primaries" of five Northeastern states on April 26. Subsequently, Trump swept all five states and greatly increased his delegate lead. In a final push to block Trump's path to the nomination, Cruz announced that one of the former candidates for the nomination, former Hewlett-Packard CEO Carly Fiorina, would be his running mate if he was the nominee. Nevertheless, after Trump won the Indiana primary on May 3, Cruz suspended his campaign, which led to the Republican National Committee Chairman Reince Priebus announcing Trump as the presumptive nominee. Kasich announced the suspension of his campaign the next day, May 4, leaving Trump as the only candidate left in the race. Trump then went on to win all of the remaining primaries, sweeping the remainder of the West, Midwest, and the entirety of the West Coast.

From March 16, 2016 to May 3, 2016, only three candidates remained in the race: Trump, Cruz and Kasich. Cruz won most delegates in four Western contests and in Wisconsin, keeping a credible path to denying Trump the nomination on first ballot with 1,237 delegates. In due course, however, Trump scored landslide victories in New York and five North-Eastern states in April, before taking every delegate in the Indiana primary of May 3. Without any further chances of forcing a contested convention,

Cruz suspended his campaign and Trump was declared the presumptive Republican nominee by the Republican National Committee chairman on May 3. Kasich dropped out the next day. After winning the Washington primary and gaining support from unbound North Dakota delegates on May 26, Trump passed the threshold of 1,237 delegates required to guarantee his nomination.

The 2016 Republican National Convention was from July 18–21 at the Quicken Loans Arena in Cleveland. The delegates selected the Republican presidential and vice presidential nominees. On the first ballot, Donald Trump clinched the nomination with 1,725 delegates, 488 more than the 1,237 majority required.

The Republican Party presidential primaries and caucuses were indirect elections in which voters allocated or elected delegates to the 2016 Republican National Convention. These delegates could have been bound or unbound to vote for a particular candidate.

Each delegation was made up of up to three kinds of delegates: party members, delegates from the congressional districts and delegates from the state at-large. They could either be bound, meaning they were legally bound to vote for a particular candidate in the first ballot at the National Convention, or they could be unbound, meaning that they were free to vote for any candidate at the National Convention. Bound delegates' voting obligations would not necessarily be in line with their own personal views. If a candidate suspended his campaign, the delegates allocated and/or elected to him could become unbound or stay bound depending on state rules.

3

HANDICAPPING THE RACE

Giving odds has become a way of generating more advertising and more income formedia pundits – "talking heads." The more likely a horse or a number, or, in politics, the candidate is likely to win, the lower the odds. For example, a "most likely will win" bet would be 1-2, which means that for ever two dollars you bet, if you win, you will get three dollars back. On the other hand, if you bet a "long shot" at, say 20-1, if you bet the same two dollars and you win, your payoff will be $40. Great monetary reward, but, like the risk-reward concept everywhere, you're not likely to win a lot of the time.

With that type of mindset, I thought I'd play a little game of oddsmaking. In June 2015, when the current political "season" began, the "professional" predictors, those with allegedly great political "wisdom" gave odds" on 2016 Presidential candidates something like the following:

Announced candidate	Party	Odds	Comment
Hillary Clinton	Dem.	1-2	Seemed a shoe-in
Jeb Bush	Rep.	2-1	Looked like it would be either the Clinton dynasty or the Bush dynasty
Donald Trump	Rep?	1000-1	You mean that nutcase from *The Apprentice?* You've got to be kidding!

Seventeen candidates were generally classed between 20-1 and 50-1 to make any serious inroads. By November 2015, there were fourteen candidates left in the race.

As of May 4, 2016, with the withdrawal of John Kasich, the world had turned upside down. The race now looked as follows:

Candidate	Party	Odds	Comment
Hillary Clinton	Dem.	1-2	The Republicans' unanimous pincushion
Donald Trump	Rep.	3-1	What???? You've got to be kidding!!!!
Ted Cruz	Rep.	10-1	**WITHDREW – MAY 3, 2016!**
Bernie Sanders	Dem	100-1	Wonderful ideas! But he's a dreamer and none of his impossible dreams could ever come true.
John Kasich	Rep.	50-1	**WITHDREW – MAY 4, 2016!**

Once thought of as serious Candidates who dropped out:

	Party	Comment

Jeb Bush — Rep. — Once thought of as the heir apparent, he was a victim of a lackluster campaign which appealed to a minuscule number of rational voters.

Ben Carson — Rep. — The only African-American candidate. A non- politician neurosurgeon from the "other side of the tracks," who was "traditionally conservative" and an ecumenical fundamentalist Christian, but who, at the end of the day, was simply too Black and too boring. After he dropped out, he endorsed DONALD TRUMP.

Chris Christie — Rep. — Popular governor of New Jersey who back in 2013 was talked about as a very serious contender by *both* parties, but a serious lapse of judgment, combined with a suspicion that he might be Mafia- related thug eventually deep-sixed his campaign. After he dropped out, he endorsed TRUMP.

Carly Fiorina — Rep. — Shrill and feisty, she positioned herself as the only real alternative to Hillary Clinton, and the only candidate with a proved track record as a business leader. However, as the race heated up, the fact that Fiorina had been fired as chief executive of more than one corporation and that she had shipped thousands of American jobs overseas did not stand her in good stead. Ultimately the capstone on the grave of her candidacy was the insulting, but very effective slam came from Donald Trump, who said, "Would you like to see a President with a face like that?"

	Party	**Comment**
Carly Fiorina *(continuation)*	Rep.	After she dropped out, Fiorina, not surprisingly, endorsed Ted Cruz. And on April 27, 2016 in what appeared to be a desperate attempt to capitalize on Trump's increasingly sexist remarks and stop the front-runner, Ted Cruz announced that his Vice Presidential running mate would be Carly Fiorina. The vice presidential run lasted less than a week when, after a blistering defeat in Indiana, Ted Cruz withdrew from the Presidential race.
Mike Huckabee	Rep.	A fundamentalist Christian minister and a retread from the 2012 Presidential primaries, he was the only one who believed he had a serious chance. After he dropped out, he endorsed TRUMP.
Martin O'Malley	Dem.	Seemed to be a highly intelligent, rational, and sensible alternative to Hillary Clinton. Unfortunately, the media gave this former governor of Maryland so little time when compared to Hillary Clinton and even Bernie Sanders that his political demise as a serious contender was doomed from the start.
Rand Paul	Rep.	A "tea party" darling and the son of the commonsense Ron Paul, a candidate in the 2012 Republican primaries, he made a lot of sense when he spoke, but the rancorous disputes with Jeb Bush coupled with the fact that he was anything but a media favorite signaled that sooner or later he would drop out.

	Party	Comment
Marco Rubio	Rep.	Up to the very end, Rubio provided a somewhat less offensive alternative to Donald Trump and Ted Cruz. His downfall started when he said about Donald Trump, "He has small hands and you know what they say about people with small hands." This led to Trump effectively demolishing Rubio's candidacy by referring to him pejoratively as "Little Marco."
Rick Santorum	Rep.	A failed, right-wing Christian fundamentalist candidate from 2012. There was simply no way he would be taken seriously – and besides, Marco Rubio was better looking when it came to the "clean young fellow" look.
Scott Walker	Rep.	Wisconsin's governor faded fast.
Rick Perry	Rep.	Texas's governor, who made noise in 2012, faded even faster.
Lindsey Graham	Rep.	South Carolina senator was never a serious factor. After he dropped out, he became the only U.S. Senator to endorse Ted Cruz.

As of April 25, 2016, John Kasich and Ted Cruz announced that Kasich conceded Indiana to Ted Cruz and Cruz said he would concede two smaller states to Kasich. Donald Trump condemned this as a "pathetic and desperate" attempt to stack the cards against him and make the Republican Convention "open" – meaning that the Republican establishment seems to be "circling the wagons" to keep Trump from being the Republican candidate in the general election. Kasich, quite sensibly, said this was no "conspiracy" – it was simply recognition that Cruz would most likely win in Indiana and it was prudent for the Ohio governor to conserve what money he had to spend it where he had the best chance. But Trump's statements drew blood – a lot of blood. Cruz spent $2.8 million to try to defeat Trump in Indiana. A "stop Trump movement" spent $2.6 million to try to defeat Trump in Indiana. Donald Trump spent $900,000 campaigning in Indiana. And by the time the Sun set in Indiana on May 3, Trump had captured the "must win" state for Cruz, 53% to 36% and a stunned Ted Cruz "suspended" his campaign (*i.e.* withdrew).

Meanwhile, Hillary Clinton sounded more like a general election candidate than competition for Bernie Sanders as she hardly mentioned Sanders at all while demonstrating that she's more than ready to take on "the Donald."

The next chapters provide a more detailed sketch of the last surviving candidates in the 2016 primaries.

4

THE TRUMP PHENOMENON

Donald John Trump is an impossible "happening!" In recent memory, no politician one has gotten away with so many gratuitous slanders, not only of his rival candidates but of virtually every minority in the country! With only one or two notable exceptions, the more outrageous his comments, the more popular he became with his core group of supporters. Trump is proof positive that polls and prognosticators may be all wet. He can take on the media with apparent impunity and demolish his opponents with no more than a facial smirk. In continuous "fact check" findings by TV pundits, he perpetually scores almost unanimous "liar" status, yet it seems that *no one gives a damn*! And with the withdrawal of his only two primary opponents, Ted Cruz on May 3 and John Kasich on May 4, the impossible came to pass. As unpopular as Trump has been with the Republican Establishment since the onset of his "it'll never happen" campaign, there was no one left to challenge him. The "Trump train" was unstoppable. Let's explore the background of this 69-year-old *wunderkind*.

Trump, born June 14, 1946, is an American businessman, politician, television personality, author, and candidate. He's the Chairman and President of The Trump Organization, as well as the founder of a gaming and hotel empire.

The son of New York City real estate developer Fred Trump, he worked for his father's firm while attending college. After graduating in 1968 he joined the company, and in 1971 was given control. He has built casinos, golf courses, hotels, and other properties. His businesses as well as his three marriages received wide media exposure. He hosted *The Apprentice*, a popular NBC reality show, from 2004 to 2015.

This is not "the Donald's" first foray into politics. He first campaigned for the U.S. presidency in 2000, winning two Reform Party primaries. On June 16, 2015, he again announced his candidacy for president, this time as a Republican. He became known for his opposition to illegal immigration and free trade agreements, as well as his frequently non-interventionist views on foreign policy, and quickly emerged as the Republican nomination front-runner.

Trump was born in Queens, the fourth of five children to Mary Anne (1912–2000) and Fred Trump (1905–1999). His mother was born on the Scottish island of Lewis and Harris. In 1930, aged 18, she visited the U.S. and met Fred, who was of German descent. They were married in 1936 and settled in Jamaica Estates, Queens. Trump has one brother, Robert (born 1948), and two sisters: Maryanne (born 1937) and Elizabeth (born 1942). Maryanne is a senior United States federal judge on the Court of Appeals for the third circuit. Another brother, Fred Jr. (1938–1981), died of complications from alcoholism.

Due to behavior problems, Donald Trump left the school at age 13 and was enrolled in the New York Military Academy. During his senior year, Trump participated in marching drills and wore a uniform, attaining the rank of captain. He claims he received "more training militarily than a lot of the guys that go into the army."

Trump attended Fordham University in the Bronx for two years, then entered the Wharton School of Business at the University of Pennsylvania. In 1968, he graduated from Wharton with a bachelor's degree in economics. Trump was eligible for the draft lottery during the Vietnam War, but was not drafted due to four student deferments while attending college, as well as a medical deferment. He was deemed fit for service after a military medical examination in 1966 and was briefly classified as 1-A by a local draft board shortly before his 1968 medical disqualification.

Trump claims that when he graduated from college in 1968, he was worth about US $200,000. At the age of 23, he made an unsuccessful commercial try at going into show business, investing $70,000 to become co-producer of the 1970 Broadway comedy "Paris Is Out!" which flopped. Trump began his real estate career at his father's company, Elizabeth Trump and Son, which focused on middle-class rental housing in the New York City boroughs of Brooklyn, Queens, and Staten Island. During his undergraduate studies, one of Trump's first projects had been the revitalization of the foreclosed Swifton Village apartment complex in Cincinnati, Ohio, which his father had purchased for $5.7 million in 1962. Fred and Donald Trump became involved in the project and, with a $500,000 investment, they turned the 1,200-unit complex's occupancy rate from 34% to 100%. Trump oversaw the company's 14,000 apartment units. In 1972, The Trump Organization sold Swifton Village for $6.75 million.

In 1971, Trump moved to Manhattan, where he became involved in larger construction projects. He first came to public attention in

1973 when he was accused by the Justice Department of violations of the Fair Housing Act in the operation of 39 buildings, including false "no vacancy" statements, and sham leases presenting higher rents to minority applicants, to facilitate the denial of housing to racial minorities.

He struck back by accusing the Justice Department of targeting his company because it was a large one, and in order to force it to rent to welfare recipients. After an unsuccessful countersuit, Trump settled the charges in 1975 without admitting guilt, saying he was satisfied that the agreement did not "compel the Trump organization to accept persons on welfare as tenants unless they were as qualified as any other tenant." The Trump Organization was hailed back into court several years later for violating the terms of the settlement.

Trump had an option to buy and made plans to develop the Penn Central Transportation Company property, which was in bankruptcy. This included the 60th Street rail yard on the Hudson River, later developed as Riverside South, as well as the land around Grand Central Terminal, for which he paid $60 million with no money down. Later, with the help of a 40-year tax abatement from the New York City government, he turned the bankrupt Commodore Hotel next to Grand Central into the Grand Hyatt and created The Trump Organization.

In 1988, Trump acquired the Taj Mahal Casino in Atlantic City, New Jersey, in a transaction with Merv Griffin and Resorts International, which led to mounting debt. By 1991 the Taj Mahal was in bankruptcy. The Taj Mahal emerged from bankruptcy on October 5, with Trump giving up 50% ownership in the casino to the bondholders in exchange for lowered interest rates and more time to pay off the debt. He also sold his financially endangered Trump Shuttle airline and his 282-foot megayacht, the *Trump*

Princess. But by the late 1990s, largely from a 25% inheritance of his father's $300 million estate, Trump's financial problems were at an end.

In 2001, Trump completed Trump World Tower, a 72-story residential structure across from the UN Headquarters, and began construction on Trump Place, a multi-building development along the Hudson River. Today, Trump owns several million square feet of prime Manhattan real estate. By 2014, Trump retained 10% ownership of Trump Entertainment Resorts, which owns the Trump Taj Mahal and Trump Plaza Hotel and Casino, both in Atlantic City. In that year, Trump Entertainment Resorts entered Chapter 11 bankruptcy and closed Trump Plaza indefinitely.

According to a July 2015 press release from his campaign manager, Trump's "income" was $362 million (which does not include dividends, interest, capital gains, rents and royalties). According to *Fortune* magazine, the $362 million figure as stated on his FEC filings is not "income" but gross revenue before salaries, interest payments on outstanding debt, and other business-related expenses; Trump's true income was most likely about one-third of what Trump publicly claimed. According to public records, Trump received a $302 New York tax rebate in 2013, given to couples earning less than $500,000 per year, who submit as proof their federal tax returns. Trump's campaign manager has suggested that Trump's tax rebate was an error, but Trump has not publicly released his federal tax returns, citing ongoing IRS audits.

Trump has licensed his name and image for the development of many real estate projects, including the Muslim owner of Trump Towers Istanbul, who pays Trump for the use of his name. In December 2015 that licensee was exploring legal means to dissociate the property after the candidate's call to ban Muslims from entering the U.S.

An analysis of Trump's business career by *The Economist* in 2016, concluded that his financial performance from 1985 to 2016 has been mediocre compared with the stock market and property in New York, noting both his successes and bankruptcies. But any real in-depth analysis is difficult because information about Trump's business is sketchy at best.

The Trump Organization operates many golf courses and resorts around the world. On February 11, 2014, Trump purchased Doonbeg Golf Club in Ireland, which he renamed Trump International Golf Links, Ireland. In 2006, Trump bought the Menie Estate in Balmedie, Aberdeenshire, Scotland, creating a highly controversial golf resort, against the wishes of local residents. Despite Trump's promises of 6,000 jobs, by his own admission, a decade later, the Scotland golf course has created only 200 jobs.

Trump has marketed his name on a large number of building projects as well as commercial products and services, achieving mixed success doing so for himself, his partners, and investors in the projects. His external entrepreneurial and investment ventures include Trump Financial (a mortgage firm), Trump Sales and Leasing (residential sales), Trump International Realty (a residential and commercial real estate brokerage firm), The failed Trump University, which is presently the subject of a large class-action lawsuit brought by former students who were allegedly bilked of their life savings, Trump Restaurants (located in Trump Tower and consisting of Trump Buffet, Trump Catering, Trump Ice Cream Parlor, and Trump Bar), GoTrump (an online travel search engine), Select By Trump (a line of coffee drinks), Trump Drinks (an energy drink for the Israeli and Palestinian markets), Donald J. Trump Signature Collection (a line of menswear, men's accessories, and watches), Donald Trump The Fragrance (2004), Success by Donald Trump (a second fragrance) Trump Ice bottled water, the former *Trump Magazine*, Trump Golf, Trump Chocolate, Trump Home (home furnishings), Trump Productions (a television production company), Trump Institute, Trump: The Game (1989 board game with a 2005 re-release version tied to The Apprentice), Donald Trump's Real Estate Tycoon (a business simulation game), Trump Books, Trump Model Management, Trump Shuttle, Trump Mortgage, Trump Network (a multi-level vitamin, cosmetic, and urinalysis marketing company), Trump Vodka, Trump Steakhouse and Trump Steaks. In addition, Trump reportedly received $1.5 million for each one-hour presentation he did for The Learning Annex.

In 2011, *Forbes'* financial experts estimated the value of the Trump brand at $200 million. Trump disputes this valuation, saying that his brand is worth about $3 billion.

Unlike past Presidential candidates, Trump has never publicly verified his income claims by releasing his tax returns; "I try to pay as little tax as possible," Trump has said.

In 2005, *The New York Times* referred to Trump's "verbal billions" in a skeptical article about Trump's self-reported wealth. At the time, three individuals with direct knowledge of Trump's finances told reporter Timothy L. O'Brien that Trump's actual net worth was between $150 and $250 million, though Trump then publicly claimed a net worth of $5 to $6 billion. Claiming libel, Trump sued the reporter and his book publisher for $5 billion, lost the case, then lost again on appeal.

Estimates of Trump's net worth have fluctuated. In 2015, *Forbes* pegged it as $4 billion, while the Bloomberg Billionaires Index estimated a net worth of $2.9 billion. On June 16, 2015, just prior to announcing his candidacy for president of the United States, Trump released to the media a one-page prepared financial disclosure statement stating a net worth of $8.7 billion. "I'm really rich," Trump said. *Forbes* called the nearly $9 billion figure a "100%" exaggeration. In July 2015, Federal election regulators released new details of Trump's self-reported wealth and financial holdings when he became a Republican presidential candidate, reporting that his assets are worth above $1.4 billion.

A July 2015 campaign press release, issued one month after Trump announced his presidential run, said that his "net worth is in excess of Ten Billion Dollars. On the same day, Trump's own stated estimates of his net worth have varied by as much as $3.3 billion. Trump has also acknowledged that past exaggerated estimates of his wealth have been "good for financing."

From 1996 until 2015, when he sold his interests, Trump owned part or all of the Miss Universe, Miss USA, and Miss Teen USA beauty pageants. In 2015, NBC and Univision both ended their business relationships with the Miss Universe Organization after Trump's presidential campaign kickoff speech on June 16, in which he stated:

"The U.S. has become a dumping ground for everybody else's problems. When Mexico sends its people, they're not sending their best. They're sending people that have lots of problems, and they're bringing those problems with us. They're bringing drugs. They're bringing crime. They're rapists. And some, I assume, are good people."

Trump subsequently filed a $500 million lawsuit against Univision, alleging a breach of contract and defamation. Cable network Reelz then acquired the rights to exclusively telecast the Miss USA pageant. Trump told *People* magazine in July 2015 that the lawsuit against Univision was part of the presidential campaign." On September 11, 2015, Trump announced that he purchased NBC's stake in the Miss Universe Organization, making him the sole owner, and had "settled" his lawsuits against the network. He sold his own interests in the pageant shortly afterwards.

Trump's hotel and casino businesses have been declared bankrupt four times between 1991 and 2009 to re-negotiate debt with banks and owners of stock and bonds. Because the businesses used Chapter 11 bankruptcy, they were allowed to operate while negotiations proceeded. Trump was quoted by *Newsweek* in 2011 saying, "I do play with the bankruptcy laws — they're very good for me" as a tool for trimming debt.

In the media, Trump is a two-time Emmy Award-nominated personality and has made appearances as a caricatured version of himself in television series and films Trump is a member of the Screen Actors Guild and receives an annual pension of more than $110,000 every year.

In 2003, Trump became the executive producer and host of the NBC reality show *The Apprentice*, in which a group of competitors battled for a high-level management job in one of Trump's commercial enterprises. Contestants were successively "fired" and eliminated from the game. In 2004, Trump filed a trademark application for the catchphrase "You're fired."

For the first year of the show, Trump earned $50,000 per episode (roughly $700,000 for the first season), but following the show's initial success, he was paid a reported $3 million per episode, making him one of the highest paid TV personalities. In a July 2015 press release, Trump's campaign manager claimed that NBC Universal had paid him $213,606,575 for his 14 seasons hosting the show, although the network did not verify the claim. In 2007, Trump received a star on the Hollywood Walk of Fame for his contribution to television.

Along with British TV producer Mark Burnett, Trump was hired as host of *The Celebrity Apprentice*, in which well-known stars compete to win money for their charities. While Trump and Burnett co-produced the show, Trump stayed in the forefront, deciding winners and "firing" losers.

In 1999, Donald Trump founded a modeling company, Trump Model Management, which operates in the SoHo neighborhood of New York City. Together with another Trump company, Trump Management Group LLC, Trump Model Management has brought nearly 250 foreign fashion models to the US to work in the fashion industry since 2000.

Trump has described his political leanings and positions in various, sometimes contradictory ways over time. He has listed his party affiliation as Republican, Independence Party, Democrat, and "decline to state." He has also run as a Reform Party candidate. Specifically, he has changed his positions on taxing the wealthy, abortion rights and health care.

A 2011 report by the Center for Responsive Politics showed that over the previous two decades of U.S. elections, Donald Trump made contributions to campaigns of both Republican Party and Democratic Party candidates, with the top 10 recipients of his political contributions being six Democrats and four Republicans. After 2011, his campaign contributions were more favorable to Republicans than to Democrats.

Trump was an early supporter of Republican Ronald Reagan for U.S. president, and in February 2012 endorsed Republican Mitt Romney for president. When asked in 2015 which recent president was best, Trump picked Democrat Bill Clinton over Republicans George H. W. Bush and George W. Bush. The Clintons' foundation has received between $100,000 and $250,000 from Trump, and they attended Trump's 2005 wedding reception. Trump wrote in 2008 that Hillary Clinton would be a "great president or vice-president."

Until 1987, he was a Democrat; he was a Republican from 1987 to 1999. He then switched to the Reform Party from 1999 to 2001. After a presidential exploratory campaign with the Reform Party, he wrote an OpEd in the New York Times stating that he was leaving the Reform Party because of the involvement of "David Duke, Pat Buchanan and Lenora Fulani. That is not company I wish to keep." From 2001 to 2009 he was a Democrat again; he switched to the Republican Party again from 2009 to 2011. An independent from 2011 to 2012, he returned to the Republican Party in 2012, where he has remained.

Trump's politics have been described as populist, nativist, protectionist, and authoritarian. On social issues, Trump describes himself as pro-life and would ban late-term abortions except in cases of rape, incest, or health. During a televised town hall event, Trump said "there has to be some sort of punishment" for the woman having an abortion, a statement he later retracted in response to outcry from his rivals and pro-life groups. He is in favor of cutting federal funding for Planned Parenthood. Trump supports the Second Amendment, is opposed to gun control in general, and has a New York concealed carry permit. He supports fixing the federal background check system so that criminal and mental health records are always put into the system. Trump opposes legalizing recreational marijuana but supports legalizing medical marijuana, while being supportive of states' rights. Trump has stated that he supports traditional marriage.

Trump has demonstrated his support of capital punishment both through his campaign speeches, and through full-page ads he purchased in 1989 in New York City.

Regarding healthcare and education, Trump favors replacing the Affordable Care Act ("Obamacare") with a free-market plan and competition to lower costs, although he has also stated support for a single-payer system in the past. Trump favors getting rid of backlogs and waitlists which are the focus of the Veterans Health Administration scandal. In a statement, he said he believes that Veterans Affairs facilities need to be upgraded with recent technology, hire more veterans to treat other veterans, increase support of female veterans, and create satellite clinics within hospitals in rural areas. Trump has stated his support for school choice and local control for primary and secondary schools. He opposes the Common Core State Standards Initiative for primary and secondary schools, and has called Common Core "a disaster" that must be ended.

Trump's views on immigration, free trade, and military interventionism, as well as his support for social security, has often put him in conflict with Republican Party establishment consensus. He identifies as a "free trader," but says that trade must be "reasonably fair." His campaign's tax plan calls for reducing the corporate tax rate to 15% concurrent with the elimination of various loopholes and deductions. Trump believes the minimum wage should not be raised because increasing it would hurt America's economic competitiveness.

On the issue of immigration, Trump has emphasized U.S. border security. During his first town hall campaign meeting in Derry, New Hampshire Trump said that if he won the election, "Day 1 of my presidency, illegal immigrants are getting out and getting out fast." Trump opposes birthright citizenship, arguing that it is not or should not be protected by the Fourteenth Amendment to the United States Constitution. On people already illegally in the United States, Trump has variously said they should all be deported, that all should be deported but some could return, that only some should be deported, or that the decision should be made after the border has been strengthened.

Regarding the environment, Trump has said that "the EPA is an impediment to both growth and jobs." Trump supports increased fracking and has criticized sustainable wind power alternatives, stating that "windmills are destroying every country they touch" while producing "unreliable and terrible" energy. He has called global warming "a total hoax."

On foreign policy, Trump has been described as non-interventionalist and nationalist. He supports increasing U.S. military defense spending, but favors decreasing U.S. spending on NATO. Trump has at various times said he favored sending U.S. troops as well as opposed sending U.S. troops to defeat the ISIS. In a 2002 interview, Trump said he favored invading Iraq. On February 18, 2016, he said that by the time the invasion occurred, he had become an opponent. In 2008, Trump said that George W. Bush should have been impeached for the war. Regarding the Israeli–Palestinian conflict, Trump has stated the importance of being a neutral party during potential negotiations, while also having stated that he is "a big fan of Israel." He endorsed Israeli Prime Minister Benjamin Netanyahu in 2013. Trump has been critical of Pakistan, comparing it to North Korea, describing it as "probably the most dangerous country" in the world, and saying that Pakistan's nuclear weapons posed a "serious problem." He has advocated improving relations with India as a "check" to Pakistan.

Trump floated the idea of running for president in 1988, 2004, and 2012, and for Governor of New York in 2006 and 2014, but did not enter those races. He was considered as a potential running mate for George H. W. Bush on the Republican Party's 1988 presidential ticket but lost out to future Vice President Dan Quayle. In 1999, Trump filed an exploratory committee to seek the presidential nomination of the Reform Party.

Trump later said that his national profile changed: "What happened was I did *The Apprentice* and it became a tremendous success. Who would have thought this was going to happen?" he told interviewer Larry King in 2005. "There's sort of nothing like having the big hot show on television."

In April 2011, Trump questioned President Barack Obama's proof of citizenship, alleging that "his grandmother in Kenya said he was born in Kenya, and she was there and witnessed the birth." Trump also questioned whether Obama had good enough grades to warrant entry to Harvard Law School. On April 25, 2011, Trump called for Obama to end the citizenship issue by releasing the long form of his birth certificate. Two days later, Obama made a formal statement in efforts by the White House to put the matter to rest with the release of the long form. Trump expressed pride at his role in the certificate's release in a press conference follow-up, saying he hoped it "checks out" and "we have to see, is it real?" When asked in July 2015 whether Obama was born in the U.S., Trump said: "I really don't know. I don't know why he wouldn't release his records."

In February 2015, Trump opted not to renew his television contract for *The Apprentice*, generating speculation that he might run for president in 2016.

On June 16, 2015, Trump announced his candidacy for President of the United States in a campaign strongly emphasized by the slogan "Make America Great Again."

Trump runs as a self-described far-right conservative, particularly as it relates to fiscal and religious matters. As it extends to social issues such as same-sex marriage and abortion, some political analysts infer Trump to be a "moderate." He campaigns on a platform that puts great emphasis on American patriotism, with disdain for political correctness. He ran counter to the Republican establishment, which widely opposed his candidacy, doubting his chances of winning the general election and fearing he could cause significant change to the image of the Republican Party. However, Trump's candidacy succeeded, partly because of widespread media coverage, his ability to self-finance his campaign and not be reliant on super PACs, frequent endorsements, and the idea that he and his supporters call "telling it like it is."

Although many of Trump's proposed policies largely appeal to working-class voters, political pundits deem some of them highly controversial and unrealistic, including the deportation of around 11 million illegal immigrants in the U.S., the erection of a substantial wall on the Mexico–United States border (with Mexico paying for it), expanded use of aggressive interrogation techniques, and a temporary ban on Muslims entering the United States. Trump's persona has also come under fire, with political contenders describing him as "divisive," and a "bully," denouncing the frequent personal attacks he makes on journalists, politicians, and competing candidates.

In response to radical Islamic terrorist attacks, Trump proposed "a total and complete shutdown of Muslims entering the United States until our country's representatives can figure out what the hell is going on." The proposal drew wide criticism from sources both within the U.S. and abroad, including foreign leaders, and leaders of Trump's own party. Figures in the Republican Party argued that a proposal banning members of a major world religion violated the party's conservative values, the Constitution's First Amendment (which grants freedom of religion), and the country's immigrant heritage. Critics pointed out that the proposal would result in the exclusion of many of the most important allies in the country's war on terror, from interpreters helping the CIA to Jordan's King Abdullah, and that it would bolster ISIL by furthering its claim that the U.S. is pitted against the Muslim faith.

The U.S. Pentagon issued a statement that "anything that bolsters ISIL's narrative and pits the United States against the Muslim faith is certainly not only contrary to our values but contrary to our national security."

During a Fox News debate, when asked about the feasibility of his plan to bar Muslims from entering the United States, Trump said that Belgium and France had been blighted by the failure of Muslims in these countries to integrate. Trump said that living in Brussels was like living in a "hellhole" because of its dire state in Muslim assimilation. Following Trump's controversial comments on Muslim immigration, the UK House of Commons held a debate on whether to ban Trump from entering the United Kingdom, after a petition was filed on Parliament's e-petition website and signed by over 500,000. The debate concluded without a vote on the matter.

Trump has had three marriages, all of which have been well documented in the tabloid media. His personal life has gained extensive media coverage. Trump married Czech model Ivana Zelníčková on April 7, 1977. They have three children: Donald, Jr. (born December 31, 1977), Eric (born January 6, 1984), and Ivanka (born October 30, 1981). By early 1990, Trump's troubled marriage to Ivana and long-running affair with actress Marla Maples had become widely documented in the tabloid press. The couple divorced in 1991. In 1992, Donald Trump sued Ivana for $25 million, alleging that she was not honoring a gag clause in their divorce agreement by disclosing facts about him.

Marla Maples gave birth to their daughter Tiffany on October 13, 1993. They married two months later. The couple formally separated in May 1997 and divorced in June 1999.

In 1998, Trump began a relationship with Slovenian-born fashion model Melania Knauss. They married on January 22,

2005. In 2006, Melania became a naturalized U.S. citizen. In March 2006, she gave birth to their son, Barron William Trump. Trump has eight grandchildren: five from his son Donald Jr. and three from his daughter Ivanka.

Trump has said of his early dating life that he felt like a great and very brave soldier and lucky to have avoided the contraction of AIDS and other sexually-transmitted diseases. "If I told the real stories of my experiences with women, often seemingly very happily married and important women, this book would be a guaranteed best-seller,"

Trump says that he is of Presbyterian faith. In April 2011 he commented: "I'm a Protestant, I'm a Presbyterian. And you know I've had a good relationship with the church over the years. I think religion is a wonderful thing. I think my religion is a wonderful religion." Trump has said that although he participates in Holy Communion, he has not asked God for forgiveness for his sins. He stated, "I think if I do something wrong, I just try and make it right. I don't bring God into that picture."

Trump maintains relationships with several prominent national evangelical and Christian leaders, including Tony Perkins and Ralph Reed. During his 2016 presidential campaign, he received a blessing from Greek Orthodox priest Emmanuel Lemelson.

In February 2016, the mainstream media issued reports of Pope Francis suggesting that Donald Trump was "not Christian" because of his advocacy for a border wall to keep out undocumented immigrants. "A person who thinks only about building walls, wherever they may be, and not about building bridges, is not a true Christian. This is not in the Gospel," the Pope replied to a reporter's questions about Trump, adding "We must see if he said things in that way and in this I give the benefit of the doubt." Trump called the Pope's criticism "disgraceful" in a Facebook post, suggesting that the Mexican government was "using the Pope as a pawn" for political purposes "because they want to continue to rip off the United States." Trump said that "if and when" the Islamic State (ISIL) attacks the Vatican, the Pope would have "wished and prayed" Trump were President because under Trump's leadership, such an attack would not happen. Trump has ties to the Jewish-American community. Trump has said: "Not only do I have Jewish grandchildren, I have a Jewish daughter [Ivanka, who converted to Judaism before her marriage to Jared Kushner] and I am very honored by that ... it wasn't in the plan but I am very glad it happened."

Over the course of his career, Trump has been involved in over 150 lawsuits in US federal courts and over 150 lawsuits in Broward County, Florida Court. In 2013, in a lawsuit filed by New York Attorney General Eric Schneiderman, Trump was accused of defrauding more than 5,000 people of $40 million for the opportunity to learn Trump's real estate investment techniques in a for-profit training program, Trump University, which operated from 2005 to 2011. A Trump counterclaim, alleging that the state Attorney General's investigation was accompanied by a campaign donation shakedown, was investigated by a New York ethics board and dismissed in August 2015. Trump filed a $1 million defamation suit against former Trump University student Tarla Makaeff, who had spent about $37,000 on seminars, after she joined the class action lawsuit and publicized her classroom experiences on social media. Trump University was later ordered by a U.S. District Judge in April 2015 to pay Makaeff and her lawyers $798,774.24 in legal fees and costs.

In 2011, Donald Trump sued Scotland for building a wind farm after assuring him it would not be built. He had recently built a golf course there and planned to build an adjacent hotel. The suit was dismissed in favor of Scotland by the Scottish Supreme Court.

In 2015, Trump initiated a $100 million lawsuit against Palm Beach County claiming that officials, in a "deliberate and malicious" act, pressured the FAA to direct air traffic to the Palm Beach International Airport over his Mar-a-Lago estate, because he said the airplanes damaged the building and disrupted its ambiance. Trump had previously sued twice over airport noise. In July 2015, Trump filed a $10 million lawsuit against chef José Andrés claiming that he backed out of a deal to open the flagship restaurant at Trump International Hotel in Washington, D.C. Andrés replied that Trump's lawsuit was "both unsurprising and without merit." Trump is suing the town of Ossining, New York over the property tax valuation on his 147-acre Trump National Golf Course, located in Briarcliff Manor in Westchester County, which Trump purchased for around $8 million at a foreclosure sale in the 1990s and to which he claimed, at the club's opening, to have added $45 million in facility improvements. Although Trump stated in his 2015 FEC filing that the property was worth at least $50 million, his lawsuit seeks a $1.4 million valuation on the property, which includes a 75,000 square foot clubhouse, five overnight suites, and permission to build 71 condominium units, in an effort to shave $424,176 from his annual local property tax obligations.

From the beginning of the campaign until May 2016, Trump has played the "anger and disdain" card very well, turning lemons into lemonade. Initially, when knocked somewhat off center by what he perceived as "hardball" questions being asked of him by Fox News's blonde bombshell, Megyn Kelly, Trump responded a day later, "She had blood coming out of her eye - and probably other places as well." (Hinting that she was acting petulant because she was probably having her monthly period). Fox News promptly came to her "aid" by rallying around her, while Trump responded by boycotting a debate organized by Fox News. Nevertheless, Fox

News, CNN, MSNBC, NBC, CBS, and ABC have given Trump more than the lion's share of coverage during the entire campaign season. Let's face it, he makes great prime time entertainment and he sells a helluva lot of advertising. No wonder Trump can trumpet that he's hardly spent any of his own money on the campaign: he gets most of the publicity for free, simply by being Donald Trump. His insults are legendary and sometimes downright hilarious.

There was one unplanned gaffe, which left a large number of voters, mainly women, upset: he told MSNBC's Chris Matthews that he thought women should be "punished" (criminally) for having an abortion. That cost him at least one state.

Although there has been precious little said about his Slovenian-born wife, former supermodel Melania Knauss Trump, she has appeared next to him in each of his victory speeches, and it is not an understatement to say that if Donald Trump can once again beat the odds, Melania will arguably be the most stunningly beautiful first lady in American history.

5

THE GAL MOST LIKELY ... HILLARY CLINTON

Hillary Diane Rodham Clinton is the Democratic nominee for President. If she wins, she will be the first woman President of the United States of America. Easily the most qualified of all the candidates, she was Secretary of State from 2009 to 2013. From 2001 to 2009, she served as a United States Senator from New York. She is the wife of the 42nd President of the United States Bill Clinton, and was First Lady of the United States during his tenure from 1993 to 2001.

A native of the Chicago area, Hillary Clinton graduated from Wellesley College in 1969 and went on to earn a J.D. from Yale Law School in 1973. After a stint as a congressional legal counsel, she moved to Arkansas, marrying Bill Clinton in 1975. She co-founded Arkansas Advocates for Children and Families in 1977, became the first female chair of the Legal Services Corporation in 1978, and was named the first female partner at the Rose Law Firm in 1979. While First Lady of Arkansas from 1979 to 1981, and 1983 to 1992, she led a task force that reformed Arkansas' public school system.

In her first major policy initiative as first lady, the president appointed her to lead the Clinton health care plan of 1993, which failed to reach a vote in Congress. In 1997 and 1999, she played a leading role in advocating the creation of the State Children's Health Insurance Program, the Adoption and Safe Families Act and the Foster Care Independence Act. The only first lady to have been subpoenaed, Clinton testified before a federal grand jury in 1996 regarding the Whitewater controversy; no charges were brought against her related to this or other investigations during her husband's presidency. Her marriage to the president was subject to considerable public discussion following the Lewinsky scandal of 1998. Her proactive role as first lady drew a polarized response from the American public, which has made her unpopular among a large segment of the conservative electorate and a pincushion for Republican politicians of every persuasion.

After moving to New York, Clinton was elected in 2000 as the first female senator from the state. Following the September 11 attacks, she voted for and supported military action in Afghanistan and Iraq, but subsequently objected to the Bush administration's conduct of the Iraq War, as well as most of George W. Bush's domestic policies. Clinton was re-elected to the Senate in 2006.

She ran for the Democratic Presidential nomination in 2008, winning more primaries and delegates than any other female candidate in American history, but ultimately she lost the nomination to Barack Obama.

As Secretary of State in the Obama administration from January 2009 to February 2013, Clinton was at the forefront of the U.S. response to the Arab Spring and advocated the U.S. military intervention in Libya. She took responsibility for security lapses related to the 2012 Benghazi attack, which resulted in the deaths of American consulate personnel, but defended her personal actions in regard to the matter. Leaving office at the end of Obama's first term, she authored her fifth book and undertook speaking engagements before announcing her second run for the Democratic nomination in April 2015.

Hillary Diane Rodham was born on October 26, 1947 in Chicago, Illinois. She was raised in a United Methodist family. Her father, Hugh Ellsworth Rodham (1911–1993), was of Welsh and English descent; he managed a successful small business in the textile industry. Her mother, Dorothy Emma Howell (1919–2011), was a homemaker of English, Scottish, French Canadian, and Welsh descent. Hillary has two younger brothers, Hugh and Tony.

Hillary Rodham attended Maine East High School, where she participated in student council, the school newspaper, and was selected for National Honor Society. In her senior year, she was a National Merit Finalist and graduated in the top five percent of her class of 1965.

Raised in a politically conservative household, Rodham helped canvass Chicago's South Side at age thirteen following the very close 1960 U.S. presidential election, where she found evidence of electoral fraud against Republican candidate Richard Nixon. She volunteered to campaign for Republican candidate Barry Goldwater in the U.S. presidential election of 1964. Rodham's early political development was shaped most by her high school history teacher (like her father, a fervent anticommunist), who introduced her to Goldwater's *The Conscience of a Conservative*, and by her Methodist youth minister (like her mother, concerned with issues of social justice), with whom she saw, and afterwards briefly met, civil rights leader Martin Luther King, Jr. at a 1962 speech in Chicago's Orchestra Hall.

In 1965, Rodham enrolled at Wellesley College, where she majored in political science. During her freshman year, she served as president of the Wellesley Young Republicans. She later stepped down from this position, as her views changed regarding the American Civil Rights Movement and the Vietnam War. In contrast to the 1960s current that advocated radical actions against the political system, she sought to work for change within it. In her junior year, Rodham became a supporter of the antiwar presidential nomination campaign of Democrat Eugene McCarthy. Following the assassination of Martin Luther King, Jr., Rodham organized a two-day student strike and worked with Wellesley's black students to recruit more black students and faculty. Even during that early period, a number of her fellow students thought she might some day become the first female President of the United States.

To help her better understand her changing political views, Professor Alan Schechter assigned Rodham to intern at the House Republican Conference, and she attended the "Wellesley in Washington" summer program. Rodham was invited by moderate New York Republican Representative Charles Goodell to help Governor Nelson Rockefeller's late-entry campaign for the Republican nomination. Rodham attended the 1968 Republican National Convention in Miami. However, she was upset by the way Richard Nixon's campaign portrayed Rockefeller and by what she perceived as the convention's "veiled" racist messages, and left the Republican Party for good.

In 1969, she graduated with a bachelor of arts, with departmental honors in political science. She became the first student in Wellesley College history to deliver its commencement address. Her speech received a standing ovation lasting seven minutes. That summer, she worked her way across Alaska, washing dishes in Mount McKinley National Park and sliming salmon in a fish processing cannery in Valdez (which fired her and shut down overnight when she complained about unhealthful conditions).

Rodham then entered Yale Law School, where she served on the editorial board of the *Yale Review of Law and Social Action.*

In the late spring of 1971 she began dating Bill Clinton, also a law student at Yale. That summer she interned in Oakland, California. Clinton canceled his original summer plans in order to live with her in California; the couple continued living together in New Haven when they returned to law school. The following summer, Rodham and Clinton campaigned in Texas for unsuccessful 1972 Democratic presidential candidate George McGovern. She received a J.D. from Yale in 1973, having stayed on an extra year to be with Clinton. He first proposed marriage to her following graduation but she declined, uncertain if she wanted to tie her future to his.

By then, Rodham was viewed as someone with a bright political future: Democratic political organizer and consultant Betsey Wright had moved from Texas to Washington the previous year to help guide her career, and Wright thought Rodham had the potential to become a future senator or president. Meanwhile, Clinton had repeatedly asked Rodham to marry him and she continued to decline. After failing the District of Columbia bar exam and passing the Arkansas exam, Rodham came to a key decision. As she later wrote, "I chose to follow my heart instead of my head". She followed Bill Clinton to Arkansas, rather than staying in Washington, where career prospects were brighter. He was then teaching law and running for a seat in the U.S. House of Representatives in his home state. In August 1974, Rodham moved to Fayetteville, Arkansas, and became one of only two female faculty members in the School of Law at the University of Arkansas. She gave classes in criminal law, where she was considered a rigorous teacher and tough grader, and was the first director of the school's legal aid clinic. She still harbored doubts about marriage, concerned that her separate identity would be lost.

Hillary Rodham and Bill Clinton bought a house in Fayetteville in the summer of 1975 and Hillary finally agreed to marry him. Their wedding took place on October 11, 1975, in a Methodist ceremony in their living room.

Bill Clinton had lost the congressional race in 1974, but in November 1976 was elected Arkansas Attorney General. The couple moved to the state capital of Little Rock. In February 1977, Rodham joined the venerable Rose Law Firm, a bastion of Arkansan political and economic influence. She specialized in patent infringement and intellectual property law while also working *pro bono* in child advocacy; she rarely performed litigation work in court.

In 1977, Rodham cofounded Arkansas Advocates for Children and Families, a state-level alliance with the Children's Defense Fund. Later that year, President Jimmy Carter (for whom Rodham had been the 1976 campaign director of field operations in Indiana) appointed her to the board of directors of the Legal Services Corporation. She served in that capacity from 1978 until the end of 1981. During her time as chair, funding for the Corporation was expanded from $90 million to $300 million; subsequently she successfully fought President Ronald Reagan's attempts to reduce the funding and change the nature of the organization.

Following her husband's November 1978 election as Governor of Arkansas, Rodham became First Lady of Arkansas in January 1979. From 1978 until they entered the White House, she had a higher salary than that of her husband. During 1978 and 1979, while looking to supplement their income, Rodham engaged in the trading of cattle futures contracts; an initial $1,000 investment generated nearly $100,000 when she stopped trading after ten months. The couple also began their ill-fated investment in the Whitewater Development Corporation real estate venture with Jim and Susan McDougal at this time. Both of these became subjects of controversy in the 1990s. On February 27, 1980, Rodham gave birth to their daughter Chelsea. In November 1980, Bill Clinton was defeated in his bid for re-election.

Bill Clinton returned to the governor's office two years later after winning the election of 1982. During her husband's campaign, Rodham began to use the name Hillary Clinton, or sometimes "Mrs. Bill Clinton", to assuage the concerns of Arkansas voters; she also took a leave of absence from Rose Law to campaign for him full-time. As First Lady of Arkansas again, she made a note of using Hillary Rodham Clinton as her name. In one of the Clinton governorship's most important initiatives, she fought a prolonged but ultimately successful battle against the Arkansas Education Association to establish mandatory teacher testing and state standards for curriculum and classroom size. She was named Arkansas Woman of the Year in 1983 and Arkansas Mother of the Year in 1984.

From 1987 to 1991, she was the first chair of the American Bar Association's Commission on Women in the Profession, created to address gender bias in the legal profession and induce the association to adopt measures to combat it. She was twice named by *The National Law Journal* as one of the 100 most influential lawyers in America: in 1988 and in 1991. When Bill Clinton thought about not running again for governor in 1990, Hillary considered running, but private polls were unfavorable and, in the end, he ran and was re-elected for the final time.

Hillary Clinton received sustained national attention for the first time when her husband became a candidate for the Democratic presidential nomination of 1992. Before the New Hampshire primary, tabloid publications printed assertions that Bill Clinton had engaged in an extramarital affair with Arkansas lounge singer

Gennifer Flowers. In response, the Clintons appeared together on *60 Minutes*, where Bill Clinton denied the affair, but acknowledged "causing pain in my marriage." This joint appearance was credited with rescuing his campaign. Bill Clinton said that in electing him, the nation would "get two for the price of one," referring to the prominent role his wife would assume.

When Bill Clinton took office as president in January 1993, Hillary Rodham Clinton became the First Lady of the United States. She was the first first lady to hold a postgraduate degree and to have her own professional career up to the time of entering the White House. She was part of the innermost circle vetting appointments to the new administration and her choices filled at least eleven top-level positions and dozens more lower-level ones. After Eleanor Roosevelt, Clinton is regarded as the most openly empowered presidential wife in American history.

Some critics called it inappropriate for the first lady to play a central role in matters of public policy. Supporters pointed out that Clinton's role in policy was no different from that of other White House advisors and that voters had been well aware that she would play an active role in her husband's presidency. Bill Clinton's campaign promise of "two for the price of one" led opponents to refer derisively to the Clintons as "co-presidents" or sometimes the Arkansas label "Billary." The pressures of conflicting ideas about the role of a first lady were enough to send Clinton into "imaginary discussions" with the also-politically-active Eleanor Roosevelt.

In January 1993, President Clinton named First Lady Clinton to chair a Task Force on National Health Care Reform, hoping to replicate the success she had in leading the effort for Arkansas education reform. Unconvinced regarding the merits of the North American Free Trade Agreement (NAFTA), she privately urged that passage of health care reform be given higher priority. The recommendation of the task force became known as the Clinton health care plan, a comprehensive proposal that would require employers to provide health coverage to their employees through individual health maintenance organizations. Its opponents quickly derided the plan as "Hillarycare," and it faced opposition from even some Democrats in Congress.

Failing to gather enough support for a floor vote in either the House or the Senate, although Democrats controlled both chambers, the proposal was abandoned in September 1994. Clinton later acknowledged that her political inexperience partly contributed to the defeat, but cited many other factors. The First Lady's approval ratings, which had generally been in the high-50s percent range during her first year, fell to 44 percent in April 1994 and 35 percent by September 1994.

Republicans made the Clinton health care plan a major campaign issue of the 1994 midterm elections, which saw a net Republican gain of fifty-three seats in the House election and seven in the Senate election, winning control of both; many analysts and pollsters found the plan to be a major factor in the Democrats' defeat, especially among independent voters. Opponents of universal health care would continue to use "Hillarycare" as a pejorative label for similar plans by others.

Along with Senators Ted Kennedy and Orrin Hatch, she was a force behind the passage of the State Children's Health Insurance Program in 1997, a federal effort that provided state support for children whose parents could not provide them with health coverage, and conducted outreach efforts on behalf of enrolling children in the program once it became law. She promoted nationwide immunization against childhood illnesses and encouraged older women to seek a mammogram to detect breast cancer, with coverage provided by Medicare. She successfully sought to increase research funding for prostate cancer and childhood asthma at the National Institutes of Health.

Together with Attorney General Janet Reno, Clinton helped create the Office on Violence Against Women at the Department of Justice. In 1997, she initiated and shepherded the Adoption and Safe Families Act, which she regarded as her greatest accomplishment as first lady. In 1999, she was instrumental in the passage of the Foster Care Independence Act, which doubled federal monies for teenagers aging out of foster care.

In a September 1995 speech before the Fourth World Conference on Women in Beijing, Clinton argued very forcefully against practices that abused women around the world and in the People's Republic of China itself, declaring that "it is no longer acceptable to discuss women's rights as separate from human rights." Delegates from over 180 countries heard her say: "If there is one message that echoes forth from this conference, let it be that human rights are women's rights and women's rights are human rights, once and for all." In doing so, she resisted both internal administration and Chinese pressure to soften her remarks. The speech became a key moment in the empowerment of women and years later females around the world would recite Clinton's key phrases. She was one of the most prominent international figures during the late 1990s to speak out against the treatment of Afghan women by the Taliban.

First Lady Clinton was a subject of several investigations by the United States Office of the Independent Counsel, committees of the U.S. Congress, and the press.

The Whitewater controversy was the focus of media attention from the publication of a *New York Times* report during the 1992 presidential campaign and throughout her time as first lady.

In 1998, the Clintons' relationship became the subject of much speculation when investigations revealed that the President had had an extramarital affair with White House intern Monica Lewinsky. Events surrounding the Lewinsky scandal eventually led to the impeachment of Bill Clinton by the House of Representatives. When the allegations against her husband were first made public, Hillary Clinton stated that they were the result of a "vast right-wing conspiracy," characterizing the Lewinsky charges as the latest in a long, organized, collaborative series of charges by Bill Clinton's political enemies rather than any wrongdoing by her husband. She later said that she had been misled by her husband's initial claims that no affair had taken place. After the evidence of President Clinton's encounters with Lewinsky became incontrovertible, she issued a public statement reaffirming her commitment to their marriage, but privately was reported to be furious at him and was unsure if she wanted to stay in the marriage.

Public reaction varied: some women admired her strength and poise in private matters made public, some sympathized with her as a victim of her husband's insensitive behavior, others criticized her as being an enabler to her husband's indiscretions, while still others accused her of cynically staying in a failed marriage as a way of keeping or even fostering her own political influence.

When New York's long-serving United States Senator Daniel Patrick Moynihan announced his retirement in November 1998, several prominent Democratic figures, including Representative Charles B. Rangel of New York, urged Clinton to run for Moynihan's open seat in the Senate election of 2000. Once she decided to run, the Clintons purchased a home in Chappaqua, New York, north of New York City, in September 1999. She became the first first lady of the United States to be a candidate for elected office. Initially, Clinton faced Rick Lazio, a Republican member of the United States House of Representatives. Throughout the campaign, opponents accused Clinton of carpetbagging, as she had never resided in New York nor participated in the state's politics before the 2000 Senate race.

Clinton won the election on November 7, 2000, with 55 percent of the vote to Lazio's 43 percent. She was sworn in as United States senator on January 3, 2001, making her the first, and so far only, woman to have held an elected office either while serving as first lady.

Upon entering the Senate, Clinton maintained a low public profile and built relationships with senators from both parties. She forged alliances with religiously inclined senators by becoming a regular participant in the Senate Prayer Breakfast. She served on five Senate committees.

Following the September 11, 2001 attacks, Clinton sought to obtain funding for the recovery efforts in New York City and security improvements in her state. Working with New York's senior senator, Charles Schumer, she was instrumental in securing $21 billion in funding for the World Trade Center site's redevelopment. Clinton voted for the USA Patriot Act in October 2001. In 2005, when the act was up for renewal, she expressed concerns with the USA Patriot Act Reauthorization Conference Report regarding civil liberties, before voting in favor of the USA Patriot Improvement and Reauthorization Act of 2005 in March 2006 that gained large majority support.

Clinton strongly supported the 2001 U.S. military action in Afghanistan, saying it was a chance to combat terrorism while improving the lives of Afghan women who suffered under the Taliban government. Clinton voted in favor of the October 2002 Iraq War Resolution, which authorized President George W. Bush to use military force against Iraq.

After the Iraq War began, Clinton made trips to Iraq and Afghanistan to visit American troops stationed there. On a visit to Iraq in February 2005, Clinton noted that the insurgency had failed to disrupt the democratic elections held earlier and that parts of the country were functioning well. Observing that war deployments were draining regular and reserve forces, she co-introduced legislation to increase the size of the regular United States Army by 80,000 soldiers to ease the strain. In late 2005, Clinton said that while immediate withdrawal from Iraq would be a mistake, Bush's pledge to stay "until the job is done" was also misguided, as it gave Iraqis "an open-ended invitation not to take care of themselves". Her stance caused frustration among those in the Democratic Party who favored quick withdrawal. Clinton supported retaining and improving health benefits for reservists and lobbied against the closure of several military bases.

Senator Clinton voted against President Bush's two major tax cut packages, the Economic Growth and Tax Relief Reconciliation Act of 2001 and the Jobs and Growth Tax Relief Reconciliation Act of 2003. Clinton voted against the 2005 confirmation of John G. Roberts as Chief Justice of the United States and the 2006 confirmation of Samuel Alito to the United States Supreme Court.

Clinton's eventual opponent in the general election was Republican candidate John Spencer, a former mayor of Yonkers. Clinton won the election on November 7, 2006, with 67% of the vote to Spencer's 31%, carrying all but four of New York's sixty-two counties. Her campaign spent $36 million for her re-election, more than any other candidate for Senate in the 2006 elections. Some Democrats criticized her for spending too much in a one-sided contest, while some supporters were concerned she did not leave more funds for a potential presidential bid in 2008. In the following months, she transferred $10 million of her Senate funds toward her presidential campaign.

Clinton opposed the Iraq War troop surge of 2007, for admittedly domestic political reasons. In March of that year, she voted in favor of a war-spending bill that required President Bush to begin withdrawing troops from Iraq by a deadline; it passed almost completely along party lines but was subsequently vetoed by Bush. In May, a compromise war funding bill that removed withdrawal deadlines but tied funding to progress benchmarks for the Iraqi government passed the Senate by a vote of 80–14 and was signed by Bush; Clinton was one of those who voted against it. Clinton responded to General David Petraeus's September 2007 Report to Congress on the Situation in Iraq by saying, "I think that the reports that you provide to us really require a willing suspension of disbelief."

In March 2007, in response to the dismissal of U.S. Attorneys controversy, Clinton called on Attorney General Alberto Gonzales to resign. Regarding the high-profile, hotly debated comprehensive immigration reform bill known as the Secure Borders, Economic Opportunity and Immigration Reform Act of 2007, Clinton cast several votes in support of the bill, which eventually failed to pass.

As the financial crisis of 2007–2008 reached a peak in September 2008, Clinton supported the proposed bailout of United States financial system, voting in favor of the $700 billion law that created the Troubled Asset Relief Program, saying that it represented the interests of the American people. It passed the Senate 74–25.

Clinton had been preparing for a potential candidacy for United States President since at least early 2003. On January 20, 2007, she announced the formation of a presidential exploratory committee for the United States presidential election of 2008, stating, "I'm in, and I'm in to win." By that time, Bill and Hillary Clinton's net worth was now more than $50 million. They had earned over $100 million since 2000, with most of it coming from Bill's books, speaking engagements, and other activities.

Throughout the first half of 2007, Clinton led candidates competing for the Democratic presidential nomination in opinion polls for the election. Senator Barack Obama of Illinois and former Senator John Edwards of North Carolina were her strongest competitors. The biggest threat to her campaign was her past support of the Iraq War, which Obama had opposed from the beginning. Clinton and Obama both set records for early fundraising.

By September 2007, polling in the first six states holding Democratic contests showed that Clinton was leading in all of them, with the races being closest in Iowa and South Carolina. By the following month, national polls showed Clinton far ahead of Democratic competitors. At the end of October, Clinton suffered a rare poor debate performance against Obama, Edwards, and her other opponents. Obama's message of change began to resonate with the Democratic electorate better than Clinton's message of experience. The race tightened considerably, especially in the early states of Iowa, New Hampshire, and South Carolina, with Clinton losing her lead in some polls by December.

In the first vote of 2008, she placed third in the January 3 Iowa Democratic caucus behind Obama and Edwards. Obama gained ground in national polling in the next few days, with all polls predicting a victory for him in the New Hampshire primary. Clinton gained a surprise win there on January 8, narrowly defeating Obama. It was the first time a woman had won a major American party's presidential primary for the purposes of delegate selection.

The nature of the contest fractured in the next few days. Several remarks by Bill Clinton and a remark by Hillary Clinton concerning Martin Luther King, Jr. and Lyndon B. Johnson, were perceived by many as, accidentally or intentionally, limiting Obama as a racially oriented candidate or otherwise denying the post-racial significance and accomplishments of his campaign.

Despite attempts by both Hillary Clinton and Obama to downplay the issue, Democratic voting became more polarized as a result, with Clinton losing much of her support among African Americans. She lost by a two-to-one margin to Obama in the January 26 South Carolina primaries, setting up an intense two-person contest for the twenty-two February 5 Super Tuesday states. Bill Clinton had made more statements attracting criticism for their perceived racial implications late in the South Carolina campaign, and his role was seen as damaging enough to her that a wave of supporters within and outside of the campaign said the former President "needs to stop." The South Carolina campaign had done lasting damage to Clinton, eroding her support among the Democratic establishment and leading to the endorsement of Obama by Ted Kennedy.

On Super Tuesday, Clinton won California, New York, New Jersey and Massachusetts, while Obama won more states; they almost evenly split the total popular vote. But Obama was gaining more pledged delegates for his share of the popular vote due to better exploitation of the Democratic proportional allocation rules.

The Clinton campaign had counted on winning the nomination by Super Tuesday and was unprepared financially and logistically for a prolonged effort; lagging in fundraising, Clinton began loaning money to her campaign. There was continuous turmoil within the campaign staff and she made several top-level personnel changes. Obama won the next eleven February contests across the country, often by large margins, and took a significant pledged delegate lead over Clinton. On March 4, Clinton broke the string of losses by winning in Ohio, where her criticism of NAFTA, a major legacy of her husband's presidency, helped in a state where the trade agreement was unpopular. Throughout the campaign, Obama dominated caucuses, for which the Clinton campaign largely ignored preparation. Obama did well in primaries where

African Americans or younger, college-educated, or more affluent voters were heavily represented; Clinton did well in primaries
where Hispanics or older, non-college-educated, or working-class
white voters predominated. Behind in delegates, Clinton's best
hope of winning the nomination came in persuading uncommit-
ted, party-appointed superdelegates.

Clinton's admission in late March, that her repeated campaign
statements about having been under hostile fire from snipers
during a March 1996 visit to U.S. troops at Tuzla Air Base in
Bosnia and Herzegovina were not true, attracted considerable
media attention. On April 22, she won the Pennsylvania primary
and kept her campaign alive. On May 6, a narrower-than-expected
win in the Indiana primary, coupled with a large loss in the North
Carolina primary, ended any realistic chance she had of winning
the nomination. She vowed to stay on through the remaining
primaries, but stopped attacks against Obama; as one advisor
stated, "She could accept losing. She could not accept quitting."
She won some of the remaining contests. Over the last three
months of the campaign she won more delegates, states, and votes
than Obama, but she failed to overcome Obama's lead.

By June 3, 2008, Obama had gained enough delegates
to become the presumptive nominee. In a speech before her
supporters on June 7, Clinton ended her campaign and endorsed
Obama. By campaign's end, Clinton had won 1,640 pledged
delegates to Obama's 1,763; at the time of the clinching, Clinton
had 286 superdelegates to Obama's 395, with those numbers
widening once Obama was acknowledged the winner. Clinton and
Obama each received over 17 million votes during the nomination
process with both breaking the previous record. Clinton was
the first woman to run in the primary or caucus of every state.
Clinton gave a passionate speech supporting Obama at the 2008
Democratic National Convention and campaigned frequently for

him in fall 2008, which concluded with his victory over McCain in the general election on November 4. Clinton's campaign ended up severely in debt; she owed millions of dollars to outside vendors and wrote off the $13 million that she lent it herself. The debt was eventually paid off by the beginning of 2013.

In mid-November 2008, President-elect Obama and Clinton discussed the possibility of her serving as U.S. Secretary of State in his administration. She was initially reluctant, but on November 20, she told Obama she would accept the position.

On December 1, President-elect Obama formally announced that Clinton would be his nominee for Secretary of State. As part of the nomination and in order to relieve concerns of conflict of interest, Bill Clinton agreed to accept several conditions and restrictions regarding his ongoing activities and fundraising efforts for the William J. Clinton Foundation and Clinton Global Initiative.

By this time, her public approval rating had reached 65%, the highest point since the Lewinsky scandal. On January 21, 2009, Clinton was confirmed in the full Senate by a vote of 94–2.

Clinton spent her initial days as Secretary of State telephoning dozens of world leaders and indicating that U.S. foreign policy would change direction: "We have a lot of damage to repair." She cited the need for an increased U.S. diplomatic presence, especially in Iraq where the Defense Department had conducted diplomatic missions.

In March 2009, Clinton prevailed over Vice President Joe Biden on an internal debate to send an additional 21,000 troops to the war in Afghanistan and supported Obama's plan to tie the surge to a timetable for eventual withdrawal. The same month, Clinton presented Russian Foreign Minister Sergey Lavrov with a "reset button" symbolizing U.S. attempts to rebuild ties with that country under its new president, Dmitry Medvedev. The policy, which became known as the Russian reset, led to improved cooperation in several areas during Medvedev's time in office, but relations would worsen considerably following Vladimir Putin's return to the position in 2012. In October 2009, on a trip to Switzerland, Clinton's intervention overcame last-minute snags and saved the signing of an historic Turkish–Armenian accord that established diplomatic relations and opened the border between the two long-hostile nations. In Pakistan, she engaged in several unusually blunt discussions with students, talk show hosts, and tribal elders, in an attempt to repair the Pakistani image of the U.S. Beginning in 2010, she helped organize a diplomatic isolation and international sanctions regime against Iran, in an effort to force curtailment of that country's nuclear program; this would eventually lead to the multinational Joint Comprehensive Plan of Action being agreed to in 2015.

Clinton and Obama forged a good working relationship without power struggles; she was a team player within the administration and a defender of it to the outside, and was careful that neither she nor her husband would upstage the president. Clinton formed an alliance with Secretary of Defense Gates as they shared similar strategic outlooks. Obama and Clinton both approached foreign policy as a largely non-ideological, pragmatic exercise. She met with him weekly but did not have the close, daily relationship that some of her predecessors had had with their presidents; moreover, certain key areas of policymaking were kept inside the White House or Pentagon. Nevertheless, the president had trust in her actions.

In a prepared speech in January 2010, Clinton drew analogies between the Iron Curtain and the free and unfree Internet. Chinese officials reacted negatively towards it and the speech garnered attention as the first time a senior American official had clearly defined the Internet as a key element of American foreign policy. In July 2010, Secretary Clinton visited Korea, Vietnam, Pakistan, and Afghanistan, all the while preparing for the July 31 wedding of daughter Chelsea amid much media attention. In late November 2010, Clinton led the U.S. damage control effort after WikiLeaks released confidential State Department cables containing blunt statements and assessments by U.S. and foreign diplomats.

The 2011 Egyptian protests posed the most challenging foreign policy crisis for the administration yet. Clinton's public response quickly evolved from an early assessment that the government of Hosni Mubarak was "stable," to a stance that there needed to be an "orderly transition to a democratic participatory government," to a condemnation of violence against the protesters. Obama came to rely upon Clinton's advice, organization, and personal connections in the behind-the-scenes response to developments. As the Arab Spring protests spread throughout the region, Clinton was at the forefront of a U.S. response that she recognized was sometimes contradictory, backing some regimes while supporting protesters against others.

As the Libyan Civil War took place, Clinton's shift in favor of military intervention aligned her with Ambassador to the U.N. Susan Rice and National Security Council figure Samantha Power and was a key turning point in overcoming internal administration opposition from Defense Secretary Gates, security advisor Thomas Donilon, and counterterrorism advisor John Brennan in gaining the backing for, and Arab and U.N. approval of, the 2011 military intervention in Libya. Secretary Clinton testified to Congress that the administration did not need congressional authorization for its military intervention in Libya, despite objections from some members of both parties that the administration was violating the War Powers Resolution, and the State Department's legal advisor argued the same when the Resolution's 60-day limit for unauthorized wars was passed. Clinton later used U.S. allies and what she called "convening power" to promote unity among the Libyan rebels as they eventually overthrew the Gaddafi regime. The aftermath of the Libyan Civil War saw the country becoming a failed state. The wisdom of the intervention and interpretation of what happened afterward would become the subject of considerable debate.

During April 2011 internal deliberations of the president's innermost circle of advisors over whether to order U.S. special forces to conduct a raid into Pakistan against Osama bin Laden, Clinton was among those who argued in favor, saying the importance of getting bin Laden outweighed the risks to the U.S. relationship with Pakistan. Following completion of the mission on May 2, which resulted in bin Laden's death, Clinton played a key role in the administration's decision not to release photographs of the dead al-Qaeda leader.

In a speech before the United Nations Human Rights Council in December 2011, Clinton said that "Gay rights are human rights," and that the U.S. would advocate for gay rights and legal protections of gays abroad. The same period saw her overcome internal administration opposition with a direct appeal to Obama and stage the first visit to Burma by a U.S. secretary of state since 1955, as she met with Burmese leaders as well as opposition leader Aung San Suu Kyi and sought to support the 2011 Burmese democratic reforms.

During the Syrian Civil War, Clinton and the Obama administration initially sought to persuade Syrian President Bashar al-Assad to engage popular demonstrations with reform, then as government violence rose in August 2011, called for him to relinquish power. The administration joined a number of allied countries in delivering non-lethal assistance to rebels opposed to the Assad government, as well as to humanitarian groups working in Syria. During mid-2012, Clinton formed a plan with CIA Director David Petraeus to further strengthen the opposition by arming and training vetted groups of Syrian rebels, but the proposal was rejected by the White House,

In December 2012, Clinton was hospitalized for a few days for treatment of a blood clot in her right transverse venous sinus. Her doctors had discovered the clot during a follow-up examination for a concussion she had sustained when she had fainted and fallen nearly three weeks earlier, after developing severe dehydration from a viral intestinal ailment acquired during a trip to Europe. The clot, which caused no immediate neurological injury, was treated with anticoagulant medication, and her doctors subsequently said she made a full recovery.

Throughout her time in office, and in her final speech concluding it, Clinton viewed "smart power" as the strategy for asserting U.S. leadership and values by combining military hard power with diplomacy and U.S. soft power capacities in global economics, development aid, technology, creativity, and human rights advocacy. As such, she became the first secretary of state to methodically implement the smart power approach. In debates over use of military force, she was generally one of the more hawkish voices in the administration. She greatly expanded the State Department's use of social media, including Facebook and Twitter, both to get its message out and to help empower people vis-à-vis their rulers.

Clinton visited 112 countries during her tenure, making her the most widely traveled secretary of state. As early as March 2011, she indicated she was not interested in serving a second term as Secretary of State should Obama be re-elected in 2012; in December 2012, following that re-election, Obama nominated Senator John Kerry to be Clinton's successor.

On September 11, 2012, the U.S. diplomatic mission in Benghazi, Libya, was attacked, resulting in the deaths of the U.S. Ambassador, J. Christopher Stevens, and three other Americans. The attack, questions surrounding the security of the U.S. consulate, and the varying explanations given afterward by administration officials for what had happened, became politically controversial in the U.S. On October 15, Clinton took responsibility for the question of security lapses and said the differing explanations were due to the inevitable fog of war confusion after such events.

On December 19, a panel led by Thomas R. Pickering and Michael Mullen issued its report on the matter. It was sharply critical of State Department officials in Washington for ignoring requests for more guards and safety upgrades and for failing to adapt security procedures to a deteriorating security environment. It focused its criticism on the department's Bureau of Diplomatic Security and Bureau of Near Eastern Affairs; four State Department officials at the assistant secretary level and below were removed from their posts as a consequence. Clinton accepted the conclusions of the report and said that changes were underway to implement its suggested recommendations.

Clinton gave testimony to two congressional foreign affairs committees on January 23, 2013, regarding the Benghazi attack. She defended her actions in response to the incident and, while still accepting formal responsibility, said she had had no direct role in specific discussions beforehand regarding consulate security. Congressional Republicans challenged her on several points, to which she sometimes responded angrily or emotionally. In particular, after persistent questioning about whether the administration had issued inaccurate "talking points" after the attack, Clinton responded with the heated and much-quoted rejoinder, "With all due respect, the fact is we had four dead Americans. Was it because of a protest or was it because of guys out for a walk one night who decided that they'd they go kill some Americans? What difference at this point does it make? It is our job to figure out what happened and do everything we can to prevent it from ever happening again." In November 2014, the House Intelligence Committee issued a report that concluded there had been no wrongdoing in the administration's response to the attack.

The House Select Committee on Benghazi was created in May 2014 and has conducted lengthy investigations related to the 2012 attack. In response to an interviewer's question in September 2015 about what the Republicans had accomplished in Congress, House Majority Leader Kevin McCarthy, credited the Benghazi hearings with lowering Clinton's poll numbers. McCarthy's answer contradicted the Republicans' previous talking points on the investigation. For example, outgoing Speaker of the House John Boehner had consistently expressed disgust at any suggestion that the hearings were politically motivated. On October 22, 2015, Clinton testified at an all-day and nighttime session before the committee. The hearing included many heated exchanges between committee members and Clinton, and between the committee members themselves. Clinton was widely seen as emerging largely unscathed from the hearing, because of what the media perceived as a calm and unfazed demeanor, and a lengthy, meandering, repetitive line of questioning from the committee.

A controversy arose in March 2015, when it was revealed by the State Department's inspector general that Clinton had exclusively used personal email accounts on a non-government, privately maintained server in lieu of email accounts maintained on Federal government servers, when conducting official business during her tenure as Secretary of State. Some experts, officials, members of Congress, and political opponents, contended that her use of private messaging system software and a private server violated State Department protocols and procedures, and Federal laws and regulations governing recordkeeping requirements.

Nearly 2,100 emails contained in Clinton's server were retroactively marked classified by the State Department, though none of the emails were marked classified at the time they were sent. 65 were later classified as "secret", more than 20 were designated "top secret", and the rest were later designated as "confidential". Government policy, reiterated in the nondisclosure agreement signed by Clinton as part of gaining her security clearance, is that sensitive information should be considered and handled as classified even if not marked as such. After allegations were raised that some of the emails in question fell into the so-called "born classified" category, an FBI probe was initiated regarding how classified information was handled on the Clinton server.

The controversy occurred against the backdrop of Clinton's 2016 presidential election campaign and hearings held by the House Select Committee on Benghazi.

When Clinton left the State Department she became a private citizen for the first time in thirty years. She and her daughter joined her husband as named members of the Bill, Hillary & Chelsea Clinton Foundation in 2013. There she focused on early childhood development efforts, including an initiative called Too Small to Fail and a $600 million initiative to encourage the enrollment of girls in secondary schools worldwide, led by former Australian Prime Minister Julia Gillard. She also led the No Ceilings: The Full Participation Project, a partnership with the Bill and Melinda Gates Foundation to gather and study data on the progress of women and girls around the world since the Beijing conference in 1995; its March 2015 report said that while "There has never been a better time in history to be born a woman ... this data shows just how far we still have to go." The foundation began accepting new donations from foreign governments, which it had stopped doing while she was secretary.

For the fifteen months ending in March 2015, Clinton earned over $11 million from her speeches, a total that rose to over $25 million when her husband's speeches were included. For the overall period 2007–14, the Clintons earned almost $141 million, paid some $56 million in federal and state taxes, and donated about $15 million to charity. As of 2015, she was estimated to be worth over $30 million on her own, or $50 million with her husband. Clinton resigned from the foundation's board in April 2015, when she began her presidential campaign.

On April 12, 2015, Clinton formally announced her candidacy for the presidency in the 2016 election. She had a campaign-in-waiting already in place, including a large donor network, experienced operatives, and the Ready for Hillary and Priorities USA Action political action committees, and other infrastructure. The campaign's headquarters were established in New York City. Focuses of her campaign have included raising middle class incomes, establishing universal preschool and making college more affordable, and improving the Affordable Care Act. Initially considered a prohibitive favorite to win the Democratic nomination, Clinton has faced an unexpectedly strong challenge from self-professed democratic socialist Senator Bernie Sanders of Vermont, whose longtime stance against the influence of corporations and the wealthy in American politics has resonated with a dissatisfied citizenry troubled by the effects of income inequality in the United States and which has contrasted with Clinton's Wall Street ties.

In the initial contest of the primaries season, Clinton only very narrowly won the Iowa Democratic caucuses, held February 1, over an increasingly popular Sanders, making her the first woman to win the Iowa caucuses. In the first primary, held in New Hampshire on February 9, she lost to Sanders by a wide margin. Sanders was an increasing threat in the next contest, the Nevada caucuses on February 20, but Clinton managed a five-percentage-point win, aided by final-days campaigning among of casino workers. She followed that with a lopsided victory in the South Carolina primary on February 27. These two victories stabilized her campaign and showed an avoidance of the management turmoil that harmed her 2008 effort.

On the March 1, the first "Super Tuesday," Clinton won seven of eleven contests, including a string of dominating victories across the South buoyed by African-American voters, and opened up a significant lead in pledged delegates over Sanders. She maintained this delegate lead over the next several weeks, with a consistent pattern through the year being that Sanders has done better among younger, whiter, more rural, and more liberal voters and in states that hold caucuses or where eligibility is open to independents, while Clinton does better among older and more diverse voter populations and in states that hold primaries or where eligibility is restricted to registered Democrats.

In a Gallup poll conducted during May 2005, 54 percent of respondents considered Clinton a liberal, 30 percent considered her a moderate, and 9 percent considered her a conservative.

In 1996, Clinton presented a vision for the children of America in the book *It Takes a Village: and Other Lessons Children Teach Us*. The book made the Best Seller list of *The New York Times* and Clinton received the Grammy Award for Best Spoken Word Album in 1997 for the book's audio recording. In 2003, Clinton released a 562-page autobiography, *Living History*, for which publisher Simon & Schuster paid Clinton a near-record advance of $8 million. The book went on to sell more than one million copies in the first month following publication, and was translated into twelve foreign languages. In 2014, Clinton published a second memoir, *Hard Choices*, which focused on her time as Secretary of State. It has sold about 250,000 copies.

Over ninety books and scholarly works have been written about Hillary Rodham Clinton, from many perspectives. A 2006 survey by *The New York Observer* found "a virtual cottage industry" of "anti-Clinton literature," put out by Regnery Publishing and other conservative imprints. Books praising Clinton did not sell nearly as well.

When she ran for Senate in 2000, a number of fundraising groups such as Save Our Senate and the Emergency Committee to Stop Hillary Rodham Clinton sprang up to oppose her. Republican and conservative groups viewed her as a reliable "bogeyman" to mention in fundraising letters, on a par with Ted Kennedy, and the equivalent of Democratic and liberal appeals mentioning Newt Gingrich. She has been the subject of many satirical impressions on *Saturday Night Live*, beginning with her time as first lady, and has made guest appearances on the show herself, in 2008 and in 2015, to face-off with her doppelgängers.

Clinton has often been described in the popular media as a polarizing figure, with some arguing otherwise. Women consistently rated Clinton more favorably than men by about ten percentage points during her first lady years. Once she became Secretary of State, Clinton's image seemed to improve dramatically among the American public and become one of a respected world figure. She gained consistently high approval ratings and her favorable-unfavorable ratings during 2010 and 2011 were the highest of any active, nationally prominent American political figure. Clinton sought to explain her popularity by saying in early 2012, "There's a certain consistency to who I am and what I do, and I think people have finally said, 'Well, you know, I kinda get her now.'" She continued to do well in Gallup's most admired man and woman poll and in 2015 she was named the most admired woman by Americans for a record fourteenth straight time and twentieth time overall. Her favorability ratings dropped, however, after she left office and began to be viewed in the context of partisan politics again, and by September 2015, with her 2016 presidential campaign underway and beset by continued reports regarding her private email usage at the State Department, her ratings had slumped to the some of her lowest levels ever.

Clinton maintained that she did not send or receive any confidential emails from her personal server. In a Democratic debate with Bernie Sanders on February 4, 2016, Clinton said, "I never sent or received any classified material – they are retroactively classifying it." In a Meet the Press interview, Clinton said, "Let me repeat what I have repeated for many months now, I never received nor sent any material that was marked classified." On July 2, 2016, Clinton stated: "Let me repeat what I have repeated for many months now, I never received nor sent any material that was marked classified."

On July 5, 2016, the FBI concluded its investigation. In a statement, FBI director James Comey said: "110 e-mails in 52 e-mail chains have been determined by the owning agency to contain classified information at the time they were sent or received. Eight of those chains contained information that was Top Secret at the time they were sent; 36 chains contained Secret information at the time; and eight contained confidential information, which is the lowest level of classification. Separate from those, about 2,000 additional e-mails were 'up-classified' to make them Confidential; the information in those had not been classified at the time the e-mails were sent."

Three emails were found to be marked as classified, although they lacked classified headers and were only marked with a small "c" in parentheses, described as "portion markings" by Comey. They found that Clinton used her personal email extensively while outside the United States, both sending and receiving work-related emails in the territory of sophisticated adversaries. The FBI assessed that it "is possible that hostile actors gained access to Secretary Clinton's personal email account." Comey stated that although Clinton was "extremely careless in their handling of very sensitive, highly classified information," the FBI expressed to the Justice Department that "no charges are appropriate in this case." On July 6, 2016, U.S. Attorney General Loretta Lynch confirmed that the investigation into Clinton's use of private email servers while secretary of state would be closed without criminal charges.

6

THE LIBERTARIAN CANDIDATE: GARY JOHNSON

In the United States, it is rare for third party and independent candidates to take large shares of the vote in elections, and even rarer for such candidates to actually win elections. Since 1990, candidates in 32 (8%) of the 380 Senate elections have won at least five percent of the vote, and two (0.5%) have won, both in 2006. In six of the 32 races, one or the other of the major parties failed to nominate any candidate, allowing third-party candidates to perform better than usual. In the 302 gubernatorial elections since 1990, 16% have won at least five percent of the vote 49 times, while 2% have won election. The last third-party or independent governor to win was Alaska's Bill Walker in 2014. No third-party or independent candidate being elected president.

The only party showing 5% of more in the 2016 Presidential elections is the Libertarian party, a political party that promotes civil liberties, non-interventionism, laissez-faire economics and the abolition of the welfare state. The LP was officially formed on December 11, 1971, in Colorado Springs, Colorado. The founding of the party was prompted in part due to concerns about the Nixon administration, the Vietnam War, conscription, and the end of the gold standard.

The party has generally promoted a classical liberal platform, in contrast to the modern liberal and progressive platform of the Democrats and the more conservative platform of the Republicans. Gary Johnson, the party's presidential nominee in 2012 and 2016, states that the LP is more culturally liberal than the Democrats, but more fiscally conservative than the Republicans. Current fiscal policy positions include lowering taxes, decreasing the national debt, allowing people to opt out of Social Security, and eliminating the welfare state, in part by utilizing private charities; current cultural policy positions include ending the prohibition of illegal drugs, supporting same-sex marriage, ending capital punishment, and supporting gun ownership rights.

There are 411,250 voters registered as Libertarian in 27 states and Washington, D.C. By that count, as well as popular vote in elections and number of candidates run per election, the LP is the country's third largest nationally organized party. It has also many firsts to its credit, such as being the first party to run an openly LGBT presidential candidate and the party under which the first electoral vote was cast for a woman for Vice President in a United States presidential election, due to a faithless elector. Though the party has never won a seat in the United States Congress, it has seen electoral success in the context of state legislatures and other local offices. Three Libertarians were elected to the Alaska House of Representatives between 1978 and 1984 and another four to the New Hampshire General Court in 1992. Neil Randall won election to the Vermont House of Representatives in 1998, which marked the last time to date a Libertarian was elected to a state house. Rhode Island State Representative Daniel P. Gordon was expelled from the Republicans and joined the Libertarian Party in 2011. In 2016, the Libertarians tied their 1992 peak of four legislators when four state legislators from four different states left the Republican Party to join the Libertarian Party: Nevada Assemblyman John Moore in January, Nebraska Senator Laura Ebke and New Hampshire Representative Max Abramson in May, and Utah Senator Mark B. Madsen in July.

Gary Johnson, the Libertarian Party's Presidential nominee in 2012, returns for a repeat try in the 2016 election.

Gary Earl Johnson (born January 1, 1953) is an American businessman, politician and the Libertarian Party nominee for President of the United States in the 2016 election. He served as the 29th Governor of New Mexico from 1995 to 2003 as a member of the Republican Party. He was the Libertarian Party's nominee for President of the United States in the 2012 election.

Johnson announced his candidacy for president on April 21, 2011, as a Republican, on a libertarian platform emphasizing the United States public debt and a balanced budget through a 43% reduction of all federal government spending, protection of civil liberties, an immediate end to the War in Afghanistan and his advocacy of the FairTax. On December 28, 2011, after being excluded from the majority of the Republican Party's presidential debates and failing to gain traction while campaigning for the New Hampshire primary, he withdrew his candidacy for the Republican nomination and announced that he would continue his presidential campaign as a candidate for the nomination of the Libertarian Party. He won the Libertarian Party nomination on May 5, 2012. The Johnson ticket received 0.99% of the popular vote, amounting to 1.27 million votes, more than all other minor candidates combined. It was the best showing in the Libertarian Party's history by vote count. On January 6, 2016, Johnson announced his candidacy for the Libertarian nomination once again in 2016, and in May he selected former Republican Governor of Massachusetts William Weld as his running mate. On May 29, 2016, Johnson won the Libertarian nomination on the second ballot with 55.8% of the delegates.

Johnson was born in Minot, North Dakota, the son of Lorraine B. (née Bostow), who worked for the Bureau of Indian Affairs, and Earl W. Johnson, a public school teacher. Johnson graduated from Sandia High School in Albuquerque in 1971, where he was on the school track team. He attended the University of New Mexico from 1971 to 1975 and graduated with a Bachelor of Science in political science. While at UNM, he joined the Sigma Alpha Epsilon fraternity, where he met his future wife, Denise "Dee" Simms.

While in college, Johnson earned money as a door-to-door handyman. His success in that industry encouraged him to start his own business, Big J Enterprises, in 1976. When he started the business, which focused on mechanical contracting, Johnson was its only employee. His major break with the firm was receiving a large contract from Intel's expansion in Rio Rancho, which increased Big J's revenue to $38 million.

Overburdened by his success, Johnson enrolled in a time management course at night school. He eventually grew Big J into a multimillion-dollar corporation with over 1,000 employees. By the time he sold the company in 1999, it was one of New Mexico's leading construction companies.

He entered politics for the first time by running for Governor of New Mexico in 1994 on a fiscally conservative, low-tax and anti-crime platform. Johnson won the Republican Party of New Mexico's gubernatorial nomination, and defeated incumbent

Democratic governor Bruce King. During his tenure as governor, Johnson became known for his low-tax libertarian views, adhering to policies of tax and bureaucracy reduction supported by a cost–benefit analysis rationale. He cut the 10% annual growth in the budget: in part, due to his use of the gubernatorial veto 200 times during his first six months in office. Johnson set state and national records for his use of veto and line-item veto powers: estimated to have been more than the other 49 contemporary governors combined, which gained him the nicknames "Veto Johnson" and "Governor Veto."

Johnson successfully sought re-election in 1998. In his second term, he concentrated on the issue of school voucher reforms, as well as campaigning for marijuana decriminalization and legalization, and opposition to the War on Drugs. Term limited, Johnson could not run for re-election at the end of his second term. After leaving office, Johnson founded the non-profit Our America Initiative in 2009, a political advocacy committee seeking to promote policies such as free enterprise, foreign non-interventionism, limited government and privatization. He endorsed the Republican presidential candidacy of Congressman Ron Paul in the 2008 election.

Commentator Andrew Sullivan quoted a claim that Johnson "is highly regarded in the state for his outstanding leadership during two terms as governor. He slashed the size of state government during his term and left the state with a large budget surplus." In an interview in *Reason* magazine in January 2001, Johnson's accomplishments in office were described as follows: "no tax increases in six years, a major road building program, shifting Medicaid to managed care, constructing two new private prisons, canning 1,200 state employees, and vetoing a record number of bills." According to one New Mexico paper, "Johnson left the state fiscally solid", and was "arguably the most popular governor

of the decade, leaving the state with a $1 billion budget surplus."
The Washington Times reported that when Johnson left office, "the
size of state government had been substantially reduced and New
Mexico was enjoying a large budget surplus."

According to a profile of Johnson in the *National Review*,
"During his tenure, he vetoed more bills than the other 49
governors combined—750 in total, one third of which had been
introduced by Republican legislators. Johnson also used his line-
item-veto power thousands of times. He credits his heavy veto
pen for eliminating New Mexico's budget deficit and cutting the
growth rate of New Mexico's government in half." According to
the *Myrtle Beach Sun News*, Johnson "said his numerous vetoes,
only two of which were overridden, stemmed from his philosophy
of looking at all things for their cost–benefit ratio and his axe fell
on Republicans as well as Democrats."

While in office, Johnson was criticized for opposing funding
for an independent study of private prisons after a series of riots
and killings at the facilities. Martin Chavez, his opponent in the
1998 New Mexico gubernatorial race, criticized Johnson for his
frequent vetoing of programs, suggesting that it resulted in New
Mexico's low economic and social standing nationally. Journalist
Mark Ames described Johnson as "a hard-core conservative" who
"ruled the state like a right-wing authoritarian" and only embraced
marijuana legalization in his second term for populist gain. This
was mainly in reference to a commercial from Johnson's reelection
campaign, featuring Johnson saying that a felon in New Mexico
would serve "every lousy second" of their prison sentence.
Johnson insisted however that the commercial was directed at "the
guy who's got his gun out" rather than non-violent drug offenders.

Johnson serves on the Advisory Council of Students for
Sensible Drug Policy, a student nonprofit organization which

advocates for drug policy reform. As of April 2011, he serves on the board of directors of Students for Liberty, a nonprofit libertarian organization. His first book, *Seven Principles of Good Government*, was published on August 1, 2012.

On April 21, 2011 Johnson announced via Twitter, "I am running for president." He was the first of an eventually large field to announce his candidacy for the Republican presidential nomination. Initially, Johnson hoped Ron Paul would not run for president so that Johnson could galvanize Paul's network of libertarian-minded voters, and he even traveled to Houston to tell Paul of his decision to run in person, but Paul announced his candidacy on May 13, 2011.

Johnson participated in the first of the Republican presidential debates, hosted by Fox News in South Carolina on May 5, 2011, appearing on stage with Herman Cain, Ron Paul, Tim Pawlenty, and Rick Santorum. Mitt Romney and Michele Bachmann both declined to debate. Johnson was excluded from the next three debates on June 13, August 11, and September 7. After the first exclusion, Johnson made a 43-minute video responding to each of the debate questions, which he posted on YouTube. The first exclusion, which was widely publicized, gave Johnson "a little bump" in name recognition and produced "a small uptick" in donations. But "the long term consequences were dismal." For the financial quarter ending June 30, Johnson raised a mere $180,000. Fox News decided that because Johnson polled at least 2% in five recent polls, he could participate in a September 22 debate in Florida, which it co-hosted with the Florida Republican Party (the party objected to Johnson's inclusion). Johnson participated, appearing on stage with Michele Bachmann, Herman Cain, Newt Gingrich, Jon Huntsman, Ron Paul, Rick Perry, Mitt Romney, and Rick Santorum. During the debate, Johnson delivered what many media outlets, including the *Los Angeles Times*, and *Time*, called the best line of the night: "My next-door neighbor's two dogs have created more shovel ready jobs than this administration."

Although Johnson had focused the majority of his campaign activities on the New Hampshire primary, he announced on November 29, 2011 that he would no longer campaign there due to his inability to gain traction with less than a month until the primary. There was speculation in the media that he might run as a Libertarian Party candidate instead. Johnson acknowledged that he was considering such a move. In December, *Politico* reported that Johnson would quit the Republican primaries and announce his intention to seek the Libertarian Party nomination at a December 28 press conference. He also encouraged his supporters to vote for Ron Paul in 2012 Republican presidential primaries.

On December 28, 2011, Johnson formally withdrew his candidacy for the Republican presidential nomination, and declared his candidacy for the 2012 presidential nomination of the Libertarian Party in Santa Fe, New Mexico. On May 5, 2012, at the 2012 Libertarian National Convention, Johnson received the Libertarian Party's official nomination for president in the 2012 election, by a vote of 419 votes to 152 votes for second-place candidate R. Lee Wrights. In his acceptance speech, Johnson asked the convention's delegates to nominate as his running mate Judge Jim Gray of California. Gray subsequently received the party's vice-presidential nomination on the first ballot.

Johnson spent the early months of his campaign making media appearances on television programs such as *The Daily Show with Jon Stewart* and *Red Eye w/Greg Gutfeld*. Starting in September 2012, Johnson embarked on a three-week tour of college campuses throughout the US. On October 23, 2012, Gary Johnson participated in a third party debate that was aired on C-SPAN, RT America, and Al Jazeera English. A post-debate online election allowed people to choose two candidates from the debate they thought had won to face each other head to head in a run-off debate. Gary Johnson and Jill Stein won the poll. They debated in Washington, D.C. on November 5, 2012.

Johnson stated that his goal was to win at least 5 percent of the vote, as winning 5 percent would allow Libertarian Party candidates equal ballot access and federal funding during the next election cycle. In a national Gallup poll of likely registered voters conducted June 7 through June 10, 2012, Johnson took 3% of the vote, while a Gallup poll conducted September 6 through September 9, 2012, showed Johnson taking 1% of likely voters. A Zogby poll released July 13, 2012, revealed Johnson took 5.3% of likely voters, while a Zogby poll released September 23, 2012, showed Johnson taking 2% of likely voters. The final results showed Johnson polling nearly 1.3 million votes and 1% of the popular vote. This established a Libertarian Party record for total votes won in a presidential election and the second-highest Libertarian percentage ever, behind Ed Clark's 1.1% in 1980. Despite falling short of his stated goal of 5%, Johnson stated, "Ours is a mission accomplished." In regards to a future presidential bid, he said "it is too soon to be talking about 2016."

Since the 2012 elections, Johnson has continued to criticize the Obama administration on various issues. In an article for *The Guardian*, Johnson called on United States Attorney General Eric Holder to let individual states legalize marijuana. In a Google Hangout hosted by Johnson in June 2013, he criticized the US government's lack of transparency and due process in regards to the NSA's domestic surveillance programs. He also said that he would not rule out running as a Republican again in the future.

In December 2013, Johnson announced the founding of his own Super PAC, Our America Initiative PAC. The Super PAC is intended to support libertarian-minded causes. "From the realities of government-run healthcare setting in to the continuing disclosures of the breadth of NSA's domestic spying, more Americans than ever are ready to take a serious look at candidates who offer real alternatives to business-as-usual," the release announcing the PAC said.

In July 2014, Johnson was named president and CEO of Cannabis Sativa Inc., a Nevada-based company that aims primarily to sell medical cannabis products in states where medicinal and/or recreational cannabis is legal.

In an April 2014, Reddit "Ask Me Anything" session, Johnson stated that he hoped to run for president again in 2016. On whether he would run as a Libertarian or a Republican, he stated that "I would love running as a Libertarian because I would have the least amount of explaining to do." In November 2014, Johnson affirmed his intention to run for the 2016 Libertarian nomination. In July 2015, Johnson reiterated his intentions for a presidential campaign but stated he was not announcing anything imminently: "I just think there are more downsides than upsides to announcing at this point, and, look, I don't have any delusions about the process. In retrospect, 90 percent of the time I spent [trying to become president] ended up to be wasted time."

In January 2016, Johnson resigned from his post as CEO of Cannabis Sativa, Inc., to pursue political opportunities, hinting to a 2016 presidential run.

On January 6, 2016, Johnson declared that he would seek the Libertarian nomination for the presidency. On May 18, Johnson named former Massachusetts Governor William Weld as his running mate. On May 29, 2016, Johnson received the Libertarian nomination on the second ballot.

Johnson's views have been described as fiscally conservative and socially liberal with a philosophy of limited government and military non-interventionism. He has identified as a classical liberal. Johnson has said he favors simplifying and reducing taxes. During his governorship, Johnson cut taxes fourteen times and never increased them. Due to his stance on taxes, political pundit David Weigel described him as "the original Tea Party candidate." Johnson has advocated for the FairTax, a proposal which would abolish all federal income, corporate and capital gains taxes, and replace them with a 23% tax on consumption of all non-essential goods, while providing a regressive rebate to households according to income level. He has argued that this would assure transparency in the tax system and incentivize the private sector to create "tens of millions of jobs." In June 2016, Johnson said that he supported the Trans-Pacific Partnership.

Johnson has said that he supports balancing the federal budget immediately. He supports "slashing government spending," including Medicare, Medicaid, and Social Security, which would involve cutting Medicare and Medicaid by 43 percent and turning them into block grant programs, with control of spending in the hands of the states to create, in his words, "fifty laboratories of innovation." He has advocated passing a law allowing for state bankruptcy and expressly ruling out a federal bailout of any states. Johnson has expressed opposition to the Federal Reserve System, which he has cited as massively devaluing the strength of the U.S. dollar, and would sign legislation to eliminate it. He has also supported an audit of the central bank, and urged Members of Congress in July 2012 to vote in favor of Ron Paul's Federal Reserve Transparency Act.

In his campaign for the Libertarian Party nomination, he stated he opposed foreign wars and pledged to cut the military budget by 43 percent in his first term as president. He would cut the military's overseas bases, uniformed and civilian personnel, research and development, intelligence, and nuclear weapons programs. He has stated his opposition to US involvement in the War in Afghanistan and opposed the US involvement in the Libyan Civil War. He does not believe Iran is a military threat, would use his presidential power to prevent Israel from attacking Iran, and would not follow Israel, or any other ally, into a war that it had initiated.

Johnson is a strong supporter of civil liberties and received the highest score of any candidate from the American Civil Liberties Union for supporting drug decriminalization while opposing censorship and regulation of the Internet, the Patriot Act, enhanced airport screenings, and the indefinite detention of prisoners. He has spoken in favor of the separation of church and state, and has said that he does not "seek the counsel of God" when determining his political agenda. Johnson endorsed same-sex marriage in 2011; he has since called for a constitutional amendment protecting equal marriage rights, and criticized Obama's position on the issue as having "thrown this question back to the states." On the other hand, Johnson opposes *Roe v. Wade*, believing states should decide the matter. He has been a longtime advocate of legalizing marijuana and has said that if he were president, he would remove it from Schedule I of the Controlled Substances Act as well as issue an executive order pardoning non-violent marijuana offenders.

Johnson opposes gun control, stating, "I'm a firm believer in the Second Amendment. I would not sign legislation banning assault weapons or automatic weapons."

Johnson was married to Dee Johnson (née Simms; 1952–2006) from 1977 to 2005. As First Lady of New Mexico, she engaged in campaigns against smoking and breast cancer, and oversaw the expansion of the Governor's Mansion. He initiated a separation in May 2005 and four months later he announced that they would divorce. At the age of 54, Dee Johnson died unexpectedly on December 22, 2006, her cause of death later attributed to hypertensive heart disease. Johnson became engaged to Santa Fe real estate agent Kate Prusack in 2009 a year after meeting her at a bike race in Santa Fe. Prusack has stated that the reason they have not yet married is because "My fiancé's always on the road."

Johnson lives in Taos, New Mexico, in a home that he built himself. He is an avid triathlete who bikes extensively. During his term in office, he competed in several triathlons, marathons and bike races. He competed three times (1993, 1997, 1999) as a celebrity invitee at the Iron Man World Championship in Hawaii, registering his best time for the 2.4-mile (3.9 km) swim, 112-mile (180 km) bike ride, and 26.2-mile (42.2 km) marathon run in 1999 with 10 hours, 39 minutes, and 16 seconds. He once ran 100 miles (160 km) in 30 consecutive hours in the Rocky Mountains. On May 30, 2003, he reached the summit of Mount Everest "despite toes blackened with frostbite." He has climbed all seven of the Seven Summits: Mount Everest, Mount Elbrus, Denali, Mount Kilimanjaro, Aconcagua, Mount Vinson, and Carstensz Pyramid— the tallest peaks in Asia, Europe, North America, Africa, South America, Antarctica, and Oceania respectively. He completed the Bataan Memorial Death March at White Sands Missile Range in New Mexico, in which participants traverse a 26.2 mile course through the desert, many of them in combat boots and wearing 35-pound packs.

On October 12, 2005, Johnson was involved in a near-fatal paragliding accident when his wing caught in a tree and he fell approximately 50 feet to the ground. Johnson suffered multiple bone fractures, including a burst fracture to his twelfth thoracic vertebra, a broken rib, and a broken knee; this accident left him 1.5 inches (3.8 cm) shorter. He used medicinal marijuana for pain control from 2005-08.

Johnson is a Lutheran and has stated that his belief in God has given him "a very fundamental belief that we should do unto others as we would have others do unto us."

7

IMMEDIATELY BELOW THE TOP TWO – BERNIE SANDERS, TED CRUZ, JOHN KASICH

Although Donald Trump and Hillary Clinton finally acceded to the positions of Republican and Democratic Presidential nominees respectively, we must give credit where credit is due to Bernie Sanders, the never-give-up, largely beloved challenger on the Democratic side, and Ted Cruz and John Kasich, erstwhile Republican Presidential candidates, who were ultimately defeated by Donald Trump.

BERNIE SANDERS

Bernard "Bernie" Sanders (born September 8, 1941), the junior United States senator from Vermont, was a serious candidate for the Democratic nomination for President. A member of the

Democratic Party since 2015, Sanders had been the longest-serving independent in U.S. congressional history, though his caucusing with the Democrats entitled him to committee assignments and at times gave Democrats a majority. Sanders became the ranking minority member on the Senate Budget Committee in January 2015; he had previously served for two years as chair of the Senate Veterans' Affairs Committee. A self-proclaimed democratic socialist, Sanders is pro-labor and favors greater economic equality.

Sanders was born and raised in Brooklyn, New York City, and graduated from the University of Chicago in 1964. While a student he was an active civil rights protest organizer for the Congress of Racial Equality and the Student Nonviolent Coordinating Committee. After settling in Vermont in 1968, Sanders ran unsuccessful third-party campaigns for governor and U.S. senator in the early to mid-1970s. As an independent, he was elected mayor of Burlington—Vermont's most populous city—in 1981, where he was reelected three times. In 1990 he was elected to represent Vermont's at-large congressional district in the US House of Representatives. He served as a congressman for 16 years before being elected to the U.S. Senate in 2006. In 2012, he was reelected with 71% of the popular vote.

Sanders rose to national prominence following his 2010 filibuster against the proposed extension of the Bush tax cuts. He favors policies similar to those of social democratic parties in Europe, particularly those instituted by the Nordic countries, and has built a reputation as a leading progressive voice on issues such as campaign finance reform, corporate welfare, global warming, income inequality, LGBT rights, parental leave, and universal healthcare. Sanders has long been critical of U.S. foreign policy and was an early and outspoken opponent of the Iraq War. He is also outspoken on civil liberties and civil rights, particularly criticizing racial discrimination in the criminal justice system as well as advocating for privacy rights against mass surveillance policies such as the USA PATRIOT Act and the NSA surveillance programs.

Bernard Sanders was born on September 8, 1941, in Brooklyn, one of New York City's five boroughs. His father, Elias Sanders, was born on September 14, 1904 in Słopnice, Poland to a Jewish family; in 1921 he immigrated to the United States at the age of 17. His mother, Dorothy Sanders (née Glassberg), was born in New York City on October 2, 1912, to Polish and Russian Jewish immigrant parents. Many of Elias's relatives who remained in Poland were killed in the Holocaust.

Sanders became interested in politics at an early age: "A guy named Adolf Hitler won an election in 1932. He won an election, and 50 million people died as a result of that election in World War II, including 6 million Jews. So what I learned as a little kid is that politics is, in fact, very important."

Sanders attended elementary school in Brooklyn, where he won a borough championship on the basketball team. He attended Hebrew school in the afternoons, and celebrated his Bar Mitzvah in 1954. The family never lacked for food or clothing, but major purchases, "like curtains or a rug," were difficult to afford.

Sanders attended James Madison High School, also in Brooklyn, where he was captain of the track team and took third place in the New York City indoor one-mile race. In high school, Sanders lost his first election, finishing last out of three candidates for the student body presidency. Shortly after his high school graduation, his mother died in June 1959 at the age of 46; his father died three years later on August 4, 1962, at the age of 57.

Sanders studied at Brooklyn College for a year in 1959–60 before transferring to the University of Chicago and graduating with a Bachelor of Arts degree in political science in 1964. He described himself as a mediocre college student because the classroom was "boring and irrelevant," while the community provided his most significant learning.

While at the University of Chicago, Sanders joined the Young People's Socialist League and was active in the Civil Rights Movement as a student organizer for the Congress of Racial Equality (CORE) and the Student Nonviolent Coordinating Committee. In January 1962, Sanders led a rally at the University of Chicago administration building to protest university president Beadle's segregated campus housing policy. "We feel it is an intolerable situation when Negro and white students of the university cannot live together in university-owned apartments," Sanders said at the protest. Sanders and 32 other students entered the building and camped outside the president's office, performing the first civil rights sit-in in Chicago history. After weeks of sit-ins, Beadle and the university formed a commission to investigate discrimination. Sanders once spent a day putting up fliers protesting against police brutality, only to eventually notice that a Chicago police car was shadowing him and taking them all down.

Sanders attended the 1963 March on Washington for Jobs and Freedom, where Martin Luther King, Jr. gave his "I Have a Dream" speech. That summer, he was convicted of resisting arrest during a demonstration against segregation in Chicago's public schools and was fined $25.

In addition to his civil rights activism during the 1960s and 1970s, Sanders was active in several peace and antiwar movements while attending the University of Chicago. Sanders applied for conscientious objector status during the Vietnam War; his application was eventually turned down, by which point he was too old to be drafted. Although he opposed the war, Sanders never criticized those who fought and has been a strong supporter of veterans' benefits.

After graduating from college, Sanders returned to New York City, where he initially worked in a variety of jobs, including Head Start teacher, psychiatric aide, and carpenter. In 1968, Sanders moved to Vermont because he had been "captivated by rural life." After his arrival there he worked as a carpenter, filmmaker, and writer who created and sold "radical film strips" and other educational materials to schools. He also wrote several articles for the alternative publication *The Vermont Freeman.*

Sanders began his electoral political career in 1971 as a member of the Liberty Union Party, which originated in the anti-war movement and the People's Party. He ran as the Liberty Union candidate for governor of Vermont in 1972 and 1976 and as a candidate for U.S. senator in 1972 and 1974. In the 1974 senatorial race, Sanders finished third behind 33-year-old Patrick Leahy and two-term incumbent U.S. Representative Dick Mallary. The 1976 campaign proved to be the zenith of Liberty Union's influence, with Sanders collecting 11,000 votes for governor and the party. This forced the races for lieutenant governor and secretary of state to be decided by the state legislature when its vote total prevented either the Republican or Democratic candidates for those offices from garnering a majority of votes. The campaign drained the finances and energy of the Liberty Union, however, and in October 1977—less than a year after the conclusion of the 1976 campaign—Sanders and the Liberty Union candidate for attorney general, Nancy Kaufman, announced their retirement from the party.

Following his resignation from Liberty Union, Sanders worked as a writer and the director of the nonprofit American People's Historical Society. While with the APHS, he made a 30-minute documentary about American Socialist leader and presidential candidate Eugene V. Debs.

In 1980, at the suggestion of his close friend and political confidant, Sanders ran for mayor of Burlington, Vermont against incumbent Democratic mayor Gordon Paquette, a five-term mayor who had served as a member of the Burlington City Council for 13 years before that, building extensive community ties and a willingness to cooperate with Republican leaders in controlling appointments to various commissions. Republicans had found Paquette so unobjectionable that they failed to field a candidate in the March 1981 race against him, leaving Sanders as his principal opponent. Sanders' effort was further aided by the decision of the candidate of the Citizens Party to exit the race so as not to split the progressive vote. Two other candidates in the race proved to be essentially non-factors in the campaign, with the battle coming down to Paquette and Sanders.

Sanders castigated the pro-development incumbent as an ally of a prominent shopping center developer, while Paquette warned of ruin for Burlington if Sanders was elected. The Sanders campaign was bolstered by a wave of optimistic volunteers as well as by a series of endorsements from university professors, social welfare agencies, and the police union. The final result came as a shock to the local political establishment, with the maverick Sanders winning by just 10 votes!

Sanders was reelected three times, defeating both Democratic and Republican candidates. He received 53% of the vote in 1983 and 55% in 1985. In his final run for mayor in 1987, Sanders defeated Paul Lafayette, a Democrat endorsed by both major parties. During his mayoralty, Sanders called himself a socialist and was so described in the press. During his first term, his supporters formed the forerunner of the Vermont Progressive Party. The

Progressives never held more than six seats on the 13-member city council, but they had enough to keep the council from overriding Sanders's vetoes. Under Sanders, Burlington became the first city in the country to fund community-trust housing.

During the 1980s, Sanders was a staunch critic of U.S. foreign policy in Latin America. In 1985, Burlington City Hall hosted a foreign policy speech by Noam Chomsky. In his introduction, Sanders praised Chomsky as "a very vocal and important voice in the wilderness of intellectual life in America" and said he was "delighted to welcome a person who I think we're all very proud of."

Sanders' administration balanced the city budget and drew a minor league baseball team, the Vermont Reds, then the Double-A affiliate of the Cincinnati Reds, to Burlington. Under his leadership, Burlington sued the local television cable franchise, winning reduced rates for customers. As mayor, Sanders led extensive downtown revitalization projects. One of his signature achievements was the improvement of Burlington's Lake Champlain waterfront. In 1981, Sanders campaigned against the unpopular plans by a Burlington developer to convert the then-industrial waterfront property owned by the Central Vermont Railway into expensive condominiums, hotels, and offices. Sanders ran under the slogan "Burlington is not for sale" and successfully supported a plan that redeveloped the waterfront area into a mixed-use district featuring housing, parks, and public space. Today, the waterfront area includes many parks and miles of public beach and bike paths, a boathouse, and a science center.

Sanders hosted and produced a public-access television program, *Bernie Speaks with the Community*, from 1986 to 1988. He collaborated with 30 Vermont musicians to record a folk album, *We Shall Overcome*, in 1987.

In 1986, Sanders unsuccessfully challenged incumbent Governor Madeleine Kunin in her run for reelection. Running as an Independent, Sanders finished in 3rd place with 14.4% of the vote. Kunin won with 47%, followed by Lt. Governor Peter P. Smith with 38%. In 1987, *U.S. News & World Report* ranked Sanders as one of America's best mayors. As of 2013, Burlington was regarded as one of the most livable cities in the nation. After serving four two-year terms, Sanders chose not to seek reelection in 1989. He lectured in political science at Harvard University's Kennedy School of Government that year and at Hamilton College in 1991.

Sanders' 1990 victory was heralded by *The Washington Post* and others as the "First Socialist Elected" to the United States House of Representatives in decades. Sanders served in the House from 1991 until he became a senator in 2007.

In 1988, incumbent Republican Congressman Jim Jeffords decided to run for the U.S. Senate, vacating the House seat representing Vermont's at-large congressional district. Former Lieutenant Governor Peter P. Smith won the House election with a plurality, securing 41% of the vote. Sanders, who ran as an independent, placed second with 38% of the vote, while Democratic State Representative Paul N. Poirier placed third with 19% of the vote. Two years later, Sanders ran for the seat again and defeated the incumbent Smith by a margin of 56% to 39%.

Sanders was the first independent elected to the U.S. House of Representatives since Frazier Reams' election to represent Ohio 40 years earlier. He served as a representative for 16 years, winning reelection by large margins except during the 1994 Republican Revolution, when he won by 3.3%, with 49.8% of the vote.

During his first year in the House, Sanders often alienated allies and colleagues with his criticism of both political parties as working primarily on behalf of the wealthy. In 1991, Sanders co-founded the Congressional Progressive Caucus, a group of mostly liberal Democrats that Sanders chaired for its first eight years. In 1993, Sanders voted against the Brady Bill, which mandated federal background checks and imposed a waiting period on firearm purchasers in the United States; the bill passed by a vote of 238–187.

In 1994, Sanders voted in favor of the Violent Crime Control and Law Enforcement Act. Sanders said he voted for the bill "because it included the Violence against Women Act and the ban on certain assault weapons". He was nevertheless extremely critical of the other parts of the bill. Though he acknowledged that "clearly, there are some people in our society who are horribly violent, who are deeply sick and sociopathic, and clearly these people must be put behind bars in order to protect society from them," he maintained in his intervention before the House that the government's ill-thought policies played a large part in "dooming tens of millions of young people to a future of bitterness, misery, hopelessness, drugs, crime, and violence". In this same intervention, he argued that the repressive policies introduced by the bill were not addressing the causes of violence, stating that "we can create meaningful jobs, rebuilding our society, or we can build more jails".

In 2005, he voted for the Protection of Lawful Commerce in Arms Act. The act's purpose was to prevent firearms manufacturers and dealers from being held liable for negligence when crimes have been committed with their products. In 2015, Sanders defended his vote, saying: "If somebody has a gun and it falls into the hands of a murderer and the murderer kills somebody with a gun, do you hold the gun manufacturer responsible? Not any more than you would hold a hammer company responsible if somebody beats somebody over the head with a hammer."

Sanders voted against the resolutions authorizing the use of force against Iraq in 1991 and 2002, and opposed the 2003 invasion of Iraq. He voted for the 2001 Authorization for Use of Military Force against Terrorists that has been cited as the legal justification for controversial military actions since the September 11 attacks. Sanders voted for a non-binding resolution expressing support for troops at the outset of the invasion of Iraq, but gave a floor speech criticizing the partisan nature of the vote and the George W. Bush administration's actions in the run-up to the war. Regarding the investigation of what turned out to be a leak of CIA agent Valerie Plame's identity by a State Department official, Sanders stated: "The revelation that the President authorized the release of classified information in order to discredit an Iraq war critic should tell every member of Congress that the time is now for a serious investigation of how we got into the war in Iraq and why Congress can no longer act as a rubber stamp for the President."

Sanders was a consistent critic of the Patriot Act. As a member of Congress, he voted against the original Patriot Act legislation. After its passage in the House, Sanders sponsored and voted for several subsequent amendments and acts attempting to curtail its effects, and voted against each re-authorization. In June 2005, Sanders proposed an amendment to limit Patriot Act provisions that allow the government to obtain individuals' library and book-buying records. The amendment passed the House by a bipartisan majority but was removed on November 4 of that year in House-Senate negotiations and never became law.

In March 2006, after a series of resolutions passed in various Vermont towns calling for him to bring articles of impeachment against George W. Bush, Sanders stated that it would be "impractical to talk about impeachment" with Republicans in control of the House and Senate. Still, Sanders made no secret of his opposition to the Bush Administration, which he regularly criticized for its cuts to social programs. Sanders was a vocal critic of Federal Reserve Chair Alan Greenspan; in June 2003, during a question-and-answer discussion with the then-Chairman, Sanders told Greenspan that he was concerned that Greenspan was "way out of touch" and "that you see your major function in your position as the need to represent the wealthy and large corporations." In October 2008, after Sanders had been elected to the Senate, Greenspan admitted to Congress that his economic ideology regarding risky mortgage loans was flawed. In 1998, Sanders voted and advocated against rolling back the Glass–Steagall Legislation provisions that kept investment banks and commercial banks separate entities.

On November 2, 2005, Sanders voted against the Online Freedom of Speech Act, which would have exempted the Internet from the campaign finance restrictions of the McCain–Feingold Bill.

Sanders entered the race for the U.S. Senate on April 21, 2005, after Senator Jim Jeffords announced that he would not seek a fourth term. Chuck Schumer, chairman of the Democratic Senatorial Campaign Committee, endorsed Sanders, a critical move as it meant that no Democrat running against Sanders could expect to receive financial help from the party. Sanders was also endorsed by Senate Minority Leader Harry Reid of Nevada and Democratic National Committee chairman and former Vermont governor Howard Dean. Dean said in May 2005 that he considered Sanders an ally who "votes with the Democrats 98% of the time". Then-Senator Barack Obama also campaigned for Sanders in Vermont in March 2006. Sanders entered into an agreement with the Democratic Party, much as he had as a congressman, to be listed in their primary but to decline the nomination should he win, which he did.

In the most expensive political campaign in Vermont's history, Sanders defeated businessman Rich Tarrant by a 2-to-1 margin. He was reelected in 2012 with 71% of the vote. Sanders was only the third senator from Vermont to caucus with the Democrats, after Jeffords and Leahy. His caucusing with the Democrats gave them a 51–49 majority in the Senate during the 110th Congress in 2007–08. The Democrats needed 51 seats to control the Senate because Vice President Dick Cheney would have broken any tie in favor of the Republicans. When he officially announced his intention to seek the Democratic nomination for president, Sanders set himself on a path to become only the second Democrat to represent Vermont in the Senate, the other being Leahy.

Polling conducted in August 2011 by Public Policy Polling found that Sanders's approval rating was 67% and his disapproval rating 28%, making him then the third-most popular senator in the country. Both the NAACP and the NHLA have given Sanders 100% voting scores during his tenure in the Senate.

As an independent, Sanders worked out a deal with the Senate Democratic leadership in which he agreed to vote with the Democrats on all procedural matters, except with permission from Democratic whip Dick Durbin (a request that is rarely made or granted). In return, he was allowed to keep his seniority and received the committee seats that would have been available to him as a Democrat; in 2013–14, he was chairman of the United States Senate Committee on Veterans' Affairs (during the Veterans Health Administration scandal). Sanders was free to vote as he pleased on policy matters, but almost always voted with the Democrats.

On September 24, 2008, Sanders posted an open letter to Treasury Secretary Henry Paulson decrying the initial bank bailout proposal; it drew more than 8,000 citizen cosigners in 24 hours.

On January 26, 2009, Sanders and Democrats Robert Byrd, Russ Feingold, and Tom Harkin were the sole majority members to vote against confirming Timothy Geithner as United States Secretary of the Treasury.

On December 10, 2010, Sanders delivered an 8 $\frac{1}{2}$-hour speech against the Tax Relief, Unemployment Insurance Reauthorization, and Job Creation Act of 2010, the proposed extension of the Bush-era tax rates that eventually became law, saying "Enough is enough! ... How many homes can you own?" In response to the speech, hundreds of people signed online petitions urging Sanders to run in the 2012 presidential election, and pollsters began measuring his support in key primary states. Progressive activists, such as Rabbi Michael Lerner and economist David Korten, publicly voiced their support for a prospective Sanders run against President Barack Obama.

In January 2015, Sanders became the ranking minority member of the Senate Budget Committee.

Sanders announced his intention to seek the Democratic Party's nomination for president on April 30, 2015, in an address on the Capitol lawn. His campaign was officially launched on May 26, 2015, in Burlington. In his announcement, Sanders said, "I don't believe that the men and women who defended American democracy fought to create a situation where billionaires own the political process," and made this a central idea throughout his campaign. Senator Elizabeth Warren welcomed Sanders's entry into the race, saying, "I'm glad to see him get out there and give his version of what leadership in this country should be." On June 19, 2015, the "Ready For Warren" organization, which had unsuccessfully tried to draft Warren to run for president, endorsed Sanders and re-branded itself "Ready to Fight".

Sanders stated that he would not pursue funding through a "Super PAC", instead focusing on small individual donations. His presidential campaign raised $1.5 million within 24 hours of his official announcement. At year's end the campaign had raised a total of $73 million from more than one million people making 2.5 million donations, with an average donation of $27.16. The campaign reached 3.25 million donations by the end of January 2016, raising $20 million in that month alone. Sanders has used social media to help his campaign gain momentum. He posts content to online platforms such as Twitter and Facebook, and has answered questions on Reddit. Sanders has also gained a large grassroots organizational following online. A July 29 meetup organized online brought 100,000 supporters to more than 3,500 simultaneous events nationwide. Sanders has received over one million individual online donations. He has credited this to his "organic" approach to social media, and to writing his campaign's online postings himself.

Sanders' campaign events in June 2015 drew overflow crowds around the country, to his surprise. When Hillary Clinton and Sanders made public appearances within days of each other in Des Moines, Iowa, Sanders drew larger crowds, even though he had already made numerous stops around the state and Clinton's visit was her first in 2015. On July 1, 2015, Sanders's campaign stop in Madison, Wisconsin, drew the largest crowd of any 2016 presidential candidate to that date, with an estimated turnout of 10,000. Over the following weeks he gained even larger crowds of 11,000 in Arizona, 15,000 in Seattle, and 28,000 in Portland.

In December 2015, the Democratic National Committee suspended the campaign's access to its voter data after a campaign staffer viewed data from Hillary Clinton's campaign during a firewall failure. The staffer denied accessing the data but the DNC confirmed it and Sanders apologized. The Sanders campaign criticized the DNC's reaction as excessive and threatened possible legal action unless the Committee restored its access. The campaign claimed it had warned the DNC about glitches in the voter file program months before. On December 18, 2015, the campaign filed a lawsuit, stating the Committee had unfairly suspended its access. Former Obama adviser David Axelrod contended on Twitter that the DNC was "putting a finger on the scale" for Clinton. The DNC and the Sanders campaign struck a deal the same day that restored the campaign's access to voter data.

Sanders narrowly lost the 2016 Iowa Democratic caucuses by 0.25% of the vote. On February 9, Sanders won the 2016 New Hampshire Democratic primary by a margin of more than 20%, one of the largest in decades. He swept nearly every demographic with the exception of those over the age of 65 and those making over $200,000 annually. Sanders became the first self-described democratic socialist and as a Jewish candidate, the first non-Christian to win a U.S. presidential primary of a major party.

In February 2016, Sanders pushed back against the Democratic National Committee's reversal of President Obama's 2008 decision to ban political contributions from lobbyists and political action committees, calling it "an unfortunate step backward," and asked Hillary Clinton to do the same. On March 8, Sanders pulled off an upset in the Michigan Democratic primary. Polls favored Hillary Clinton by significant margins. On April 8, Sanders accepted an invitation to speak at Vatican City on April 15 to address income inequality and the environment.

The DNC announced on May 5, 2015, that there would be six debates, much fewer than the 26 debates and forums during the 2008 Democratic primary. Critics, including the Sanders campaign, have alleged that the debate schedule is part of the DNC's deliberate attempt to protect the front-runner, Hillary Clinton. Clinton has expressed willingness to hold more debates.

In November 2015, Sanders announced that he would be a Democrat from then on, and will run in any future elections as a Democrat.

Sanders is a self-described socialist, democratic socialist, and progressive who admires the Nordic model of social democracy and is a proponent of workplace democracy. In November 2015, Sanders gave a speech at Georgetown University about his view of democratic socialism, including its place in the policies of presidents Franklin D. Roosevelt and Lyndon B. Johnson. In defining what democratic socialism means to him, Sanders said: "I don't believe government should take over the grocery store down the street or own the means of production, but I do believe that the middle class and the working families who produce the wealth of America deserve a decent standard of living and that their incomes should go up, not down. I do believe in private companies that thrive and invest and grow in America, companies that create jobs here, rather than companies that are shutting down in America and increasing their profits by exploiting low-wage labor abroad." Many journalists have likened his policies to the New Deal.

Many commentators have noted the consistency of Sanders's views throughout his political career. Calling international trade agreements a "disaster for the American worker", Sanders voted against and has spoken for years against NAFTA, CAFTA, and PNTR with China, saying that they have resulted in American corporations moving abroad. He also strongly opposes the Trans-Pacific Partnership, which he says was "written by corporate America and the pharmaceutical industry and Wall Street."

Sanders focused on economic issues such as income and wealth inequality, raising the minimum wage, universal healthcare, reducing the burden of student debt, making public colleges and universities tuition-free by taxing financial transactions, and expanding Social Security benefits by eliminating the cap on the payroll tax on all incomes above $250,000. He has become a prominent supporter of laws requiring companies to give their workers parental leave, sick leave, and vacation time, noting that such laws have been adopted by nearly all other developed countries. He also supports legislation that would make it easier for workers to join or form a trade union.

Sanders has advocated for greater democratic participation by citizens, campaign finance reform, and the overturn of *Citizens United v. FEC*. He also advocates comprehensive financial reforms, such as breaking up "too big to fail" financial institutions, restoring Glass–Steagall legislation, reforming the Federal Reserve Bank and allowing the Post Office to offer basic financial services in economically marginalized communities. Sanders strongly opposed the U.S. invasion of Iraq and has criticized a number of policies instituted during the War on Terror, particularly mass surveillance and the USA Patriot Act.

Sanders has liberal stances on social issues, having advocated for LGBT rights and against the Defense of Marriage Act. Sanders considers himself a feminist. He is also pro-choice regarding abortion, and opposes the de-funding of Planned Parenthood. He has denounced institutional racism and called for criminal justice reform to reduce the number of people in prison, advocates a crackdown on police brutality, and supports abolishing private, for-profit prisons and the death penalty. Sanders supports legalizing marijuana at the federal level. On November 15, 2015, in response to the Islamic State of Iraq and the Levant (ISIL)'s attacks in Paris, Sanders cautioned against "Islamophobia" and said, "We gotta be tough, not stupid" in the war against ISIL, further stating that the U.S. should continue to welcome Syrian refugees.

Sanders advocates bold action to reverse global warming and substantial investment in infrastructure, with "energy efficiency and sustainability" and job creation as prominent goals. Sanders considers climate change as the greatest threat to national security.

In 1963, Sanders and Deborah Shiling, whom he met in college, volunteered for several months on the Israeli kibbutz

Sha'ar HaAmakim. They married in 1964 and bought a summer home in Vermont; they had no children and divorced in 1966. Sanders's son, Levi Sanders, was born in 1969 to girlfriend Susan Campbell Mott. In 1988, Sanders married Jane O'Meara Driscoll, who later became president of Burlington College, in Burlington, Vermont. With her he has three stepchildren—Dave Driscoll, Carina Driscoll, and Heather Titus —whom he considers to be his own children. He also has seven grandchildren.

In December 1987, during his tenure as mayor, Sanders recorded a folk album titled *We Shall Overcome* with 30 Vermont musicians. As Sanders was not skilled at singing, he performed his vocals in a talking blues style. On February 6, 2016, Sanders was a guest star alongside Larry David on *Saturday Night Live*, playing a Polish immigrant on a steamship that was sinking near the Statue of Liberty. Sanders's elder brother, Larry, lives in England. He was a Green Party county councillor until he retired from the Council in 2013.

Sanders had a typical upbringing for his generation of American Jews: his father generally attended synagogue only on Yom Kippur; he attended public schools while his mother "chafed" at his yeshiva Sunday schooling at a Hebrew school; and their religious observances were mostly limited to Passover Seders with their neighbors. Larry Sanders said, "They were very pleased to be Jews, but didn't have a strong belief in God." Bernie had a Bar Mitzvah ceremony at the historic Kingsway Jewish Center in Midwood, Brooklyn, where he grew up.

In 1963, in cooperation with the Labor Zionist youth movement Hashomer Hatzair, Sanders and his first wife volunteered at Sha'ar HaAmakim, a kibbutz in northern Israel. His motivation for the trip was as much socialistic as it was Zionistic.

As mayor of Burlington, Sanders allowed a Chabad public menorah to be placed at city hall, an action contested by the local

ACLU chapter. He publicly inaugurated the Hanukkah menorah and performed the Jewish religious ritual of blessing Hanukkah candles. His early and strong support played a significant role in the now widespread public menorah celebrations around the globe. When asked about his Jewish heritage, Sanders has said he is "proud to be Jewish."

Sanders has rarely spoken about religion and has avoided directly answering or downplayed questions about it. He has stated he is "not particularly religious" and "not actively involved" with organized religion. He has been described as a "secular Jew who does not practice any religion" and a "secular Jew" who lacks "God talk," and he has called himself a "secular Jew without strong ties to organized religion". A press package issued by his office states, without elaboration, "Religion: Jewish", while the *Washington Post* describes him as potentially "one of the few modern presidents to present himself as not religious." He has said he believes in God, though not necessarily in a traditional manner: "I think everyone believes in God in their own ways," he said. "To me, it means that all of us are connected, all of life is connected, and that we are all tied together." In October 2015, on the late-night talk show *Jimmy Kimmel Live!*, Kimmel asked Bernie, "You say you are culturally Jewish and you don't feel religious; do you believe in God and do you think that's important to the people of the United States?" Bernie replied:

"I am who I am, and what I believe in and what my spirituality is about is that we're all in this together. That I think it is not a good thing to believe as human beings we can turn our backs on the suffering of other people ... and this is not Judaism, this is what Pope Francis is talking about, that we can't just worship billionaires and the making of more and more money. Life is more than that."

Sanders does not regularly attend any synagogue, and works on Rosh Hashanah, a day when Jews typically take a holiday from work. He has attended yahrzeit observances in memory of the deceased, for the father of a friend, and attended a Tashlikh, an atonement ceremony, with the mayor of Lynchburg on the afternoon of Rosh Hashanah in 2015. Sanders's wife is Roman Catholic, and he has frequently expressed admiration for Pope Francis, saying that "the leader of the Catholic Church is raising profound issues. It is important that we listen to what he has said." Sanders has said he feels "very close" to Francis' economic teachings, describing him as "incredibly smart and brave". In April 2016, Sanders accepted an invitation from Marcelo Sánchez Sorondo, an aide close to the pope, to speak at a Vatican conference on economic and environmental issues. While at the Vatican, Sanders met briefly with the pontiff.

JOHN KASICH

With the shocking departure of runner-up Ted Cruz on May 3, 2016, John Kasich, who had started out the campaign as the "also ran among also-rans" was the "last man standing" in the way of Donald Trump's ascendancy to the Republican candidate for President of the United States. That honor lasted less than twenty-four hours. As CNN prognosticators said after Ted Cruz's decision to opt out of the race, "John Kasich has moved from Number 4 in a 3-man race to Number 4 in a two-man race." Still, it appeared that the traditional Republican party simply no other viable candidate on the horizon. With his departure from the race, there seemed to be no impediment to Trump's accession to the standard bearer of the Republican Party for 2016.

John Richard Kasich born May 13, 1952) is the current governor of Ohio, first elected in 2010 and re-elected in 2014. On July 21, 2015, he announced his candidacy for the 2016 Republican nomination for President. Kasich served nine terms as a member of the United States House of Representatives. His tenure in the House included 18 years on the House Armed Services Committee and six years as chairman of the House Budget Committee. He was a key figure in the passage of both welfare reform and the Balanced Budget Act of 1997. He was a commentator on Fox News Channel, hosting *Heartland with John Kasich* from 2001 to 2007. He also worked as an investment banker, serving as managing director of the Lehman Brothers office in Columbus, Ohio. In the 2010 Ohio gubernatorial election, Kasich defeated Democratic incumbent Ted Strickland. He was re-elected in 2014, defeating Democrat Ed FitzGerald by 30 percentage points.

Kasich was born in McKees Rocks, Pennsylvania, an industrial town near Pittsburgh. He is the son of Anne (Vukovich) and John Kasich, who worked as a mail carrier. Kasich's father was of Czech descent, while his mother was of Croatian ancestry. Both his father and mother were children of immigrants and were practicing Roman Catholics. He has described himself as "a Croatian and a Czech." After attending public schools in McKees Rocks, Kasich enrolled at Ohio State University, where he joined the Alpha Sigma Phi .

Earning a Bachelor of Arts degree in political science from Ohio State in 1974, he went on to work as a researcher for the Ohio Legislative Service Commission. From 1975 to 1978, he served as an administrative assistant to then-state Senator Buz Lukens.

In 1978, Kasich ran against Democratic incumbent Robert O'Shaughnessy for State Senate. At age 26, Kasich won with 56% of the vote, the youngest person ever elected to the Ohio Senate. One of his first acts as a State Senator was to refuse a pay raise. Republicans gained control of the State Senate in 1980; but Kasich went his own way by opposing a budget proposal he believed would raise taxes and writing his own proposal instead.

In 1982, Kasich ran for Congress. He won the Republican primary with 83% of the vote and defeated incumbent Democrat U.S. Congressman Bob Shamansky in the general election by a margin of 50%–47%. He was re-elected eight times after 1982, winning at least 64% of the vote each time. During his congressional career, Kasich was considered a fiscal conservative, taking aim at programs supported by Republicans and Democrats. He worked with Ralph Nader in seeking to reduce corporate tax loopholes.

Kasich was a member of the House Armed Services Committee for 18 years. He developed a "fairly hawkish" reputation on that committee, although he challenged defense spending he considered wasteful. He participated extensively in the passage of the Goldwater–Nichols Act of 1986, which reorganized the U.S. Department of Defense. He also pushed through the bill creating the 1988 Base Realignment and Closure Commission, which closed obsolete U.S. military bases, and successfully opposed a proposed $110 million expansion of the Pentagon building at the end of the Cold War.

Kasich said he was "100% for" the first Persian Gulf War as well as the 2001 invasion of Afghanistan, but said that he did not favor U.S. military participation in the Lebanese Civil War or in Bosnia. In 1997, with fellow Republican representative Floyd Spence, he introduced legislation (supported by some congressional Democrats) for the U.S. to pull out of a multilateral peacekeeping force in Bosnia. In the House, he supported the Comprehensive Anti-Apartheid Act, a Dellums-led initiative to impose economic sanctions against apartheid-era South Africa.

In 1993, Kasich became the ranking Republican member of the House Budget Committee. Kasich and other House Budget Committee Republicans proposed an alternative to President Bill Clinton's deficit reduction bill, the Omnibus Budget Reconciliation Act of 1993. That proposal included funds to implement Republican proposals for health care, welfare, and crime control legislation and for a child tax credit. The Penny-Kasich Plan, named after Kasich and fellow lead sponsor Tim Penny, was supported by Republicans and conservative Democrats. It proposed $90 billion in spending cuts over five years, almost three times as much in cuts as the $37 billion in cuts backed by the Clinton administration and Democratic congressional leaders. About one-third ($27 billion) of the proposed Penny-Kasich cuts would come from means-testing Medicare, specifically by reducing Medicare payments to seniors who earned $75,000 or more in adjusted gross income. This angered the AARP, which lobbied against the legislation. The proposal was narrowly defeated in the House by a 219-213 vote.

As ranking member of the Budget Committee, Kasich proposed his own health care reform plan as a rival to the Clinton health care plan of 1993 championed by First Lady Hillary Rodham Clinton, but more market-based.

On November 17, 1993, Kasich voted to approve the North American Free Trade Agreement, casting a "yea" vote for the North American Free Trade Agreement Implementation Act.

In 1994, Kasich was one of the Republican leaders to support a last-minute deal with President Bill Clinton to pass the Federal Assault Weapons Ban. After a series of meetings with Clinton's Chief of Staff, Leon Panetta, a longtime friend of Kasich, the assault weapons ban was passed when 42 Republicans crossed party lines and voted with Democrats to ban assault weapons. His support of the assault-weapons ban angered the National Rifle Association, which gave Kasich an "F" rating in 1994.

In 1995, when Republicans gained the majority in the United States Congress following the 1994 election, Kasich became chairman of the House Budget Committee. In 1996, he introduced the Personal Responsibility and Work Opportunity Act in the House, an important welfare reform bill signed into law by President Clinton. During the 1996 presidential campaign, Republican nominee Bob Dole was reported to have considered Kasich as a vice presidential running mate but instead selected Jack Kemp, a former congressman and Secretary of Housing and Urban Development.

In 1997, Kasich rose to national prominence after becoming the chief architect of a deal that balanced the federal budget for the first time since 1969, the Balanced Budget Act of 1997. In 1998, Kasich voted to impeach President Clinton on all four charges made against him. In 1999, while the Senate prepared to vote on the charges, he said: "I believe these are impeachable and removable offenses."

Kasich did not seek re-election in 2000. In February 1999, he formed an exploratory committee to run for president. In March 1999 he announced his campaign for the Republican nomination. After very poor fundraising, he dropped out in July 1999, and endorsed Governor George W. Bush of Texas.

After leaving congress, Kasich went to work for Fox News, hosting *Heartland with John Kasich* on the Fox News Channel and guest-hosting *The O'Reilly Factor*, filling in for Bill O'Reilly as needed. He occasionally appeared as a guest on *Hannity & Colmes*.

Kasich served on the board of directors for several corporations, including Invacare Corporation and the Chicago-based Norvax Inc. In 2001, Kasich joined Lehman Brothers' investment banking division as a managing director, in Columbus, Ohio. He remained at Lehman Brothers until it declared bankruptcy in 2008. That year, Lehman Brothers paid him a $182,692 salary and a $432,200 bonus. He stated that the bonus was for work performed in 2007.

Republicans tried to recruit Kasich to run for Ohio governor in 2006, but he declined to enter the race. In 2008, Kasich formed Recharge Ohio, a political action committee (PAC) with the goal of raising money to help Republican candidates for the Ohio House of Representatives and Ohio Senate, in an effort to retain Republican majorities in the Ohio General Assembly. Kasich served as honorary chairman of the PAC.

On May 1, 2009, Kasich filed papers to run for governor of Ohio against incumbent Democratic governor Ted Strickland. He formally announced his candidacy on June 1, 2009. On January 15, 2010, Kasich announced Ohio State Auditor Mary Taylor as his running mate. During a speech before Ashtabula County Republicans in March 2009, Kasich talked about the need to "break the back of organized labor in the schools," according to the Ashtabula *Star Beacon*.

Ohio teachers' unions supported Democrat Ted Strickland, and after Kasich's gubernatorial victory, he said, "I am waiting for the teachers' unions to take out full-page ads in all the major newspapers, apologizing for what they had to say about me during this campaign." Elsewhere, he said he was willing to work with "unions that make things."

On May 4, 2010, Kasich won the Republican nomination for governor, having run unopposed. On November 2, 2010, Kasich defeated incumbent Democrat Ted Strickland in a closely contested race to win the governorship.

In the 2014 Ohio gubernatorial election Kasich won 86 of the 88 counties.

Kasich, who was elected with Tea Party support in 2010, faced some backlash from some Tea Party activists. His decision to accept the Patient Protection and Affordable Care Act's expansion of Medicaid caused some Tea Party activists to refuse to support his campaign. Kasich supported longtime ally and campaign veteran Matt Borges over Portage County Tea Party chairman Tom Zawistowski for the position of chairman of the Ohio Republican Party. Zawistowski secured just three votes in his run for the chairmanship. Tea Party groups announced they would support a primary challenger, or, if none emerged, the Libertarian nominee. Ultimately, Zawistowski failed to field anyone on the ballot and the Libertarian nominee was removed from the ballot after failing to gain the required number of valid signatures necessary for ballot access.

Kasich is sometimes billed as a moderate due to his "unassuming image," but has a record in the House and as Ohio governor that puts him a big step to the right of what many Americans would consider in the middle.

Kasich is a firm abortion opponent and describes himself as pro-life. Since 2011, Kasich has signed 16 anti-abortion measures into law. In June 2013, Kasich signed into law a state budget which stripped $1.4 million in federal dollars from Planned Parenthood by placing the organization last on the priority list for family-planning funds; provided funding to crisis pregnancy centers; and required women seeking abortions to undergo ultrasounds. The budget also barred abortion providers from entering into emergency transfer agreements with public hospitals, requiring abortion providers to find private hospitals willing to enter into transfer agreements. Another provision of the bill requires abortion providers to offer information on family planning and adoption services in certain situations. Under the budget, rape crisis centers could lose public funding if they counseled sexual assault victims about abortion.

In 2015, Kasich said in an interview that Planned Parenthood ought to be de-funded but Republicans in Congress should not force a government shutdown over the issue.

In a speech in April 2012, Kasich acknowledged that climate change is real and is a problem. In the same speech Kasich said that the Environmental Protection Agency should not regulate carbon emissions and that instead states and private companies should be in charge of regulating coal-fired power plant emissions. In 2015, Kasich stated that he does not know all the causes of climate change. In 2014, Kasich signed into law a bill freezing Ohio's renewable portfolio standard, which required the state to acquire 12.5% of its energy portfolio from renewable sources and to reduce energy consumption by 22% by 2025 for two years. The legislation signed by Kasich to stop the program was supported by Republican legislative leaders, utility companies, and some industry groups, and opposed by environmentalists, some manufacturers, and the American Lung Association.

In his 2015 budget plan, Kasich proposed raising the tax rate on hydraulic fracturing (fracking) activities. Specifically, Kasich's plan called for imposing a 6.5% severance tax on crude oil and natural gas extracted via horizontal drilling and sold at the source and for an additional 4.5 percent tax per thousand cubic feet on natural gas and liquefied natural gas. The proposal would not affect conventional drilling taxes.

In April 2015, Kasich signed a bill aimed at protecting Lake Erie's water quality.[The bill places restrictions on the spread of manure and other fertilizers that contribute to toxic algal blooms and requires large public water treatment plants to monitor phosphorus levels. The bill had been unanimously approved by both chambers of the Ohio Legislature the previous month. Kasich is a supporter of the Keystone XL oil pipeline project; along with other Republican governors, Kasich signed an open letter in support of federal approval for the project in February 2015.

To offset a state budget deficit, Kasich proposed selling five state prisons to the for-profit prison industry. Following the separate fatal police shootings of John Crawford III and Tamir Rice, a 12-year-old boy in Ohio, while each were holding BB guns, where grand juries decided not to indict any of the officers involved, Kasich created the Ohio Collaborative Community-Police Advisory Board "to address what he described as frustration and distrust among some Ohioans toward their police departments, particularly among the black community." The 23-member task force (with 18 members appointed by Kasich) was appointed in January 2015 and issued its 629-page final report and recommendations in April 2015. The report recommended greater accountability and oversight for police agencies and officers, further community education and involvement in policing, and new use-of-force and recruitment, hiring, and training standards for police agencies. In April 2015, Kasich created the Ohio Collaborative Community-Police Advisory Board, a twelve-member board tasked (in conjunction with the Ohio Office of Criminal Justice Services and the Ohio Department of Public Safety) with developing statewide standards for the recruiting, hiring and screening of police officers, and for the use of force (including deadly force) by police. The advisory board, the first of its kind in Ohio, was also tasked by Kasich with developing "model policies and best practice recommendations to promote better interaction and communication between law enforcement departments and their home communities." In August 2015, the board issued its recommendations, which placed "an emphasis on the preservation of human life and restrict officers to defending themselves or others from death or serious injury." In August 2015, Kasich said that he was open to the idea of requiring police officers to wear body cameras.

As of July 2015, Kasich had presided over the executions of twelve inmates and commuted the death sentences of five inmates. In January 2015, Kasich announced that, due to pending litigation and other issues, he was delaying all seven executions scheduled through January 2016. At that time, the most recent execution had occurred in January 2014. Kasich granted 66 of 1,521 requests for executive clemency, about 4.4 percent of the non-death-penalty cases he received and acted upon from 2011 to 2014. This was the lowest clemency rate of any Ohio governor since at least the 1980s, when records began to be kept.

Kasich supports various criminal justice reform efforts. In 2011, Kasich signed sentencing reform legislation which allowed judges to sentence defendants convicted of non-violent fourth- and fifth-degree felonies to "community-based halfway house facilities" instead of prison; expanded the earned credit system to allow inmates to reduce their sentences; and allowed felons who have already served 80 percent or more of their sentences to be immediately released. In 2012, Kasich signed into law a bill, sponsored by Cleveland Democratic Senator Shirley Smith and Cincinnati Republican Senator Bill Seitz, easing the collateral consequences of criminal conviction. In September 2014, Kasich touted the Ohio's prison system's recidivism rate, which is one of the lowest in the nation. U.S. Senator Rob Portman, a Republican, attributed a drop in Ohio's recidivism rate "to the bipartisan work of the state legislature, Governor Kasich, Ohio's re-entry leaders and the success of programs made possible at the federal level by the Second Chance Act," which Portman sponsored. In 2015, Kasich proposed a state budget including $61.7 million for addiction treatment services for prisoners.

Kasich initially expressed opposition to medical marijuana in 2012, saying "There's better ways to help people who are in pain." However, in late 2015 and early 2016, Kasich said he was open to legalization of medical marijuana. Kasich opposed "Issue 3," an Ohio ballot measure in 2015 that proposed the legalization of recreational marijuana, saying it was a "terrible idea."

In March 2014, in an effort to address the opioid epidemic, Kasich signed legislation (passed unanimously in both chambers of the state legislature) expanding the availability of naloxone, a lifesaving antidote to opioid overdoses; the measure allowed friends and family members of addicts to obtain access to naloxone and for first responders to carry naloxone. In July 2015, Kasich signed legislation further expanding the availability of naloxone, making it available without a prescription.

During Kasich's tenure, the state has eliminated a budget shortfall that his administration has estimated at $8 billion. Ohio also increased its "rainy day fund" from effectively zero to more than $2 billion. Kasich closed the budget shortfall in part by cutting aid to local governments, forcing some of them to raise their own taxes or cut services. And increasing sales taxes helped make the income tax cuts possible." In March 2008, Kasich called for "phasing out" Ohio's state income tax. During Kasich's time as governor, Ohio ranked 22nd out of the 50 states for private-sector job growth, at 9.3%.

Kasich signed a state budget in 2011 which eliminated the state's estate tax effective January 1, 2013.

In 2013, Kasich signed into law a $62 billion two-year state budget. The budget provided for a 10-percent state income tax cut phased in over three years, and an increase in the state sales tax from 5.5 percent to 5.75 percent. It also included a 50% tax cut for small business owners on the first $250,000 of annual net income. Kasich used his line-item veto power to reject a measure that would stop the Medicaid expansion (which Kasich had accepted from the federal government) to cover nearly 275,000 working poor Ohioans.

In 2015, Kasich signed into law a $71 billion two-year state budget after using his line-item veto power to veto 44 items. The overall 2015 budget provides a 6.3 percent state income-tax cut as a part one component of a $1.9 billion net tax reduction and lowers the top income-tax rate to slightly below 5 percent. The budget also "spends $955 million more in basic state aid for K-12 schools than the last two-year period"; "boosts state funding for higher education to help offset a two-year tuition freeze at public universities"; expands the Medicaid health program; increases cigarette taxes by 35 cents a pack; and "prohibits independent health care and child care workers under contract with the state from unionizing."

On March 31, 2011, in his first year as governor, Kasich signed into law a controversial labor law which restricted collective bargaining rights of public employees, such as police officers, firefighters, and teachers. The legislation, championed by Kasich, prohibited all public employees from striking and restricted their ability to negotiate health care and pension benefits. The final version of the legislation signed by Kasich had passed the state Senate in a 17-16 vote (with six Senate Republicans joining all of the Senate Democrats in voting no) and the state House in a 53-44 vote, with two members abstaining. Democrats and labor unions opposed the legislation and placed a referendum on the November 2011 ballot to repeal the law. Kasich and other supporters of the law characterized the legislation as a necessary measure "to help public employers control labor costs" and reduce tax burdens to make Ohio more competitive with other states, while labor unions and other opponents characterized the bill as "a union-busting attack on the middle class." Ohio voters rejected Senate Bill 5 in a 61 percent to 39 percent vote, which was viewed as a rebuke to Kasich. On election night, Kasich said in a speech at the Ohio Statehouse that "It's clear the people have spoken. I heard their voices. I understand their decision. And frankly, I respect what the people have to say in an effort like this." Following this defeat,

Kasich dropped efforts for a broad-based collective bargaining restrictions, although in 2012 he supported a bill including "provisions reminiscent of Senate Bill 5" but applying only to the Cleveland Metropolitan School District.

In May 2015, Kasich rescinded executive orders issued by his predecessor Ted Strickland in 2007 and 2008 that provided the right to home health care contractors and in-home child care contractors to collectively bargain with the state.

Kasich has campaigned for a balanced budget amendment to the U.S. Constitution.

In speaking in the 2016 campaign on domestic surveillance, Kasich has "straddled the line," praising Rand Paul for saying that "we need to get warrants," but also saying "if there's information they need, the government needs to get it." Kasich has said there needs to be "a balance between good intelligence and the need to protect Americans from what can become an aggressive government somewhere down the road." On one occasion, Kasich spoke out against proposals to mandate that technology companies provide a "backdoor" for the government to access encrypted devices, saying that this could end up aiding hackers. On a subsequent occasion, Kasich said that encryption was dangerous because it could stymie government antiterrorism investigations. Kasich has condemned whistleblower Edward Snowden as a traitor.

Kasich proposed new legislation which would increase funding to charter schools and poor school districts. He canceled the school-funding formula put into place by his Democratic predecessor, Governor Ted Strickland. During Kasich's tenure as governor, he pushed to expand charter schools, increase the number of school vouchers that use public money to pay for tuition at private schools, implement a "merit pay" scheme for teachers, and evaluate teachers by student standardized test scores in math and reading. Kasich supports the Common Core State Standards and has criticized Republicans who turned against it.

During Kasich's tenure, funding for traditional public schools declined by about $500 million, while funding for charter schools has increased at least 27 percent. Analysts disagree "on whether Kasich's education budgets give increases beyond inflation." In the 2015 state budget, Kasich used his line-item veto power "to cut more than $84 million of funding from public schools." Kasich favors allowing public school districts "to teach alternatives to evolution, such as intelligent design, if local school officials want to, under the philosophy of 'local control.

In November 2002, Kasich urged the invasion of Iraq, telling a crowd of students at Ohio State University, "We should go to war with Iraq. It's not likely that Saddam Hussein will give up his weapons. If he did he would be disgraced in the Arab world."

In an interview in August 2015, Kasich said: "I would never have committed ourselves to Iraq." A Kasich spokesman subsequently said that "Kasich was not revising history" but was instead saying that the Iraq War was a mistake given the facts available now.

Kasich has said that the U.S. "should've left a base in Iraq" instead of withdrawing troops in 2011.

In 2015, Kasich said that airstrikes were insufficient to combat the Islamic State of Iraq and the Levant, and he would send U.S. ground troops to fight ISIL. Kasich opposed the landmark 2015 international nuclear agreement with Iran, and in September 2015 was one of fourteen Republican governors who sent a letter to President Obama stating "that we intend to ensure that the various state-level sanctions against Iran that are now in effect remain in effect," despite the agreement. Kasich has expressed support for the U.S.'s drone program. He has said, however, that the program should be overseen by the Department of Defense, and not by the

CIA. Kasich has said that he wants to lift budget sequestration for military spending, and "spend more if necessary." In November 2015, Kasich said that if elected president, he "would send a carrier battle group through the South China Sea" to send a message to China regarding their claims of sovereignty there.

In the U.S. House of Representatives in 1996, Kasich voted for the Defense of Marriage Act, which barred federal recognition of same-sex marriage. During this period, Kasich supported a ban on same-sex marriage in Ohio and stated that he did not approve of the gay lifestyle. As governor of Ohio, Kasich signed an executive order banning discrimination on the basis of sexual orientation for state employees; this was narrower than the previous executive order signed by his predecessor because it omitted protections for gender identity.

During the 2016 presidential campaign, Kasich struck a more moderate tone compared to his Republican opponents. In June 2015, following the U.S. Supreme Court's decision in *Obergefell v. Hodges*, which held that there is a fundamental right to same-sex marriage under the Fourteenth Amendment, Kasich said that he was "obviously disappointed" and that he believes in "traditional marriage," but that the ruling was "the law of the land and we'll abide by it" and that it was "time to move on" to other issues. Kasich indicated that he did not support an amendment to the U.S. Constitution to overturn the decision. In response to a debate question about how he would explain his position on same-sex marriage to one of his daughters if she were gay, Kasich responded, "The court has ruled, and I said we'll accept it. And guess what, I just went to a wedding of a friend of mine who happens to be gay. Because somebody doesn't think the way I do doesn't mean that I can't care about them or can't love them. So if one of my daughters happened to be that, of course I would love them and I would accept them. Because you know what? That's what we're taught when we have strong faith."

In September 2015, Kasich commented on the highly publicized case of Kim Davis (the Rowan County, Kentucky clerk who refused to comply with a federal court order directing her to issue marriage licenses to same-sex couples), saying: "Now, I respect the fact that this lady doesn't agree but she's also a government employee, she's not running a church, I wouldn't force this on a church. But in terms of her responsibility I think she has to comply. I don't think —I don't like the fact that she's sitting in a jail, that's absurd as well. But I think she should follow the law."

While in the U.S. House of Representatives, Kasich had a mixed record on gun policy. He was one of 215 Representatives to vote for the Federal Assault Weapons Ban, which became law in 1994, but voted against the Brady Handgun Violence Prevention Act ("Brady Bill"), which established current background check laws.

As governor, Kasich shifted to more pro-gun positions. In 2011, he signed one bill permitting concealed handguns in bars and another making it easier for people with misdemeanor drug convictions to purchase guns. In 2012, Kasich signed a bill allowing gun owners to transport weapons with loaded magazines in their vehicles and expanding concealed carry permit reciprocity. In December 2014, Kasich signed legislation that reduced the numbers of hours of training required to obtain a concealed carry permit and eliminated the training requirement for permit renewals.

Kasich opted to accept Medicaid-expansion funding provided by the Patient Protection and Affordable Care Act (ACA or "Obamacare") in Ohio. This decision angered many Statehouse Republicans, who wanted Kasich to reject the expansion.

Total spending on Medicaid by the state was almost $2 billion (or 7.6 percent) below estimates for the fiscal year ending in

June 2015, according to a report by Kasich's administration. The lower-than-expected costs were attributed to expanded managed care, shorter nursing home stays and increased in-home care for seniors, capitated reimbursement policies, increased automation to determine eligibility for the program and pay care providers, and an improving economy in the state which allowed some participants to move out of the program.

In an October 2014 interview, Kasich said that repeal of the ACA was "not gonna' happen" and stated that "The opposition to it was really either political or ideological. I don't think that holds water against real flesh and blood, and real improvements in people's lives." Kasich later said that he was referring solely to the law's Medicaid expansion, and that "my position is that we need to repeal and replace" the rest of the law. In 2015, Kasich expressed support for many provisions of the ACA (ensuring coverage for people with preexisting conditions, the use of insurance exchanges, and Medicaid expansion), but opposed mandates.

In 2010, while running for governor, Kasich expressed support for amending the U.S. Constitution to abolish the Fourteenth Amendment's guarantee of *jus soli* (birthright) citizenship for people born in the United States. Kasich also told the *Columbus Dispatch* at the time that "One thing that I don't want to reward is illegal immigration." In 2014, Kasich acknowledged that his stance on immigration has "evolved" because "maybe I'm a little smarter now," stating: "I don't want to see anybody in pain. So I guess when I look at this now, I look at it differently than I did in '10. ... When I look at a group of people who might be hiding, who may be afraid, who may be scared, who have children, I don't want to be in a position of where I make it worse for them." That year, Kasich expressed openness to a path to citizenship for undocumented immigrants, saying at a Republican Governors Association (RGA) meeting in Florida, "I don't like the idea of citizenship when people jump the line, but we may have to do it." Kasich was the only governor at the RGA conference "to express openly a willingness to create a pathway to citizenship for undocumented immigrants." In August 2015, while running for president, Kasich called for a path to legal status (but not necessarily citizenship) for undocumented immigrants and for a guest worker program. Kasich also appeared to disavow his earlier stance against birthright citizenship, stating "I don't think we need to go there"; called for completion of a fence along the U.S.-Mexico border; and noted that undocumented immigrants who were brought to the U.S. as young children may obtain driver's licenses in Ohio.

In October 2015, Kasich criticized Donald Trump's "plan to build a wall along the Mexican border and remove immigrants who entered the United States illegally," calling these notions "just crazy."

In February 2014, Kasich signed into law a bill which cut six days from Ohio's early voting period, including the "golden week" (a period at the beginning of early voting when voters could both register to vote and cast an in-person absentee ballot). The measures were hotly contested in the state legislature, passing on a party-line vote, with Republicans in favor and Democrats opposed.

In April 2015, he had announced the formation of his "New Day for America" group. In May 2015, sources close to him had said he was "virtually certain" to run for the Republican nomination for president. On July 21, 2015, Kasich announced his candidacy for the Republican presidential nomination during a speech at Ohio State University. On January 30, 2016, the *New York Times* endorsed Kasich for the Republican nomination. The *Times* editorial board strongly rebuked leading candidates Donald

Trump and Senator Ted Cruz and wrote that Kasich, "though a distinct underdog, is the only plausible choice for Republicans tired of the extremism and inexperience on display in this race."

On the campaign trail, Kasich sought to project a sunny, optimistic message, describing himself as "the prince of light and hope." This marked a change in tone for Kasich, who had developed a reputation as an abrasive governor. Kasich came in second place in the New Hampshire primary on February 9, 2016, behind winner Trump. The *Cincinnati Enquirer* reported that this was "the best possible result" for Kasich and lent "credence to the notion that he can emerge" as a Republican alternative to Trump and Cruz.

Kasich did not win any of the first 22 primaries and caucuses, but on March 15, 2016, came in first place in his home state of Ohio, a winner-take-all primary for Republicans with 66 delegates at stake. Kasich still faces a steep delegate deficit against his rivals. Kasich's campaign strategy hinges on the possibility of a contested (or brokered) Republican National Convention, in which no single candidate has enough delegates to win the nomination on the first ballot, something that has not happened in either of the two major parties' presidential nominating conventions since 1952.

Kasich has been married twice. His first marriage was to Mary Lee Griffith from 1975 to 1980, and they had no children. Griffith has campaigned for Kasich since their divorce. Kasich and his current wife, Karen Waldbillig, a former public relations executive, were married in March 1997 and have twin daughters, Emma and Reese.

Kasich was raised a Catholic, but considers denominations irrelevant, and stated that "there's always going to be a part of me that considers myself a Catholic." He drifted away from his religion as an adult, but came to embrace an Anglican faith after both his parents were killed in a car crash by a drunk driver on August 20, 1987. Kasich has said he "doesn't find God in church" but does belong to the St. Augustine church in Westerville, Ohio, which is part of the Anglican Church in North America, a conservative church that broke off from the Episcopal Church.

TED CRUZ

With Ted Cruz's departure from the race on May 3, the attempt to stop Donald Trump rattled in its death throes. Rafael Edward "Ted" Cruz (born December 22, 1970) is the junior United States Senator from Texas. He was a candidate for the Republican nomination for President.

Cruz graduated from Princeton University in 1992, and from Harvard Law School in 1995. Between 1999 and 2003, he was the Director of the Office of Policy Planning at the Federal Trade Commission, an Associate Deputy Attorney General at the United States Department of Justice, and domestic policy advisor to George W. Bush in the 2000 George W. Bush presidential campaign. He served as Solicitor General of Texas, from 2003 to 2008. He was the first Hispanic, and the longest-serving, Solicitor General in Texas history. From 2004 to 2009, Cruz was an adjunct professor at the University of Texas School of Law in Austin, where he taught U.S. Supreme Court litigation.

Cruz ran for the Senate seat vacated by fellow Republican Kay Bailey Hutchison, and in July 2012, defeated Lieutenant Governor David Dewhurst, during the Republican primary runoff, 57%–43%. Cruz then defeated former state Representative Paul Sadler in the November 2012 general election, winning 56%–41%. He is the first Hispanic American to serve as a U.S. senator representing Texas, and is one of three senators of Cuban descent. He chairs the Senate Judiciary Subcommittee on Oversight, Federal Rights and Agency Activities and is also the chairman of the Senate Commerce Subcommittee on Space, Science and Competitiveness. In November 2012, he was appointed vice-chairman of the National Republican senatorial committee.

Cruz began campaigning for the Republican presidential nomination in March 2015. During the primary campaign, his base of support has mainly been among social conservatives, though he has had crossover appeal to other factions within his party, including libertarian conservatives. His victory in the February 2016 Iowa caucuses marked the first time a Hispanic person won a presidential caucus or primary.

Cruz was born on December 22, 1970, in Calgary, Alberta, Canada, to parents Eleanor Elizabeth (Darragh) Wilson and Rafael Bienvenido Cruz. At the time of his birth, Cruz's parents had lived in Calgary for three years and were working in the oil business as owners of a seismic-data processing firm for oil drilling. In 1974, his father left the family and moved to Texas. Later that year, his parents reconciled and relocated to Houston. Cruz's father was born in Cuba. His mother was born in Wilmington, Delaware, and is three quarters of Irish descent and one quarter of Italian descent. His father left Cuba in 1957 to attend the University of Texas at Austin and obtained political asylum in the United States after his four-year student visa expired. Rafael Cruz claimed Canadian citizenship in 1973 and became a naturalized U.S. citizen in 2005. Eleanor and Rafael Cruz divorced in 1997. Cruz had two older half-sisters, Miriam Ceferina Cruz and Roxana Lourdes Cruz, from his father's first marriage. Miriam died in 2011.

Cruz attended two private high schools: Faith West Academy in Katy, Texas; and Second Baptist High School in Houston, from which he graduated as valedictorian in 1988. During high school,

Cruz participated in a Houston-based group known at the time as the Free Market Education Foundation, a program that taught high school students the philosophies of economists such as Milton Friedman and Frédéric Bastiat.

Cruz graduated *cum laude* from Princeton University in 1992 with a Bachelor of Arts in Public Policy from the Woodrow Wilson School of Public and International Affairs. While at Princeton, he competed for the American Whig-Cliosophic Society's Debate Panel and won the top speaker award at both the 1992 U.S. National Debating Championship and the 1992 North American Debating Championship. In 1992, he was named U.S. National Speaker of the Year. Princeton's debate team named their annual novice championship after Cruz. Cruz argued that the drafters of the Constitution intended to protect the rights of their constituents, and that the last two items in the Bill of Rights offer an explicit stop against an all-powerful state.

After graduating from Princeton, Cruz attended Harvard Law School, graduating *magna cum laude* in 1995 with a Juris Doctor degree. While at Harvard Law, he was a primary editor of the *Harvard Law Review*, and executive editor of the *Harvard Journal of Law and Public Policy*, and a founding editor of the *Harvard Latino Law Review*. Referring to Cruz's time as a student at Harvard Law, Professor Alan Dershowitz said, "Cruz was off-the-charts brilliant." At Harvard Law, Cruz was a John M. Olin Fellow in Law and Economics.

Cruz served as a law clerk to J. Michael Luttig of the United States Court of Appeals for the Fourth Circuit in 1995 and William Rehnquist, Chief Justice of the United States in 1996, the first Hispanic to clerk for a Chief Justice of the United States.

After Cruz finished his clerkships, he took a position with Cooper, Carvin & Rosenthal from 1997 to 1998. While with the firm, Cruz worked on matters relating to the National Rifle Association, and helped prepare testimony for the impeachment proceedings against President Bill Clinton. Cruz also served as private counsel for Congressman John Boehner during Boehner's lawsuit against Congressman Jim McDermott for releasing a tape recording of a Boehner telephone conversation.

Cruz joined the George W. Bush presidential campaign in 1999 as a domestic policy adviser, advising then-Governor George W. Bush on a wide range of policy and legal matters, including civil justice, criminal justice, constitutional law, immigration, and government reform. He assisted in assembling the Bush legal team, devising strategy, and drafting pleadings for filing with the Supreme Court of Florida and U.S. Supreme Court, in the case *Bush v. Gore*, during the 2000 Florida presidential recounts, leading to two wins for the Bush team. Cruz recruited future Chief Justice John Roberts and noted attorney Mike Carvin to the Bush legal team. After Bush took office, Cruz served as an associate deputy attorney general in the U.S. Justice Department and as the director of policy planning at the U.S. Federal Trade Commission.

Appointed to the office of Solicitor General of Texas by Texas Attorney General Greg Abbott, Cruz served in that position from 2003 to 2008. The office had been established in 1999 to handle appeals involving the state, but Abbott hired Cruz with the idea that Cruz would take a "leadership role in the United States in articulating a vision of strict constructionism." As Solicitor General, Cruz argued before the Supreme Court of the United States nine times, winning five cases and losing four. Cruz has authored 70 U.S. Supreme Court briefs and presented 43 oral arguments, including nine before the United States Supreme Court. Cruz's record of having argued before the Supreme Court nine times is more than any practicing lawyer in Texas or any current member of Congress.

After leaving the Solicitor General position in 2008, Cruz worked in a private law firm in Houston, often representing corporate clients, until he was sworn in as U.S. senator from Texas in 2013. In 2009 and 2010, he formed and then abandoned a bid for state attorney general when the incumbent Attorney General Greg Abbott, who hired Cruz as Solicitor General, decided to run for re-election.

Cruz's victory in the Republican primary was described by the *Washington Post* as "the biggest upset of 2012 ... a true grassroots victory against very long odds." On January 19, 2011, after U.S. Senator Kay Bailey Hutchison said she would not seek reelection, Cruz announced his candidacy via a blogger conference call. In the Republican senatorial primary, Cruz ran against sitting Lieutenant Governor David Dewhurst. Cruz was endorsed first by former Alaska Governor Sarah Palin and then by the Club for Growth, a fiscally conservative political action committee; Tea Party Express; Young Conservatives of Texas; and U.S. Senators Tom Coburn, Jim DeMint, Mike Lee, Rand Paul and Pat Toomey. He was also endorsed by former Texas Congressman Ron Paul, George P. Bush, and former U.S. senator from Pennsylvania Rick Santorum. Former Attorney General Edwin Meese served as national chairman of Cruz's campaign.

Cruz won the runoff for the Republican nomination with a 14-point margin over Dewhurst. Cruz defeated Dewhurst despite being outspent by Dewhurst who held a statewide elected office. Dewhurst spent $19 million and Cruz only spent $7 million. Dewhurst raised over $30 million and outspent Cruz at a ratio of nearly 3-to-1.

In the November 6 general election, Cruz faced Democratic candidate Paul Sadler, an attorney and a former state representative from Henderson, in east Texas. Cruz won with 4.5 million votes (56.4%) to Sadler's 3.2 million (40.6%). Two minor candidates garnered the remaining 3% of the vote. According to a poll by Cruz's pollster, Cruz received 40% of the Hispanic vote, vs. 60% for Sadler, outperforming Republican Presidential candidate Mitt Romney with the Hispanic vote in Texas.

In January 2016, *The New York Times* reported that Cruz and his wife had taken out low-interest loans from Goldman Sachs (where she worked) and Citibank, and failed to report the nearly $1 million in loans on Federal Election Commission disclosure statements as required by law. Cruz disclosed the loans on his Senate financial disclosure forms in July 2012, but not on the Federal Election Commission form. There is no indication that Cruz's wife had any role in providing any of the loans, or that the banks did anything wrong. The loans were largely repaid by later campaign fundraising. A spokesperson for Cruz said his failure to report the loans to the FEC was "inadvertent" and said he would be filing supplementary paperwork.

Cruz has sponsored 25 bills of his own, including:

1. A bill to repeal the Patient Protection and Affordable Care Act and the health-care related provisions of the Health Care and Education Reconciliation Act of 2010, introduced January 29, 2013

2. A bill to prohibit the use of drones to kill citizens of the United States within the United States, introduced March 7, 2013

3. Two bills to investigate and prosecute felons and fugitives who illegally purchase firearms, and to prevent criminals from obtaining firearms through straw purchases and trafficking, introduced March 15, 2013

4. A bill to permit States to require proof of citizenship for registering to vote in federal elections, introduced July 17, 2013

5. A bill to increase coal, natural gas, and crude oil exports, to approve the construction of the Keystone XL Pipeline, to expand oil drilling offshore, onshore, in the National Petroleum Reserve–Alaska, and in Indian reservations, to give states the sole power of regulating hydraulic fracturing, to repeal the Renewable Fuel Standard, to prohibit the Environmental Protection Agency (EPA) from regulating greenhouse gases, to require the EPA to assess how new regulations will affect employment, and to earmark natural resource revenue to paying off the federal government's debt, introduced March 27, 2014

6. A bill to amend the Federal Election Campaign Act of 1971 to eliminate all limits on direct campaign contributions to candidates for public office, introduced June 3, 2014

Cruz was involved with the October 2013 government shutdown. He gave a 21-hour Senate speech in an effort to hold up a federal budget bill and therefore defund the Affordable Care Act. Cruz persuaded the House of Representatives and House Speaker John Boehner to include an ACA defunding provision in the bill. In the U.S. Senate, former Majority Leader Harry Reid Senate, blocked the filibuster attempt because only eighteen Republican Senators supported the filibuster. To supporters, the move signaled the depth of Cruz's commitment to rein in government. To critics, including some Republican colleagues such as Senator Lindsey Graham, the move was ineffective.

On April 1, 2014, Cruz introduced a bill that would allow the President of the United States to deny visas to any ambassador to the United Nations who has been found to have been engaged in espionage activities or a terrorist activity against the United States or its allies and may pose a threat to U.S. national security interests. The bill was written in response to Iran's choice of Hamid

Aboutalebi as their ambassador. Aboutalebi was involved in the Iran hostage crisis, in which of a number of American diplomats from the US embassy in Tehran were held captive in 1979.

Under the headline "A bipartisan message to Iran", Cruz thanked President Barack Obama for signing the bill into law. The letter, published in the magazine *Politico* on April 18, 2014, starts with "Thanks to President Obama for joining a unanimous Congress and signing S 2195 into law". Cruz also thanked senators from both political parties for "swiftly passing this legislation and sending it to the White House."

In his first two years in the Senate, Cruz attended 17 of 50 public Armed Services Committee hearings, 3 of 25 Commerce Committee hearings, 4 of the 12 Judiciary Committee hearings, and missed 21 of 135 roll call votes during the first three months of 2015.

In a November 2014 Senate speech, Cruz accused the president of being "openly desirous to destroy the Constitution and this Republic." In the same speech, Cruz invoked the speeches of the ancient Roman senator Cicero against Catiline to denounce Obama's planned executive actions on immigration reform. Classics professor Jesse Weiner, writing in *The Atlantic*, said that Cruz's analogy was "deeply disquieting" because "in casting Obama in the role of Catiline, Cruz unsubtly suggests that the sitting president was not lawfully elected and is the perpetrator of a violent insurrection to overthrow the government...In effect, he accuses the president of high treason. Regardless of one's views on immigration reform and the Obama administration at large, this is dangerous rhetoric."

Cruz has repeatedly said that the 2015 international nuclear agreement with Iran "will make the Obama administration the world's leading financier of radical Islamic terrorism."

In response, Obama called Cruz's statements an example of "outrageous attacks" from Republican critics that crossed the line of responsible discourse: "We've had a sitting senator, who also happens to be running for president, suggest that I'm the leading state sponsor of terrorism. Maybe this is just an effort to push Mr. Trump out of the headlines, but it's not the kind of leadership that is needed for America right now." Former Republican presidential nominee Mitt Romney also criticized Cruz for his remarks, writing that although he, too, was opposed to the Iran agreement, Cruz's statement connecting Obama to terrorism was "way over the line" and "hurts the cause."

After the death of Associate Justice Antonin Scalia, Cruz expressed his view that the winner of the 2016 U.S. presidential election, rather than President Obama, should appoint a new Justice.

Cruz has used harsh rhetoric against fellow Republican politicians, and his relationships with various Republican members of Congress have been strained. In 2013, Cruz referred to Republicans who he thought were insufficiently resistant to the proposals of President Obama as a "surrender caucus." Cruz also called fellow Republicans out as "squishes" on gun-control issues during a Tea Party rally. Cruz's role in the United States federal government shutdown of 2013 in particular attracted criticism from a number of Republican colleagues. Republican Senator John McCain is reported to particularly dislike Cruz; in a Senate floor speech in 2013, McCain denounced Cruz's reference to Nazis when discussing the Affordable Care Act. In March 2013, McCain also called Cruz and others "wacko birds" whose beliefs are not "reflective of the views of the majority of Republicans."

In a heated Senate floor speech in July 2015, Cruz accused Senate Republican Leader Mitch McConnell of telling "a flat-out lie" over his intentions to reauthorize the Export-Import Bank of the United States, which Cruz opposes. "What we just saw today was an absolute demonstration that not only what he told every Republican senator, but what he told the press over and over and over again was a simple lie," Cruz said of Senate Republican Leader McConnell. Cruz's "incendiary outburst" was "unusual in the cordial atmosphere of the Senate", according to *Reuters*. In the same speech, Cruz assailed the "Republican majority in both houses of Congresses" for what Cruz termed an insufficiently conservative record. Cruz's speech, and especially his accusation against McConnell, was condemned by various senior Republican senators, with John McCain saying that the speech was "outside the realm of Senate behavior" and "a very wrong thing to do." Orrin Hatch expressed a similar opinion: "I don't condone the use of that kind of language against another senator unless they can show definitive proof that there was a lie....And I know the leader didn't lie." Cruz had alleged that McConnell scheduled a vote on the Ex-Im Bank as part of a deal to persuade Democrats like Maria Cantwell to stop blocking a trade bill, whereas McConnell denied there was any "deal", and that denial is what Cruz termed a "lie"; Hatch says McConnell did pledge to help Cantwell get a vote on the Ex-Im Bank.

Among Cruz's few close allies in the Senate is Mike Lee of Utah. Cruz has expressed pride in his reputation for having few allies, saying in June 2015 that he has been vilified for fighting "the Washington cartel."

When Boehner announced in September 2015 that he would step down and resign from the House, Cruz expressed his concern that before resigning Boehner may have "cut a deal with Nancy Pelosi to fund the Obama administration for the rest of its tenure". The following month, the budget agreement passed in the House by a vote of 266 to 187, with unanimous support from Democrats and from Boehner, lifting the debt ceiling through March 2017, and Cruz called the agreement "complete and utter surrender.

As early as 2013, Cruz was widely expected to run for the presidency in 2016. On March 14, 2013, he gave the keynote speech at the annual Conservative Political Action Conference (CPAC) in Washington DC. In October 2013, Cruz won the Values Voter Summit presidential straw poll with 42% of the vote. Cruz finished first in two presidential straw polls conducted in 2014 with 30.33% of the vote at the Republican Leadership Conference and 43% of the vote at the Republican Party of Texas state convention.

On April 12, 2014, Cruz spoke at the Freedom Summit, an event organized by Americans for Prosperity, and Citizens United. The event was attended by several potential presidential candidates. In his speech, Cruz mentioned that Latinos, young people and single mothers are the people most affected by the recession, and that the Republican Party should make outreach efforts to these constituents. He also said that the words, "growth and opportunity" should be tattooed on the hands of every Republican politician.

On March 23, 2015, Cruz announced his 2016 presidential candidacy for the GOP primaries and caucuses, in a morning speech delivered at Liberty University in Lynchburg, Virginia. At the same hour, Cruz posted on his Twitter page: "I'm running for President and I hope to earn your support!" He was the first announced major Republican presidential candidate for the 2016 campaign. During the primary campaign, his base of support has been mainly among social conservatives, though he has had crossover appeal to other factions within his party, including in particular libertarian conservatives.

On February 1, 2016, Cruz won the Iowa caucuses. The Iowa win made him the first Hispanic to win either a presidential primary election or caucus. Cruz received 28% of the vote. On February

10, 2016, Cruz placed third in the New Hampshire primary, with about 12% of the vote. On February 21, 2016 he placed third in the South Carolina Republican primary with about 22.3% of the vote. On March 1, 2016, the first Super Tuesday primary day, Cruz won Texas by 17%, along with Alaska and Oklahoma, providing him with four state primary victories total. On March 5, 2016, Cruz won the Kansas and Maine caucuses, giving him six statewide wins. Cruz won his widest margin up to that point in Kansas, where he beat Trump by 25 points. With his victories over Trump in Texas, Kansas, and Maine, Cruz established himself as the candidate with the best opportunity to defeat Trump, the leading contender for the nomination.

On March 8, 2016, Cruz won the Idaho primary with 45% of vote, defeating Trump by 17% and earning his seventh statewide victory. He placed second in Michigan, Mississippi, and Hawaii. On March 12, 2016, Cruz won the Wyoming county conventions with 67% of the vote and 9 delegates, giving him his eighth statewide win.

On March 22, 2016, Cruz won the Utah Caucus with 69.2% of the vote, versus John Kasich with 16.8% and Donald Trump with 14%. Because Cruz surpassed the 50% winner-take-all threshold, he won all 40 of Utah's delegates. This win was his ninth.

On April 6, 2016, Cruz won the Wisconsin primary with 48.2% of the vote, with Trump receiving 35.1%. It was Cruz's tenth statewide win. Cruz won 36 of the possible 42 delegates available in Wisconsin. Trump received the other 6 delegates. On April 2 and 7-9, 2016, Cruz swept the Colorado congressional district and state conventions taking all 34 delegates. This gave Cruz his eleventh state win. On April 16, 2016, Cruz won all 14 of Wyoming's at-large delegates in the state convention. This secured the majority of state delegates for him and gave him the majority of delegates in eight states.

Cruz has stated that when he was a child, his mother told him that she would have to make an affirmative act to claim Canadian citizenship for him, so his family assumed that he did not hold Canadian citizenship. In August 2013, after the *Dallas Morning News* pointed out that Cruz had dual Canadian-American citizenship, he applied to formally renounce his Canadian citizenship and ceased being a citizen of Canada on May 14, 2014. Several lawsuits and ballot challenges asserting that Cruz is ineligible have been filed. No lawsuit or challenge has been successful, and in February 2016, the Illinois Board of Elections ruled in Cruz's favor, stating, "The candidate is a natural born citizen by virtue of being born in Canada to his mother who was a U.S. citizen at the time of his birth."

On abortion, Cruz is "strongly pro-life" and "would allow the procedure only when a pregnancy endangers the mother's life." He is in favor of cutting federal funding to Planned Parenthood. Cruz opposes both same-sex marriage and civil unions. He believes that marriage should be legally defined as only "between one man and one woman," but believes that the legality of same-sex marriage should be left to each state to decide. Cruz referred to the Supreme Court's decision to allow same-sex marriage as "among the darkest hours of our nation."

In 2015, Cruz voted in favor of the USA Freedom Act, which reauthorized the USA Patriot Act but reformed some of its provisions. Cruz is a proponent of school choice and opposes the Common Core State Standards Initiative. He is a strong critic of the Patient Protection and Affordable Care Act ("Obamacare"). He has sponsored legislation that would repeal the health care reform law and its amendments in the Health Care and Education Reconciliation Act of 2010.

Cruz is a gun-rights supporter. He adopted a "hard-line stance" on immigration issues during the 2014 border crisis and is an opponent of comprehensive immigration reform. He advocates for an increase from 65,000 to 325,000 annually in skilled foreign workers entering the United States using H-1B visas. Cruz opposes the legalization of marijuana, but believes it should be decided at the state level.

The candidate opposes net neutrality, arguing that the Internet economy has flourished in the United States simply because it has remained largely free from government regulation.

Cruz has called for an end to "overcriminalization, harsh mandatory minimum sentences, and the demise of jury trials." He supports the death penalty. In his 2012 Senate campaign, Cruz frequently mentioned his role as counsel for the State of Texas in *Medellín v. Texas*, a 2008 case in which the U.S. Supreme Court found that Texas has the legal right to ignore an order from the International Court of Justice directing the U.S. to review the convictions and sentences of dozens of Mexican nationals on death row. Cruz has referred to *Medellín* as the most important case of his tenure as Texas solicitor general.

In an interview with radio host Hugh Hewitt discussing the attack that killed three people at a Planned Parenthood clinic in Colorado Springs, Cruz said that "the simple and undeniable fact is the overwhelming majority of violent criminals are Democrats", and that the reason Democrats are soft on crime, is that convicted felons tend to vote Democratic. In August 2015, in the wake of the ambush death of a Texas police officer who was gunned down while filling up at a gas station, Cruz said that police are "feeling the assault from the President, from the top on down, as we see — whether it's in Ferguson or Baltimore, the response from senior officials, the President or the Attorney General, is to vilify law enforcement. That's wrong. It's fundamentally wrong. It's endangering all of our safety and security."

Cruz has been described as a "free trader" and as a "free-trade advocate" by the *Wall Street Journal*. In 2013, Cruz proposed the abolition of the IRS and the implementation of a flat tax "where the average American can fill out taxes on a postcard." Cruz is "adamantly opposed to a higher minimum wage." He wants to decrease the size of the government significantly. In addition to eliminating the IRS as described above, Cruz has promised to eliminate four other cabinet-level agencies. Cruz proposes to eliminate the Department of Energy, the Department of Education, Department of Commerce, and the Department of Housing and Urban Development.

Cruz is a supporter of TransCanada's Keystone XL Pipeline, and along with every other Republican senator was a cosponsor of legislation in support of the pipeline.

Cruz rejects the scientific consensus on climate change. He has said that "the scientific evidence doesn't support global warming." He has stated: "They call anyone who questions the science who even points to the satellite data – they call you a, quote, 'denier.' Denier is not the language of science. Denier is the language of religion. It is heretic. You are a blasphemer. It's treated as a theology. But it's about power and money. At the end of the day, it's not complicated. This is liberal politicians who want government power." In March 2015, he said that some people are "global warming alarmists" and, citing satellite temperature measurements, said that there had been no significant warming in 18 years.

He voted against the Water Resources Development Act of 2013, that would have created the National Endowment for the Oceans and authorized more than $26 billion in projects to be built by the Army Corps of Engineers, at least $16 billion of which would have come from federal taxpayers. Cruz voted against the bill because it neglected "to reduce a substantial backlog of projects, to the detriment of projects with national implications, such as the Sabine–Neches Waterway". Cruz stated that the Corps' responsibilities were expanded without providing adequate measures for state participation. Proponents of the bill argued that it would provide steady funding to support research and restoration projects, funded primarily by dedicating 12.5% of revenues from offshore energy development, including oil, gas, and renewable energy, through offshore lease sales and production based royalty payments, distributed through a competitive grant program.

Cruz has been an adamant opponent of the Joint Comprehensive Plan of Action, a 2015 international nuclear agreement with Iran negotiated by the U.S. and other world powers, calling it "catastrophic" and "disastrous." He is a critic of the rapprochement between Cuba and the United States, saying that the thaw in relations was a "manifestation of the failures of the Obama-Clinton-Kerry foreign policy" that "will be remembered as a tragic mistake."

In 2013, Cruz stated that America had no "dog in the fight" during the Syrian Civil War and stated that America's armed forces should not serve as "al-Qaeda's air force". In 2014, Cruz criticized the Obama administration: "The president's foreign policy team utterly missed the threat of ISIS, indeed, was working to arm Syrian rebels that were fighting side by side with ISIS", calling ISIS "the face of evil". In a statement opposing US intervention for regime change in Syria, Cruz said, "If President Obama and Hillary Clinton and Sen. Rubio succeed in toppling (Syrian President Bashar) Assad, the result will be the radical Islamic terrorists will take over Syria, that Syria will be controlled by ISIS, and that is materially worse for U.S. national security interests."

Cruz married Heidi Nelson in 2001. The couple has two daughters, Caroline and Catherine. Cruz met his wife while working on the George W. Bush presidential campaign of 2000. She is currently taking leave from her position as head of the Southwest Region in the Investment Management Division of Goldman, Sachs & Co. and previously worked in the White House for Condoleezza Rice and in New York as an investment banker. Cruz has said, "I'm Cuban, Irish, and Italian, and yet somehow I ended up Southern Baptist,"

In what many viewed as a desperate attempt to beat Trump in Indiana – since media pundits stated that if Cruz did not win Indiana his campaign was effectively doomed – Cruz announced on stage that he had picked former Presidential primary candidate Carly Fiorina as his running mate. If Cruz anticipated that the abrasive Fiorina would be an antidote to Hillary Clinton, he may have grossly miscalculated the attractiveness of Fiorina as a viable candidate. The charmless former head of Hewlett Packard, who had been fired from her position, then came on stage and sang a rather silly political ditty.

Things went from bad to worse the following day when John Boehner, former Speaker of the House, who had effectively been cashiered by the Tea Party Republicans in 2015, and who'd never enjoyed a good relationship with Cruz, made a public statement at Stanford University that Cruz was "Lucifer (the devil) in the flesh," that he was a "Son of a B----" (he never outright used the word), and that his attempted shutdown of the government in 2013 unless the Affordable Health Care Act was repealed was a stupid bit of grandstanding, since there was no way ObamaCare was going to be repealed in this Congress.

PART THREE

THE POLITICS OF

INSANITY – 2016

WE'RE OFF TO THE RACES

8

THE REPUBLICAN NATIONAL CONVENTION

The 2016 Republican National Convention, in which delegates of the United States Republican Party chose the party's nominees for President of the United States and Vice President of the United States in the United States presidential election, 2016, was held July 18–21, 2016, at Quicken Loans Arena in Cleveland, Ohio The event marked the third time Cleveland has hosted this event, the first since 1936. In addition to determining the party's national ticket, the convention ratified the party platform.

There were 2,472 delegates to the Republican National Convention, with a simple majority of 1,237 required to win the presidential nomination. Most of those delegates were bound for the first ballot of the convention based on the results of the 2016 Republican presidential primaries. The convention formally nominated Donald Trump as the party's nominee and Mike Pence as his running mate.

On May 3, Republican National Committee chairman Reince Priebus declared Donald Trump the presumptive nominee after

Texas senator Ted Cruz dropped out of the race. The next day, Ohio Governor John Kasich suspended his campaign, effectively making Trump the presumptive Republican presidential nominee. Trump was the first presidential nominee of a major party since Wendell Willkie, the Republican candidate in 1940, who has held neither political office nor a high military rank prior to his nomination. He was also the first presidential nominee of a major party without political experience since General Dwight D. Eisenhower first captured the Republican presidential nomination in 1952.

The convention was designated as a National Special Security Event, meaning that ultimate authority over law enforcement goes to the Secret Service and Department of Homeland Security. A highly publicized online petition by gun activists to allow the open carry of guns inside Quicken Loans Arena garnered 45,000 signatures; however, the Secret Service, which is in charge of convention security, announced that it would not allow guns in the arena or the small "secure zone" immediately outside it during the event.

The Cleveland Police Department has received $50 million in federal grants to support local police operations during the event. With this grant money, the City of Cleveland purchased over 2,000 riot control personnel gear sets prior to the convention for $20 million, and the remaining $30 million went toward personnel expenses. Items such as water guns, swords, tennis balls and coolers were banned by the City of Cleveland from the 1.7-square-mile "event zone" outside the convention hall by the City of Cleveland, but because of a statewide open-carry law permitting the open carrying of guns, firearms were permitted. The Cleveland Police Union asked Governor John Kasich to temporarily suspend Ohio's state open-carry gun law so as to block the carrying of guns within the event zone, but Kasich rejected the request, writing: "Ohio governors do not have the power to arbitrarily suspend federal and state constitutional rights or state laws as suggested."

Before the convention there were a number of online phishing expeditions that may have been hackers looking for weak spots in the convention's network. The computer network of the Democratic National Committee had already been penetrated by compromising, among other things, the database of opposition research on Trump.

In May 2016, the American Civil Liberties Union threatened to file a lawsuit on behalf of two activist groups, Citizens for Trump and a progressive group called Organize Ohio, asserting that protesters were being inhibited in their attempts to organize effectively by the city's delay in granting permits. As of May 19, six groups had filed for permits, but none had been granted. Cleveland stalled on approving and making public the demonstration applications it received, while Philadelphia (which hosted the 2016 Democratic National Convention) had already granted an application. The ACLU sued the city in federal district court on June 14, 2016. As of May 20, 2016, groups that filed for protest permits included the AIDS Healthcare Foundation; Global Zero; Organize Ohio, a group of progressive activists; the Citizens for Trump/Our Votes Matter March; Coalition to March on the RNC and Dump Trump; Stand Together Against Trump, an anti-Donald Trump group; People's Fightback Center/March Against Racism; and Created Equal, an anti-abortion group. A pro-Trump group, Trump March RNC, withdrew its application after Trump became the presumptive nominee.

As Trump rose to become the presumptive presidential nominee of the Republican Party, a number of prominent Republicans announced they would not attend the convention. Of the living former Republican nominees for president, only

1996 nominee Bob Dole announced that he would attend the convention; Romney, John McCain, George W. Bush and George H. W. Bush all announced that they would skip the convention. A number of Republican Governors, U.S. Representatives and U.S. Senators, particularly those facing difficult reelection campaigns, also indicated that they would not attend, seeking to distance themselves from Trump and spend more time with voters in their home states. Most notably, Governor Kasich chose to avoid the convention, while Ohio Senator Rob Portman attended the convention but avoided taking a major role in its proceedings. On July 8, 2016, Nebraska Senator Ben Sasse announced that he would not attend the convention. Many Republican senators did not attend the convention at all: Senator Steve Daines of Montana went "fly-fishing with his wife"; Senator Jeff Flake of Arizona, said he had to "mow his lawn"; and Senator Lisa Murkowski of Alaska, went traveling in Alaska by bush plane.

A number of prominent businesses and trade groups, including Coca-Cola, Microsoft and Hewlett-Packard, scaled back participation in the convention, sharply reducing their contributions for convention events and sponsorship. In June, six major companies that sponsored the 2012 Republican convention—Wells Fargo, UPS, Motorola, JPMorgan Chase, Ford and Walgreens Boots—announced they would not sponsor the 2016 Republican convention. Apple Inc. followed suit, announcing that it, too, would be withdrawing funding from the convention over Trump's position on certain election issues.

Seating arrangements for state and territorial delegations were announced on July 16, two days before the convention began. The Ohio and Texas delegations were assigned to the back of the convention hall, a move viewed as punishment for the delegations, as they did not back Trump in their respective primaries (Ohio and Texas voted for Kasich and Cruz, respectively).

The Rules Committee, which sets the rules of the convention and the standing rules that govern the party until the next convention, met on July 14. The rules it passes must be adopted by the full convention to take effect. This committee is regarded as the most powerful. The Rules Committee was chaired by Enid Mickelsen of Utah and Ron Kaufman of Massachusetts.

Republican delegate Kendal Unruh led an effort among other Republican delegates to change the convention rules to include a 'conscience clause' that would allow delegates bound to Trump to vote against him, even on the first ballot at the July convention. Following a marathon 15-hour meeting on July 14, 2016, the Rules Committee voted down a move to send a "minority report" to the floor allowing the unbinding of delegates, thereby guaranteeing Trump's nomination. The committee then voted 87–12 to include rules language specifically stating that delegates were required to vote based on their states' primary and caucus results. By unanimous vote, the Rules Committee also voted to change Rule 40(b), a controversial rule that had provided that "a candidate had to win a majority of the vote in eight states to have his or her name placed into nomination at the convention." The committee voted to return to the pre-2012 rule, which required a candidate to receive only a plurality of the vote in at least five states to have his or her name placed in nomination.

The Platform Committee met for two days of open hearings on July 11 and 12 to generate a draft party platform, which must had to be ratified by the full convention. The Platform Committee was chaired by Senator John Barrasso of Wyoming. The Republican National Committee organized up to ten closed-door meetings with business lobbyists and officials from a number of groups, including the American Petroleum Institute, Edison Electric Institute, National Association of Manufacturers, Hudson Institute, Institute for Energy Research, and America's Health Insurance Plans, to discuss platform issues.

The Credentials Committee handled disputes on the eligibility of convention delegates. The Committee on Contests reviewed contested delegates; if the Contests Committee recommends that a delegate be de-certified, the Credentials Committee considers the recommendation. The Rule Committee was chaired by Mike Duncan, former chairman of the Republican National Committee, and co-chaired by Arkansas Republican Party chairman Doyle Webb.

Conservative views on social issues, especially centering around homosexuality, were adopted by the platform committee. The platform committee adopted its platform on July 12. The platform was "staunchly conservative" and reflected the party's drift further to the hard right. The most contentious discussions at the platform committee dealt with social issues, particularly those dealing with LGBT people. The convention adopted a "strict, traditionalist view" on social issues, expressing deep criticism "of how the modern American family has evolved."[77] Many platform planks expressing "disapproval of homosexuality, same-sex marriage or transgender rights." The committee moved to overturn *Obergefell v. Hodges*, the Supreme Court decision on same-sex marriage, by a constitutional amendment. The platform also called for the appointment of judges "who respect traditional family values." The platform promoted state bathroom bills to restrict the public restrooms that transgender persons can use; stated that "natural marriage" is between a man and a woman and is less likely to result in children who become drug addicts; and expressed support for allowing parents to seek conversion therapy for their gay minor children. The platform called internet pornography "a public health crisis that is destroying the life of millions" and encouraged states to fight it. The platform also called for the teaching of the Bible in public schools.

The party's platform language was strengthened to condemn all types of abortion without exceptions. The platform committee adopted a provision, proposed by Kansas Secretary of State Kris Kobach, expressing opposition to any restriction on magazine capacity in firearms. The platform called for certain federally controlled public lands to be immediately transferred to state ownership, where it could be privatized. The platform did not specify whether the lands would include national parks, national forests, or wilderness areas.

On foreign policy, the members of the platform committee were split between "libertarian-minded isolationists" and "national security hawks. The hawks won on almost every point, voting down measures that would have condemned ongoing U.S. involvement in Middle Eastern wars and approving language promoting increased military spending. One plank reflected a more isolationist approach, eliminating references to giving weapons to Ukraine in its fight with Russia and rebel forces, after Trump staffers reportedly intervened with delegates. The platform opposed a two-state solution to the Israeli–Palestinian conflict. While the 2012 Republican platform called for passage of the Trans-Pacific Partnership (TPP), the 2016 platform adopted by the convention committee omits mention of the agreement, reflecting the influence of presumptive nominee Donald Trump, who opposes the trade pact. The platform expressly calls for a wall to be built on the U.S.-Mexico border, as Trump requested.

On the afternoon of July 18, 2016, a group of delegates opposed to Trump launched a "last-ditch effort" to force a roll-call vote on the convention rules. These delegates sought to change the party rules package to "unbind" delegates so that on the first ballot, delegates could "vote their conscience" and conceivably block Trump from being nominated on the first ballot; such a move would also "allow Trump opponents a platform to argue against" Trump. The effort was rejected. It was reported that Trump campaign aides and RNC staff worked on the floor to persuade delegates to withdraw their support and "challenged the validity of various signatures." This prompted the Colorado delegation to walk out in protest.

Jeff Sessions, U.S. Senator from Alabama, formally nominated Trump for president. Trump won the presidential nomination on the first ballot with 69.8% of the delegates, the lowest percentage of delegates won by the Republican nominee since the 1976 Republican National Convention. The vice presidential nomination was held immediately after the presidential nomination. Indiana Governor Mike Pence, Trump's choice for his preferred running mate, won the vice presidential nomination by acclamation.

In April 2016, Trump vowed to bring "some showbiz" to the convention, criticizing the party's 2012 convention in Tampa, Florida, as "the single most boring convention I've ever seen." The convention's lineup of speakers lacked "many of the party's rising stars" and featured some of Trump's "eclectic collection of friends, celebrities and relatives." Trump was directly involved in details of convention plans, seeking "to maximize the drama and spectacle" of the four-night event. A large number of prominent Republican elected officials said they were not interested in attending the convention or even speaking at it, seeking to distance themselves from Trump. The Trump campaign considered the idea of having Trump speak all four nights at the convention – a break from the traditional practice of the presidential nominee taking the stage only on the final night of the convention. Ultimately, Trump decided *not* to speak every night.

A number of figures that Trump said he would invite to speak, including boxing promoter Don King, former Alaska governor Sarah Palin and New England Patriots quarterback Tom Brady, were not included in the early lineup. Trump wanted King to speak at the convention and raised the issue several times, reportedly until Republican National Committee chairman Reince Priebus "firmly explained" to Trump that King should not be invited due to his past manslaughter conviction. Former Chicago Bears coach Mike Ditka, a Trump supporter, declined an invitation to speak. An early roster of speakers obtained by the media listed former NFL quarterback Tim Tebow as a speaker, but Tebow later dismissed this as a rumor and did not appear at the convention. Haskel Lookstein, a prominent Orthodox rabbi, was initially set to appear at the convention to deliver the opening prayer (having accepted an invitation to do so from Ivanka Trump, a congregant), but after hundreds of American Modern Orthodox Jews urged him to withdraw from the convention, Lookstein pulled out.

Trump sought to bar those who have not endorsed him from addressing the convention, making comments aimed at the former primary rivals who have declined to endorse him – Bush, Carly Fiorina, Lindsey Graham and George Pataki. However, both Senator Marco Rubio of Florida and Senator Ted Cruz of Texas, who ran against Trump for the Republican nomination and lost, were eventually placed on the speakers' schedule, although "neither paid the expected price of that spotlight by offering an explicit endorsement." Cruz met with Trump two weeks before the convention and accepted an invitation to speak. Rubio was initially not offered a speaking slot and was expected to skip the convention, but on July 17, 2016, it was confirmed that Rubio would address the convention via recorded video and release all 173 delegates to Trump. Neither Rubio nor Cruz were listed as "headliner" speakers.

Governor Kasich did not enter the convention hall or speak at the convention, despite overtures from Trump allies. Kasich said: "If I'm going to show up at the convention and I'm not going to be saying all these great things about the host, then I think it's inappropriate. I don't think that's the right thing to do." Kasich attended events outside the convention hall in support of down-ballot Republican candidates. As the convention began, the Trump campaign lashed out at Kasich for his failure to endorse, prompting an exchange that *The New York Times* called "remarkably bitter" and "the latest extraordinary turn in a campaign that has veered sharply away from political precedent." Manafort called Kasich "petulant" and accused him of "embarrassing his party," prompting Kasich chief political aide John Weaver to mock Trump and criticize Manafort for his work on behalf of foreign "thugs and autocrats" abroad.

On July 17, 2016, the convention planners released the convention's official schedule of events and speakers, along with themes. The schedule of speakers included the following:

Monday, July 18– "Make America Safe Again": Mark Burns of South Carolina, televangelist, prosperity gospel preacher. Burns' controversial prayer was described as "perhaps the most politically charged benediction ever heard at a national convention"; Burns stated that "our enemy is not other Republicans, but is Hillary Clinton and the Democratic Party;" Willie Robertson, star of the reality television show *Duck Dynasty;* Rick Perry, former Governor of Texas, unsuccessful candidate for 2016 Republican presidential nomination; Scott Baio, actor and television producer; Patricia Smith, mother of Benghazi victim Sean Smith; Antonio Sabàto Jr., soap opera actor and ex-underwear model; David A. Clarke Jr., sheriff of Milwaukee County, Wisconsin, known for anti–Black Lives Matter views; U.S. Senator Jeff Sessions, Republican of Alabama; Rudy Giuliani, former mayor of New York City; Melania Trump, wife of Donald Trump – listed as headliner; Michael T. Flynn, retired U.S. Army lieutenant general – listed as headliner; and U.S. Senator Joni Ernst, Republican of Iowa – listed as headliner.

Tuesday, July 19–"Make America Work Again:" Michael Mukasey, former U.S. Attorney General; Chris W. Cox, executive director, National Rifle Association Institute for Legislative Action; Natalie Gulbis, professional golfer; U.S. Senator Mitch McConnell, Senate majority leader, Republican of Kentucky; U.S. Representative Paul Ryan, speaker of the United States House of Representatives, Republican of Wisconsin. Ryan's speech was largely ceremonial role. He called for Republican unity in the speech; U.S. Representative Kevin McCarthy, House majority leader, Republican of California; Chris Christie, Governor of New Jersey, unsuccessful candidate for 2016 Republican presidential nomination; Tiffany Trump, Trump's daughter – listed as headliner; Kerry Woolard, general manager of Trump Winery; Donald Trump Jr., Trump's son – listed as headliner; Ben Carson – retired neurosurgeon, unsuccessful candidate for 2016 Republican presidential nomination – listed as headliner; Kimberlin Brown, actor.

Wednesday, July 20–"Make America First Again:" Rick Scott, Governor of Florida; Phil Ruffin, Las Vegas casino owner; Michelle Van Etten — Van Etten was "billed as a small business owner employing more than 100,000 people" in the convention's official schedule, but she was in fact an independent retailer through a multi-level marketing firm who did not employ anyone; Scott Walker, Governor of Wisconsin, unsuccessful candidate for 2016 Republican presidential nomination; Marco Rubio, U.S. Senator from Florida, unsuccessful candidate for 2016 Republican presidential nomination (video); Ted Cruz, U.S. Senator from Texas, unsuccessful candidate for 2016 Republican presidential nomination; Eric Trump, Trump's son – listed as headliner; Newt Gingrich, former speaker of the U.S. House of Representatives, listed as a headliner; Mike Pence, Governor of Indiana and Republican vice-presidential nominee – listed as headliner.

Thursday, July 21–"Make America One Again:" Jerry Falwell Jr., president of Liberty University; Joe Arpaio, sheriff of Maricopa County, Arizona; Fran Tarkenton, former NFL quarterback; Reince Priebus, chairman of the Republican National Committee; Ivanka Trump, Trump's daughter – listed as headliner; Donald Trump, Republican presidential nominee – listed as headliner.

Of the 19 speakers billed as "headliners," six are members of the Trump family: Trump himself, his wife Melania and four of his children, Ivanka, Don Jr., Eric and Tiffany.

Some of the speeches received a significant amount of media attention.

Melania Trump's Speech

Melania Trump's speech almost immediately came under scrutiny when striking similarities were discovered between her speech and Michelle Obama's speech at the 2008 Democratic National Convention. The Trump campaign at first denied allegations of plagiarism. Campaign manager Paul Manafort argued that the speech contained "not that many similarities" and the words used are not unique words "that belong to the Obamas." Following Mrs. Trump's speech, various media outlets reported similarities as alleged plagiarism and suggested that members of Donald Trump's presidential campaign should respond to the accusations, which they did a few hours after the speech in the form of the following statement: "In writing the speech, Melania's team of writers took notes on her life's inspirations, and in some instances included fragments that reflected her own thinking."

Reince Priebus, chairman of the Republican National Committee, described the speech as "inspirational" but said if plagiarism were found, he thought "it certainly seems reasonable" to fire the person who wrote the speech. Paul Manafort, Donald Trump's campaign chairman, called it a "great speech" and said "obviously Michelle Obama feels very similar sentiments toward her family". He later said "to think that she would be cribbing Michelle Obama's words is crazy", adding "This is once again an example of when a woman threatens Hillary Clinton, she seeks out to demean her and take her down. It's not going to work against Melania Trump."

On July 20, 2016, the Trump campaign issued a statement by Meredith McIver which included the following: In working with Melania on her recent first lady speech, we discussed many people who inspired her and messages she wanted to share with the American people. A person she has always liked is Michelle Obama. Over the phone, she read me some passages from Mrs. Obama's speech as examples. I wrote them down and later included some of the phrasing in the draft that ultimately became the final speech. On July 20, two days after Melania's speech, McIver wrote that Donald Trump declined her offer to resign.

Chris Christie's speech

In the second night of the convention, Governor Chris Christie gave a speech in a style of a mock trial. After a series of statements regarding Hillary Clinton that his audience described as "guilty", the crowd chanted "lock her up". The crowd's reaction has received widespread coverage following the speech. Clinton responded to the chant in an interview on *60 Minutes* by saying that she was saddened by it.

Ted Cruz's speech

Donald Trump's top rival during the primaries, Ted Cruz, spoke in prime time on the third night of the convention. Cruz did not endorse Trump during his speech. Instead urged listeners to "vote your conscience, vote for candidates up and down the ticket who you trust to defend our freedom and to be faithful to the Constitution." Pro-Trump delegates were enraged at Cruz's speech, shouting him down and booing him off the stage, in what was described by the *New York Times* as "the most electric moment of the convention." Convention security personnel and Cruz advisor Ken Cuccinelli escorted Cruz's wife Heidi out of the hall, fearing for her safety.[Newt Gingrich spoke after Cruz and said: "I had the text of what Ted Cruz was gonna say, and I thought it was funny," Gingrich said. "I mean, Ted gets up and he says, 'Look, vote your conscience for someone who will support the Constitution.' Well, in this particular election year, that by definition cannot be for Hillary Clinton." The following morning, Cruz attended a contentious meeting with delegates representing Texas that resulted in what CNN labeled "a remarkable 25-minute back-and-forth with his own constituents, defying appeals from his own Texas delegation to put the party above his inhibitions and back Trump."

Cruz's speech sparked a backlash and elicited negative reactions from prominent Republicans supporting Trump. New Jersey governor and former presidential candidate Chris Christie called the speech "awful" and "selfish." New York Congressman Peter T. King called Cruz a "fraud" and a "self-centered liar." Senator Dan Coats of Indiana responded that Cruz was a "self-centered, narcissistic, pathological liar." Representative Marsha Blackburn of Tennessee, when asked about Cruz's speech, responded that she "would tell [Cruz] the same thing I would tell my kids, 'get over yourself.'" Susan Hutchison, chair of the Washington State

Republican Party, confronted Cruz after his speech and labeled Cruz a "traitor to the party." In addition, Cruz was denied entry to influential Republican donor Sheldon Adelson's suite at the convention. Conservative radio host Rush Limbaugh speculated that Cruz was trying to mimic Ronald Reagan's speech at the 1976 Republican National Convention, in that "he wanted to deliver a speech that was Reaganesque in that the delegates would walk out of there thinking that they should have nominated him. He didn't get there." Instead, Limbaugh compared his speech to Ted Kennedy's at the 1980 Democratic National Convention, in which he failed to endorse President Jimmy Carter, the nominee, by putting his own interests ahead of the interests of the party.

Donald Trump's speech

Trump, having been formally nominated as the Republican presidential nominee on the second night of the convention, spoke on the fourth and final night of the convention. Trump's speech was leaked hours in advance by Correct the Record, a liberal-leaning Super PAC, though Trump had already given copies of his speech to the network press pool. Trump's daughter Ivanka introduced him in a speech immediately before his own speech. "Here Comes the Sun" was used as the entrance music for Ivanka Trump. The George Harrison estate complained about the use of this song, which his family said was "offensive and against the wishes of the George Harrison estate."

Trump spoke for 75 minutes, the longest since the 1972 Republican National Convention and one of the longest acceptance speeches ever in major-party convention history. In his speech, Trump stated that America faces a "crisis" due to "attacks on our police" and "terrorism in our cities," and emphasized an important theme in his campaign: law and order. In evaluating the speech,

Glenn Thrush of *Politico* noted the influence of Richard Nixon, Spiro Agnew, Ronald Reagan, and Rudy Giuliani, all of whom sounded similar themes earlier in American history in attempts to win over the "Silent Majority". Trump also promised to limit American participation and global crises and trade deals. When Trump turned to the subject of illegal immigration, many in the audience began shouting "Build the wall, build the wall," referring to a signature promise of Trump's campaign to build a wall on the Mexico–United States border. Trump also repeatedly attacked President Barack Obama and the Democratic presumptive nominee, Hillary Clinton, arguing that the country and world had become less safe during their time in office. However, Trump attempted to reach out to supporters of defeated Democratic candidate Bernie Sanders, as well as down-and-out urbanites.

Philip Rucker and David Fahrenthold of the *Washington Post* found Trump's speech to be "relentlessly gloomy," and observed that Trump painted himself as an agent of change, while he cast Clinton as a defender of the status quo. Trump's speech was variously dubbed the "Mourning in America" speech and the "Evening in America" speech. Niall Stanage of *The Hill* argued that Trump's speech brought stability to a turbulent convention and showed Trump at his "most comfortable and energized." A *Politico* poll found largely positive reactions among "GOP political insiders" while Democrats argued that Trump's "dark" speech would prove damaging. *The New York Post* released a cover story the next day by Michael Goodwin praising Trump's speech, declaring it "the speech of his life," and also saying that the speech "could signal the start of an American revival." Ratings figures released by the major networks showed that approximately 32 million viewers watched Trump's speech, slightly ahead of the number that watched Mitt Romney's 2012 speech.

A Gallup survey found that 35% of Americans saw Trump's speech positively while 36% saw it negatively. 36% of Americans say the convention made them more likely to vote for Trump, while 51% said it made them less likely to vote for him. This is the highest "less likely to vote" percentage for a candidate in the 15 times Gallup has asked this question after a convention. It is also the first time in Gallup's convention polling that a Democratic or Republican convention has made more say that they are less likely to vote for the party's nominee.

According to FiveThirtyEight, poll averages suggested a post-convention bounce of 3 to 4 percentage points for Trump.

The number of demonstrators was significantly lower than expected, and according to Cleveland records, three of five officially permitted protests planned for the first three days of the convention did not occur. Lower-than-expected was attributed to a variety of factors, including "fear of violence from the police and fear of violence from the Trump supporters"; Cleveland's relatively small size compared to cities such as Chicago or New York; and a heavy police presence. Overall the demonstrations were generally peaceful. Some demonstrators expressed disappointment to the low turnout. In contrast, the 2016 Democratic National Convention saw a larger turnout and more arrests than the Republican Convention.

Viewership (10:00 to 11:45 PM Eastern)

Network	Viewers			
	Night 1	Night 2	Night 3	Night 4
Fox News	6,348,000	5,262,000	7,337,000	9,353,000
CNN	3,943,000	3,064,000	3,504,000	5,476,000
NBC	3,913,000	4,682,000	5,071,000	4,587,000
ABC	3,643,000	2,329,000	2,326,000	3,861,000
CBS	2,963,000	2,537,000	2,590,000	3,809,000
MSNBC	1,995,000	1,533,000	1,980,000	2,953,000
TOTAL	**22,805,000**	**19,407,000**	**22,808,000**	**30,039,000**

9

THE DEMOCRATIC NATIONAL CONVENTION

The 2016 Democratic National Convention was the gathering at which delegates of the United States Democratic Party chose their nominees for President of the United States and Vice President of the United States in the 2016 national election. It began on July 25, 2016, and concluded on July 28, 2016, at the Wells Fargo Center in Philadelphia, Pennsylvania, with some caucus meetings at the Pennsylvania Convention Center, beginning exactly one week after the 2016 Republican National Convention.

Former Secretary of State Hillary Clinton won the Democratic presidential nomination, becoming the first female major party presidential candidate. At the convention, she was endorsed by her primary rival, Bernie Sanders, along with President Barack Obama and other major party leaders. Clinton's running mate, Senator Tim Kaine of Virginia, won the vice presidential nomination by acclamation.

A cache of more than 19,000 e-mails was leaked on July 22, 2016. This caused Democratic National Committee chair Debbie

Wasserman Schultz to resign. Julian Assange, the founder of Wikileaks, timed the release of the e-mails to occur shortly before the Democratic convention in hopes of maximizing its impact.

By May 19, 2016, five organized groups of Sanders supporters had applied for demonstration permits from the Philadelphia police department. A joint rally between the Poor People's Economic Human Rights Campaign and the Green Party of the United States was denied a protest permit, but both groups planned to go ahead with their protest regardless. The Poor People's Economic Human Rights Campaign, the Green Party, and other groups obtained permits for their demonstrations on July 7 after the American Civil Liberties Union filed a lawsuit that resulted in the city lifting its ban on rush-hour protests during the DNC. The city of Philadelphia expected 35,000 to 50,000 protesters throughout the convention.

The Democratic presidential ballot was held on July 26, with Mayor Stephanie Rawlings-Blake of Baltimore presiding over the roll call of states. Senator Barbara Mikulski, the longest-serving woman in the history of Congress, nominated Clinton.

After all states had voted, Bernie Sanders stated, "I move that the convention suspend the procedural rules. I move that all votes, all votes cast by delegates be reflected in the official record, and I move that Hillary Clinton be selected as the nominee of the Democratic Party for president of the United States." Clinton had made a similar motion during the 2008 convention roll call; however, Sanders (unlike Clinton in 2008) did not move to nominate Clinton by acclamation. Clinton became the first woman to be nominated for president by a major U.S. political party.

Clinton had announced her selection of Senator Tim Kaine of Virginia as her running mate on July 22. Some Sanders supporters had discussed the possibility of challenging Kaine's nomination, but Kaine was nominated by acclamation on the third day of the convention. Kaine became the first Virginian since Woodrow Wilson to be on a major party's ticket.

The Platform Committee is co-chaired by former Atlanta mayor Shirley Franklin and Connecticut governor Dannel P. Malloy. Prior to the meeting of the full Platform Drafting Committee, eight meetings in four regions were held. The drafting committee concluded its work on June 25, sending the draft platform to the full platform committee.

The full Platform Committee approved the Democratic platform following heated debate in Orlando on July 10, 2016; the platform was formally approved at the convention itself in Philadelphia.[49]

The platform adopted by the platform committee was the most progressive in party history, largely reflecting the influence of platform-committee members appointed by Bernie Sanders. The platform committee-drafted platform was praised by both Hillary Clinton's campaign and Bernie Sanders' campaign, with Sanders policy director Warren Gunnells saying his campaign achieved "at least 80 percent" of its goals. Although Sanders could have chosen, under party rules, to force a vote on the convention floor using a "minority report" process, he decided not to do so.

The platform expresses support for raising the federal minimum wage to $15 an hour and indexing it to inflation, a plank supported by Sanders. The adoption of this point was a boost for the Fight for $15 movement. The platform also calls for ending the sub-minimum wage for tipped workers and workers with disabilities, and for twelve weeks of paid family and medical leave.

On health care, the platform committee adopted a provision supporting a public option for the Affordable Care Act and for legislation to allow Americans ages 55 and over to buy into Medicare. The platform repeats the Democratic Party pledge to empower Medicare to negotiate lower prices for prescription drugs and also calls for doubling support for community health centers that provide primary health-care services, particularly in rural areas.

The platform expresses support for Wall Street reform, the expansion of Social Security and the abolition of the death penalty, all points supported by Sanders. This marked the first time that a major U.S. party had called for ending capital punishment in its platform. On financial regulation (Wall Street reform), the platform supports a 21st-century Glass-Steagall Act to keep banks from gambling with taxpayer-guaranteed deposits, calls for the breakup of "too big to fail" financial institutions, and supports a tax on excessive speculation.

The platform expresses support for criminal justice reform, calls for an end to private prisons, and reforms to boost police accountability to communities. It calls for shutting "the revolving door between Wall Street and Washington," calling for "a ban on golden parachutes for bankers taking government jobs, limits on conflict of interest, and a two-year ban on financial services regulators 'from lobbying their former colleagues.'"

On taxation, the platform pledges "tax relief" to middle-class families. The platform also calls for the end of overseas tax deferral and the carried interest tax loophole, as well as a crackdown on corporate inversions. On K–12 education, the party's platform was revised in important ways, backing the right of parents to opt their children out of high-stakes standardized tests, qualifying support for charter schools, and opposing using test scores for high-stakes purposes to evaluate teachers and students. The platform calls for "democratically governed great neighborhood public schools and high-quality public charter schools, and opposes for-profit charter schools focused on making a profit off of public resources."

On workers' rights, the platform endorses expanding and defending the right of workers to organize unions and bargain collectively. The platform supports the ability of workers to organize via card check and calls for a 'model employer' executive order that would give preference in government procurement to employers who provide their workers with a living wage, benefits and the opportunity to form a union. The platform committee approved compromise language on the controversial practice of hydraulic fracturing (fracking), calling for increased federal, state and local regulation of the practice but not a wholesale ban, as Sanders had pushed for.

In a close, 81-80 vote, the platform committee approved language supporting the removal of marijuana from Schedule I of the Controlled Substances Act, providing a reasoned pathway for future legalization of marijuana.

The platform maintained the Democratic Party's long-standing support for Israel, with DNC chair Debbie Wasserman Schultz terming it the strongest pro-Israel platform in the party's history. The platform includes a provision condemning the BDS movement and calling for a two-state solution to the Israeli-Palestinian conflict that guarantees Israel's future as a secure and democratic Jewish state with recognized borders and provides the Palestinians with independence, sovereignty, and dignity. Proposals for language that would have condemned settlements and called for an end to the Israeli occupation were rejected in the platform committee.

On abortion, the platform states, "We believe unequivocally, like the majority of Americans, that every woman should have access to quality reproductive health care services, including safe and legal abortion — regardless of where she lives, how much money she makes, or how she is insured." It also promises action to overturn the Helms Amendment and the Hyde Amendment, and against efforts to defund Planned Parenthood. This marked the first time the Democratic platform had an explicit call to repeal the Hyde Amendment.

The platform urged U.S. ratification of the Convention on the Elimination of All Forms of Discrimination Against Women and supported passage of the Equal Rights Amendment, saying: "After 240 years, we will finally enshrine the rights of women in the Constitution."

On July 23, party officials announced that Democratic National Committee chairwoman Debbie Wasserman Schultz would not preside over or speak at the convention. The announcement came after the leak of 20,000 emails by seven DNC staffers from January 2015 to May 2016, during the Democratic primary season. The emails showed the staffers favoring Clinton and disparaging Sanders. Wasserman Schultz's removal from convention activities was approved by both the Clinton and Sanders campaigns. In her place, the Rules Committee named Representative Marcia Fudge of Ohio as convention chair.

On July 24, the DNC Rules Committee voted overwhelmingly, 158–6, to adopt a superdelegate reform package. The new rules were the result of a compromise between the Clinton and the Sanders campaigns; in the past, Sanders had pressed for the complete elimination of superdelegates. Under the reform package, in future Democratic conventions about two-thirds of superdelegates would be bound to the results of state primaries and caucuses. The remaining one third—Democratic senators, Democratic governors and Democratic U.S. representatives— would remain unbound and free to support the candidate of their choice.

Mayor of Baltimore Stephanie Rawlings-Blake, the secretary of the Democratic National Committee, gaveled in the convention on the afternoon of July 25. 257 speakers addressed the convention from the podium over the course of the convention. These speakers included the following:

First night (Monday, July 25): Theme: "United Together": U.S. Representative Steny Hoyer of Maryland, the House Democratic Whip; Governor Dan Malloy of Connecticut, chairman of the Democratic Governors Association; John Podesta, chairman of Hillary Clinton's 2016 campaign; Lily Eskelsen Garcia, president of the National Education Association; Richard Trumka, president of the AFL-CIO; Randi Weingarten, president of the American Federation of Teachers; U.S. Senator Bob Casey Jr. of Pennsylvania; U.S. Senator Al Franken of Minnesota and comedian Sarah Silverman - performed a comedy sketch together; Eva Longoria, actress; First Lady Michelle Obama (headliner); U.S. Representative Joe Kennedy III of Massachusetts (introduced Warren); U.S. Senator Elizabeth Warren of Massachusetts (keynote speaker); U.S. Senator Bernie Sanders of Vermont (headliner)— final speaker of the night; Rabbi Julie Schonfeld, delivered closing benediction.

Second night (Tuesday, July 26): Theme: "A Lifetime of Fighting for Children and Families": U.S. Representative Tulsi Gabbard of Hawaii, nominating Bernie Sanders for president; Senator Barbara Mikulski of Maryland, nominating Hillary Clinton for president; House Minority Leader Nancy Pelosi of California, appearing alongside several other female House Democrats; U.S. Senator Chuck Schumer of New York; Donna Brazile, Democratic National Committee Vice Chair of Voter Registration and Participation and future interim chair of the Democratic National Committee (effective at the end of the convention); Former Attorney General Eric Holder; Cecile Richards, president of Planned Parenthood; Lena Dunham and America Ferrara, actresses; U.S. Senator Barbara Boxer of California; Debra Messing, actress; Former Governor Howard Dean of Vermont; U.S. Senator Amy Klobuchar of Minnesota; Ima Matul, Indonesian survior of human trafficking, who spoke on the anti-slavery and human trafficking programs championed by Hillary Clinton; Former Secretary of State Madeleine Albright; Former President Bill Clinton (headliner); Meryl Streep, actress.

Third night (Wednesday, July 27): Theme: "Working Together": Reverend William J. Byron, S.J., invocation; Mayor Bill de Blasio of New York City; The Reverend Jesse Jackson; Mayor Karen Weaver of Flint, Michigan; U.S. Representative G.K. Butterfield of North Carolina, chair of the Congressional Black Caucus; U.S. Senate Democratic Leader Harry Reid of Nevada; Lieutenant Governor Gavin Newsom of California; Former Governor Martin O'Malley of Maryland; Sigourney Weaver, actress; Governor Jerry Brown of California; Angela Bassett, actress; Former U.S. Representative Gabby Giffords & Captain Mark Kelly, both of Arizona; Former CIA Director and Secretary of Defense Leon Panetta; Second Lady of the United States Jill Biden; Vice President Joe Biden (headliner); Former Mayor Michael Bloomberg of New York; U.S. Senator Tim Kaine of Virginia, accepting the 2016 Democratic vice presidential nomination (headliner); President Barack Obama (headliner).

Fourth night (Thursday, July 28): Theme: "Stronger Together": Former State Representative Bakari Sellers of South Carolina; Dolores Huerta, civil rights leader; Governor Mark Dayton of Minnesota; House Minority Leader Nancy Pelosi of California; U.S. Representative Joaquín Castro of Texas; Governor Andrew Cuomo of New York; Ted Danson and Mary Steenburgen, actors; Governor Tom Wolf of Pennsylvania; Former Governor Jennifer Granholm of Michigan; Doug Elmets, former Reagan administration official; Reverend William Barber, II, of North Carolina; Kareem Abdul-Jabaar, professional basketball player; Khizr Khan, with Ghazala Khan, father and mother of fallen Army Captain Humayun S. M. Khan; General John R. Allen, U.S. Marine Corps (retired 4-star General), surrounded by dozens of veterans; Captain Florent Groberg (retired), recipient of the Medal of Honor; Chelsea Clinton, daughter of Bill and Hillary Clinton (headliner); 2016 Democratic presidential nominee Hillary Clinton (headliner).

Unlike previous conventions, sitting Cabinet members did not speak at the event; the White House decided that barring Cabinet officers from addressing the convention would send a signal about the primacy of the Obama administration's responsibility to manage the government and serve the American people and avoid legal or political difficulties.

NOTABLE SPEECHES

Sarah Silverman

Minnesota Senator Al Franken introduced fellow comedian Sarah Silverman, who is also a Bernie Sanders supporter. In her speech, she urged other Sanders supporters to back Hillary Clinton and later said that Bernie or Bust people "are being ridiculous". *The Washington Post* and *Politico* called this one of the most memorable moments of the night. *The New York Times* called her speech "the perfect breath of fresh air."

Michelle Obama

In her speech, First Lady Michelle Obama defended Hillary Clinton and urged Democrats to vote for Hillary focusing on Clinton's role as a woman and a mother. Obama alluded to Donald Trump's actions as reasons to vote for Clinton, while attempting to heal the fractures within the party. Referencing her experience as a black woman in the White House, she said that although she lives in a "house that was built by slaves," seeing her children play on the White House lawn fills her with hope. She said: "Don't let anyone ever tell you that this country is not great, that somehow we need to make it great again. Because this right now is the greatest country on Earth." *The Atlantic* described the speech as the best of the night and called it a speech "for the ages," a qualification echoed in other publications. David Smith of *The Guardian* called it a "profound, moving and devastating riposte to Donald Trump".

Bernie Sanders

Vermont Senator and former Democratic candidate Bernie Sanders spoke on the first day of the Democratic Convention, urging his supporters to vote for presumptive nominee Hillary Clinton. In his speech, Sanders told supports that he understood and shared their disappointment about the final results of the nominating process, but urged them to "take enormous pride in the historical accomplishments we have achieved," saying: "Together, my friends, we have begun a political revolution to transform America and that revolution – our revolution – continues."

Sanders offered a strong endorsement of Hillary Clinton, saying that American needed leadership that would "improve the lives of working families, children, the elderly, the sick and poor" and "bring our people together," and that "By these measures, any objective observer will conclude that – based on her ideas and her leadership – Hillary Clinton must become the next president of the United States." Sanders said "I am proud to stand with her."

On the second day of the convention, Sanders' delegates, with his approval, voted for him in the formal roll-call vote, although at the end of the roll-call vote Sanders moved to suspend the rules to and formally nominate Clinton for president, an important unifying gesture.

Bill Clinton

Former President Bill Clinton spoke on the second night of the convention, telling the story of his life with his wife, Hillary Clinton. Clinton described his wife as someone who had fought for change throughout her entire life, beginning with their first meeting in law school in 1971. Clinton contrasted the Republican portrayal of his wife with what he argued is the "real one," relating anecdotes regarding Clinton's friends and family. Dylan Matthews of Vox called the speech a "typical first lady address," noting that the former president rarely touched on his own political career. Chris Cillizza of the *Washington Post* stated that Clinton talked about his wife in an "engaging, funny and, yes, sweet way."

Michael Bloomberg

Former New York City Mayor Michael Bloomberg spoke on the third night of the convention, where he emphasized that he is not a Democrat, but endorsed Clinton anyway to "defeat a dangerous demagogue." Bloomberg's speech aimed to convince centrist voters that voting for Clinton is the "responsible" thing to do, as Bloomberg argued Trump would be a dangerous and unpredictable president. Chris Cillizza of the *Washington Post* wrote that Bloomberg gave a "searing and effective critique" of a fellow New York billionaire. After the speech, Reihan Salam of *Slate* wondered whether Bloomberg's speech foreshadowed future ideological battles in the Democratic Party between moderate "Bloombourgeoisie" and liberal "Sandernistas."

Tim Kaine

Having been nominated by acclamation earlier in the day, Kaine accepted the Democratic vice presidential nomination on the night of July 27. In one of his first major national speeches, Kaine discussed his life story, including his childhood as the son of an ironworker, his time in Honduras, and his response to the Virginia Tech shooting. Kaine also attacked Trump, arguing that, in contrast to Clinton, Trump had failed to explain what he would do once in office. Kaine performed an impression of Trump, mockingly repeating "believe me," and then arguing that Trump's past showed that he cannot be trusted. Kaine also strongly endorsed Clinton as the most qualified candidate for president, calling her *lista,* Spanish for "ready." After the speech, Morgan Winsor of ABC News noted the many Twitter users who described Kaine as "your friend's overly nice dad."

Barack Obama

In one of the last major speeches of his presidency, Obama strongly endorsed Clinton as the nominee, saying, "There has never been a man or woman more qualified than Hillary Clinton." Obama contrasted his and Clinton's hopeful view of America with that of Trump, which he called "deeply pessimistic." Obama argued that Trump is unqualified for the office, and is attempting to use fear to get elected. Michael Grunwald of Politico called it a "stirring but fundamentally defensive speech." Conservative blogger Erick Erickson tweeted "I disagree with the President on so much policy and his agenda, but appreciate the hope and optimism in this speech." After the speech, Clinton appeared on the stage for the first time in the convention, embracing her 2008 primary rival.

Khizr Khan

Khizr Khan, the father of Captain Humayun Khan, a Muslim-American soldier killed during Operation Iraqi Freedom, criticized Donald Trump's proposed ban on Muslim immigration. His was clearly the most moving speech of the evening and Trump's combative reaction to it created a firestorm backlash that knocked 4-5 percentage points off his previous 4-point bounce after the Republican convention.

Chelsea Clinton

Chelsea Clinton introduced her mother, Hillary Clinton, the Democratic nominee, by sharing her personal story about her relationship with her mother when she was younger. She also praised her for being a great mother, and said that her (Chelsea's) kids are proud of Hillary.

Hillary Clinton

After being introduced by her daughter, Clinton accepted the Democratic presidential nomination on July 28, the final night of the convention. In her speech, Clinton asked voters to trust in her experience, judgment, and compassion based on her long public career. Clinton discussed what her priorities would be as president, saying that creating jobs would be her "primary mission," and that she would also seek to combat climate change, make college more affordable, and institute new gun laws. Clinton contrasted her hopeful vision and specific policy proposals with what she sees as Trump's fearmongering and vague ideas. Eyder Peralta of NPR also noted that Clinton's "grounded" speech contrasted with the "soaring" speeches of President Obama. To supporters of her rival

Bernie Sanders, Clinton stated "I want you to know, I've heard you," complimenting their energy and passion.

A Politico poll of "Democratic insiders" found highly positive reactions, though the insiders had slightly better reviews for the speeches of Michelle Obama and Barack Obama. A CNN instant poll showed that 86% of viewers had a positive reaction to the speech (71% very positive, 15% somewhat positive) and 12% had a negative reaction. According to CNN's instant polls at both conventions, viewers had a more favorable view of her speech than Trump's speech at the Republican National Convention the week earlier. A Gallup poll showed that Clinton's speech was viewed about 24 points more positively than negatively. Also, according to Gallup, 45% were more likely to vote for Clinton versus 41% who were less likely to vote for her based on what they saw/read about the convention.

Sam Wang reported a 7% post-convention bounce for Clinton in general election polling (on the basis of the six polls released by 1 August 2016). According to *FiveThirtyEight*, Clinton's post-convention bounce was larger than Trump's.

Viewership (10:00 to 11:45 PM Eastern)

Network	Viewers			
	Night 1	**Night 2**	**Night 3**	**Night 4**
CNN	6,208,000	5,929,000	6,169,000	7,505,000
MSNBC	4,597,000	3,834,000	4,918,000	5,272,000
NBC	4,293,000	5,281,000	4,167,000	4,516,000
ABC	4,107,000	3,463,000	3,550,000	3,846,000
Fox News	3,330,000	2,851,000	3,031,000	2,394,000
CBS	3,206,000	2,945,000	2,860,000	3,653,000
TOTAL	**26,054,000**	**24,303,000**	**24,695,000**	**28,638,000**

10

THE VICE PRESIDENTIAL CANDIDATES

Alben Barkley (1877-1056), who served as Vice President under President Harry S. Truman (1949-1953), once famously remarked, "The Vice Presidency isn't worth a bucket of warm spit. While that may or may not have been true in his day, the Vice President today is one of the President's closest and most important confreres and advisers, the President pro-tempore of the Senate, the tie-breaker in the event the Senate is deadlocked, and he or she must be ready to step into the Presidency on a moment's notice, such as Lyndon Johnson, who took the helm of state when President John F. Kennedy was assassinated; or Gerald Ford, who succeeded President Richard M. Nixon when he resigned. The current Vice President, Joe Biden, has served with distinction as a universally popular "nice guy" – everyone's favorite uncle, a long-term public servant, and a courageous survivor of the early death by cancer of his son and protégé.

The 2016 candidates for the second highest office in the land are Senator Tim Kaine, former Governor of Virginia for the Democrats, and Mike Pence, current governor of Indiana for the

Republican. The following thumbnail sketch tells you something about each of these Vice Presidential hopefuls.

TIM KAINE

Timothy Michael "Tim" Kaine (born February 26, 1958) is an American attorney and politician serving as the junior United States Senator from Virginia. Kaine was elected to the Senate in 2012. Born in Saint Paul, Minnesota, Kaine grew up in Overland Park, Kansas, graduated from the University of Missouri, and earned a law degree from Harvard Law School before entering private practice and becoming a lecturer at the University of Richmond School of Law. He was first elected to public office in 1994, when he won a seat on the Richmond, Virginia City Council. He was then elected mayor of Richmond in 1998, serving in that position until being elected Lieutenant Governor of Virginia in 2001. Kaine was elected governor of Virginia in 2005, serving from 2006 to 2010. He served as chairman of the Democratic National Committee from 2009 to 2011.

On July 22, 2016, Hillary Clinton announced that she had selected Kaine to be her vice presidential running mate in the 2016 presidential election. The 2016 Democratic National Convention nominated him on July 27.

Kaine is the eldest of three sons born to Mary Kathleen (née Burns), a home economics teacher, and Albert Alexander Kaine, Jr., a welder and the owner of a small iron-working shop. He was raised Catholic. Kaine's father is of Scottish and Irish ancestry, and his mother is of Irish descent. Kaine's family moved to Overland Park, Kansas, when Kaine was two years old, and he grew up in the Kansas City area. In 1976, he graduated from Rockhurst High School, a Jesuit all-boys preparatory school in Kansas City,

Missouri. At Rockhurst, Kaine joined the debate team and was elected student body president.

Kaine received his B.A. in economics from the University of Missouri in 1979, completing his degree in three years, and graduating summa cum laude. He entered Harvard Law School in 1979, but interrupted his law studies after his first year to work in Honduras for nine months from 1980 to 1981, helping Jesuit missionaries who ran a Catholic school in El Progreso. While running a vocational center that taught carpentry and welding, he also helped increase the school's enrollment by recruiting local villagers. Kaine is fluent in Spanish as a result of his year in Honduras.

After returning from Honduras, Kaine met his future wife, first-year Harvard Law student, Anne Holton. He graduated from Harvard Law School with a J.D. degree in 1983. Kaine and Holton moved to Holton's hometown of Richmond, Virginia, after graduation, and Kaine was admitted to the Virginia Bar in 1984.

After graduating from law school, Kaine served as law clerk to Judge R. Lanier Anderson III of the United States Court of Appeals for the Eleventh Circuit, in Macon, Georgia. Kaine then joined the Richmond law firm of Little, Parsley & Cluverius. In 1987, Kaine became a director with the law firm of Mezzullo & McCandlish. Kaine practiced law in Richmond for 17 years, specializing in fair housing law and representing clients discriminated against on the basis of race or disability. He represented the Virginia chapter of Housing Opportunities Made Equal in a landmark redlining discrimination lawsuit against Nationwide Mutual Insurance Co.'s practices in Richmond. Kaine won a $100.5 million verdict in the case; the judgment was overturned on appeal, and Kaine and his colleagues negotiated a $17.5 million settlement.

Kaine regularly did pro bono work. In 1988, he started teaching legal ethics at the University of Richmond School of Law for six years. He was a founding member of the Virginia Coalition to End Homelessness.

Kaine became interested in politics in part due to the influence of his wife's family and his experience attending Richmond city council meetings. In May 1994, he was elected to the city council of Richmond, defeated the incumbent city councilman by 97 votes. Kaine served four terms on the council, the latter two as mayor.

On July 1, 1998, Kaine was elected mayor of Richmond on an 8-1 vote, becoming the city's first white mayor in more than ten years, which was viewed as a surprise. Previous mayors had treated the role as primarily a ceremonial one, with the city manager effectively operating the city; Kaine treated the office as a full-time job, taking a more hands-on role.

Along with Commonwealth's Attorney David Hicks, U.S. Attorney James Comey, and Police Chief Jerry Oliver, Kaine was a supporter of Project Exile, which a reporter described as a controversial but effective program, that shifted gun crimes to federal court, where armed defendants faced harsher sentences. The effort won broad political support and the city's homicide rate fell by 55% during Kaine's tenure in office. He later touted Project Exile during his campaign for lieutenant governor in 2001.

On several occasions, Kaine voted in opposition to tax increases, and supported a tax abatement program for renovated buildings, which was credited for a housing renovation boom in the city. Richmond was named one of the 10 best cities in America to do business by *Forbes* magazine during Kaine's term.

The *New York Times* wrote that Kaine was by all accounts instrumental in bridging the city's racial divide. In the early part of his term, Kaine issued an apology for the city's role in slavery; the apology was generally well received as a genuine, heartfelt expression.

During his tenure as mayor, Kaine drew criticism for spending $6,000 in public funds on buses to the Million Mom March, an anti-gun-violence rally in Washington, D.C.; after a backlash, Kaine raised the money privately and reimbursed the city.

Kaine ran for Lieutenant Governor of Virginia in 2001, joining the race after state senator Emily Couric dropped out due to pancreatic cancer and endorsed Kaine as her replacement. Kaine won the nomination, garnering 39.7% of the vote. In the general election, Kaine won with 50.35%, of the vote, edging out his Republican opponent, who received 48.06%. Kaine was inaugurated on January 12, 2002, and was sworn in by his wife Anne Holton, a state judge.

In 2005, Kaine ran for governor of Virginia. He was considered an underdog for most of the race, trailing in polls for most of the election. Kaine ultimately prevailed, winning 51.7% to his Republican opponent's 46.0%.

Kaine emphasized fiscal responsibility and a centrist message. He expressed support for controlling sprawl and tackling longstanding traffic issues, an issue that resonated in the exurbs of northern Virginia. He benefited from his association with the popular outgoing Democratic governor, Mark Warner, who had performed well in traditionally Republican areas of the state. On the campaign trail, Kaine referred to the "Warner-Kaine administration" in speeches and received the strong backing of Warner. Kilgore later attributed his defeat to Warner's high popularity and the plummeting popularity of Republican President George W. Bush, who held one rally with Kilgore on the campaign's final day.

The campaign turned sharply negative in its final weeks, with Kilgore running television attack ads that claimed, incorrectly, that Kaine believed that "Hitler doesn't qualify for the death penalty." The ads also attacked Kaine for his service ten years earlier as a court-appointed attorney for a death-row inmate. The Republican ad was denounced by the editorial boards of the *Washington Post* and a number of Virginia newspapers as a "smear" and "dishonest." Kaine responded with an ad in which he told voters that he opposes capital punishment but would take an oath and enforce the death penalty. In later polls, voters said they believed Kaine's response and were angered by Kilgore's negative ads.

Kaine was sworn in as governor at the colonial Capitol at Williamsburg, on January 14, 2006, the first governor since Thomas Jefferson to be inaugurated there. He served as chairman of the Southern Governors' Association from 2008 to 2009.

On January 31, 2006, Kaine gave the Democratic response to President George W. Bush's 2006 State of the Union address. In it, Kaine criticized the Bush administration's No Child Left Behind Act for wreaking havoc on local school districts; criticized congressional Republicans for cutting student loan programs; and condemned as reckless Bush's spending increases and tax cuts. Kaine praised bipartisan initiatives in Virginia to make record investments in education and to improve veterans' access to veterans' benefits. Kaine criticized the Bush administration's conduct of the Iraq War and treatment of U.S. soldiers; saying that the American people were given inaccurate information about reasons for invading Iraq; "our troops in Iraq were not given the best body armor or the best intelligence"; and "the administration wants to further reduce military and veterans' benefits."

As governor, Kaine successfully protected 400,000 acres of Virginia land from development, fulfilling a promise he made in 2005. Kaine's conservation efforts focused on conservation easements (voluntary easements that preserve the private ownership of a piece of land while also permanently protecting it from development); a substantial Virginia land preservation tax credit encouraged easements. From 2004 to 2009, the Virginia

Outdoors Foundation (a quasi-governmental entity set up in 1966 to preserve open land in the state) protected more land than it had in the previous forty years, a fact touted by Kaine as his term drew to a close.

As governor, Kaine established the Climate Change Commission, a bipartisan panel to study climate change issues. Kaine supported a coal-fired power plant project in Wise County, clashing with environmentalists who opposed the project. In 2009, Kaine expressed support for tighter restrictions on mountaintop removal coal mining imposed by the Obama administration.

In October 2006, Kaine signed an executive order banning smoking in all government buildings and state-owned cars as of January 1, 2007. He signed legislation banning smoking in restaurants and bars, with some exceptions, in March 2009, making Virginia the first Southern state to do so.

In 2007, Kaine secured increases in state funding for nursing in the Virginia General Assembly and announced a 10% salary increase for nursing faculty above the normal salary increase for state employees, plus additional funds for scholarships for nursing master's programs. The initiatives were aimed at addressing a shortage of practicing nurses.

Following the 2007 Virginia Tech shooting, in which 32 people were killed, Kaine appointed an eight-member Virginia Tech Review Panel, chaired by retired Virginia State Police superintendent W. Gerald Massengill to probe the event. The commission members included specialists in psychology, law, forensics and higher education as well as former Secretary of Homeland Security Tom Ridge. The commission issued its findings and recommendations in August 2007. Among other recommendations, the panel proposed many mental health reforms. Based on the panel's recommendations, Kaine proposed $42 million of investment in mental health programs and reforms, included boosting access to outpatient and emergency mental health services, increasing the number of case managers and improving monitoring of community-based providers. In April 2007, Kaine signed an executive order instructing state agencies to step up efforts to block gun sales to people involuntarily committed to inpatient and outpatient mental health treatment centers. Kaine, who had been in Japan on a trade mission at the time of the shootings, received widespread praise for his quick return to the state and his handling of the issue .

Among Kaine's greatest challenges as governor came during the 2008–09 economic crisis; the *Washington Post* wrote that perhaps his greatest success was keeping the state running despite the crisis. In the midst of the Great Recession, unemployment in Virginia remained lower than the national average. During Kaine's tenure as governor, the unemployment rate in Virginia rose from 3.2% to 7.4%, a smaller increase than the national unemployment rate which rose from 4.7% to 9.9% during the same period.

As governor, Kaine approved $3.31 billion in general fund spending cuts. After the end of Kaine's term in office, the Virginia General Assembly adopted about $1.33 billion in additional budget cuts that Kaine had recommended, for a total of $4.64 billion in cuts. Virginia was one of three states to earn the highest grade in terms of management in a report by the non-partisan Pew Center on the States. Virginia took first place each year from 2006 to 2009 in the "Best States for Business" rankings published by *Forbes.*

In July 2007, during the debate on the Silver Line of the Washington Metro through Tysons Corner, Kaine supported an elevated track solution in preference to a tunnel, citing costs and potential delays that would put federal funding at risk.

In 2008, Kaine backed a $22 million proposal in the Virginia General Assembly to make pre-kindergarten education more accessible to at-risk four-year-olds. Virginia was rated as the best state to raise a child in a 2007 report by *Education Week* and the Pew Center on the States.

As governor, Kaine made a number of appointments to the Virginia state courts. Kaine made two appointments[c] to the Supreme Court of Virginia, naming Chesapeake Circuit Judge S. Bernard Goodwyn to the Court in 2007 and Virginia Court of Appeals Judge LeRoy F. Millette, Jr. to the Court in 2008.

Kaine announced his support for Senator Obama's presidential bid in February 2007. Kaine's endorsement was the first from a statewide elected official outside of Illinois. Because Kaine was a relatively popular governor of a Southern state, there was media speculation that he was a potential nominee for vice president. Obama had supported Kaine in his campaign for governor and had said about him: "Tim Kaine has a message of fiscal responsibility and generosity of spirit. That kind of message can sell anywhere." On July 28, 2008, Politico reported that Kaine was "very, very high" on Obama's shortlist for vice president, a list which also included then Senator Hillary Clinton of New York, Governor Kathleen Sebelius of Kansas, Senator Evan Bayh of Indiana, and Senator Joe Biden of Delaware. Obama ultimately selected Biden to become the vice-presidential nominee.

In January 2009, Kaine became the Chairman of the Democratic National Committee. Kaine had turned down the position the first time it was offered to him, expressing misgivings about accepting a partisan position, but nonetheless took the job at the request of President Obama. During his tenure, he oversaw a significant expansion of the party's grassroots focus through Organizing for America, the political operation for the White House. In February 2011, after Kaine spoke to union leaders in Madison, Organizing for America got involved in Wisconsin's budget battle and opposed Republican-sponsored anti-union legislation. They made phone calls, sent emails, and distributed messages via Facebook and Twitter to build crowds for rallies.

After completing his term as governor in January 2010, Kaine taught part-time at the University of Richmond. Kaine explained that he had chosen to teach at a private university, rather than public university, "because it would not have been right for a sitting governor to be seeking employment at an institution when he writes the budget and appoints the board of the institution."

United States Senate

After Senator Jim Webb's decision not to seek reelection, Kaine announced on April 5, 2011, that he would run for Webb's seat. He was initially reluctant to return to public office, but Webb, Senator Mark Warner, and other Virginia Democrats saw Kaine as the strongest potential Democratic candidate and convinced him to run. Kaine filmed announcement videos in English and Spanish and was unopposed for the Democratic nomination. He defeated former Senator and Governor George Allen in the general election.

Kaine was sworn in for a six-year term on January 3, 2013, reuniting him with Mark Warner, the senior senator. Kaine was lieutenant governor when Warner was governor of Virginia.

On June 11, 2013, Kaine delivered a speech on the Senate floor in support of the bipartisan immigration bill. The speech was entirely in Spanish, marking the first time a senator had ever made a speech on the Senate floor in a language other than English.

As a member of the Senate Committee on Foreign Affairs, Kaine pushed for a new Congressional authorization of military force for the American operations against Islamic State of Iraq and the Levant (ISIL). Kaine supported the Joint Comprehensive Plan of Action with Iran, though he also helped Republican Senator Bob Corker hold a vote on a resolution of disapproval on the deal. Kaine has taken several trips throughout the Middle East, meeting with the leaders of states such as Turkey and Israel.

While in the Senate, Kaine has continued to teach part-time at the University of Richmond, receiving a salary of $16,000 per year. Kaine voted with his party more than 90% of the time. He reportedly has good relations with both Democratic and Republican senators.

In the 113th Congress (2013–15), Kaine served on the Committee on Armed Services, the Committee on the Budget, and the Committee on Foreign Relations. In the current Congress, Kaine serves on the same three committees, plus the Special Committee on Aging. In July 2013, Kaine was named chairman of the United States Senate Foreign Relations Subcommittee on Near East, South Asia, Central Asia and Counterterrorism. Within the Senate Armed Services Committee, Kaine serves on the Subcommittee on Emerging Threats and Capabilities, the Subcommittee on Readiness and Management Support (for which he is the ranking member), and the Subcommittee on Sea Power.

Within the Senate Foreign Affairs Committee, Kaine serves on the Subcommittee on State Department and USAID Management, International Operations, and Bilateral International Development (for which he is the ranking member), the Subcommittee on Europe and Regional Security Cooperation, the Subcommittee on Near East, South Asia, Central Asia, and Counterterrorism, and the Subcommittee on Western Hemisphere, Transnational Crime, Civilian Security, Democracy, Human Rights and Global Women's Issues.

In January 2014, Kaine, with Republican Senator Rob Portman of Ohio, established the bipartisan Senate Career and Technical

Education Caucus (CTE Caucus), which focuses on vocational education and technical education. Kaine and Portman co-chair the caucus. In 2014, Kaine and Portman introduced the CTE Excellence and Equity Act to the Senate; the legislation would provide $500 million in federal funding, distributed by competitive grants, to high schools to further CTE programs. The legislation, introduced as an amendment to the omnibus Carl D. Perkins Career and Technical Education Act of 2006, would promote apprenticeships and similar initiatives.

Kaine endorsed Hillary Clinton's presidential bid in 2016 and campaigned actively for Clinton in seven states during the primaries. He had been the subject of considerable speculation as a possible running mate for Clinton, with several news reports indicating that he was at or near the top of Clinton's list of people under consideration alongside Elizabeth Warren and Julian Castro. The *New York Times* reported that Clinton's husband, former President Bill Clinton, privately backed Kaine as his wife's vice-presidential selection, noting his domestic and national security résumé. On July 22, 2016, she picked Kaine to be her running mate in the election. Clinton introduced Kaine as her choice in a joint appearance at a rally at Florida International University in Miami the following day. The 2016 Democratic National Convention nominated him their vice presidential candidate on July 27, 2016.

Kaine is the first Virginian since Woodrow Wilson to be on a major party's ticket, and is the first Virginian to run for vice president on a major party's ticket since John Tyler in 1840; he is also the first Senator from Virginia to be on a major party's ticket since Tyler.

According to the *New York Times*, Kaine is widely described by people in his political orbit as a likable if less than charismatic figure...guided by moral convictions that flow from his deep

Christian faith. Kaine described himself on *Meet the Press* as "boring."

In terms of political ideology, *FiveThirtyEight* characterizes him as a mainstream Democrat and notes that his ideology score is very similar to that of Vice President Joe Biden. Three conservative groups gave Kaine zero percent ratings in the few years before 2016, while the liberal group Americans for Democratic Action gave Kaine a 90% rating in 2014. The *New York Times* wrote that in hyperpartisan Washington, he is often seen as a centrist while also describing him as an "old-fashioned liberal driven by Jesuit ideals."

Kaine acknowledges the scientific consensus on climate change, and in a 2014 Senate speech criticized climate change deniers, as well as those who "may not deny the climate science, but deny that the U.S. can or should be a leader in taking any steps" to address the issue. Kaine has expressed concern about sea level rise (a major consequence of climate change), and in particular its effect on coastal Virginia.

Kaine endorses making coal energy production cleaner saying that it is imperative to convert coal to electricity with less pollution than we do today. He has criticized those who "frame the debate as a conflict between an economy and the environment," saying that "protecting the environment is good for the economy." Kaine co-sponsored the Advanced Clean Coal Technology Investment in Our Nation Act, legislation to increase investment in clean coal technologies. He voted against passage of legislation to approve the Keystone XL pipeline. Kaine supports the use of hydraulic fracturing (fracking) to harvest natural gas from shale formations. He believes this will reduce carbon pollution.

Like his fellow senator from Virginia, Mark Warner, Kaine applauded the U.S. Forest Service's plan to close most, but not all, of the George Washington National Forest to hydraulic fracturing and other horizontal drilling activities. Kaine supports oil and gas exploration off the coast of Virginia, saying, "I have long believed that the moratorium on offshore drilling, based on a cost-benefit calculation performed decades ago, should be re-examined." He also supports the development of solar energy and offshore wind turbines. Based on his votes on environmental issues in the Senate, the League of Conservation Voters has given Kaine an 88% score for 2015, and a 91% lifetime score.

Kaine, a Roman Catholic, is personally against abortion, but is "largely inclined to keep the law out of women's reproductive decisions." Kaine has said: "I'm a strong supporter of *Roe v. Wade* and women being able to make these decisions. In government, we have enough things to worry about. We don't need to make people's reproductive decisions for them." Kaine supports some legal restrictions on abortion, such as requiring parental consent for minors (with a judicial bypass procedure) and banning late-term abortions in cases where the woman's life is not at risk.

In 2009, Kaine previously criticized the Obama administration for not providing a broad enough religious employer exemption in the contraceptive mandate of the Affordable Care Act, but praised a 2012 amendment to the regulations that allowed insurers to provide birth control to employees when an employer was an objecting religious organization. In 2005, when running for governor, Kaine said he favored reducing abortions by: (1) "Enforcing the current Virginia restrictions on abortion and passing an enforceable ban on partial birth abortion that protects the life and health of the mother"; (2) "Fighting teen pregnancy through abstinence-focused education"; (3) "Ensuring women's access to health care (including legal contraception) and economic opportunity"; and (4) "Promoting adoption as an alternative for women facing unwanted pregnancies."

In 2007, as governor, Kaine cut off state funding for abstinence-only sex education programs, citing studies which showed that such programs were ineffective, while comprehensive sex education programs were more effective. Kaine believes that both abstinence and contraceptives must be taught, and that education should be evidence-based.

As a senator, he has received perfect scores from Planned Parenthood and the abortion-rights advocacy group NARAL. He has received a score of zero from the anti-abortion National Right to Life Committee.

In 2006, Kaine campaigned against an amendment to the Virginia State Constitution to bar same-sex marriage, and in March 2013, Kaine announced his support of same-sex marriage. In the Senate, Kaine co-sponsored the Employment Non-Discrimination Act, which would bar employment discrimination on the basis of sexual orientation.

Kaine is generally pro-union and has received a 96 percent lifetime Senate voting rating from the AFL-CIO, which praised his selection as vice presidential nominee. However, Kaine supports Virginia's longstanding "right-to-work" law, which "frees union nonmembers from any legal obligation to pay fees to a union that bargains collectively on their behalf." Kaine supports the Lilly Ledbetter Fair Pay Act, which expands the cases in which worker can sue against gender pay discrimination. Following his selection by Clinton as a running mate in 2016, Kaine was praised by the National Organization for Women. Kaine favors an increase in the minimum wage.[131]

In the Senate, Kaine has supported the normalization of U.S.–Cuban relations and has supported the international nuclear agreement with Iran. On the issue of the war in Afghanistan, Kaine's website states "The main mission in Afghanistan—destroying Al Qaeda—is nearly complete and we should bring our troops home as quickly as we can, consistent with the need to make sure that Afghanistan poses no danger in the broader region."

Kaine and Republican Senator John McCain of Arizona introduced the War Powers Consultation Act of 2014, which would replace the War Powers Act of 1973, bringing the Congress back into decisions on the deployment of U.S. military forces. The bill would establish a Congressional Consultation Committee, with which the President would be required to consult regularly regarding significant foreign policy matters; before ordering the deployment of the Armed Forces into a significant armed conflict; and at least every two months for the duration of any significant armed conflict. Kaine argued for the bill by citing his frustration over the sloppiness of process and communication over decisions of war, noting that Presidents tend to overreach and Congress sometimes willingly ducks tough votes and decisions. We all have to do better. Kaine has stated that war powers questions are a personal obsession of his.

On December 11, 2014, after a five-month campaign by Kaine, the U.S. Senate Foreign Relations Committee approved by 10–8 (straight party lines) a measure authorizing military force against ISIL, but barring the use of ground troops. In 2015, Kaine criticized Obama's approach to the Syrian civil war, saying that the establishment of humanitarian no-fly zones would have alleviated the humanitarian crisis in Syria.

Kaine personally opposes capital punishment, but presided over eleven executions while governor. Kaine said: "I really struggled with [capital punishment] as governor. I have a moral position against the death penalty. But I took an oath of office to uphold it. Following an oath of office is also a moral obligation." During his time in office he commuted one death sentence in June 2008 on grounds of mental incompetence. Kaine vetoed a number of bills to expand the death sentence to more crimes, saying: "I do not believe that further expansion of the death penalty is necessary to protect human life or provide for public safety needs." Some of the vetoes were overridden, while others were sustained.

Kaine is a gun owner. He has supported expanded background checks for weapons purchases as well as restrictions on the sale of combat-style weapons and high-capacity magazines. As governor, Kaine oversaw the closing of loopholes in Virginia law that allowed some who had failed background checks to purchase guns. In the Senate, Kaine has supported legislation which would require background checks to be performed for weapons sold via gun shows and via the internet. He also supports legislation to bar weapons sales to suspected terrorists on the No Fly List.

Kaine is strongly for the regulation of the financial industry and he supports the Dodd–Frank Wall Street Reform and Consumer Protection Act. In July 2016, Kaine signed a bipartisan letter that urged the Consumer Financial Protection Bureau to carefully tailor its rulemaking under Dodd-Frank regarding community banks and credit unions so as not to unduly burden these institutions with regulations aimed at commercial banks. The letter prompted criticism from progressives who viewed it as anti-regulation. Kaine responded to the criticism by saying, "It's important you don't treat every financial institution the same. It wasn't credit unions that tanked the economy, it wasn't local community banks that tanked the economy, it wasn't regional banks that did things that tanked the economy." Kaine also signed a letter urging that a requirement that regional banks report liquidity levels on a daily basis be loosened.

Kaine supports allowing the Bush tax cuts to expire for those with incomes above $500,000. In 2012, Kaine supported raising the cap on income subject for the FICA (Social Security) payroll tax so that it covers a similar percentage of income as it did in the 1980s under President Reagan, which would greatly extend the solvency of the Social Security program. In the Senate, Kaine has supported the Marketplace Fairness Act, which would allow states to require online retailers to collect sales taxes in the same manner as traditional brick-and-mortar retailers.

Kaine supported granting President Obama Trade Promotion Authority to allow him to negotiate free trade agreements. Kaine stated that the goal should be to negotiate deals that protect workers' rights, environmental standards and intellectual property, while knocking down tariffs and other barriers that some countries erect to keep American products out. In July 2016, Kaine said that the Trans-Pacific Partnership (TPP) agreement was an improvement of the status quo in terms of it being an upgrade of labor standards, environmental standards, and intellectual property protections, but maintained that he had not yet decided how to vote on final approval of the agreement, citing significant concerns over TPP's dispute resolution mechanism. Later in July, Kaine said he could not support the TPP in its current form. He has been a proponent of NAFTA.

Kaine supports President Obama's Deferred Action for Childhood Arrivals and Deferred Action for Parental Accountability programs, which would allow up to five million undocumented immigrants to gain deferral of deportation and authorization to legally work in the United States. Alongside fellow Virginia senator Mark Warner and many other members of Congress, Kaine signed on to an amicus brief in support of the program in the Supreme Court case of *United States v. Texas*. Kaine also supports comprehensive immigration reform, which would allow persons illegally present in the U.S. to earn legal status by paying a fine and taxes.

Kaine strongly disagrees with the ruling in *Citizens United v. FEC* (2010). In 2015, he joined a group of Senate Democrats in a letter to Securities and Exchange Commission Chairwoman Mary

Jo White that said the ruling reversed long-standing precedent and has moved our country in a different and disturbing direction when it comes to corporate influence in politics. They urged the SEC to require publicly traded companies to disclose political spending to their shareholders to increase transparency in the U.S. political process following the U.S. Supreme Court decision in *Citizens United.*

Kaine supported passage of the Patient Protection and Affordable Care Act of 2009 ("Obamacare"), saying in 2012: "I was a supporter and remain a supporter of the Affordable Care Act. I felt like it was a statement that we were going to put some things in the rear-view mirror." In 2013, Kaine said that he agreed that changes to the ACA should be debated, but criticized Republicans for wrapping them up with the threat of a federal government shutdown.

In 1984, Kaine married Anne Bright Holton, the daughter of former Virginia governor A. Linwood Holton, Jr. The couple met while they were both students at Harvard Law School. Holton has served as a judge for the Virginia Juvenile and Domestic Relations District Court in Richmond. After serving as first lady of Virginia during her husband's term, she was appointed by Governor Terry McAuliffe in January 2014 to be Virginia's secretary of education, and served in that position until July 2016, when she stepped down after her husband was named as the Democratic vice presidential candidate. The couple has three children: Nat (b. 1990), Woody (b. 1992), and Annella (b. 1995). Nat, the elder son, is a United States Marine. Kaine and his wife have been congregants of the St. Elizabeth Catholic Church in Richmond, a mostly black congregation, for 30 years. Kaine has played the harmonica for over twenty years, and often travels with several.

Kaine has received the Humanitarian Award from the Virginia Center for Inclusive Communities, then the Virginia Region of the National Conference for Community and Justice (2000), the Virginia Council of Churches' Faith in Action Award (2009), the University of Richmond School of Law's William Green Award for Professional Excellence (2012), the Appalachian Trail Conservancy's Congressional Award (2015), and the Center for the National Interest's Distinguished Service Award (2016).

MIKE PENCE

Michael Richard "Mike" Pence (born June 7, 1959) is an American politician and attorney, and the Republican Party nominee for Vice President of the United States, in the 2016 election. He has been serving since 2013 as the governor of Indiana. Pence previously represented Indiana's 2nd congressional district and Indiana's 6th congressional district in the United States House of Representatives from 2001 to 2013 and served as chairman of the House Republican Conference from 2009 to 2011. Pence is a conservative and a supporter of the Tea Party movement. On July 15, 2016, Donald Trump announced that he had selected Pence as his vice presidential running mate in the 2016 presidential election.

Pence was born in Columbus, Indiana, one of six children of Nancy Jane (née Cawley) and Edward J. Pence, Jr., who ran a string of gas stations. His family were Irish Catholic Democrats. He was named after his grandfather, a Chicago bus driver and Irish immigrant who came from County Sligo to the United States through Ellis Island. His maternal grandmother's parents were from Doonbeg, County Clare.

Pence graduated from Columbus North High School, in 1977. He earned a B.A. in history from Hanover College, in 1981 and a J.D. from the Indiana University Robert H. McKinney School of Law in Indianapolis, Indiana, in 1986. While at Hanover, Pence joined the Phi Gamma Delta fraternity, serving as his chapter's president. After graduating from Hanover, Pence worked as an admissions counselor at the college, from 1981 to 1983. After graduating from law school in 1986, Pence worked as an attorney in private practice. He ran unsuccessfully for a congressional seat in 1988 and 1990. He returned to his law practice following his second unsuccessful run. In 1991, he became the president of the Indiana Policy Review Foundation, a self-described free-market think tank and a member of the State Policy Network.

In 1994, he began a career in talk radio. He hosted *The Mike Pence Show*, which was based in WRCR-FM in Rushville. Pence called himself "Rush Limbaugh on decaf" since he considered himself politically conservative while not as outspoken as Limbaugh. The show was syndicated by Network Indiana and aired weekdays 9 a.m. to noon (ET) on 18 stations throughout the state, including WIBC in Indianapolis. From 1995 to 1999, Pence also hosted a weekend political talk show out of Indianapolis.

In 1988, Pence ran for Congress against Democratic incumbent Phil Sharp. Pence lost the election. He ran against Sharp again in 1990, quitting his job in order to work full-time in the campaign. Sharp won again. During the race, Pence used political donations to pay the mortgage on his house, his personal credit card bill, groceries, golf tournament fees and car payments for his wife. While the spending was not illegal at the time, it undermined his campaign.

During the 1990 campaign, Pence ran an ad in which an actor, dressed in a robe and headdress and speaking in a thick Middle Eastern accent, thanked his opponent for doing nothing to wean the United States off imported oil as chairman of a House subcommittee on energy and power. In response to criticism, Pence's campaign responded that the ad was not about Arabs, it was about Sharp's lack of leadership. In 1991, Pence published an essay, "Confessions of a Negative Campaigner," in which he apologized for running negative ads against Sharp.

In November 2000, Pence was elected to the U.S. House of Representatives in Indiana's 2nd Congressional District after six-year incumbent David M. McIntosh opted to run for governor of Indiana. The district comprises all or portions of 19 counties in eastern Indiana. Pence was re-elected four more times by comfortable margins. In the 2006 House elections, he defeated Democrat Barry Welsh.

On November 8, 2006, Pence announced his candidacy for leader of the Republican Party (minority leader) in the United States House of Representatives. Pence's release announcing his run for minority leader focused on a return to the values of the 1994 Republican Revolution. On November 17, Pence lost to Representative John Boehner of Ohio by a vote of 168–27.

Pence defeated Welsh in the 2008 House election. In January 2009, Pence was elected by his GOP colleagues to become the Republican Conference Chairman, the third-highest-ranking Republican leadership position. He ran unopposed and was elected unanimously. He was the first representative from Indiana to hold a House leadership position since 1981. In 2008, *Esquire* magazine listed Pence as one the ten best members of Congress, writing that Pence's unalloyed traditional conservatism has repeatedly pitted him against his party elders.

In 2010, Pence was encouraged to run against incumbent Democratic Senator Evan Bayh, but opted not to enter the race, even after Bayh unexpectedly announced that he would retire.

After the November 2010 election, Pence announced that he would not run for re-election as the Republican Conference Chairman. On May 5, 2011, Pence announced that he would seek the Republican nomination for governor of Indiana in 2012.

Pence served as the chairman of the Republican Study Committee, a group of conservative House Republicans, from 2005 to 2007.

While in Congress, Pence belonged to the Tea Party Caucus. During Pence's twelve years in the House, he introduced 90 bills and resolutions; none became law.

Pence began seeking to defund Planned Parenthood in 2007 by introducing legislation aimed at preventing any organization that provides abortion services from receiving Title X funding.

In 2009, Pence opposed birthright citizenship (the legal principle set forth by the Citizenship Clause of the Fourteenth Amendment to the United States Constitution that all persons born on U.S. soil are citizens). He co-sponsored a bill that would have limited citizenship to children born to at least one parent who is a citizen, immigrants living permanently in the U.S. or non-citizens performing active service in the U.S. Armed Forces.

Pence praised the 2010 Supreme Court ruling in *Citizens United v. FEC* when it was announced. Pence described the McCain–Feingold Act, which regulated the financing of political campaigns, as oppressive restrictions on free speech.

Pence was a co-sponsor of a 2011 spending limit amendment to the U.S. Constitution. This amendment would limit federal spending to the average annual revenue collected in the three prior years, adjusted in proportion to changes in population and inflation. In regards to adopting the gold standard, Pence stated in 2011, "The time has come to have a debate over gold and the proper role it should play in our nation's monetary affairs." Pence proposed legislation to end the dual mandate of the Federal Reserve (maximizing employment and stabilizing prices), requiring the Fed to just focus on price stability and not full employment.

He has been a proponent of a flat federal tax rate. Pence opposed the Troubled Asset Relief Program (TARP) (the "Wall Street bailout") of 2008. Pence also opposed the auto industry rescue package of 2008–09, which guided General Motors and Chevrolet through bankruptcy. In 2007, Pence voted against raising the federal minimum wage to $7.25 (from $5.15) an hour over two years. While in the House, Pence voted against the Employee Free Choice Act ("card check").

He voted against the American Recovery and Reinvestment Act of 2009. He had publicly opposed the bill, denouncing it as a failure, and called for a federal spending freeze. He later wrote a letter to the Department of Transportation requesting stimulus money for his district. In 2010, Pence hosted a job fair for stimulus-backed employers.

He voted against Dodd–Frank Wall Street Reform and Consumer Protection Act. Pence voted against the No Child Left Behind Act.

While in the House, Pence voted to eliminate funding for climate education programs and to prohibit the Environmental Protection Agency from regulating greenhouse gas emissions. Pence also repeatedly voted against energy efficiency and renewable energy funding and rules and voted for several bills that supported fossil fuel development, including legislation promoting offshore drilling. The League of Conservation Voters, an environmentalist group, gave Pence a lifetime rating of 4 percent.

Pence was a supporter of earmark reform. He voted against the $139.7 billion transportation-treasury spending bill in June 2006, and in favor of a series of amendments proposed that same month by Jeff Flake that would strip other members' earmarks from the federal budget. On occasion, however, Pence secured earmarks for projects in his district.

Pence supported the Iraq War Resolution, which authorized military action against Iraq. During the Iraq War, Pence opposed setting a public withdrawal date from Iraq. During an April 2007 visit to Baghdad, Pence and John McCain visited Shorja market, the site of a deadly attack in February 2007 that claimed the lives of 61 people. Pence and McCain described the visit as evidence that the security situation in Iraqi markets has improved.

Pence chaired the House Foreign Affairs Subcommittee on the Middle East and was a prominent supporter of George W. Bush's Iraq War troop surge of 2007. At the time, Pence stated that "the surge is working" and defended the initial decision to invade in 2003. Pence has opposed closing the Guantanamo Bay detention camp and trying the suspected terrorists in the U.S. Pence believes that the Obama administration must overturn this wrongheaded decision. As an alternative, Pence has said that the enemy combatants should be tried in a military tribunal. Pence has stated his support of Israel and its right to attack facilities in Iran to prevent them from developing nuclear weapons, has defended the actions of Israel in its use of deadly force in enforcing the blockade of Gaza, and has referred to Israel as America's most cherished ally. He visited Israel in 2014 to express his support, and in 2016 signed into law a bill which would ban Indiana from having any commercial dealings with a company that boycotts Israel.

Two weeks prior to the NATO intervention in Libya, Pence thanked the Obama administration and Secretary of State Hillary Clinton for their efforts to isolate the Gaddafi regime. Pence expressed support for a no-fly zone and stated that Gaddafi must go. Pence voted against the act that created Medicare Part D, a Medicare prescription-drug benefit. He also voted against the Patient Protection and Affordable Care Act.

Pence supported the USA Patriot Act on its passage in 2001, and in 2005 called the act essential to our continued success in the war on terror here at home. Pence was a sponsor of legislation in 2009 to extend three expiring provisions of the Patriot Act (the library records provision, the roving-wiretap provision, and the lone-wolf provision) for an additional ten years.

In June 2006, Pence unveiled an immigration plan that would include increased border security, followed by strict enforcement of laws against hiring illegal aliens, and a guest worker program. This guest worker program would have required participants to apply from their home country to government-approved job placement agencies that match workers with employers who cannot find Americans for the job. The plan received support from conservatives such as Dick Armey, but attracted criticism from other conservatives such as Phyllis Schlafly, Richard A. Viguerie, and Pat Buchanan, who viewed Pence as lending his conservative prestige to a form of liberal amnesty.

In 2010, Pence voted against the DREAM Act, which would grant the undocumented children of illegal immigrants conditional non-immigrant status if they met certain requirements. In 2010, Pence stated that Arizona S.B. 1070, which at the time of passage in 2010 was the US's broadest and strictest anti-illegal immigration legislation, was a good faith to try and restore order to their communities.

Pence does not accept the scientific consensus that human activity is the primary driver of climate change. In 2001, Pence wrote in an op-ed that "Global warming is a myth," saying (inaccurately) that "the earth is actually cooler today than it was about 50 years ago." In 2006 and 2009, Pence expressed the view that it was unclear whether climate change was driven by human activity, and in 2009 he told Chris Matthews that there was a growing skepticism in the scientific community about global warming.

In 2009, Pence led the Republican effort to defeat the American Clean Energy and Security Act, a Democratic-backed bill to cut greenhouse gas emissions (and therefore combat climate change) through a cap-and-trade system.

Pence opposed President Obama's executive order eliminating restrictions on embryonic stem-cell research. Pence stated, "I believe it is morally wrong to create human life to destroy it for research. I believe it is morally wrong to take the tax dollars of millions of pro-life Americans." He asserted that scientific breakthroughs have rendered embryonic stem-cell research obsolete.

When asked if he believes in evolution, Pence answered "I believe with all my heart that God created the heavens and the earth, the seas and all that's in them. How he did that I'll ask him about some day."

In 2001, Pence wrote an op-ed arguing against the tobacco settlement and tobacco regulation, saying that they would create new government bureaucracies and encroach on private lives. He stated that despite the hysteria from the political class and the media, smoking doesn't kill. Pence asserted, "2 out of every three smokers does not die from a smoking related illness and 9 out of ten smokers do not contract lung cancer," while acknowledging that smoking isn't good for you and people who smoke should quit. In 2009, Pence voted against the Family Smoking Prevention and Tobacco Control Act, which allows the FDA to regulate tobacco products.

In 2002, Pence criticized a speech by then-Secretary of State Colin Powell where Powell stated that it was important for young people to protect themselves from the possibility of acquiring any sexually transmitted disease through the use of condoms. Pence called Powell's comments a sad day, and expressed his support for abstinence education. Pence asserted that condoms are a very,

very poor protection against sexually transmitted diseases and that Powell was inadvertently misleading millions of young people and endangering lives.

Pence supported President George W. Bush's unsuccessful 2005 proposal to partially privatize Social Security by allowing workers to invest part of their Social Security payroll taxes in private investment accounts and reduce the increase in benefits for high-income participants. Pence had previously proposed a similar but more aggressive reform plan than Bush's. When asked in 2010 if he would be willing to make cuts to Social Security, Pence answered, "I think everything has to be on the table." When asked if he would raise the retirement age, he said, "I'm an all-of-the-above guy. We need look at everything on the menu."

Pence has been a longtime, aggressive advocate of trade deals between the U.S. and foreign countries. Pence is a supporter of the North American Free Trade Agreement (NAFTA), and during his tenure in the House, he voted for every free-trade agreement that came before him. Pence voted in favor of the Central American Free Trade Agreement (CAFTA); in favor of keeping the U.S. in the World Trade Organization; and in favor of permanent normal trade relations with China. Pence also supported bilateral free-trade agreements with Colombia, South Korea, Panama, Peru, Oman, Chile and Singapore. Pence's strong stance in favor of free trade sharply differs from the stance of his running mate Trump, who has condemned globalization and the liberalization of trade. Pence voted against the Trade and Globalization Act of 2007, which would have expanded trade adjustment assistance to American workers adversely affected by globalization.

In 2000, Pence stated "Congress should oppose any effort to recognize homosexuals as a discrete and insular minority entitled to the protection of anti-discrimination laws similar to those extended to women and ethnic minorities." He called for an audit to ensure that federal dollars were no longer being given to organizations that celebrate and encourage the types of behaviors that facilitate the spreading of the HIV virus and instead advocated for resources to be directed toward conversion therapy programs, for those seeking to change their sexual behavior. Pence has said that homosexuals should not serve in the military, saying, "Homosexuality is incompatible with military service because the presence of homosexuals in the ranks weakens unit cohesion." Pence opposed the repeal of don't ask, don't tell, saying in 2010 that allowing gays and lesbians to openly serve in the military would have an impact on unit cohesion.

In 2007, Pence voted against the Employment Non-Discrimination Act, which would have banned workplace discrimination on the basis of sexual orientation. Pence opposed the 2009 Matthew Shepard Hate Crimes Act, saying that Barack Obama wanted to advance a radical social agenda and said that pastors could be charged or be subject to intimidation for simply expressing a Biblical worldview on the issue of homosexual behavior.

Pence opposes both same-sex marriage and civil unions. While in the House, he said that societal collapse was always brought about following an advent of the deterioration of marriage and family. He has advocated a constitutional same-sex marriage ban but did not champion such a proposed ban for his first year as governor.

In 2005, after Hurricane Katrina struck the Louisiana coast, Pence favored offsetting the costs of the hurricane with $24 billion in other spending reductions.

Pence is an advocate of federal restrictions of online gambling. In 2006, he was one of 35 cosponsors of H.R. 4411, the Goodlatte–Leach Internet Gambling Prohibition Act, and H.R. 4777, the Internet Gambling Prohibition Act.

Pence was mentioned as a possible Republican candidate for president in 2008 and 2012. In September 2010, Pence was the top choice for president in a straw poll conducted by the Values Voter Summit.

In June 2012, after the U.S. Supreme Court upheld the Affordable Care Act in *NFIB v. Sebelius*, Pence likened the ruling to the September 11 terrorist attacks in a closed-door meeting of the House Republican Conference. He immediately apologized for making the statement.

On May 5, 2011, Pence announced that he would be seeking the Republican nomination for governor of Indiana in 2012. Incumbent Republican Governor Mitch Daniels was term-limited. On November 6, 2012, Pence won the gubernatorial election, defeating the Democratic and Libertarian nominees. He was sworn in as governor of Indiana on January 14, 2013.

Pence made tax reform, namely a 10% income-tax rate cut, a priority for 2013. While he did not get the 10% cut he advocated, Pence did accomplish his goal of cutting state taxes. Legislators cut the income tax by 5% and also killed the inheritance tax. The legislative package was the largest tax cut in Indiana history, about $1.1 billion dollars.

During Pence's term as governor, the unemployment rate reflected the national average. Indiana's job growth lagged slightly behind the national trend. In 2014, Indiana's economy was among the slowest-growing in the U.S., with 0.4% GDP growth, compared to the national average of 2.2%; this was attributed in part to sluggish manufacturing sector.

Carrier Corp. and United Technologies Electronic Controls announced in 2016 that they would be closing two facilities in Indiana, sending 2,100 jobs to Mexico; Pence expressed deep disappointment with the moves. Pence was unsuccessful in his efforts to persuade the companies to stay in the state, although the companies agreed to reimburse local and state governments for certain tax incentives that they had received.

In 2013, Pence signed a law blocking local governments in Indiana from requiring businesses to offer higher wages or benefits beyond those required by federal law. In 2014, Pence supported the Indiana Gateway rail improvement project.

In 2014, Pence called for the swift adoption of the Trans-Pacific Partnership (TPP), urging Indiana's congressional delegation to support the trade deal.

As governor, Pence has pressed for a balanced budget amendment to the state's constitution. He initially proposed the initiative in January 2015. The legislation has passed the state Senate and is progressing through the House.

Indiana has had AAA credit ratings with the three major credit-rating agencies since 2010, before Pence took office; these ratings been maintained through Pence's tenure. Pence inherited a $2 billion budget reserve from his predecessor, Mitch Daniels, and the state has added to that reserve under his watch, though not before requiring state agencies, including public universities, to reduce funding in years in which revenue fell below projections. The state finished fiscal year 2014 with a reserve of $2 billion; budget cuts ordered by Pence for the $14 billion annual state budget include $24 million cut from colleges and universities; $27 million cut from the Family and Social Services Administration; and $12 million cut from the Department of Corrections. In October 2015, Pence announced plans to pay off a $250 million federal loan to cover unemployment insurance payments that spiked during the recession. In March 2016, Pence signed legislation to fund a $230 million two-year road-funding package.

Indiana enacted right-to-work legislation under Pence's predecessor, Republican governor Mitch Daniels. Under Pence, the state successfully defended this legislation against a labor challenge. In 2015, he signed legislation that repealed an eighty-year-old Indiana law that required construction companies working on publicly funded projects to pay a prevailing wage that was determined by local boards of taxpayers and contractors.

Pence has questioned proposals to decrease penalties for low-level marijuana offenses in Indiana, saying that the state should focus on reducing crime, not reducing penalties. In 2013, Pence expressed concern that a then-pending bill to revise the state's criminal code was not tough enough on drug crimes, and successfully lobbied to limit the reduction in sentencing of marijuana offenses. In 2016, Pence signed into law a measure that reinstated a ten-year mandatory minimum prison sentence for certain drug offenders.

During 2014, Governor Pence sent a letter to U.S. Attorney General Eric Holder which said that Indiana would not comply with federal prison rape standards because they were too expensive. According to the Indiana Department of Corrections, it would cost the state $15-20 million annually to comply with the guidelines. Pence said that a number of rape prevention measures had already been implemented. In 2015, Pence signed Senate Bill 94, which lengthened the statute of limitations for rape, continuing for five years after sufficient DNA evidence is uncovered, enough recorded evidence is brought forth or discovered, or the offender confesses to the crime. By Pence signing Senate Bill 8, the death penalty for beheadings was allowed if the victim was alive at the time of the offense.

In 2014, over the opposition of Indiana school organizations, Pence signed a bill which allows firearms to be kept in vehicles on school property. In 2015, following a shooting in Chattanooga, Pence recruited the NRA to train the Indiana National Guard on concealed carry. Some National Guard officials from other states questioned why a civilian organization would be involved in a military issue. In May 2015, Pence signed into law Senate Bill 98, which limited lawsuits against gun and ammunition manufacturers and sellers and retroactively terminated the City of Gary's still-pending 1999 lawsuit against gun manufacturers and retailers that allegedly made illegal sales of handguns. The bill was supported by Republicans, who hoped that the measure would attract more gun-related businesses to Indiana, but opposed by Gary mayor and former Indiana attorney general Karen Freeman-Wilson, who viewed the measure as an unprecedented violation of the separation of powers between the legislative and judicial branches of state government.

In 2016, Pence signed Senate Bill 109 into law, legalizing the captive hunting of farm-raised deer in Indiana.

Since December 2014, there has been an HIV outbreak in Southern Indiana. In 2011, Planned Parenthood ran five rural clinics in Indiana. They tested for HIV and offered prevention, intervention and counseling for better health. The one in Scott County performed no abortions. The Republican controlled legislature and Pence defunded Planned Parenthood. Scott County has been without an HIV testing center for two years. Pence had long been a vocal opponent of needle exchange programs, which allow drug users to trade in used syringes for sterile ones in order to stop the spread of diseases, despite evidence that they work. Since March 2015, he has allowed at least five counties to open needle exchanges but has not moved to lift the state ban on funding for needle exchanges.

In March 2016, Pence signed into law H.B. 1337, a controversial bill that both banned certain abortion procedures and placed new restrictions on abortion providers. The bill banned abortion if the reason for the procedure given by the pregnant person was the fetus' race or gender or a fetal abnormality. In addition, the bill required that all fetal remains from abortions or miscarriages at any stage of pregnancy be buried or cremated, which according to the Guttmacher Institute is not currently required in any other state.

The law was described as exceptional for its breadth; if implemented, it would have made Indiana the first state to have a blanket ban on abortions based solely on race, sex or suspected disabilities, including evidence of Down syndrome.

Days after the U.S. Supreme Court issued its decision in *Whole Woman's Health v. Hellerstedt*, a federal court issued a preliminary injunction blocking the bill from taking effect, with U.S. District Judge Tanya Walton Pratt determining that the bill was likely to be unconstitutional and that the State of Indiana would be unlikely to prevail at trial.

In 2015, Pence and the Obama administration agreed to expand Medicaid in Indiana, in accordance with the Affordable Care Act. As part of the expansion, Pence negotiated modifications to the program for Indiana that included co-payments by participants. The co-payments are linked to healthy behaviors on the part of the participants, so that, for example, a participant who quit smoking would receive a lower co-payment. Participants can lose benefits for failing to make the payments.

During his tenure as governor, Pence supported significant increases in education funding to voucher programs and charter schools. In 2015, Pence secured significant increases in charter-school funding from the Legislation, although he did not get everything he had proposed. The number of students receiving vouchers in Indiana has increased 10 times since 2012 to 33,000, and almost 60% of students in the state now qualify for vouchers. Indiana has the largest and fastest growing voucher program in the country.

Pence opposes the Common Core State Standards, calling for the repeal of the standards in his 2014 State of the State address.

The Indiana General Assembly then passed a bill to repeal the standards, becoming the first state to do so. Pence helped establish a small $10 million state preschool pilot program in Indiana in 2014, a little after one year after taking office, and testified personally before the state Senate Education Committee in favor of the program to convince fellow Republicans (several of whom opposed the proposal) to approve the plan. Although the plan was initially defeated, Pence successfully managed to revive it, getting Indiana off the list of just 10 U.S. states that spent no direct state funds to help poor children attend preschool. Demand for enrollment in the program far outstripped capacity, and Pence at first refused to apply for up to $80 million in federal Health and Human Services Preschool Development Grant program funding, arguing that Indiana must develop its own pre-K program without federal intrusion. After coming under sustained criticism for this position, Pence reversed course and sought to apply for the funds. Pence has clashed repeatedly with the Indiana Superintendent of Public Instruction (a separately elected position in the state). In one of his first acts as governor, Pence removed control of the Educational Employment Relations Board, which is in charge of handling conflicts between unions and school boards, from the Superintendent. Pence created a new Center for Education and Career Innovation to coordinate efforts between schools and the private sector; the Superinendent opposed the Center, viewing it as a power grab and encroachment on her own duties. Pence eventually disestablished the Center in order to help defuse the conflict.

During Pence's term in office, the Republican-controlled Indiana General Assembly has repeatedly tried to roll back renewable energy standards and successfully ended Indiana's energy efficiency efforts. Pence is an outspoken supporter of the coal industry, declaring in his 2015 State of the State address that Indiana is a pro-coal state, expressing support for an all-of-the-above energy strategy, and stating that Indiana must continue to oppose the overreaching schemes of the EPA until it brings their war on coal to end. In 2015, Pence sent a letter to President Obama denouncing the EPA's Clean Power Plan (which would regulate carbon emissions from existing power plans) and stating that Indiana would refuse to comply with the plan. Indiana joined other states in a lawsuit seeking to invalidate the plan. In 2016, Pence stated that even if legal challenges failed, Indiana would continue to defy the rule and would not come up with its own plan to reduce emissions.

On January 26, 2015 it was widely reported that Pence had planned to launch a state-run, taxpayer-funded news service for Indiana. The service, called "JustIN" was to be overseen by a former reporter for *The Indianapolis Star*, and would feature breaking news, stories written by press secretaries, and light features. At the time, it was reported that the two employees who would run the news service would be paid a combined $100,000 yearly salary. The target audience was small newspapers that had limited staff, but the site would also serve to communicate directly with the public. The idea was met with revulsion both by small Indiana newspapers and by the national news media. The publisher of the *Portland Commercial Review* said, "I think it's a ludicrous idea, the notion of elected officials presenting material that will inevitably have a pro-administration point of view is antithetical to the idea of an independent press." Many news stories compared the new JustIN service to state-run news agencies in Russia, China, and North Korea. There was speculation that the news service would publish pro-administration stories that would make Pence look good in the event of a presidential run.

It was especially surprising coming from Pence, because of his history in radio and his former role as a media advocate in Congress, when he supported shield laws protecting confidentiality of media sources and opposed the Fairness Doctrine, which would have given the government more control over political speech. *The Atlantic* regarded the announcement of JustIN as evidence of a disturbing changing trend in how the public gets news. After a week or so of controversy about the idea, Pence scrapped the idea.

On March 26, 2015, Pence signed Indiana Senate Bill 101, also known as the Indiana Religious Objections bill into law. The law's signing was met with widespread criticism by people and groups who felt the law was carefully worded in a way that would permit discrimination against LGBT persons. Such organizations as the NCAA, the gamer convention Gen Con, and the Disciples of Christ spoke out against the law. Apple CEO Tim Cook and Salesforce. com CEO Marc Benioff condemned the law, with Salesforce.com saying it would halt its plans to expand in the state. Angie's List announced they would cancel a $40 million expansion of their Indianapolis based headquarters due to concerns over the law. The expansion would have moved 1000 jobs into the state. The mayors of San Francisco and Seattle banned official travel to Indiana. Thousands protested against the policy. Five GOP state representatives voted against the bill, and the Republican mayor of Indianapolis, criticized it as sending the wrong signal about the state.

Pence repeatedly defended the law, stating that it was not about discrimination. Pence stated, "We are not going to change this law," while refusing to answer whether examples of discrimination against LGBT people given by Eric Miller of anti-LGBT group Advance America would be legal under the law. Pence denied the law permitted discrimination and wrote in a March 31, 2015, *Wall Street Journal* op-ed, "If I saw a restaurant owner refuse to serve a gay couple, I wouldn't eat there anymore. As governor of Indiana, if I were presented a bill that legalized discrimination against any person or group, I would veto it." In the wake of the backlash against the RFRA, on April 2, 2015, Pence signed legislation revising the law to prevent potential discrimination.

As of March 2016, Pence attempted unsuccessfully to prevent Syrian refugees from being resettled in Indiana. In December 2015, Pence stated that calls to ban Muslims from entering the U.S. are offensive and unconstitutional.

Pence ran for a second term as governor. He was unopposed in the May 3, 2016, Republican primary for governor. He was to face Democrat John R. Gregg, former speaker of the Indiana House of Representatives, in a rematch of the 2012 race. However, Pence filed paperwork ending his campaign on July 15, 2016, as Trump announced his selection of Pence as his vice presidential running mate.

Pence endorsed Senator Ted Cruz of Texas in the 2016 Republican presidential primaries.

Donald Trump considered naming Pence as his vice presidential running mate along with other finalists New Jersey Governor Chris Christie and former House speaker Newt Gingrich. Trump officially announced on Twitter that Pence would be his running mate. Immediately after the announcement, Pence said that he was very supportive of Donald Trump's call to temporarily suspend immigration from countries where terrorist influence and impact represents a threat to the United States. Pence said that he was absolutely in sync with Trump's Mexican wall proposal, stating that Mexico is absolutely going to pay for it. According to a FiveThirtyEight rating of candidates' ideology, Pence is the most conservative vice-presidential candidate in the last forty years.

Pence and his wife Karen have been married since 1985. They have three children: Michael, Charlotte, and Audrey. During his service in the U.S. House, the Pence family lived in Arlington, Virginia, when Congress was in session. Michael Pence is a second lieutenant in the United States Marine Corps. Pence was raised in a Catholic family, serving as an altar boy and attending parochial school. He became a born-again Christian in college, while a member of a nondenominational Christian student group in college, identifying his freshman year, and specifically a Christian music festival in Asbury, Ky., in the spring of 1978, as the moment he made a commitment to Christ. After that point, however, Pence continued to attend Mass (where he met his wife) and worked as a Catholic youth minister. Pence called himself Catholic in a 1994 news piece, although by 1995, Pence and his family had joined an evangelical megachurch, the Grace Evangelical Church. In 2013, Pence said that his family was kind of looking for a church. Pence has described himself as "a Christian, a conservative and a Republican, in that order," and as a born-again, evangelical Catholic.

PART FOUR

THE RACE TO THE WHITE HOUSE

11

THE POLITICS OF INSANITY – TRYING TO GET TO THE ISSUES

The run-up to November 8, 2016, the day on which the United States elects its next Chief Executive Officer, has been unlike any other in recent memory. The general campaign has, at least on one side, focused much more on personality assassination than on the issues.

What's even more bizarre, because of the smears concerning events that happened no later than 2012, and more likely nearly eight years ago – events that were precipitated by a Republican administration, the heirs of which are trying to dredge them up and recast the blame for their own advantage, the *issues* that are important have been relegated to the back burner.

Legitimate debate has disappeared since, it seems, Mr. Trump's refusal to directly answer questions is immediately followed by deflecting the subject to his attacks on Hillary Clinton's character. As of September 11, 2016, the fifteenth anniversary of the 9-1-1 attack on the United States, Trump has provided _no_ specific details of _any_ of his "programs." And unlike any presidential candidate in the past forty years, he steadfastly refuses to release his Income Tax returns to the voting populace, hiding behind the charade that "he's being audited – he's been audited more times than any other businessman in history." What this has to do with his current fitness for the highest office in the land is ambiguous at best. More likely, it is a reflection of _his own character_.

Each candidate's "base," its core supporters, shows the extraordinary schism that presently divides the two aspirants. The division could not be more clearly defined.

Hillary Clinton's core supporters are women, more highly educated voters, African-Americans, Hispanics, minorities, those generally viewed as liberals, those who are perceived as "establishment" types, and voters more interested in the "issues."

The contrast with Donald Trump's supporters couldn't be sharper. Donald Trump's core supporters consist of uneducated or undereducated lower middle class white males who feel disenfranchised by "the system;" Tea Party hardliners; Big Oil; the gun lobby; antitax zealots; climate-change deniers; those who want to get rid of "Obamacare" at any price; those who think America has kowtowed too much to "foreigners;" and xenophobes who perceive anyone who is not white, Christian, and "American" as _the enemy,_ who must be purged from "our" society. It often seems as though these folks stand for an incoherent mess of ideas unrelated to any theory of where the world is going or how America will actually "become great again" in the 21st century. Those who believe anything Trump says, not because it has a semblance of truth, but because they _want_ to believe it. "And it's better than crooked Hillary."

Indeed, there is one thing that stands head and shoulders above everything else that unites Trump's followers more than all other aspects of this campaign: an absolutely visceral, often totally irrational, *hatred* of Hillary Clinton. Does Donald Trump, who has made substantial contributions to the Clintons' earlier campaigns as well as to the Clinton Foundation, truly believe the hateful, inconsistent rhetoric which he spouts on any given day? Or is he simply saying what he has to say to his faithful, dogged followers who lap up everything he says much like the adoring German public followed Hitler's blandishments during the 1932 campaign?

Have we as a people lost all ability to seriously question such demonstrable fabrications? Or are we so hypnotized by this consummate showman that we fail to see that "the Emperor has no clothes?"

Consider the charges which the Trump campaign has leveled at Hillary Clinton since even before the start of the general campaign:

1. She's a liar.

2. She's a liar.

3. She's a liar.

4. You can't believe anything she says.

5. Can you believe how stupid she was, using her own private email servers when he was Secretary of State?

6. That's *treason*, for God's sake.

7. And she lied about it to the FBI.

8. And she lied about it to the American people.

9. And she's still lying about it.

10. She's a liar.

11. And she shouldn't be allowed to run for President of the United States. She should be locked up in the Federal

Penitentiary (and maybe while we're getting rid of all the Muslims and the illegals (Mexicans) we should get rid of her, too). Here, the Trump loyalists start to chant at every rally, "Lock her up! Lock her up! Lock her up."

12. She doesn't have the stamina to be President. (Translation: she's a *woman* and everyone knows men have more strength and stamina than women).

13. She was an enabler who let her philandering husband get away with adultery.

14. She and her husband have made millions from the Clinton Foundation.

15. The Clinton Foundation has accepted money from all kinds of evil foreigners and dictators – and guess who got favored treatment when she was Secretary of State?

16. She's a racist. She talks like she's not, but when have any minorities gotten any help from her?

17. She's in the pocket of Wall Street.

18. She's in the pocket of the insurance companies.

19. She's in the pocket of the big pharmaceutical companies.

20. And she's a goddamned liar!

If you have listened to Trump's speeches anywhere in America during the general campaign, *that* has been the theme of almost every single speech. There's a deeper, darker undercurrent to Trump's message to his faithful: *We've had a Nigger in the White House for the past eight years and this country's more f****d up than ever. And now do you want to follow that with a* <u>woman</u> *in the White House? What the hell is this country coming to?*

Sometimes is seems very difficult to separate rhetoric for facts and even the all-powerful media seems stunned when they demonstrate Trump's inconsistencies – all, right, let's be frank, his downright 180° changes of positions back and forth and back again, sometimes in a single speech or on a single day – and his followers absolutely ignore these inconsistencies as if they don't exist and immediately turn back to, "Well you know, Hillary's the biggest liar in the history of politics!"

To demonstrate the viciousness of this campaign, I received an email exchange within the past week from people I hardly knew which, better than anything else I've recently read, amply describes the degree of insanity in this election:

Email No. 1 (Pro-Clinton)

"I am really sick and tired of people saying both candidates are equally horrible choices, how much America thoroughly hates both of them to the core, that there's not a single positive trait in either one of them and wow, if only we had voted for that guy behind the deli counter or the neighbor's cat, America would be way better off.

"There are only 2 candidates who stand any mathematical chance of prevailing in this year's election. One of them is, in fact, eminently qualified to become the 45th President of the United States, perhaps more so than any of the other 44 previous office holders. She (that's right...*she*) has been dedicated to public service in one capacity or another since 1971. To name a few:

"First ever student commencement speaker at Wellesley College; Distinguished graduate of Yale Law School; Editorial board of the Yale Review of Law and Social Action; Co-founded Arkansas Advocates for Children and Families; Former civil litigation attorney; Staff attorney for Children's Defense Fund;

Faculty member in the School of Law at the University of Arkansas; Former Director of the Arkansas Legal Aid Clinic; First female chair of the Legal Services Corporation; First female partner at Rose Law Firm, the oldest and one of the largest law firms in Arkansas; Twice named by The National Law Journal as one of the 100 Most Influential Lawyers in America; Arkansas Woman of the Year in 1983; Chair of the American Bar Association's Commission on Women in the Profession; Created Arkansas's Home Instruction Program for Preschool Youth; Instrumental in passage of the State Children's Health Insurance Program; First Lady of the United States; Promoted nationwide immunization against childhood illnesses; Successfully sought to increase research funding for prostate cancer and childhood asthma at the National Institutes of Health; Worked to investigate reports of an illness that affected veterans of the Gulf War (now recognized as Gulf War Syndrome); Helped create the Office on Violence Against Women at the Department of Justice; Initiated and shepherded the Adoption and Safe Families Act; Helped create Vital Voices, an international initiative to promote the participation of women in the political processes of their countries; Two-term New York Senator; Served on five Senate committees: Budget (2001–2002), Armed Services (2003–2009), Environment and Public Works (2001–2009), Health, Education, Labor and Pensions (2001–2009) and the Special Committee on Aging; Member of the Commission on Security and Cooperation in Europe; Leading role in investigating the health issues faced by 9/11 first responders; Worked with Sen. Chuck Schumer of New York on securing $21.4 billion in funding for the World Trade Center redevelopment; Former United States Secretary of State; Brokered a ceasefire deal between Israel and Hamas in 2012.

"The other candidate who is supposedly 'equally bad' is a real estate developer and television personality who was born into a family whose wealth has been estimated to exceed $300 million and makes racism, sexism, misogyny, nihilism and ultra-nationalism the pillars of his candidacy. So far he has called for:

"Building a wall across the southern border that Mexico is supposedly going to pay for; The deportation, by force if necessary, of 11 million undocumented immigrants; Banning and deporting all members of a religious faith that total over 1 billion adherents worldwide, even if they are American citizens, because 'everybody knows' they're just a bunch of murdering terrorists; Lists among his associates known white supremacists and eugenicists; Speaks admiringly of ruthless foreign despots and encourages espionage against the United States by hostile governments; Ruminates about not defending our NATO allies against Russian invasion; States openly and freely that using nuclear weapons should always be an option simply to make him more 'unpredictable.' That's not a strategy. That's insanity.

"Did I mention his blithe refusal to offer concrete policy proposals on how any of this neo-Nazi wish list could possibly be achieved?

"But they're supposedly 'equally awful' and 'everybody hates them both.' Yes, you can't vote for Hillary Clinton over Donald Trump because, you know…emails. And Benghazi. And Foundations. And Wall Street. And secret assassinations. And pantsuits. And, and, and….

"OK, listen up. Nobody cares about emails that show Bono wanted State Department assistance to stream his music from the International Space Station. So far all we have seen is a public official in extraordinary circumstances who should have known better demonstrate 'extreme carelessness' to which she has owned up sufficiently and which, by the way, **no** wrongdoing was ever uncovered even after a year-long investigation by the FBI. We all know that trustworthiness is important in a President. But if absolutely no slack is given at all, and I mean none, if this is how we treat people who make public service their life and profession, then you will always get 'crooks' as politicians because who in their right mind would want the job? It's like being a firefighter. When there's a fire everybody runs out. You run in. It's a maniac's job but it has to be done so let's have the best do it and not get wrapped up in what amounts to paperwork. That's all this really is. Paperwork. You would rather stay at home or vote for someone George Orwell or Edgar Allan Poe couldn't have dreamed up over emails?

"Furthermore, I want to know why everyone has their knickers in a twist over the tragic deaths of 4 State Department personnel in Benghazi in 2012 when nobody raised a peep about, count 'em, 241 armed and ready US servicemen who were blown to bits by a suicide bomber in Beirut in 1983? Well? *Why not?* We all know why but I won't denigrate the deaths of brave people serving their country in the diplomatic corps and the military while performing what is often a filthy and difficult job. But other people love to bring it up as often as possible as a *political weapon.* They want you to believe she is some kind of cold and diabolical monster without any concern for the lives of people who often must work in really dangerous places in the name of peace and diplomacy. There have been 9 House and Senate hearings and not one has found any wrongdoing and the Republicans have admitted openly that they are conducting the hearings for political reasons to stop Clinton's presidency, not because there is anything to uncover or change. Nine hearings should confirm this fact. That is a complete waste of millions of taxpayer dollars.

"Wouldn't it be nice if we could just forget all of that pesky accomplishment stuff of hers and remember that what really matters is the thrill of waiting for indictments which makes for great television? That way we could finally 'lock her up' and enough with these stupid women who think they can run a country.

Well, enough. This isn't the lesser of two evils. This is a choice between one great and qualified candidate for the nation's highest office who you really should be excited about and a dolt with a bad toupee who, if you were honest with yourself, you wouldn't trust to manage a Dairy Queen much less the Oval Office.

"As for the others, don't give me any nonsense about Bernie, Martin, Ted, John, Marco, Jeb, Chris, Rand, Carly, Ben, Lindsey or any of the others because they aren't running anymore. And I certainly don't want to hear some load of tripe about Gary or Jill, because they can't win either and that's simply the way it is. Those two are just like all of the other hundreds of people legitimately on the ballot to become President in November who are never going to get within spitting distance of the White House. Ever heard of Rod Silva? Me neither, but he's running for President on the Nutrition Party ticket. Look him up. Here's the bottom line: only two people can win and it's not going to be anyone on this Rogue's Gallery of wannabes…or the guy behind the deli counter or your neighbor's cat.

"We have a great opportunity here. We also have the potential for real catastrophe and that's not being hyperbolic. You know good and well which is which. Don't be stupid."

Email #2 (Pro-Trump)

"Choose wisely, indeed:

"I'm not a Trump fan – I think there are a lot of better candidates. I simply cannot, though, vote for someone who has habitually lied to the American people about her actions:

• No classified material on her personal e-mail? The FBI says not true.

- Only one electronic device used? The FBI says 13.
- All e-mails turned over? FBI says they just found another 14,900.
- Benghazi was a response to a video? E-mail interchange clearly shows she knew it was a terrorist attack, yet lied to the American people for days afterwards. And sent Susan Rice to make her false statements.
- No relationship between State Dept. and Clinton Foundation? E-mails clearly show influence peddling.

"Do you know why she was fired from her first job out of law school? For lying.

"The e-mails I saw clearly show requests from the foundation to the State Department for foundation contributors. She even accepted donations from foreign governments. Over half of the non-standard meetings on her calendar were for people who made donations. The e-mail interchange clearly shows the influence peddling between the Clinton Foundation and the Secretary of State."

Email #3 (Pro-Clinton)

"When Clinton was Secretary of State, there was no prohibition against using a personal smart phone or a private server nor was there a law or rule saying she (or any other government official) had to use the government's .gov server. Despite Colin Powell saying he doesn't specifically remember telling her 8 years ago to use a private server so the public couldn't demand to see all her truly personal e-mails, both Condi Rice and General Powell, the previous two Secretaries of State, used private phones and servers just like Hillary Clinton. If using a private server was such a big deal, one would think that in the 4 years that Hillary Clinton was Secretary of State (not to mention sending and receiving over 50,000 or more e-mails), that someone would have noticed that she wasn't using the .gov address, and said to her that she should change. Again, it wasn't an issue because it was common practice 4 - 8 years ago. The point is being brought up after Hillary is no longer Secretary of State.

"Also, no one (including the FBI) has found any evidence that any one hacked in to Clinton's private server and read classified e-mails. The FBI did a thorough check of what transpired. The investigation lasted a full year. The FBI was/is headed by a Republican, so no one may claim bias or 'looking the other way' in favor of Ms. Clinton. The Director of the FBI said that no wrong doing on the part of Clinton was found; there was nothing illegal or culpable. He did say that the approximately 20-30 e-mails he found that could have been considered classified, were not labeled so by the sender of the e-mails to Secretary Clinton. He also said Secretary Clinton was sloppy and should have used the .gov server at all times. That's it. In hindsight (and going forward), all government employees, including the Secretary of State, should use .gov when sending and receiving e-mails. But remember, even the Pentagon was hacked into recently. Using .gov does not insure that no one will ever see classified information transmitted over the internet. There is nothing here to disqualify her from becoming the President.

"Benghazi was a terrible and tragic situation. Most people forget that a couple of years before the incident, a Republican Congress passed a bill to reduce spending for security at U.S. Embassies around the world. Hillary Clinton had nothing to do with that. Next, the attack came on an embassy where the nearest U. S. military base that could send help was about 10 hours away.

Help was sent as soon as possible but it was too late to do any good. During the shelling and charge through the gate, communications to help outside the country were obviously extremely difficult... the embassy was under serious attack. There were also no reporters to send up-dates. The local government didn't react to stop the attack. The U.S. Ambassador and 3 other staff were shot. Rumors of what occurred were rampant. Was it al-Qaeda, Boko Haram, or some other terrorist group? Was it in response to the admittedly disrespectful, anti-Muslim video/movie that had just been released in the U.S.? No one knew...and, what caused the attack wasn't the first thing on anyone's mind. Helping the survivors was primary. Remember Mitt Romney trying to claim that President Obama was too slow to declare that the attack was the work of terrorists? He made a big deal out of this in a debate but was shown that he had his facts wrong. President ''Obama did claim the attack was done by terrorist. <u>But, so what</u>?!? Merely calling out the attackers as "terrorists" doesn't seem to be a priority issue. Call the attackers the Boy Scouts of Libya or the Red Brigade —again, so what? The label means nothing. Hillary had no reason to lie or suppress facts about the attack. **NINE (9)** Senate and House hearings over that past several years, all called for and chaired by Republicans, with hundreds of hours of testimony–found nothing wrong with the way the Benghazi Embassy was run nor anything that Secretary Clinton (or anyone else) could have done to prevent the attack or stop it any earlier. A Republican on the last committee to hold a hearing on Benghazi admitted, publically, that nothing new was learned in the hearing and that the hearing was only to thwart Hillary Clinton's bid for the Presidency. Check it out, you'll find the statement quite easily. Last, Benghazi was an awful, heartbreaking event. But we must recognize that there are something like 160 U.S. embassy's around the world. It's impossible to make sure each embassy is absolutely impregnable. Attacks like Benghazi have happened before and may happen again. There is always a potential risk of harm for each diplomat from the United States in a foreign country. To seek political capital from this tragedy by Donald Trump is disgusting.

"Hundreds of people ask to speak with officials every hour of every day to have their government do something for them. That's the job of the government … to serve the people. It's done informally and formally (lobbyists). But Hillary Clinton has had nothing to do with the Clinton Foundation for many years. Being Secretary of State and running for President had been her full time job. The Foundation is run by her husband, Bill, and her daughter, Chelsea. It has helped millions of people. The Clinton Foundation itself is above reproach. I've never heard or read any negative comment from anyone about the services provided and work done by the Clinton Foundation over the years. It is truly an example of the good a former President may do after leaving office (see also, Presidents Carter and Bush -41 for other current examples). President Bill Clinton has raised millions of dollars for this charity—that's how charities work; they are not government sponsored. Bill Clinton has taken nothing for himself from this humanitarian effort. The money to operate the Foundation has come from thousands of sources - domestic and foreign – including Trump himself. Do any of the donors also deal with the U.S. government? Undoubtedly. But, there is not one piece of evidence that shows that while serving as the Secretary of State, Hillary Clinton did any favors for or did anything inappropriate for anyone because of a donation made to the Foundation. Trump keeps saying 'I am not saying it's true but "people" tell me that there is a problem,' so I am going to label her 'Crooked" Hillary.' Then he repeats the salacious name over and over and over, even though it is baseless, reckless and false. Someone who doesn't truly look into the matter to seek the truth, will begin repeating the untrue claim.

"It's absurd and obscene but that's how Trump runs his campaign – use falsehood and innuendo and may be something will stick. See 'Lying Ted,' 'Little Marco,' 'Low energy-Jeb,' etc. attacks from the recent primaries! Remember this one from a few months ago …'I've seen an old picture of Lee Harvey Oswald, with a man standing behind him who people think looks a lot like Ted Cruz's father…I'm not saying it's true, but people say Ted's dad was involved in the assassination of President Kennedy.' Or, 'My investigators have found proof that Barak Obama is not a natural American--he was born in Kenya. I show you the proof.' That was said about 7 plus years ago and no proof has ever been presented.

"Or, after the 9-1-1 attack on the World Trade Center in 2001, 'I saw thousands of Muslims cheering in the streets.' Absolutely not true! All pathetic lies! The most pathetic lie by Trump— something close to -- I get my information from talk shows and I consult myself for guidance on finding solutions to problems…'I know more about how to deal with the terrorists and end wars than the generals.'

"Donald Trump's tactic is clearly to tell people that other people have caused their problems, to tell people that the country has been destroyed by its leadership and only he can save the people…'What do you have to lose?!?' This is crazy. But for some strange reason people want to hear that if someone like Trump gets rid of the troublemakers (Muslims, Mexicans, etc.) all will be well again—there will be jobs, no crime, etc.. It's nonsense, scary and dangerous. Hitter used the same approach to get elected in Germany in the 1930s. And let us not forget that Hitler's propaganda chief, Josef Goebbels, is believed to have said. "If you tell a lie big enough and keep repeating it often enough, people will eventually come to believe it.

Hillary Clinton is probably the most experienced, qualified person to run for President we've ever had. To slander her with false and twisted statements is the only way that a lightweight huckster like Donald Trump, can run against her. I hope that the American people take the time to learn the facts and then to vote for Hillary. Trump is not qualified or experienced enough in his own right to represent our country. I agree with President Obama's comment made a week or two ago…that when he first ran against John McCain and then against Mitt Romney for President, he had very different ideas from each opponent about how to deal with the issues confronting the country. President Obama went on to state that he also knew that, despite the different philosophical approaches on what to do as President, if he lost to either man, our country would still be in good, competent hands. He does not feel the same if Donald Trump becomes President--our country would not be in competent hands. …"

* * *

On August 9, 2016 *Time* magazine interviewed Donald Trump. A segment of that interview appears below:

TIME: It's been a difficult stretch for your campaign over the last two weeks. What's going on in the polls?

TRUMP: Well, I think we're doing well. We have tremendous crowds. We have the same level of enthusiasm that we've had, if not more. Some of the polls are down a little bit. We have some polls that are not down very much. But I think we're moving along. I think we're doing fine.

TIME: You had a couple of conversations with Reince Priebus (Chairman of the Republican National Committee) last week. He was pretty direct with you about the state of the campaign, saying that you were running behind some key Senate

races. It was reported to us that he issued what amounted
to an ultimatum that they would potentially support Senate
candidates over your campaign if the numbers didn't reverse
themselves by September. Could you shed a little bit of light
on this?

TRUMP: He never said that. We never had a conversation about
that. We do very well together. We never had that conversation.
Doesn't exist. And by the way, Reince Priebus is a terrific guy.
He never said that. It was never stated. Why would they state that
when I'm raising millions of dollars for them?

TIME: Going back to the polls, some showed you down six,
seven, eight points nationally and in swing states by a similar
margin. You won the primary, but the general election is
obviously a very different electorate. What do you have to do
differently?

TRUMP: Well, I'm running it differently than I did the primaries.
I am listening to so-called experts to ease up the rhetoric, and so
far, I'm liking the way I ran in the primaries better. I got more votes
than anybody in the history of the primaries, I got 14 million votes
and won most of the states. But I'm now listening to people that
are telling me to be easier, to be nicer, be softer. That's OK, and
I'm doing that. Personally, I don't know if that's what the country
wants. When we're having heads chopped off in the Middle East,
when things are happening that have never happened before in
terms of the atrocities, in terms of giving $400 million in cash and
all other things, I think maybe they want tougher rhetoric. They
would like me to be a little bit different than I was in the primaries.
And in the primaries, I broke the all-time record for votes.

TIME: So do you intend to revert?

TRUMP: I'm not agreeing or disagreeing with anybody. I think I
may do better the other way. They would like to see it be a little bit

different, a little more modified. I don't like to modify. But that's what I've done. We'll see where it takes me.

TIME: You've said that you intend to win black and Latino voters in the general election, but some of the surveys right now have you at less than 3% with African-American voters, about 20% with some Latino voters. How do you intend between now and Election Day to turn it around?

TRUMP: All I can do is tell the truth. That's all I can do. And we'll see what happens. All I can do is be honest and tell the truth. I'm looking to tell it like it is. I'm going to bring jobs back. We'll stop the illegal immigration. And all I want to do is be honest and be truthful. If that does it, that's great. And if that doesn't do it, that's fine too.

TIME: Let me ask you about the debates. Secretary Clinton has just accepted an invitation to all three presidential debates scheduled by the commission. Can you also commit now to attending all three debates under the conditions negotiated by the commission?

TRUMP: Well, I haven't seen the conditions, I'll be seeing the conditions this afternoon or tomorrow, so I'll let you know then. But I want a debate very badly.

TIME: Is there anyone that would be unacceptable to you as a moderator?

TRUMP: Well, I don't know. Who would be the moderators? … I'll have to see who the moderators are. I would say that certain moderators would be unacceptable, absolutely. By the way, I will absolutely do three debates. I did very well in the debates on the primaries. So I look forward to the debates. I will demand fair moderators. I think the moderator has to be impartial and there's some people that aren't.

TIME: You mentioned you want to see the conditions. You've talked a lot about how you want to negotiate better deals. Is that something that you would like to reopen?

TRUMP: Well, I did it once before. I re-negotiated the debates in the primaries, remember? They were making a fortune on them and they had us in for three and a half hours and I said that's ridiculous. I said, you know, that's unacceptable. And they changed the whole format of the debate. I'm sure they'll be open to any suggestions I have, because I think they'll be very fair suggestions.

TIME: How would you address criticism of the plan that it would benefit disproportionately those at the higher incomes rather than the middle class?

TRUMP: No, it benefits corporations, and the middle class gets benefited, big league. But no, it doesn't, because we have a 12% tax rate. The middle class gets benefited very substantially. But the big beneficiaries are the jobs and what's happening with business. This is very good.

TIME: If Putin continues his provocations, should the U.S. provide lethal assistance to the Ukrainians?

TRUMP: First of all, I answered the question perfectly previously but only about 70% of the media covered it that way. When Obama is talking about Russia, and when he's talking about the Ukraine, it was under Obama, and his so-called tough stance, that Crimea went to the Ukraine. This wasn't under Trump. And so when I answered that question I said they've already got Crimea. But it was under Obama that Crimea was taken. And you know, so then he talks about me with Russia. Well, I don't think that would have happened if I were in his position. … And of course, as you know, he reset the relationship with Russia. But it was under Obama's reign, under Obama's presidency, that Crimea went to Russia. And you know he's talking about toughness and he's talking about all of these different things, but you know, the Ukraine is having a lot of problems. But one of the problems is Crimea goes over to Russia during Obama's reign. So when Obama criticizes various policy of, let's say, of Trump, all I said was that was taken during Obama's time.

TIME: You talk about the strategists and the wise people counseling you. Are you still having fun? You seem to want to return to the way things used to be during the primary.

TRUMP: I am having a good time. Again, you see the difference. Let's say between yesterday and go back into the rallies. I would say that I like the previous better. I can always revert to that if I want. It was more of an attacking style, which perhaps is a more natural style for me. There's always a chance that I will do that and can go back to that.

TIME: Given that you had success with that attacking style and you enjoy it more, why did you decide to make the switch?

TRUMP: I listen to people, despite what people say. I'm not sure if I agree with them. I'll let you know in a couple of weeks.

TIME: Do you feel you got yourself off-message in the last two weeks? Did you get yourself back on message yesterday?

TRUMP: I was hit hard during the Democrat convention. I think we had very successful Republican convention, frankly. But the one that goes last has a big advantage because it's the last. All they did was negative, negative, negative. So, you know that could have had an impact. Now I'm going to North Carolina. It's a packed house. There are people waiting outside. Nobody has that. When Hillary goes out, I look at her so-called rallies, she gets 250 people and there's empty seats all over the place. I may be wrong, but I think we're doing much better than anybody understands.

And I said that after Wisconsin, when everyone said, well, that's the end of Trump, it looks like he lost. And I said, I don't feel it. So, we've had this conversation before and I actually feel more strongly now than I did then. We'll see. We're five points behind, or six points behind. That's not a lot.

TIME: Do you think the polls are getting your support wrong?

TRUMP: I think so. Some people get good crowds the last week of the campaign. I had about 18,000 people in Jacksonville, Florida, three days ago. And 4,000 or 5,000 walked away; they couldn't get in. In Daytona we had thousands of people. So, yeah, I think there's something out there. And I think the Clinton campaign understands that. They've spent $240 million on ads. I've spent nothing. Zero. Purposely. We've also raised a lot of money. We started in June and we did $51 million and people fell off their seat. And $27 million of it was small contributions, $61 dollars. No Republican's ever gotten that. And they said, 'that must be a blip, that won't happen, and that was a blip.' Except for one problem: in the next month we did $82 million, much of it in small donations. So I'm putting up millions of dollars and we're also raising millions of dollars for the RNC.

* * *

On September 7, 2016, Clinton and Trump engaged in a "Commander-in-Chief Forum" aboard the *Intrepid*, a World War II naval ship, now a military museum, moderated by Matt Lauer, host of the popular morning show *Today* on NBC. The candidates did not debate one another face to face, but many thought it was a precursor of the first Presidential debate, which was set to be held on September 26, 2016. Although there was instant and often harsh criticism of the way Lauer handled the task, which continued a week later, a partial transcript of that forum seemed to be indicative of how the actual debate would go.

LAUER: … Ladies and gentlemen, please welcome Hillary Clinton. … Let me ask you something ahead of time that I'll ask Mr. Trump in a half an hour. **To the best of your ability tonight, can we talk about your qualities and your qualifications to be commander-in-chief and not use this as an opportunity to attack Mr. Trump, all right? And I'll ask him the exact same thing.**

CLINTON: I think that's an exactly right way to proceed.

LAUER: OK.

CLINTON: This is a very important decision for our country. And each of us should be presenting our experience, our expertise, and our plans to protect and defend the United States and our allies around the world.

LAUER: What is the most important characteristic that a commander-in-chief can possess?

CLINTON: Steadiness. An absolute rock steadiness, and mixed with strength to be able to make the hard decisions. Because I've had the unique experience of watching and working with several presidents. And these are not easy decisions. If they were, they wouldn't get to the president in the first place. And when you're sitting in the Situation Room, as I have on numerous occasions, particularly with respect to determining whether to recommend the raid against bin Laden, what you want in a president, a commander-in-chief, is someone who listens, who evaluates what is being told to him or her, who is able to sort out the very difficult options being presented…

LAUER: So judgment is a key.

CLINTON: Temperament and judgment, yes.

274   THE POLITICS OF INSANITY – HUGO N. GERSTL

LAUER: The word "judgment" has been used a lot around you, Secretary Clinton, over the last year-and-a-half, and in particular concerning your use of your personal e-mail and server to communicate while you were secretary of state. You've said it's a mistake.

CLINTON: Mm-hmm.

LAUER: You said you made not the best choice. You were communicating on highly sensitive topics. Why wasn't it more than a mistake? Why wasn't it disqualifying, if you want to be commander-in- chief?

CLINTON: Well, Matt, first of all, as I have said repeatedly, it was a mistake to have a personal account. I would certainly not do it again. I make no excuses for it. It was something that should not have been done. But the real question is the handling of classified material, which is I think what the implication of your question was. And for all the viewers watching you tonight, I have a lot of experience dealing with classified material, starting when I was on the Senate Armed Services Committee going into the four years as secretary of state. Classified material has a header which says "top secret," "secret," "confidential." Nothing — and I will repeat this, and this is verified in the report by the Department of Justice — none of the e-mails sent or received by me had such a header. …

LAUER: You said you thought your communications on that were fairly routine?

CLINTON: Well, let me say, the FBI just released their report about their investigation, they discussed drone matters in the unclassified section of their report.

LAUER: But Director Comey also said this after reviewing all the information. He said there is evidence to support a conclusion that any reasonable person in Secretary Clinton's position should have known that an unclassified system was no place for that conversation.

CLINTON: Well, Matt, I just respectfully point to the hundreds of experienced foreign policy experts, diplomats, defense officials who were communicating information on the unclassified system because it was necessary to answer questions and to be able publicly to go as far as we could, which was not acknowledging the program. But I would be in Pakistan, as I was on several occasions. There might very well have been a strike. I would be asked in a public setting, in an interview, about it. It was known to have happened. We had to have an answer that did not move into classified area. And I think we handled that appropriately.

LAUER: Let us bring in Hallie Jackson of NBC News who's been covering this campaign. She's getting questions from our veterans ...

QUESTION [from the audience]: Secretary Clinton, thank you very much for coming tonight. As a naval flight officer, I held a top secret sensitive compartmentalized information clearance. And that provided me access to materials and information highly sensitive to our war fighting capabilities. Had I communicated this information not following prescribed protocols, I would have been prosecuted and imprisoned. Secretary Clinton, how can you expect those such as myself who were and are entrusted with America's most sensitive information to have any confidence in your leadership as president when you clearly corrupted our national security?

CLINTON: Well, I appreciate your concern and also your experience. But let me try to make the distinctions that I think are important for me to answer your question. First, as I said to Matt, you know and I know classified material is designated. It is marked. There is a header so that there is no dispute at all that what is being communicated to or from someone who has that access is marked classified. And what we have here is the use of an unclassified system by hundreds of people in our government to send information that was not marked, there were no headers, there was no statement, top secret, secret, or confidential. I communicated about classified material on a wholly separate system. I took it very seriously. When I traveled, I went into one of those little tents that I'm sure you've seen around the world because we didn't want there to be any potential for someone to have embedded a camera to try to see whatever it is that I was seeing that was designated, marked, and headed as classified. So I did exactly what I should have done and I take it very seriously, always have, always will.

LAUER: Secretary Clinton, let's talk about your vote in favor of the war in Iraq. You've since said it was a mistake.

CLINTON: Mm-hmm.

LAUER: Obviously, it was not something you said you would do again. ... How do you think these people [in the audience] feel when the person running to be their commander-in-chief says her vote to go to war in Iraq was a mistake?

CLINTON: I think that the decision to go to war in Iraq was a mistake. And I have said that my voting to give President Bush that authority was, from my perspective, my mistake. I also believe that it is imperative that we learn from the mistakes, like after-action reports are supposed to do, and so we must learn what led us down that path so that it never happens again. I think I'm in the best possible position to be able to understand that and prevent it.

But I will say this. I'm asking to be judged on the totality of my record, what I've done for our veterans as first lady, as senator, what I've done for Gold Star Families, working with them to increase the death benefit from $12,000 to $100,000, working with Republicans, like Lindsey Graham, to get TRICARE for our National Guard members who didn't have health care unless they were deployed, working to provide more support for the care of our veterans, those who are wounded, working with the Fisher family, now into the third generation of caring for our fallen heroes, working with John McCain to raise money for Brooke Medical Center's Intrepid Center to take care of those who are coming back with profound injuries, working on TBI and PTSD and so much more, working with groups to end veteran suicide, like TAPS. So, yes... there was a mistake. Now, my opponent was for the war in Iraq. He says he wasn't. You can go back and look at the record. He supported it. He told Howard Stern he supported it. So he supported it before it happened, he supported it as it was happening, and he is on record as supporting it after it happened. I have taken responsibility for my decision. ...

QUESTION [another person in the audience]: Secretary Clinton, you have had an extensive record with military intervention. How do you respond to progressives like myself who worry and have concerns that your hawkish foreign policy will continue? And what is your plan to end wasteful war campaigns in which our peers, servicewomen and men, continue to be killed and wounded?

CLINTON: I assume you're talking about Iraq, because of my vote, and you probably are talking about Libya, because of the role that I played in the administration's decision about whether to take on Gaddafi. But before I get to that, let me say very clearly: I view force as a last resort, not a first choice. I will do everything in my power to make sure that our men and women in the military are fully prepared for any challenge that they may have to face on our behalf. But I will also be as careful as I can in making the most significant decisions any president and commander-in-chief can make about sending our men and women into harm's way. With respect to Libya, again, there's no difference between my opponent and myself. He's on record extensively supporting intervention in Libya, when Gaddafi was threatening to massacre his population. I put together a coalition that included NATO, included the Arab League, and we were able to save lives. We did not lose a single American in that action. And I think taking that action was the right decision. Not taking it, and permitting there to be an ongoing civil war in Libya, would have been as dangerous and threatening as what we are now seeing in Syria.

LAUER: Let me ask you about the Iran nuclear deal. It was signed under Secretary Kerry; it was begun under you. You started those talks.

CLINTON: Right, I did.

LAUER: You have said you expect the Iranians to cheat, you think they'll buy time, and perhaps stay along their course to building a nuclear weapon. If they cheat, Secretary Clinton, will you have any course of action other than a military course of action? Would you enter into negotiations with again (ph)? Would you go back to economic sanctions knowing they cheated and are then closer to a nuclear weapon?

CLINTON: Let me put this in context, because this is one of the most important strategic questions we face. When I became secretary of state, the Iranians were on a fast track to acquiring the material necessary to get a nuclear weapon. That had happened the prior eight years. They mastered the nuclear fuel cycle, they built covert facilities, they stocked them with centrifuges, and they were moving forward. What was our decision? Our decision was to try to put together an international coalition that included Russia and China to exert the kind of pressure through sanctions that the United States alone could not do. ... So, yes, I put together the coalition. We imposed the sanctions. We got them to the negotiating table. And after I left, we got the agreement. That agreement put a lid on their nuclear weapons program and imposed intrusive inspections. I have said we are going to enforce it to the letter.

LAUER: Do you think they're playing us?

CLINTON: On the nuclear issue, no. I think we have enough insight into what they're doing to be able to say we have to distrust but verify. What I am focused on is all the other malicious activities of the Iranians - ballistic missiles, support for terrorists, being involved in Syria, Yemen, and other places, supporting Hezbollah, Hamas. But here's the difference. I would rather as president be dealing with Iran on all of those issues without having to worry as much about their racing for a nuclear weapon. So we have made the world safer; we just have to make sure it's enforced. ...

QUESTION [from the audience]: Secretary Clinton, last October you said that surveys of veterans show that they're overall satisfied with their treatment and that the problems with the V.A. aren't as widespread as they're made out to be. So do you think the problems with the V.A. have been made to seem worse than they really are?

CLINTON: I was outraged by the stories that came out about the V.A. And I have been very clear about the necessity for doing whatever is required to move the V.A. into the 21st century, to provide the kind of treatment options that our veterans today desperately need and deserve. And that's what I will do as president. But I will not let the V.A. be privatized. And I do think there is an agenda out there, supported by my opponent, to do just that. I think that would be very disastrous for our military veterans. So I'm going to do everything I can - I'm going to have a meeting every week in the Oval Office. We're going to bring the V.A. people, we're going to bring the DOD people, because we've got to have a better fit between getting mustered out and getting into the V.A. system, sometimes - and you probably know this, Sergeant - I've met so many vets who get mustered out, who leave the service, they can't find their records from DOD, and those records never make it to the V.A. They feel like they're living in a funhouse. They have to go over the same things over and over. We're living in a technological world. You cannot tell me we can't do a better job getting that information. And so I'm going to focus on this. I'm going to work with everybody. I'm going to make them work together. And we're going to fix the problems in the V.A.

LAUER: Let's talk about veterans and suicide. … It's an alarming, alarming story. The population of veterans has a rate of suicide far above the general population.

CLINTON: Twenty suicides a day.

LAUER: What are you going to do to stop it?

CLINTON: Well, this month is Suicide Prevention Awareness Month. I've spent a lot of time with family members, survivors, who've lost a loved one after he or she came home, sometimes suffering from PTSD or TBI or sexual assault, being handed bags of opioids, not being given an appropriate treatment to help that particular person, which is something we have to change. So I rolled out my mental health agenda last week, and I have a whole section devoted to veterans' mental health. And we've got to remove the stigma. We've got to help people currently serving not to feel that if they report their sense of unease, their depression, that somehow it's going to be a mark against them. We have to do more about addiction, not only drugs, but also alcohol. So I have put forth a really robust agenda, working with a lot of the VSOs and other groups, like TAPS, who have been thinking about this and trying to figure out what we're going to do to help our veterans re-enter civilian life and live full, productive lives.

QUESTION [from the audience]: Secretary Clinton, as an Army veteran, a commander-in-chief's to empathize with servicemembers and their families is important to me. The ability to truly understand implications and consequences of your decisions, actions, or inactions. How will you determine when and where to deploy troops directly into harm's way, especially to combat ISIS?

CLINTON: We have to defeat ISIS. That is my highest counterterrorism goal. And we've got to do it with air power. We've got to do it with much more support for the Arabs and the Kurds who will fight on the ground against ISIS. We have to squeeze them by continuing to support the Iraqi military. They've taken back Ramadi, Fallujah. They've got to hold them. They've got to now get into Mosul. We're going to work to make sure that they have the support — they have special forces, as you know, they have enablers, they have surveillance, intelligence, reconnaissance help. They are not going to get ground troops. We are not putting ground troops into Iraq ever again. And we're not putting ground troops into Syria. We're going to defeat ISIS without committing American ground troops. So those are the kinds of decisions we have to make on a case-by-case basis. And, remember, when I became secretary of state, we had 200,000 troops deployed in Iraq and Afghanistan. And I'm very grateful that we have brought home the vast majority of those. We have a residual force, as you know, in Afghanistan. We have built up several thousands of the folks that I've talked about who are assisting in the fight against ISIS. But it is in our national security interest to defeat ISIS. And I intend to make that happen. And as part of it, we're going after Baghdadi, the leader, because it will help us focus our attention, just like going after bin Laden helped us focus our attention in the fight against Al Qaeda in the Afghanistan-Pakistan theater.

LAUER: Would your message as the next president of the United States or potential next president be to Americans that we simply are living in the reality that those attacks will happen? And can you guarantee people that after four years of a Clinton presidency, they will be safer on the streets of San Bernardino or Boston than they are today?

CLINTON: … I'm going to do everything in my power to make sure that that's the result. I'm not going to promise something that I think most thinking Americans know is going to be a huge challenge, and here's why. We've got to have an intelligence surge. We've got to get a lot more cooperation out of Europe, out of the Middle East. We have to do a better job of not only collecting and analyzing the intelligence we do have, but distributing it much more quickly down the ladder to state and local law enforcement. We also have to do a better job combating ISIS online, where they recruit, where they radicalize. And I don't think we're doing as much as we can. We need to work with Silicon Valley. We need to work with our experts in our government. We have got to disrupt, we have got to take them on in the arena of ideas that, unfortunately, pollute and capture the minds of vulnerable people. So we need to wage this war against ISIS from the air, on the ground, and online, in cyberspace. And here at home, for goodness's sakes, we have to finally pass a law prohibiting people on the terrorist watch list from being able to buy a gun in the United States of America. So we've got work to do. I know we can do that work. I'm meeting with a group of terror experts, counterterrorism experts. But I want to just say one additional thing. Matt Olsen, the former director of the National Center on Counterterrorism, has a great article out today saying the last thing we need to do is to play into the hands of ISIS. Going after American Muslims, defaming a Gold Star family, the family of Captain Khan, making it more difficult for us to have a coalition with Muslim majority nations, that is not going to help us to succeed in defeating ISIS and protecting our American homeland. …

LAUER: Now, please welcome the Republican nominee for president, Donald Trump. ... You heard me say to Mrs. Clinton, Secretary Clinton, and it didn't completely work out toward the end there, as much as possible I'd like you to tell our veterans and our people at home why you are prepared for the role of commander-in-chief and try to keep the attacks to a minimum. We've had a year of that and maybe 60 more days of it.

TRUMP: To a minimum, absolutely.

LAUER: Any time you talk to a president, they'll tell you the most daunting part of the job is the role of commander-in-chief.

TRUMP: Right.

LAUER: What have you experienced in your personal life or your professional life that you believe prepares you to make the decisions that a commander-in-chief has to make?

TRUMP: Well, I've built a great company. I've been all over the world. I've dealt with foreign countries. I've done very well, as an example, tremendously well dealing with China and dealing with so many of the countries that are just ripping this country. They are just taking advantage of us like nobody's ever seen before. And I've had great experience dealing on an international basis. I look today and I see Russian planes circling our planes. They're taunting us. I see in Iran, I see the boats taunting our ships, our destroyers, and I think...

LAUER: But what have you done in your life that prepares you to send men and women of the United States into harm's way?

TRUMP: Well, I think the main thing is I have great judgment. I have good judgment. I know what's going on. I've called so many of the shots. And I happened to hear Hillary Clinton say that I was not against the war in Iraq. I was totally against the war in Iraq. From a — you can look at Esquire magazine from '04. You can look at before that. And I was against the war in Iraq because I said it's going to totally destabilize the Middle East, which it has. It has absolutely been a disastrous war, and by the way, perhaps almost as bad was the way Barack Obama got out. That was a disaster.

LAUER: People talk about you and commander-in-chief, and not just Secretary Clinton, but some of your Republican opponents in the primary season, and they wonder about your temperament. They say, does Donald Trump have the temperament to be commander-in-chief? You said something recently that I found interesting. You admitted that sometimes in the heat of a debate or when you're talking about a lot of issues you say things that you later regret. So can we afford that with a commander-in-chief — to have a commander-in-chief who says things that he later regrets?

TRUMP: Well, when you say regret, yeah, sure, I regret. But in the meantime, I beat 16 people and here I am. So, you know, to a certain extent there is a regret. I would have liked to have done it in a nicer manner. But I had 16 very talented people that I had to go through. And that was a lot of people. That was a record, Matt. That was a record in the history of Republican politics. I was able to get more votes than anybody ever has gotten in the history of Republican politics.

LAUER: But when you say inflammatory things in a presidential campaign, it's different than saying them when you're commander-in-chief. If you say things you regret… when you're commander-in-chief, you can spark a conflict, you can destabilize a region, you can put American lives at risk. Can we afford to take that risk with you?

TRUMP: Well, I think absolutely. I think if you saw what happened in Mexico the other day, where I went there, I had great relationships, everything else. I let them know where the United States stands. I mean, we've been badly hurt by Mexico, both on the border and with taking all of our jobs or a big percentage of our jobs. And if you look at what happened, look at the aftermath today where the people that arranged the trip in Mexico have been forced out of government. That's how well we did. And that's how well we're going to have to do, Matt.

LAUER: Back in August, when you admitted that you regret some of the things you said, you also said this. "I can promise you this: I will always tell you the truth."

TRUMP: It's true.

LAUER: So let me read some of the things you've said. "I know more about ISIS than the generals do. Believe me." Was that the truth?

TRUMP: Well, the generals under Barack Obama and Hillary Clinton have not been successful. ISIS...

LAUER: Do you know more about ISIS than they do?

TRUMP: I think under the leadership of Barack Obama and Hillary Clinton, the generals have been reduced to rubble. They have been reduced to a point where it's embarrassing for our country. You have a force of 30,000 or so people. Nobody really knows. But probably 30,000 people. And I can just see the great - as an example - General George Patton spinning in his grave as ISIS we can't beat. We had the greatest...

LAUER: Yeah, you've said if we had MacArthur today or if we had Patton today, we would not have ISIS, that the rise of these military commanders that we have today, they come up the chain of command, and by the time they get to the top, they're too politically correct. And we know that's not a compliment coming from you. Have you lost faith in the military commanders?

TRUMP: I have great faith in the military. I have great faith in certain of the commanders, certainly. But I have no faith in Hillary

Clinton or the leadership. You look at what's happened. And, you know, when she comes in and starts saying, oh, I would have done this, I would have - she's been there for 30 years. I mean, we need change, Matt. We have to have it, and we have to have it fast.

QUESTION [from the audience]: Mr. Trump, over the past 15 years, a lot of U.S. troops have bled and died securing towns and provinces from Iraq to Afghanistan, only to have insurgent groups like ISIS spring back the moment we leave. Now, you've claimed to have a secret plan to defeat ISIS. But you're hardly the first politician to promise a quick victory and a speedy homecoming. So assuming we do defeat ISIS, what next? What is your plan for the region to ensure that a group like them doesn't just come back?

TRUMP: Sure. I mean, part of the problem that we've had is we go in, we defeat somebody, and then we don't know what we're doing after that. We lose it, like as an example, you look at Iraq, what happened, how badly that was handled. And then when President Obama took over, likewise, it was a disaster. It was actually somewhat stable. I don't think could ever be very stable to where we should have never gone into in the first place. But he came in. He said when we go out - and he took everybody out. And really, ISIS was formed. This was a terrible decision. And frankly, we never even got a shot. And if you really look at the aftermath of Iraq, Iran is going to be taking over Iraq. They've been doing it. And it's not a pretty picture. … I've always said we shouldn't be there, but if we're going to get out, take the oil. If we would have taken the oil, you wouldn't have ISIS, because ISIS formed with the power and the wealth of that oil.

LAUER: How were we going to take the oil? How were we going to do that?

TRUMP: Just we would leave a certain group behind and you would take various sections where they have the oil. They have - people don't know this about Iraq, but they have among the largest oil reserves in the world, in the entire world. And we're the only ones, we go in, we spend $3 trillion, we lose thousands and thousands of lives, and then, Matt, what happens is, we get nothing. You know, it used to be to the victor belong the spoils. Now, there was no victor there, believe me. There was no victor. But I always said: Take the oil. One of the benefits we would have had if we took the oil is ISIS would not have been able to take oil and use that oil to fuel themselves.

LAUER: Let me stay on ISIS. When we've met in the past and we've talked, you say things like I'm going to bomb the expletive out of them very quickly. And when people like me press you for details like that gentleman just said on what your plan is, you very often say, I'm not going to give you the details because I want to be unpredictable.

TRUMP: Absolutely. The word is unpredictable.

LAUER: But yesterday, you actually told us a little bit about your plan in your speech. You said this. Quote, "We're going to convene my top generals and they will have 30 days to submit a plan for soundly and quickly defeating ISIS." So is the plan you've been hiding this whole time asking someone else for their plan?

TRUMP: No. But when I do come up with a plan that I like and that perhaps agrees with mine, or maybe doesn't - I may love what the generals come back with. I will convene…

LAUER: But you have your own plan?

TRUMP: I have a plan. But I want to be - I don't want to - look. I have a very substantial chance of winning. Make America great again. We're going to make America great again. I have a substantial chance of winning. If I win, I don't want to broadcast to the enemy exactly what my plan is. And let me tell you, if I like maybe a combination of my plan and the generals' plan, or the generals' plan, if I like their plan, Matt, I'm not going to call you up and say, "Matt, we have a great plan." This is what Obama does. "We're going to leave Iraq on a certain day."

LAUER: But you're going to convene a panel of generals, and you've already said you know more about ISIS than those generals do.

TRUMP: Well, they'll probably be different generals, to be honest with you. I mean, I'm looking at the generals, today, you probably saw, I have a piece of paper here, I could show it, 88 generals and admirals endorsed me today.

LAUER: It's a numbers game. Hillary Clinton claims more numbers.

TRUMP: Well, it's not really - it's not - yeah, numbers. People that have been losing for us for a long period of time. I mean, the fact is, we have had the worst and you could even say the dumbest foreign policy. Our results are so bad. We would have been better off had we never, ever spent $2 in that part of the world.

LAUER: You recently received two intelligence briefings.

TRUMP: Yes, I did.

LAUER: Did anything in that briefing, without going into specifics, shock or alarm you?

TRUMP: Yes. Very much so.

LAUER: Did you learn new things in that briefing?

TRUMP: First of all, I have great respect for the people that gave us the briefings. They were terrific people. They were experts on Iraq and Iran and different parts of - and Russia. But, yes, there was one thing that shocked me. And it just seems to me that what they said President Obama and Hillary Clinton and John Kerry, who is another total disaster, did exactly the opposite.

LAUER: Did you learn anything in that briefing - again, not going into specifics - that makes you reconsider some of the things you say you can accomplish, like defeating ISIS quickly?

TRUMP: No, I didn't learn anything from that standpoint. What I did learn is that our leadership, Barack Obama, did not follow what our experts and our truly - when they call it intelligence, it's there for a reason - what our experts said to do. And I was very, very surprised in almost every instance. And I could tell you. I have pretty good with the body language. I could tell they were not happy. Our leaders did not follow what they were recommending.

QUESTION [from the audience]: Mr. Trump. Do you believe that an undocumented person who serves - who wants to serve in the U.S. armed forces deserves to stay in this country legally?

TRUMP: I think that when you serve in the armed forces, that's a very special situation, and I could see myself working that out, absolutely. ... As you know, under DACA, we already have people who are undocumented who are serving.

TRUMP: I think military is a very special thing. If they plan on serving, if they get in, I would absolutely hold those people - now, we have to be very careful. We have to vet very carefully. Everybody would agree with that. But the answer is, it would be a very special circumstance, yes. Thank you.

QUESTION [from the audience]: Mr. Trump, as you know, tensions between the United States and Russia have been at the highest level since the Cold War. In your first 120 days of presidency, how would you de-escalate the tensions? And more importantly, what steps would you take to bring Mr. Putin and the Russian government back to negotiating table?

TRUMP: I think I would have a very good relationship with many foreign leaders. I think it's very sad, when you look at Barack

Obama, as an example, lands Air Force One in China, and they don't want to put out stairs to get off the plane. And he has to use the stairs that mechanics use to get up and down to fix the plane. They wouldn't give him stairs. I think it's very sad, when he lands in Saudi Arabia, and he lands in Cuba, and there aren't high officials to even greet him. This is the first time in the history — the storied history of Air Force One. I think I would have a very, very good relationship with Putin. And I think I would have a very, very good relationship with Russia. As I said, take a look today. Take a look at what happened with their fighter jets circling one of our aircraft in a very dangerous manner. Somebody said less than 10 feet away. This is hostility. And I saw, just two or three days ago, they looked like they were not exactly getting along, but I looked at President Obama and Putin staring at each other. These were not two people that were getting along. And, you know, the beautiful part of getting along, Russia wants to defeat ISIS as badly as we do. If we had a relationship with Russia, wouldn't it be wonderful if we could work on it together and knock the hell out of ISIS? Wouldn't that be a wonderful thing?

LAUER: Let me ask you about some of the things you've said about Vladimir Putin. You said, I will tell you, in terms of leadership, he's getting an "A," our president is not doing so well. And when referring to a comment that Putin made about you, I think he called you a brilliant leader, you said it's always a great honor to be so nicely complimented by a man so highly respected within his country and beyond.

TRUMP: Well, he does have an 82 percent approval rating, according to the different pollsters, who, by the way, some of them are based right here. Look, look…

LAUER: He's also a guy who annexed Crimea, invaded Ukraine, supports Assad in Syria, supports Iran, is trying to undermine our influence in key regions of the world, and according to our intelligence community, probably is the main suspect for the hacking of the DNC computers...

TRUMP: Well, nobody knows that for a fact. But do you want me to start naming some of the things that President Obama does at the same time?

LAUER: But do you want to be complimented by that former KGB officer?

TRUMP: Well, I think when he calls me brilliant, I'll take the compliment, OK? The fact is, look, it's not going to get him anywhere. I'm a negotiator. We're going to take back our country. You look at what's happening to our country, you look at the depleted military. You look at the fact that we've lost our jobs. We're losing our jobs like we're a bunch of babies. We're going to take back our country, Matt. The fact that he calls me brilliant or whatever he calls me is going to have zero impact.

LAUER: But the fact that you say you can get along with him, do you think the day...

TRUMP: I think I'd be able to get along with him.

LAUER: Do you think the day that you become president of the United States, he's going to change his mind on some of these key issues?

TRUMP: Possibly. It's possible. I don't know, Matt. It's possible. And it's not going to have any impact. If he says great things about me, I'm going to say great things about him. I've already said, he is really very much of a leader. I mean, you can say, oh, isn't that a terrible thing - the man has very strong control over a country. Now, it's a very different system, and I don't happen to like the system. But certainly, in that system, he's been a leader, far more than our president has been a leader. We have a divided country.

We have a country where you have Hillary Clinton with her e-mails that nobody's ever seen where she deletes 33,000 e-mails, and that's after getting a subpoena from Congress. If you do that in private business, you get thrown in jail.

QUESTION [from the audience]: I like what you say about supporting veterans and how they're important. But I haven't heard what the actual plans are to continue that support beyond words. How do you translate those words to action after you take office?

TRUMP: Well, I love that question, because I've been very close to the vets. You see the relationship I have with the vets just by looking at the polls. In fact, today a poll came out. And my relationship has been very good. I have a very, very powerful plan that's on my website that you possibly saw. One of the big problems is the wait time. Vets are waiting six days, seven days, eight days. And by the way, Hillary Clinton six months ago said the vets are being treated essentially just fine, there's no real problem, it's over-exaggerated. She did say that.

LAUER: No, no, she went on after that and laid out a litany of problems within the V.A.

TRUMP: Look, I mean, she made up half of the things she said about me. I'm telling you, this is - she said she was satisfied with what was going on in the Veterans Administration. Now, under my plan, if you've got to wait — and, by the way, people are dying on line. They're dying, waiting, waiting to get to see a doctor. They're waiting five days and six days. Under a part of my plan, if they have that long wait, they walk outside, they go to the local doctor, they choose the doctor, they choose the hospital, whether it's public or private, they get themselves better. In many cases, it's a minor procedure or a pill or just a prescription. And they end up dying because they can't get to see the doctor. We will pay the bill.

They go outside, they get a doctor, they get a prescription, they do what they have to do, and we pay the bill. That is something that I have been praised - and, by the way, I never said take the V.A.- take the Veterans Administration private. I wouldn't do that. Too much respect for our people. I would never do that. I heard it was said that I said that. I would not do that. But I do believe — I do believe, when you're waiting in line for six, seven days, you should never be in a position like that. You go out, you see the doctor, you get yourself taken care of.

QUESTION [from the audience]: I do. Mr. Trump, I wanted to ask what your plan will be to stop 20 veterans a day from killing themselves.

TRUMP: And actually it's 22. And it's almost impossible to conceive that this is happening in our country, 20 to 22 people a day are killing themselves. A lot of it is they're killing themselves over the fact that they can't - they're under tremendous pain and they can't see a doctor. We're going to speed up the process. We're going to create a great mental health division. They need help. They need help. They need tremendous help. And we're doing nothing for them. The V.A. is really almost, you could say, a corrupt enterprise. If you look at what's going on, as an example, Matt, in Arizona, where they caught people stealing, and they can't even do anything about it, they can't even fire the people. So we are going to make it efficient and good. And if it's not good, you're going out to private hospitals, public hospitals, and doctors. Thank you very much.

QUESTION [from the audience]: Mr. Trump, I have a daughter who is interested in joining the service, but when she researched the military, she saw the stats on sexual assault and decided not to go. I have a concern about the rape of women in our armed forces. As president, what specifically would you do to support all victims of sexual assault in the military?

TRUMP: It's a great question. And it's a massive problem. The numbers are staggering, hard to believe, even. But we're going to have to run it very tight. I at the same time want to keep the court system within the military. I don't think it should be outside of the military. But we have to come down very, very hard on that. And your daughter is absolutely right, it is a massive problem. But we have to do something about that problem. And the best thing we can do is set up a court system within the military. Right now, the court system practically doesn't exist. It takes too long.

LAUER: In 2013, on this subject, you tweeted this, quote, "26,000 unreported sexual assaults in the military, only 238 convictions. What did these geniuses expect when they put men and women together?"

TRUMP: Well, it is - it is - it is a correct tweet. There are many people that think that that's absolutely correct. And we need to have a...

LAUER: So this should have been expected? And does that mean the only way to fix it is to take women out of the military?

TRUMP: Well, it's happening, right? And, by the way, since then, it's gotten worse. No, not to take them out, but something has to be happen. Right now, part of the problem is nobody gets prosecuted. You have reported and - the gentleman can tell you, you have the report of rape and nobody gets prosecuted. There are no consequences. When you have somebody that does something so evil, so bad as that, there has to be consequence for that person. You have to go after that person. Right now, nobody's doing anything. Look at the small number of results. I mean, that's part of the problem.

LAUER: So many of the issues that we've talked about with you, Mr. Trump, tonight, and Secretary Clinton, are so complex that even career military people and career diplomats and politicians have trouble getting their arms around them.

TRUMP: Right.

LAUER: You've had a very different background, in business. So nobody would expect you to have taken over the last 20 years really deep dives into some of these issues. But I'm curious about what you're doing now. What kind of research are you doing now? What kind of homework are you doing? What kind of things are you reading as you prepare for the day in two months where you might be elected the next president of the United States?

TRUMP: Sure. Well, in the front row, you have four generals. You have admirals. We have people all throughout the audience that I'm dealing with. Right here is a list that was just printed today of 88 admirals and generals that I meet with and I talk to.

LAUER: How much time are you spending on this?

TRUMP: I'm also - a lot. A lot. And I'm doing a lot of different things. Don't forget, we're running a big campaign. We're doing very well. I'm also, you know, and I'm very much giving it to my children and my executives to run, I'm also partially running a business. I'm campaigning, I'm running a business. I've got a lot of hats right now. But we're doing very well. But in the meantime, I am studying. And I'm meeting constantly - you see General Flynn and you see some of the folks that we have, and they're scattered throughout the audience. So we have admirals, we have generals, we have colonels. We have a lot of people that I respect. And I think I've learned a lot. But I think, also, I certainly — I really feel I have a common sense on the various issues that you're talking about, Matt.

LAUER: You said in the speech today, you said history shows that when America is not prepared is when the danger is the greatest.

TRUMP: And we're not prepared.

LAUER: Will you be prepared on day one, if you're elected president of the United States, to tackle these complex national security issues?

TRUMP: One hundred percent. Again, she made a mistake on Libya. She made a terrible mistake on Libya. And the next thing, I mean, not only did she make the mistake, but then they complicated the mistake by having no management once they bombed you know what out of Gaddafi. I mean, she made a terrible mistake on Libya. And part of it was the management aftereffect. I think that we have great management talents, great management skills.

LAUER: But you are prepared?

TRUMP: Totally prepared. But remember this. I found this subject and these subjects of interest all of my life, Matt. This hasn't been over the last 14 months. I've found these substantiates of tremendous interest. That's why they were asking me about Iraq 14 years ago. They were asking me these questions. They don't ask businesspeople those questions.

LAUER: Have you given much thought, Mr. Trump, if you're elected president and commander-in-chief, to that moment where you're going to have to make that first decision that puts American men and women in harm's way?

TRUMP: I think it's the most difficult decision you can possibly ever make. You're talking about death. And we're talking death to not just our side. We're talking death all over. I would be very, very cautious. I think I'd be a lot slower. She has a happy trigger. You look, she votes for the wars, she goes in Libya…

LAUER: Have you thought about personally the emotional burden of that moment?

TRUMP: I think it's a tremendous burden. I think there is no greater burden that anybody could have. I've been preparing this for a long time. And, you know, my theme is make America great again. We're going to make America great again. But, Matt, we've also got to make America strong again. And right now, we are not strong. Believe me. We have a depleted military. We have the greatest people in the world in our military. But it is very sadly depleted.

Now, it's time to move on to what the candidates see as the issues and to explore their proposed programs for dealing with those issues.

12

WHAT THE CANDIDATES FEEL THE ISSUES ARE - AND HOW THEY WOULD DEAL WITH THOSE ISSUES.

A. FOREIGN POLICY ISSUES

CHINA

CLINTON:

Hillary Clinton says the next administration must continue to cultivate trust and cooperate with China on a range of international challenges, like North Korea and climate change, while keeping competition within acceptable limits. The U.S.-China relationship is not one that "fits neatly into categories like friend or rival," In 2015, she criticized China for "trying to hack into everything that doesn't move in America," and called on the United States to remain vigilant. "China's military is growing very quickly, they're establishing military installations that again threaten countries we have treaties with, like the Philippines, because they are building on contested property," .

As secretary of state, Clinton was a central actor in the Obama administration's strategic "pivot" to Asia. Her first official trip abroad as the top U.S. diplomat in 2009 included visits to Japan, Indonesia, South Korea, and China, which she said was intended to highlight the emerging strategic importance of China and the Asia-Pacific region.

In July 2009, she and Treasury Secretary Tim Geithner inaugurated an annual program of high-level talks with Beijing known as the Strategic and Economic Dialogue. Clinton laid out the Obama administration's multi-pronged strategy for the region in an in 2011. "Our challenge now is to build a web of partnerships and institutions across the Pacific that is as durable and as consistent with American interests and values as the web we have built across the Atlantic," she wrote.

Clinton's remarks at a security forum in Vietnam in 2010 generated great international interest, in particular her reference to the "national interest" the United States has "in freedom of navigation, open access to Asia's maritime commons, and respect for international law in the South China Sea."

She has also regularly criticized China's record on human rights. As first lady in 1995, she delivered an address at a UN conference in Beijing in which she tacitly rebuked the Chinese government for its treatment of women and one-child policy. "It is a violation of human rights when women are denied the right to plan their own families, and that includes being forced to have abortions or being sterilized against their will," she said. In 2008, she called on President George W. Bush to boycott the opening of the Olympic Games in Beijing, pointing to political violence in Tibet and China's failure to pressure Sudan to halt the violence in Darfur.

TRUMP:

China has bested the United States in recent years, particularly with regard to trade and economic policy, according to Donald Trump. He singled China out for criticism, accusing the country of dumping its exports and of devaluing its currency, the Yuan. Trump said that as president he would impose tariffs on Chinese goods to change Beijing's economic policies. "If they don't come to the table, they're going to have a tax when they put their products into this country. And they're going to behave."

In November 2015, Trump outlined his plan for reforming U.S. trade relations with China.. He would as president formally designate China a currency manipulator, crack down on what he says is its theft of U.S. intellectual property, and expose its various export subsidy practices. As president, he would also seek to lower the U.S. corporate income tax rate, decrease the national debt, and ramp up the U.S. military presence in the Asia-Pacific region, all of which he says would bolster Washington's bargaining position with respect to Beijing.

CUBA

CLINTON:

The former secretary of state embraces the normalization of ties with Cuba and in July 2015 called for lifting the economic embargo. "The Cuba embargo needs to go, once and for all." "We should replace it with a smarter approach that empowers the Cuban private sector, Cuban civil society, and the Cuban-American community to spur progress and keep pressure on the regime." She called the embargo an "albatross" on U.S. diplomacy in Latin America and said, "Most Republican candidates still view Cuba—

and Latin America more broadly—through an outdated Cold War lens."

Clinton said that as president, if Congress does not lift the embargo, she would use executive authority to further reduce travel restrictions to the island. She wrote in her 2014 book, *Hard Choices*, that as secretary of state she urged President Obama to reconsider the embargo. "Since 1960, the United States had maintained an embargo against the island in hopes of squeezing Castro from power, but it only succeeded in giving him a foil to blame for Cuba's economic woes," she wrote.

Her recent positions mark a shift from a tougher posture toward Cuba. As first lady, Clinton supported the 1996 Helms-Burton Act, which strengthened the U.S. embargo against Cuba. (President Bill Clinton signed it into law.) During her 2008 presidential campaign, Clinton said she opposed lifting the embargo on an undemocratic Cuba. She has since said she changed her mind on Cuba policy when she realized the embargo wasn't achieving its goals. "I thought we should shift the onus onto the Castros to explain why they remained undemocratic and abusive," she wrote in *Hard Choices*.

TRUMP:

In a break with much of his party, Donald Trump says he supports diplomacy with Cuba. "The concept of opening with Cuba is fine," he said in September 2015, adding, "but we should have made a better deal." In 1999, the real-estate developer wrote in favor of the embargo, claiming that he had turned down offers to partner with European investment groups to develop properties on the island. "I had a choice to make: huge profits or human rights," Trump wrote. "For me, it was a no-brainer."

DEFENSE

CLINTON:

Hillary Clinton advocates the use of "smart power" in the pursuit of U.S. foreign policy objectives, which she says means "choosing the right combination of tools—diplomatic, economic, military, political, legal, and cultural—for each situation." As secretary of state, she sought close collaboration with her counterparts at the Pentagon, Secretaries of Defense Robert Gates and Leon Panetta. She referred to the Obama's administration's intervention in Libya in 2011, which was authorized by the United Nations and supported by the Arab League, as "smart power at its best." She said the United States provided essential military capabilities, like intelligence, but that NATO allies in Europe took the lead in combat operations.

Clinton voted for the U.S. invasion of Iraq in 2003 and was an early supporter for arming and training "vetted" Syrian rebels in 2012. She also supported the surge in Afghanistan in 2009 and for keeping U.S. troops in Iraq beyond 2011. In 2015, she supported the creation of a no-fly zone in Syria.

In a 2014 interview, Clinton said she was "thinking a lot about containment, deterrence, and defeat" and applying some of the U.S. strategy used during the Cold War to current foreign policy challenges, including the self-proclaimed Islamic State and Russia.

Clinton's campaign website lists several foreign policy priorities that could involve the U.S. military: prohibiting Iran from gaining a nuclear weapon; defeating the Islamic State; holding China accountable on issues like cybersecurity, containing and deterring Russian aggression; and strengthening alliances, particularly with Israel. Additionally, she says the government must take better care of veterans and military families.

TRUMP:

Donald Trump has said he would increase the size, power, and reach of the military, but has offered few specifics. He has also criticized the readiness of U.S. nuclear forces.

Trump has opposed some recent U.S. military interventions, including the 2003 invasion of Iraq. "I do not believe that we made the right decision going into Iraq, but, you know, hopefully, we'll be getting out," he said in 2004. He supported the U.S. invasion of Afghanistan in 2001, although he has criticized the length of U.S. involvement there.

In the days after the Brussels attacks in March 2016 that left more than thirty people dead, Trump questioned the utility of NATO. He called the Cold War-era institution "obsolete" for, among other things, focusing too little on terrorism, and said the United States was paying much more than its fair share for the alliance. "It's become very bureaucratic, extremely expensive and maybe is not flexible enough to go after terror. Terror is very much different than what NATO was set up for."

Meanwhile, Trump said that as president he would be willing to withdraw U.S. military forces from allied countries like Japan and Korea if they did not "increase their contribution significantly." In 2011, Trump listed seven core principles of his foreign policy doctrine, which emphasizes defense: 1) American interests come first; 2) Maximum firepower and military preparedness; 3) Only go to war to win; 4) Stay loyal to your friends and suspicious of your enemies; 5) Keep the technological sword razor sharp; 6) See the unseen. Prepare for threats before they materialize; and 7) Respect and support our present and past warriors.

ENERGY AND CLIMATE CHANGE

CLINTON:

Hillary Clinton describes herself as "a proven fighter against the threat of climate change," having led the Obama administration's 2012 establishment of a global initiative to reduce short-lived climate pollutants. In July 2015, Clinton said that as president she would aim to "make the United States the world's clean energy superpower," and announced two proposals to fight climate change: the installation of more than half a billion solar panels by the end of her first term, and the generation of enough renewable energy to power every U.S. home within ten years. She has vowed to fight Republican efforts in Congress and the courts to undo President Obama's Clean Power Plan, which set carbon emission limits on U.S. states.

She also says as president she would unveil a "Clean Energy Challenge" (CEC), a broad federal program that would partner with states, cities, and rural communities on renewable energy, power grid resilience, and air pollution control. Among other things, the CEC would extend clean energy tax incentives, expand R&D efforts, and increase U.S. hydropower generation.

Clinton opposes drilling in the U.S. Arctic and says she is very skeptical of the need for energy production off the coast of southeastern states like the Carolinas. She also opposes construction of the Keystone XL pipeline, saying the project distracts from U.S. efforts to combat climate change.

Clinton has referred to the positive effects of the U.S. natural gas boom, but has said she would tighten regulations on the practice of hydraulic fracturing. "By the time we get through all of my conditions, I do not think there will be many places in America where fracking will continue to take place," she said in a March 2016 debate. Meanwhile, she says she will work to cut federal subsidies for oil and gas businesses, and will maintain the moratorium on new coal-mining leases while the federal process is reviewed.

TRUMP:

Donald Trump says he does not believe climate change is a significant environmental challenge, and he doubts that humans are contributing factors. In a May 2016 speech outlining his energy reform plan, he pledged to lead the country toward total energy independence while accounting for "rational environmental concerns" like clean air and water. His proposal called for, among other things, expanding domestic production of oil and gas, lifting moratoriums on energy production on federal lands, permitting the construction of the Keystone XL oil pipeline, voiding the Obama administration's Clean Power Plan, and walking away from the Paris climate deal. The United States should pursue all forms of energy, including renewables, but should not preference one source over another, he said.

IMMIGRATION

CLINTON:

Hillary Clinton has described immigration reform as an economic and "at heart, a family issue," saying that she will fight for comprehensive immigration legislation that includes a path to full and equal citizenship for the more than eleven million undocumented immigrants in the United States. She has pledged to introduce omnibus legislation during her first 100 days in the White House. Meanwhile, the candidate has vowed to expand on President Obama's executive actions that defer deportation and grant temporary work visas for nearly half of the undocumented

306	THE POLITICS OF INSANITY – HUGO N. GERSTL

population, despite a Supreme Court ruling in June 2016 that upheld a temporary ban on one of them.

Clinton has said that U.S. immigration enforcement and detention practices need to be "more humane," sparing children and other "vulnerable" people from confinement in large facilities. She has said that as president she would create a new federal agency, the Office of Immigrant Affairs, to coordinate immigration policy across all levels of government and help immigrants integrate into their communities.

In October 2015, Clinton said the United States should accept as many as sixty-five thousand Syrian refugees, substantially more than the ten thousand President Obama proposed. Weeks later, after the terrorist attacks in Paris and San Bernardino, she called for greater vigilance in screening migrants coming to the United States, but warned against denying entry based on country of origin or religion. "It would be a cruel irony indeed if ISIS can force families from their homes, and then also prevent them from ever finding new ones. We should be doing more to ease this humanitarian crisis, not less," she said at the Council on Foreign Relations in November 2105.

In 2014, Clinton supported the deportation of thousands of child immigrants from Central America. "We have to send a clear message just because your child gets across the border doesn't mean your child gets to stay," she said. "We don't want to send a message contrary to our laws or encourage more to come."

As a presidential candidate in 2007, she supported a pathway to legalization for undocumented immigrants, but opposed states allowing them to obtain driver's licenses, a policy she now supports. As a legislator, Senator Clinton for several years cosponsored the DREAM Act, legislation to create a pathway to citizenship for undocumented immigrants who came to the United

States as children. She also voted for the Secure Fence Act of 2006, a bill providing for the construction of seven hundred miles of double fencing along the U.S.-Mexico border.

TRUMP:

Donald Trump has made illegal immigration a signature issue of his presidential campaign, generating headlines with controversial remarks about the nature of the challenge and his plans for reform. When he announced his candidacy in June 2015, he claimed that Mexico was sending violent criminals, including rapists, into the United States. (Mexico denies doing this.) He has also called for the deportation of the more than eleven million undocumented immigrants living in the United States. "We're rounding 'em up in a very humane way, in a very nice way. And they're going to be happy because they want to be legalized," he said in September 2015.

Trump issued a policy paper in August 2015 outlining his three point plan for immigration reform. First, he pledges to construct a wall across the entire southern U.S. border, which he says the Mexican government should either finance or be subject to a number of penalties. These will include, Trump says, the United States withholding billions of dollars in remittance payments to Mexico; hiking fees and possibly cancelling visas issued to Mexicans; and increasing fees at ports of entry to the United States from Mexico. "The cost of building a permanent border wall pales mightily in comparison to what American taxpayers spend every single year on dealing with the fallout of illegal immigration on their communities, schools and unemployment offices," he writes.

Second, he pledges to ramp up law enforcement, including tripling the number of Immigration and Customs Enforcement agents, imposing nationwide e-verify, deporting all criminal non-citizens, defunding so-called sanctuary cities (municipalities that critics say do not fully enforce federal immigration laws), raising penalties for those who overstay their visa, and ending birthright citizenship. "[The guarantee of birthright citizenship] remains the biggest magnet for illegal immigration," he says.

Lastly, he says he will restrict legal immigration, including the flow of guest workers and refugees, and legally require U.S. businesses to hire U.S. citizens before others.

Trump has said that if elected president he would not only prevent Syrian refugees from coming to the United States, but he would also deport those already in the country. After the December 2015 attacks in San Bernardino, California, Trump proposed temporarily banning all Muslims from entering the country. The candidate in June 2016 said that he would "suspend immigration from areas of the world when there is a proven history of terrorism against the United States, Europe or our allies." The ban could be lifted, Trump said, once the United States is "in a position to properly and perfectly screen those people coming into our country."

The Republican candidate applauded the Supreme Court's ruling in June that upheld a temporary ban on one of President Obama's so-called deferred action programs.

IRAN

CLINTON:

Hillary Clinton supports the multinational deal with Iran to stop its nuclear program but says the United States must ensure that Tehran complies. "My approach will be distrust and verify. We should anticipate that Iran will test the next president. They'll want to see how far they can bend the rules. That won't work if I'm in the White House," she said in September 2015. She says as president, she would penalize Iran for any violation of the agreement and reintroduce sanctions unilaterally, if necessary. In the event Iran attempts to acquire a nuclear weapon, she "will not hesitate to take military action," she says.

Previously, Clinton said Iran had no right to enrich uranium. (The current agreement allows Iran limited enrichment capacity.) "Contrary to their claim, there is no such thing as a right to enrich," she said in August 2014.

Iran and allied militant groups continue to destabilize the broader region and pose an existential threat to Israel, Clinton says. "We cannot ever take that lightly, particularly when Iran ships advanced missiles to Hezbollah, and the Ayatollah outlines an actual strategy for eliminating Israel or talks about how Israel won't exist in twenty-five years.". Her administration would continue to maintain Israel's military superiority by providing it the latest U.S. weapons technology, including F-35 fighters and missile defense systems.

As secretary of state, Clinton played a central role in gaining UN Security Council support for international sanctions against Iran in 2010, and she pressed many countries, including India and China, to stop purchasing Iranian oil. "In the end our efforts led to every major Iranian customer, even the most reluctant, agreeing to reduce their purchases of Iran's oil," she wrote in her 2014 memoir *Hard Choices*. Meanwhile, she says she regrets that the Obama administration did not speak out more forcefully against Iran's crackdown on democratic protests known as the Green Movement in 2009.

TRUMP:

The Republican candidate has criticized the multinational nuclear agreement with Iran and has said he would renegotiate it, if he's elected. He opposes all aspects of the deal, including its duration, sanctions relief, and inspections regime. During a March 2016 speech, Trump labeled Iran the "biggest sponsor of terrorism around the world" and pledged as U.S. president to dismantle its terror network and counter its "aggressive push to destabilize and dominate the region." He did not offer specifics about this proposed effort.

THE ISLAMIC STATE

CLINTON:

Hillary Clinton says President Obama waited too long to begin arming and training "moderate" Syrian rebels, a delay she says has contributed to the rise of the self-proclaimed Islamic State and other militant groups in the Middle East. As secretary of state, Clinton led the U.S diplomatic effort to end the conflict in Syria and remove President Bashar al-Assad from power after his crackdown on anti-government protests beginning in 2011. After leaving government, she supported the president's decision to seek approval from Congress to conduct airstrikes in Syria in retaliation for Assad's use of chemical weapons in 2013. And she supported the administration's agreement with Russia, reached days later, to eliminate the Assad regime's chemical weapons stockpile.

In the aftermath of the Islamic State's November 2015 attacks on Paris and Beirut, Clinton presented a plan to defeat the group that called on the United States and its allies to intensify military and diplomatic efforts. "Our strategy should have three main elements," she said at CFR. "One, defeat ISIS in Syria, Iraq, and across the Middle East. Two, disrupt and dismantle the growing terrorist infrastructure that facilitates the flow of fighters, financing, arms, and propaganda around the world. Three, harden our defenses and those of our allies against external and homegrown threats."

Clinton supports President Obama's decision ruling out the deployment of a large number of U.S. combat troops to defeat the Islamic State, and says that a ground force should be drawn from the region, particularly Sunni Arabs and Kurds in both Iraq and Syria. However, Clinton says U.S. special forces should be given greater freedom to train Iraqi forces and Syrian rebels and to accompany them into battle, if necessary.

Meanwhile, she says the United States and its coalition partners should step up intelligence gathering, conduct more airstrikes, and establish a no-fly zone over Syria to provide refugees with a sanctuary.

In December, Clinton called on U.S. government agencies to work with top technology companies to shut down the online presence of violent extremist groups like the Islamic State. She also called for greater screening of certain migrants coming to the United States, including requiring those who have traveled to a country with "serious problems with terrorism and foreign fighters" in the past five years to undergo a full visa inquiry.

As U.S. senator, Clinton voted in 2002 to authorize the U.S. invasion of Iraq, a decision she says in 2015 was a mistake. However, she says the Iraqi government was wrong not to allow several thousand U.S. troops to remain in Iraq after 2011.

TRUMP:

In September 2015, Trump said the United States should wait out the conflict in Syria, and allow militants of the self-proclaimed Islamic State to wage war on the forces of President Bashar al-Assad. "Why aren't we letting ISIS go and fight Assad and then we pick up the remnants?" he said. After the November 2015 Paris attacks, he said he would intensify military attacks on the Islamic State and restrict the group's ability to use the Internet as a recruiting tool. "We've got to take back the Internet because they are taking people. They're literally brainwashing people." In a March 2016 debate, the candidate seemed to indicate he would be willing as president to deploy on the ground tens of thousand of U.S. troops to battle the Islamic State. "We really have no choice. We have to knock out ISIS," he said. "I would listen to the generals, but I'm hearing numbers of 20,000 to 30,000." Days later, Trump said that he would likely suspend U.S. purchases of Saudi Arabian oil if the Gulf country did not contribute troops to the fight against ISIS. Meanwhile, Trump called for a greater U.S. effort to disrupt the Islamic State's access to oil revenues and "dark banking channels."

Meanwhile, Trump has favored the creation of so-called "safe zones" for refugees in parts of Syria. He said the U.S. military could lead efforts to protect these areas but that other countries, particularly the Gulf States and Germany, should pay for the operation.

NATIONAL SECURITY

CLINTON:

In December 2015, Clinton put forth a multipronged plan to defend the U.S. homeland from terrorist attacks. Among other things, she called on government agencies to work with top tech companies to shut down the online presence of violent extremist groups like the Islamic State. She also called for greater screening of certain migrants coming to the United States, particularly those who have traveled to a country with "serious problems with terrorism and foreign fighters" in the past five years. Additionally, the United States needs an "intelligence surge" to counter groups like the Islamic State, Clinton said, which should include hiring more operations officers and linguists, as well as increasing electronic surveillance and aerial reconnaissance.

As secretary of state, Hillary Clinton advocated a counterterrorism approach that leveraged the work of many federal agencies, including the U.S. Agency for International Development, as well as international security partnerships. In 2011, the year the White House released its National Strategy for Counterterrorism, she launched the Global Counterterrorism Forum, a venue intended to allow national security professionals from dozens of countries to share best practices. She also supported the Obama administration's efforts to incorporate traditional law enforcement practices, including civilian trials, with the counterterrorism operations of the CIA and the Department of Defense.

She wrote in her memoir *Hard Choices* that drone strikes, particularly on suspected al-Qaeda terrorists in Pakistan, provided the Obama administration with an "important alternative" in instances where such individuals could not be captured and prosecuted. She says she supported some of these strikes because she felt they were important to national security and met certain legal and military guidelines, while she opposed others. "But in every case I thought it was crucial that these strikes be part of a larger smart power counterterrorism strategy that included diplomacy, law enforcement, sanctions, and other tools," she wrote.

Clinton has long advocated for the closure of the Guantanamo Bay detention center, saying the facility undermines U.S. foreign policy objectives. "It represents in the eyes of the world abuse, secrecy, and contempt for the rule of law. Rather than keeping us more secure, Guantanamo is harming our national security." As a U.S. senator in 2004, Clinton cosponsored the Intelligence Reform and Terrorist Prevention Act, which aimed to improve coordination among U.S. intelligence agencies and, most notably, created a director of national intelligence to serve as the top adviser to the president on intelligence matters. She also voted for the 2001 Authorization for the Use of Military Force that launched the war against al-Qaeda and its affiliates, as well as the Patriot Act, which gave the government sweeping powers to collect intelligence for counterterrorism operations.

As a private individual in 2015, Clinton came out in favor of the Freedom Act, which reformed government surveillance practices under the Patriot Act and, in particular, ended the NSA's bulk collection of U.S. telephone records. "Congress should move ahead now with the USA Freedom Act — a good step forward in ongoing efforts to protect our security & civil liberties."

Clinton has adopted somewhat of an even-handed approach to the debate over encryption, refraining from coming down in favor of either Apple or the FBI in their legal battle over access to a terrorism suspect's iPhone. In February 2016, Clinton said she saw both sides and called on government and tech companies to cooperate on a solution. "As smart as we are, there's got to be some way on a very specific basis we could try to help get information around crimes and terrorism," she said.

TRUMP:

Donald Trump generally supports robust U.S. counterterrorism practices, including some controversial government surveillance and interrogation programs. "We have to err on the side of security," he said in June 2015, speaking about NSA's program to collect bulk data on U.S. phone calls. "It's certainly not something I like," he said, "but when you have all these maniacs over the world, we probably have to go that little bit of an extra step."

He also supports the use of harsh interrogation techniques against suspected terrorists, including waterboarding. "I would support and endorse the use of these techniques if the use of these methods would enhance the protection and safety of the nation. Though the effectiveness of many of these methods may be in dispute, nothing should be taken off the table when American lives are at stake," he wrote in February 2016. However, weeks later, Trump said that he would not as president order U.S. personnel to violate domestic or international law.

In early 2016, he supported a California federal court's order compelling Apple to help the FBI crack the password of a terrorism suspect's iPhone. Furthermore, Trump called on Americans to boycott the technology company until it complied with the FBI's demands.

Meanwhile, he opposes President Obama's efforts to close the Guantanamo Bay detention center in Cuba, saying that, if elected, he would probably expand the number of detainees held there.

After the December 2015 attacks in San Bernardino, California, Trump proposed temporarily banning all Muslims from entering the country. In June 2016 he said that he would "suspend immigration from areas of the world when there is a proven history of terrorism against the United States, Europe or our allies." The ban could be lifted, Trump said, once the United States is "in a position to properly and perfectly screen those people coming into our country."

NORTH KOREA

CLINTON:

Clinton supports using sanctions to isolate North Korea until the regime gives up its nuclear arsenal. In January 2016, after North Korea tested a nuclear device for the fourth time, she said the United States must work with the United Nations to impose additional sanctions and called on China to use its influence to deter Pyongyang's "irresponsible actions." The United States and its allies in the Asia-Pacific region should also bolster their missile defenses, she said.

During her tenure as secretary of state from 2009 to 2013, North Korea broke off multi-party talks and violated UN prohibitions against testing long-range rockets and conducting nuclear weapons tests. Clinton continued the U.S. policy of calling on Pyongyang to abide by a September 2005 joint statement that sought a "verifiable denuclearization of the Korean peninsula in a peaceful manner." The United States, working through the UN, helped put together a multilateral regime of sanctions on North Korea aimed at pressuring it to give up its nuclear weapons program. Additionally, Clinton said she supported the Obama administration's so-called pivot to Asia in part because the United States needed a greater military presence in the region to counter the North Korean threat.

TRUMP:

Donald Trump has said the U.S. government should be paying more attention to North Korea, a nuclear-armed country he said is led by a "maniac," referring to Kim Jong-un. The candidate stated, in May 2016, that he would be willing to speak to Kim-Jong-un. After North Korea tested a nuclear device in January 2016, Trump said China and South Korea should put pressure on Pyongyang. He said China has "total control" over North Korea and that if Beijing doesn't "solve the problem, we should make trade very difficult with China." Weeks later, following the North's launch of a satellite that Western countries suspect was a front for a ballistic missile test, Trump again called on China to intervene. "I would get China to make [Kim Jong-un] disappear in one form or another very quickly."

Trump indicated that as president he might support Japan's developing its own nuclear weapons capability in response to the threat from North Korea. Additionally, he said he would be willing to withdraw U.S. forces from South Korea and Japan if these treaty allies did not contribute more financially to these relationships.

In 2000, Trump wrote that he would preemptively strike North Korea if it continued to pursue nuclear weapons technology: "I would let Pyongyang know in no uncertain terms that it can either get out of the nuclear arms race or expect a rebuke similar to the one Ronald Reagan delivered to Muammar Gaddafi in 1986."

RUSSIA

CLINTON:

Hillary Clinton says the United States needs to work with Russia on issues of common interest where possible, like arms control, but partner with allies to limit Russia's transgressions when needed, as in Ukraine. Russian President Vladimir Putin views the United States as a "competitor" and wants to reestablish a Russian sphere of influence in its neighborhood while projecting its power in other places like the Mideast, Clinton says.

The United States should respond by strengthening the NATO alliance and improving the energy security of European states, many of which rely on Russian natural gas. Clinton has called for tougher measures against Putin to punish him for invading Ukraine and annexing Crimea as well as for supporting Syrian President Bashar al-Assad. "I remain convinced that we need a concerted effort to really up the cost on Russia and, in particular, on Putin," Clinton said in September 2015. "I think it's important too that the United States make it very clear to Putin that it's not acceptable for him to be in Syria creating more chaos, bombing people on behalf of Assad, and we can't do that if we don't take more of a leadership position, which is what I'm advocating," .

As secretary of state, Clinton was an architect of the so-called "reset" in U.S. relations with Russia, a diplomatic approach that sought greater cooperation with Russia, but that some critics say fell short and encouraged Russian aggression. She says the reset had a number of early victories, including sanctions on Iran and North Korea, supply lines in Afghanistan, Russia's entering the World Trade Organization, UN support for a no-fly zone in Libya, and wider cooperation on counterterrorism.

TRUMP:

Donald Trump says that Russian President Vladimir Putin does not respect President Obama and that this has encouraged Russia's intervention in Ukraine. "President Obama is not doing what he should be doing in Ukraine," he said in September 2015, although he did not give specifics on what U.S. policy should be. He did, however, call on other European states to support Kiev. "With respect to Ukraine, people have to band together from other parts of Europe to help," Trump said.

In early 2016, Trump questioned whether NATO was still relevant in today's security environment. Moreover, he said the

United States was paying much more than its fair share for the alliance. "It's become very bureaucratic, extremely expensive and maybe is not flexible enough to go after terror. Terror is very much different than what NATO was set up for." Despite his criticisms, however, Trump said that as president he would honor U.S. treaty commitments under NATO, including defending the Baltic States from potential Russian encroachment.

At times, Trump has praised Putin's brand of leadership and said he would enjoy meeting the Russian leader. "I will tell you in terms of leadership he is getting an 'A,' and our president is not doing so well." He has said that because of his business background and his frequent trips to Moscow, he would likely have a "great relationship with Putin."

In the Middle East, Trump has suggested that the United States let Russian forces destroy the self-declared Islamic State in Syria. In October 2015, he characterized Russian airstrikes in Syria as a "positive thing," adding that Russia would likely suffer the same fate as the United States in the region. "We just get bogged down in the Middle East and Russia will get bogged down in the Middle East."

TRADE

CLINTON:

Hillary Clinton has supported trade liberalization throughout her many decades in politics, but at times she has criticized and even opposed major agreements she said did not adequately protect workers. As a candidate for president in 2015-2016, she has distanced herself from the Trans-Pacific Partnership, urging President Obama to heed the warnings of some leading congressional Democrats who say the twelve-nation initiative could displace thousands of American jobs. "Any trade deal has to produce jobs and raise wages and increase prosperity and protect our security." In October, after the twelve member states signed on to the TPP, Clinton said the proposed trade deal failed to meet her standards. "I have said from the very beginning that we had to have a trade agreement that would create good American jobs, raise wages and advance our national security, and I still believe that is the high bar we have to meet. I don't believe it's going to meet the high bar I have set."

Clinton officially supported the TPP during her time as secretary of state. In 2011 she wrote that the agreement was central to the Obama administration's strategic pivot to Asia, and described it in 2012 as "the gold standard in trade agreements." In her 2014 memoir *Hard Choices*, she wrote: "It's safe to say that TPP won't be perfect—no deal negotiated among a dozen countries ever will be—but its higher standards, if implemented and enforced, should benefit American businesses and workers."

Clinton favored reauthorizing the U.S. Export-Import Bank, a decades-old trade promotion agency that many Republicans say distorts the free market. "Across our country, the Export-Import Bank supports up to 164,000 jobs," Clinton said weeks before the bank lost its charter in June 2015.

As a senator from New York (2001–2009), Clinton's record on trade was mixed: She voted in favor of bilateral agreements with Australia, Chile, Jordan, Morocco, Oman, Peru, and Singapore, but voted against the Central American Free Trade Agreement on grounds that it lacked robust protections for foreign workers. As a candidate for president in 2007, she called NAFTA, an accord signed into law by President Bill Clinton in 1993, "flawed" and vowed to renegotiate some of its components.

TRUMP:

Donald Trump says he favors free trade, but he has opposed several U.S. trade agreements because he says they were poorly negotiated and resulted in Americans losing jobs. In September 2015, he called the North American Free Trade Agreement a disaster, saying that his administration would "either renegotiate it or we will break it" if he becomes president. Trump says he would penalize U.S. companies that shift manufacturing outside the country. He called out Ford Motor Company specifically in his June 2015 speech announcing his candidacy, saying he would impose a 35 percent tax on vehicles the automaker exports to the United States from new plants in Mexico. (Ford says its recent investments in Mexico help keep it globally competitive.)

Trump also opposes the Trans-Pacific Partnership (TPP), the Obama administration's free trade agreement with Pacific Rim nations. He says the deal was concluded in secrecy and it will primarily benefit other countries, particularly China (not part of the TPP) and Japan, and large U.S. corporations.

In November 2015, Trump outlined his plan for reforming U.S. trade relations with China. He would as president formally designate China a currency manipulator, crack down on what he says is its theft of U.S. intellectual property, and expose its various export subsidy practices. Trump would also seek to lower the U.S. corporate income tax rate, decrease the national debt, and ramp up the U.S. military presence in the Asia-Pacific region, all of which he says would bolster Washington's bargaining position with respect to Beijing.

B. ACROSS THE BOARD ISSUES

	CLINTON	TRUMP
1. Should the death penalty be allowed?	YES	YES
2. Should the United States abide by its treaties with Native American tribes?	YES	?
3. Should private prisons be slowed in the United States?	NO	YES
4. Should Law Enforcement by allowed to use Racial profiling?	NO	YES
5. Should Supreme Court Justice Scalia's replacement be chosen by President Obama?	YES	NO
6. Should the U.S. continue the War on Drugs?	NO	No position
7. Should Churches, Temples, Mosques, Synagogues, etc. remain tax exempt?	?	YES
8. Does lowering the Corporate Income Tax rate create jobs?	No position	YES
9. Should the Federal Government continue to subsidize oil companies?	NO	NO
10. Should any federal taxes be increased?	YES	NO
11. Should there be a flat tax on income?	NO	No position

	CLINTON	TRUMP
12. Should Glass-Steagall be reinstated?	NO	No position
13. Should the U.S. return to the gold standard in which coin and currency are backed by gold?	No position	No position
14. Should Social Security be privatized?	NO	No position
15. Is the Trans-Pacific Partnership Agreement (TPP) good for America?	NO	NO
16. Is the growth of Charter Schools good for education in America?	No position	YES
17. Are the common core standards good for education in America?	No position	NO
18. Should and public colleges or universities be tuition free?	YES	NO
19. Was the *Citizens United* Supreme Court decision good for America?	NO	NO
20. Should the Presidential Debates include third party candidates?	No position	YES
21. Should felons who have completed their Sentences be allowed to vote?	YES	No position
22. Should voters be required to show photo identification in order to vote?	NO	No position
23. Should U.S. election campaigns be publicly financed?	YES	No position

	CLINTON	TRUMP
24. Should new fossil fuel leases on federal Land be allowed?	No position	YES
25. Should fracking be allowed?	YES	YES
26. Is China an economic or military threat to the U.S.?	YES	YES
27. Should the United States maintain its embargo against Cuba?	NO	NO
28. Is the nuclear arms deal with Iran good for America?	YES	NO
29. Should there be an independent Palestinian state?	YES	No position
30. Should more gun control laws be enacted?	YES	NO
31. Should schools be gun-free zones?	YES	No position
32. Should people on the no-fly list or the terror watch list be allowed to purchase guns?	NO	NO
33. Should aborti0on be legal?	YES	YES
34. Should any vaccines be required for children?	No position	No position
35. Is Obamacare good for America?	YES	NO
36. Should parental consent be required for pregnant minors to have abortions?	NO	?

	CLINTON	TRUMP
37. Should euthanasia or physician-assisted suicide be legal?	YES	?
38. Should Planned Parenthood receive federal funding?	YES	NO
39. Should all Americans have the right (be entitled to) health care?	YES	No position
40. Should the federal government use raids to enforce Immigration law?	NO	YES
41. Should checking immigration status for all employees be mandatory for all employers	?	YES
42. Should the United States continue to build the fence/wall along the U.S. / Mexico border?	No position	YES
43. Should undocumented immigrants in the U.S. be allowed to become legal residents?	YES	NO
44. Should Sanctuary Cities be continue to receive federal funding for Law Enforcement?	No position	NO
45. Should the United States allow Syrian refugees into the country?	YES	NO
46. Should the federal government guarantee paid family and medical leave?	YES	No position
47. Should the federal minimum wage be increased?	YES	UES
48. Do labor unions provide an overall benefit to their workers in the United States?	YES	No position

	CLINTON	TRUMP
49. Should marijuana be a medical option?	YES	YES
50. Should recreational marijuana be legal?	No position	No position
51. Should the U.S. and Russia collaborate to Combat terrorism?	No position	YES
52. Should the U.S. continue its drone strikes abroad?	YES	No position
53. Should the U.S. send ground troops to combat ISIS?	NO	YES
54. Should the U.S. close the Guantanamo Bay Detention Camp?	YES	NO
55. Should the U.S. military budget be increased?	No position	VARIES
56. Should the U.S. have mandatory military or civilian national service?	NO	?
57. Should the National Security Agency (NSA) continue to collect phone and email metadata on U.S. citizens?	NO	YES
58. Should waterboarding or other extreme interrogation techniques be a legal option?	NO	YES
59. Should women be allowed to serve in military combat positions?	YES	No position
60. Should colleges and universities use Affirmative Action for admissions?	YES	YES

	CLINTON	TRUMP
61. Is the Black Lives Matter movement good for U.S.?	YES	No position
62. Is the criminal justice system unfair to Black people?	YES	No position
63. Is human activity responsible for global climate change?	YES	NO
64. Should genetically modified foods (GMO's) have mandatory labeling?	YES	NO
65. Should the U.S. authorize the Keystone XL pipeline to import tar sand oil from Canada?	NO	YES
66. Should the U.S. transition away from fossil fuels and toward renewable energy?	YES	NO
67. Was the U.S. Supreme Court decision legalizing same sex marriages a good decision?	YES	No position
68. Should religious liberty give people the right to deny goods and services for gay marriage?	NO	No position
69. Should transgender people be allowed to use the bathroom of their choice?	YES	No position

13

THE CANDIDATES' PLATFORM ISSUES

A. HILLARY CLINTON

(Source: Hillary Clinton's Official Website)

1. TAX SYSTEM

Hillary Clinton believes that we need an economy that works for everyone, not just those at the top. But when it comes to taxes, too often the wealthiest and the largest corporations are playing by a different set of rules than hardworking families.

Hillary is committed to restoring basic fairness in our tax code and ensuring that the wealthiest Americans and large corporations pay their fair share, while providing tax relief to working families. That's not only fair, it's good for economic growth, because she will use the proceeds to create good-paying jobs here in America—and make bold investments that leave our economy more competitive over the long run.

As president, Hillary will:

- **Restore basic fairness to our tax code.** Hillary will implement a "fair share surcharge" on multi-millionaires and billionaires and fight for measures like the Buffett Rule to ensure the wealthiest Americans do not pay a lower tax rate than hardworking middle-class families. She'll close loopholes that create a private tax system for the most fortunate, and she'll ensure multi-million-dollar estates are paying their fair share of taxes.

- **Close corporate and Wall Street tax loopholes and invest in America.** Hillary will close tax loopholes like inversions that reward companies for shifting profits and jobs overseas. She will charge an "exit tax" for companies leaving the U.S. to settle up on their untaxed foreign earnings. She will close tax loopholes that let Wall Street money managers pay lower rates than some middle-class families. And she'll reward businesses that invest in good-paying jobs here in the United States.

- **Simplify and cut taxes for small businesses so they can hire and grow.** The smallest businesses, with one to five employees, spend 150 hours and $1,100 per employee on federal tax compliance. That's more than 20 times higher than the average for far larger firms. We've got to fix that.

- **Provide tax relief to working families from the rising costs they face.** For too many years, middle-class families have been squeezed by rising costs for everything from child care to health care to affording college. Hillary will offer relief from these rising costs, including tax relief for Americans facing excessive out-of-pocket health care costs and for those caring for an ill or elderly family member.

- **Pay for ambitious investments in a fiscally responsible way.** Hillary believes that we can afford to pay for ambitious, progressive investments in good-paying jobs, debt-free college, and other measures to strengthen growth, broaden opportunity, and reduce inequality. Hillary will use the proceeds from ensuring the wealthiest and the largest corporations pay their fair share to pay for these investments without adding to the debt.

2. ADDICTION AND SUBSTANCE ABUSE

Nearly 23 million Americans suffer from a substance use disorder, yet only about one in 10 receive treatment. Addiction and substance use disorders touch the lives of people in big cities and small towns, across every income level. We can't arrest or incarcerate our way out of it—we need a new approach. That's why Hillary Clinton is proposing a bold plan to prevent and treat addiction, support people in recovery, and take on this epidemic once and for all. Hillary will launch a $7.5 billion fund to support new federal-state partnerships that empower local leaders to implement programs that work for their communities.

As president, Hillary will focus on:

- **Prevention:** Let's empower communities to implement programs to teach adolescents about drug use and addiction.

- **Treatment and recovery:** Substance use disorders are chronic diseases, and recovery is only possible through effective and ongoing care—not neglect or stigmatization. Everyone who needs treatment and ongoing support should be able to get it. We should invest in and empower our recovery community organizations.

- **First responders:** All first responders should have access to naloxone, a drug that can prevent opioid overdoses from becoming fatal.

- **Prescribers:** Drug prescribers will have to meet standards for training and go through a prescription drug monitoring program before writing a prescription for controlled medications.

- **Criminal justice reform:** Let's prioritize rehabilitation and treatment over prison for low-level and nonviolent drug offenses and work to end the era of mass incarceration.

3. ECONOMY – 5 POINT PLAN

Despite the progress we've made in coming back from the Great Recession, we face a set of core challenges to building an economy that works for everyone—including a political system that is doing too little to help working Americans, an economic system that encourages too many corporations to favor short-term profits over long-term investments, and outdated workplace policies that aren't meeting the needs of modern families.

As president, Hillary has a five-point plan to meet these challenges:

- **A 100-days jobs plan: Break through Washington gridlock to make the boldest investment in good-paying jobs since World War II.** Hillary will fight to pass a plan in her first 100 days in office to invest in infrastructure, manufacturing, research and technology, clean energy, and small businesses. She will strengthen trade enforcement, and she'll say no to trade deals like TPP that don't meet a high enough bar of creating good-paying jobs. And she will make the U.S. the clean energy superpower of the world—with half a billion solar panels installed by the end of her first term and enough clean, renewable energy to power every home in America within 10 years of her taking office.

- **Make debt free college available to all Americans.** Hillary will make college debt-free, and she'll provide relief for Americans with existing debt by allowing them to refinance their student loans.

- **Rewrite the rules so that more companies share profits with employees—and fewer ship profits and jobs overseas.** Hillary will reward companies that share profits and invest in their workers, and she will raise the minimum wage to a living wage. She will crack down on companies that shift profits overseas to avoid paying U.S. taxes, and she'll make companies that export jobs give back the tax breaks they've received in America. She will defend existing Wall Street reform and push for new measures to strengthen it.

- **Make certain that corporations, the wealthy, and Wall Street pay their fair share.** Hillary will pay for her economic priorities and avoid adding to the national debt by ensuring the wealthiest Americans and the biggest corporations pay their fair share. For example, she'll fight for the Buffett Rule, close the carried interest loophole, and impose a new surcharge on multi-millionaires and billionaires.

- **Enact policies that meet the challenges families face in the 21st-century economy.** Hillary will make it possible for parents to succeed at work and at home by updating outdated laws so they match how families work today. She will fight for equal pay and guarantee paid leave, two changes that are long overdue. And she will provide relief from the rising costs of necessities like child care and housing, while taking steps to provide Americans with greater retirement and health care security.

4. ALZHEIMER'S DISEASE

Alzheimer's disease is the sixth leading cause of death in the United States. It's the only cause of death in the top 10 that we can't prevent, cure, or even delay.

As the population of our country ages, the number of people suffering from Alzheimer's is expected to grow to nearly 15 million Americans—and could cost more than $1 trillion per year—by 2050.

As president, Hillary will:

- **Commit to preventing, effectively treating, and making a cure possible for Alzheimer's disease by 2025.**

- **Invest $2 billion per year in research for Alzheimer's and related disorders**, the level leading researchers have determined necessary to prevent and effectively treat Alzheimer's and make a cure possible by 2025.

- **Make sure that funding is reliable and consistent so researchers can work steadily toward effective treatment.**

- **Put the best and brightest on the case.** Hillary will appoint a top-flight team of research and health experts to oversee this ambitious initiative.

Alzheimer's disease affects a growing number of Americans and their families. To support those families, Hillary will:

- **Make it easier for families and individuals with Alzheimer's to get the care they need.** Medicare should cover comprehensive Alzheimer's care-planning sessions and the cost of properly documenting every diagnosis and care plan.

- **Help protect loved ones who wander.** Hillary will work with Congress to reauthorize the Missing Alzheimer's Disease Patient Alert Program to help find individuals who are reported missing.

- **Ensure our seniors are aware and can take advantage of their Medicare benefits.** Hillary will direct the Social Security Administration to raise awareness about the wellness visits, cognitive screenings, and other preventive benefits covered by Medicare.

Hillary's plan builds on her long record of working across the aisle on behalf of patients and families dealing with Alzheimer's disease:

- In the U.S. Senate, she consistently pushed for greater funding for Alzheimer's research, including federally funded stem cell research.

- She also co-chaired the Congressional Task Force on Alzheimer's Disease and introduced legislation to restore funding for the Alzheimer's Association 24/7 Contact Center and for Alzheimer's disease demonstration grants.

5. AUTISM

More than 3.5 million Americans are believed to have autism spectrum disorder (ASD)—including an estimated one in every 68 children. And the cost of treatment and services is more than most families can afford. Improving support for children and adults with autism can vastly improve their lives—and make the cost more sustainable for families.

Hillary Clinton is proposing a new, wide-ranging autism initiative that will:

- **Expand insurance coverage for autism services.** Hillary will improve access to autism services through healthcare. gov and private health insurance plans.

- **Conduct a nationwide early screening outreach campaign.** Hillary's plan will boost early screening rates so that kids can get diagnosed and receive the services that will make a difference in their lives.

- **Invest in more research to deepen our understanding of autism.** As president, Hillary will significantly increase funding for autism-related research and call for the first-ever nationwide study of the prevalence of adult autism.

- **Increase employment opportunities for individuals with autism.** Hillary will work to close the employment gap by launching a new Autism Works Initiative that will include a post-graduation transition plan for every student with autism, along with a public-private partnership to connect people with autism to employment opportunities.

- **Keep students with autism safe at school.** Hillary will work to ensure students with disabilities, including autism, are protected from bullying at school.

Hillary has a long record of advocating for children and families affected by autism, describing the disease in 2007 as "one of the most urgent—and least understood—challenges facing our children."

- As first lady, she fought hard for more awareness and funding for autism, including supporting the bipartisan Children's Health Act of 2000, which had a special focus on autism research.

- In the Senate, she introduced the bipartisan Expanding the Promise for Individuals with Autism Act (EPIAA) to expand access to interventions and support for Americans with autism. And she cosponsored legislation in 2006 that authorized hundreds of millions of dollars in new spending on autism-related programs, including research, education, early detection, and intervention.

6. CAMPAIGN FINANCE REFORM

Americans are understandably cynical about a political system that has been hijacked by billionaires and special interests. That's why Hillary Clinton is putting forward a plan for aggressive campaign finance reform. She'll work to curb the outsized influence of big money in American politics, shine a light on secret spending, and fight to make our democracy work for everyone— not just the wealthy and well-connected.

As president, Hillary will:

- **Overturn** *Citizens United*—**the Supreme Court case that unleashed hundreds of millions of dollars in corporate and special-interest money into U.S. elections.** Hillary will appoint Supreme Court justices who will protect Americans' right to vote over the right of billionaires to buy elections. She will also propose a constitutional amendment to overturn *Citizens United* within her first 30 days in office.

- **End secret, unaccountable money in politics.** We need federal legislation to require outside groups to publicly disclose significant political spending. And until Congress acts, Hillary will sign an executive order requiring federal government contractors to do the same. She'll also push for an SEC rule requiring publicly traded companies to disclose political spending to shareholders.

- **Amplify the voices of everyday Americans.** Hillary will establish a small-donor matching system for presidential and congressional elections to give small donors greater influence.

7. CAMPUS SEXUAL ASSAULT

An estimated one in five women reports being sexually assaulted while in college. Hillary Clinton will fight to bring an end to sexual assault on America's campuses—because every student deserves a safe environment where they can learn and thrive, not live in fear.

Thanks to the efforts of advocates and survivors, we are seeing the beginnings of good work around the country. President Obama's administration has worked hard to shine a light on campus sexual assault.

Hillary's plan to end campus sexual assault is guided by three core principles:

1. **Provide comprehensive support to survivors.** Every campus should offer survivors the support they need—no matter their gender, sexual orientation, ethnicity, or race. Those services, from counseling to critical health care, should be confidential, comprehensive, and coordinated.

2. **Ensure a fair process for all.** Too often, the process of addressing a sexual assault on campus is confusing and convoluted. Many who choose to report sexual assault in the criminal justice system fear that their voices will be dismissed instead of heard. We need a fair process for all involved, whether that's in campus disciplinary proceedings or in the

criminal justice system. All parties involved should have notice and transparency in campus disciplinary proceedings, and complaints filed in the criminal justice system must be treated seriously.

3. **Increasing prevention efforts.** It's not enough to address this problem by responding only once sexual assault occurs—we need to redouble our prevention efforts and start them earlier. We should increase sexual violence prevention education programs that cover issues like consent and bystander intervention and make sure we have programs not only in college but also in secondary school.

Hillary has led efforts to address violence against women her entire career:

- As first lady, Hillary supported the creation of the Department of Justice's Office on Violence against Women. She cast a global spotlight on the issue in her historic 1995 Beijing speech, where she denounced violence against women as a clear violation of human rights.

- As senator, Hillary co-sponsored the 2005 reauthorization of the Violence against Women Act. Additionally, Hillary intro-duced the CARE Act twice, to ensure that rape and incest victims had access to emergency contraception in hospital emergency rooms. In response to the spike in reports of sex-ual assault cases in the military, she introduced legislation to make emergency contraception available to servicewomen.

- As secretary of state, Hillary rallied the international community to take collective action to end violence against women. She drew attention to the use of rape as a weapon of war and spearheaded a U.N. Resolution that established guidelines for an international response to sexual assault in war-torn areas.

8. CLIMATE CHANGE

Climate change is an urgent threat and a defining challenge of our time. It threatens our economy, our national security, and our children's health and futures. We can tackle it by making America the world's clean energy superpower and creating millions of good-paying jobs, taking bold steps to slash carbon pollution at home and around the world, and ensuring no Americans are left out or left behind as we rapidly build a clean energy economy.

On day one, Hillary Clinton will set bold, national goals that will be achieved within 10 years of taking office:

- Generate enough renewable energy to power every home in America, with half a billion solar panels installed by the end of Hillary's first term.

- Cut energy waste in American homes, schools, hospitals and offices by a third and make American manufacturing the cleanest and most efficient in the world.

- Reduce American oil consumption by a third through cleaner fuels and more efficient cars, boilers, ships, and trucks.

Hillary's plan will deliver on the pledge President Obama made at the Paris climate conference—without relying on climate deniers in Congress to pass new legislation. She will reduce greenhouse gas emissions by up to 30 percent in 2025 relative to 2005 levels and put the country on a path to cut emissions more than 80 percent by 2050.

As president, Hillary will:

Defend, implement, and extend smart pollution and efficiency standards, including the Clean Power Plan and standards for cars, trucks, and appliances that are already helping clean our air, save families money, and fight climate change.

- **Launch a $60 billion Clean Energy Challenge** to partner with states, cities, and rural communities to cut carbon pollution and expand clean energy, including for low-income families.

- **Invest in clean energy infrastructure, innovation, manufacturing and workforce development** to make the U.S. economy more competitive and create good-paying jobs and careers.

- **Ensure safe and responsible energy production.** As we transition to a clean energy economy, we must ensure that the fossil fuel production taking place today is safe and responsible and that areas too sensitive for energy production are taken off the table.

- **Reform leasing** and expand clean energy production on public lands and waters tenfold within a decade.

- **Cut the billions of wasteful tax subsidies oil and gas companies** have enjoyed for too long and invest in clean energy.

- **Cut methane emissions across the economy** and put in place strong standards for reducing leaks from both new and existing sources.

- **Revitalize coal communities** by supporting locally driven priorities and make them an engine of U.S. economic growth in the 21st century, as they have been for generations.

- **Make environmental justice and climate justice central priorities** by setting bold national goals to eliminate lead poisoning within five years, clean up the more than 450,000 toxic brownfield sites across the country, expand solar and energy efficiency solutions in low-income communities, and create an Environmental and Climate Justice Task Force.

- **Promote conservation and collaborative stewardship.**
  Hillary will keep public lands public, strengthen protections
  for our natural and cultural resources, increase access to
  parks and public lands for all Americans, as well as harness
  the immense economic potential they offer through expanded
  renewable energy production, a high quality of life, and a
  thriving outdoor economy.

9. COMBATTING TERRORISM: KEEP THE HOMELAND SAFE

The threat we face from terrorism is real, urgent, and knows
no boundaries. Horrific attacks like the ones in Paris, Brussels,
Orlando, and San Bernardino have made it all too clear: It is not
enough to contain ISIS and the threat of radical jihadism—we
have to defeat it. Hillary Clinton has laid out a comprehensive
plan to do that:

1. Take out ISIS's stronghold in Iraq and Syria

We have to defeat ISIS on the battlefield by:

- Intensifying the coalition air campaign against ISIS fighters,
  leaders, and infrastructure;

- Stepping up support for local Arab and Kurdish forces on the
  ground and coalition efforts to protect civilians; and

- Pursuing a diplomatic strategy aimed at resolving Syria's
  civil war and Iraq's sectarian conflict between Sunnis and
  Shias—both of which have contributed to the rise of ISIS.

2. Work with our allies to dismantle global terror networks

**We have to stem the flow of jihadists from Europe and America
to and from Iraq, Syria, and Afghanistan.** To that end, we must

work with our allies to dismantle the global terror network that supplies radical jihadists with money, weapons, and fighters. That means:

- Working hand in hand with European intelligence services to identify and go after enablers who help jihadists forge documents and travel undetected;

- Targeting efforts to deal with ISIS affiliates from Libya to Afghanistan; and

- Working with tech companies to fight jihadist propaganda online, intercept ISIS communications, and track and analyze social media posts to stop attacks—while protecting security and privacy.

3. Harden our defenses at home

We have to do more to identify and stop terrorists—including so-called "lone wolves"—from carrying out attacks in the United States, including:

- Supporting first responders, law enforcement, and intelligence officers with the right tools, resources, intelligence, and training to prevent attacks before they happen;

- Launching an intelligence surge to get security officials the tools they need to prevent attacks;

- Keeping assault weapons and other tools of terror out of terrorists' hands by allowing the FBI to stop gun sales to suspected terrorists, enacting comprehensive background checks, and keeping military-style assault weapons off our streets; and

- Supporting law enforcement to build trustful and strong relationships with American Muslim communities. We need every American community invested in this fight, not fearful and sitting on the sidelines.

10. CRIMINAL JUSTICE REFORM

People are crying out for criminal justice reform. Families are being torn apart by excessive incarceration. Young people are being threatened and humiliated by racial profiling. Children are growing up in homes shattered by prison and poverty. They're trying to tell us. We need to listen.

The United States has less than 5 percent of the world's population but almost 25 percent of the total prison population. A significant percentage of the more than 2 million Americans incarcerated today are nonviolent offenders. African American men are far more likely to be stopped and searched by police, charged with crimes, and sentenced to longer prison terms than white men found guilty of the same offenses.

To successfully reform our criminal justice system, we must work to strengthen the bonds of trust between our communities and our police, end the era of mass incarceration, and ensure a successful transition of individuals from prison to home. As president, Hillary will focus on a few key areas.

Strengthen bonds of trust between communities and police

Effective policing and constitutional policing go hand in hand. We can—and must—do both by:

- Bringing law enforcement and communities together to develop national guidelines on the use of force by police officers, making it clear when deadly force is warranted and when it isn't and emphasizing proven methods for de-escalating situations.

- **Acknowledging that implicit bias still exists across society—even in the best police departments—and tackle it together.** Hillary will commit $1 billion in her first budget to find and fund the best training programs, support new research, and make this a national policing priority.

- **Making new investments to support state-of-the-art law enforcement training programs at every level** on issues like use of force, de-escalation, community policing and problem solving, alternatives to incarceration, crisis intervention, and officer safety and wellness.

- **Supporting legislation to end racial profiling** by federal, state, and local law enforcement officials.

- **Strengthening the U.S. Department of Justice's pattern or practice unit**—the unit that monitors civil rights violations—by increasing the department's resources, working to secure subpoena power, and improving data collection for pattern or practice investigations.

- **Doubling funding for the U.S. Department of Justice "Collaborative Reform" program.** Across the country, there are police departments deploying creative and effective strategies that we can learn from and build on. Hillary will provide assistance and training to agencies that apply these best practices.

- **Providing federal matching funds to make body cameras available to every police department in America.**

- **Promoting oversight and accountability in use of controlled equipment,** including by limiting the transfer of military equipment to local law enforcement from the federal government, eliminating the one-year use requirement, and requiring transparency from agencies that purchase equipment using federal funds.

- **Collecting and reporting national data** to inform policing strategies and provide greater transparency and accountability when it comes to crime, officer-involved shootings, and deaths in custody.

End the era of mass incarceration

Today in America, more than one out of every 100 adults is behind bars. This mass incarceration epidemic has an explicit racial bias, as one in three black men can expect to go to prison in their lifetime. A significant number of those incarcerated are held for low-level, nonviolent offenses. We must end the era of mass incarceration by:

- **Reforming mandatory minimum sentencing.** Excessive federal mandatory minimum sentences keep nonviolent drug offenders in prison for too long—and have increased racial inequality in our criminal justice system. Hillary will reform this system by:
  - ◊ Cutting mandatory minimum sentences for nonviolent drug offenses in half.
  - ◊ Allowing current nonviolent prisoners to seek fairer sentences.
  - ◊ Eliminating the sentencing disparity for crack and powder cocaine so that equal amounts of crack and powder cocaine carry equal sentences, and applying this change retroactively.
  - ◊ Reforming the "strike" system, so that nonviolent drug offenses no longer count as a "strike," reducing the mandatory penalty for second- and third-strike offenses.
- **Focusing federal enforcement resources on violent crime, not simple marijuana possession.** Marijuana arrests, including for simple possession, account for a large number of drug arrests. Significant racial disparities exist in marijuana enforcement—black men are significantly more likely to be

arrested for marijuana possession than their white counter-parts, despite the fact that their usage rates are similar. Hillary will allow states that have enacted marijuana laws to act as laboratories of democracy and reschedule marijuana from a Schedule I to a Schedule II substance.

- **Prioritizing treatment and rehabilitation—rather than incarceration—for low-level, nonviolent drug offenders.** More than half of prison and jail inmates suffer from a mental health problem. Up to 65 percent of the correctional population meets the medical criteria for a substance use disorder. Hillary will ensure law enforcement is properly trained for crisis intervention and referral to treatment as appropriate, direct the attorney general to urge federal prosecutors to seek treatment over incarceration for low-level, nonviolent drug crimes.

- **Dismantling the school-to-prison pipeline.** Hillary will work to dismantle the school-to-prison pipeline by providing $2 billion in support to schools to reform overly punitive disciplinary policies, calling on states to reform school disturbance laws, and encouraging states to use federal education funding to implement social and emotional support interventions.

- **Ending the privatization of prisons.** Hillary believes we should move away from contracting out this core responsibility of the federal government to private corporations. We must not create private industry incentives that may contribute—or have the appearance of contributing—to over-incarceration. The campaign does not accept contributions from federally registered lobbyists or PACs for private prison companies and will donate any such direct contributions to charity.

Promote successful re-entry by formerly incarcerated individuals

This year, the number of people released from state or federal prison will reach approximately 600,000. For the sake of everyone given a second chance—as well as the health and safety of the communities to which they return—the pathway to re-entry should offer a fair opportunity for success. Hillary will work to remove barriers and create pathways to employment, housing, health care, education, and civic participation, including:

- **Taking executive action to "ban the box" for federal employers and contractors,** so that applicants have an opportunity to demonstrate their qualifications before being asked about their criminal records.

- **Investing $5 billion in re-entry job programs for formerly incarcerated individuals** so that individuals can have a fair shot at getting back on their feet and becoming productive, contributing members of society.

- **Supporting legislation to restore voting rights to individuals who have served their sentences.**

11. DISABILITY RIGHTS

We should acknowledge how the disabilities community has played such an important role in changing things for the better in our country.

The Americans with Disabilities Act (ADA) was a tremendous step forward: It opened educational opportunities, expanded transportation, made sure everyone can enter buildings, and ensured that no one would be turned down for a job because of a disability. Hillary Clinton is committed to realizing the promise of the ADA and continuing to expand opportunity for the 50 million Americans living with a disability—because we're stronger together.

As president, Hillary will:

- Work to fulfill the promise of the Americans with Disabilities Act.

- Expand support for Americans with disabilities to live in integrated community settings.

- Improve access to meaningful, gainful employment for people with disabilities.

- Provide tax relief to help the millions of families caring for aging relatives or family members with chronic illnesses or disabilities.

Hillary has spent her life fighting for the rights of Americans with disabilities.

- Hillary's first job out of law school was with the Children's Defense Fund, and one of her first tasks was going door to door to figure out why so many children were missing school. She found that many parents were not sending their children to school because schools did not accommodate disabilities. The evidence she gathered was presented to Congress, and it helped build the case for the passage of the law that ensures all children with disabilities have access to school.

- As secretary of state, Hillary worked to build strong support for the United States to join the United Nations Convention on the Rights of Persons with Disabilities. But despite a broad, bipartisan coalition, the Republican-controlled Senate blocked its passage.

- Today, Hillary recognizes that there is still much work to do, including improving access to meaningful and gainful employment, as well as housing in integrated community settings, for people with disabilities. Too many Americans with disabilities continue to be left out of the workforce, and for those who are employed, too many are in under-stimulating jobs that don't fully allow them to use their talents. And too many end up having to live in separate facilities when they should have the opportunity to live at home and be in their communities.

- As a presidential candidate, Hillary has been proud to partner with the disabilities community. She's stood up to those who bully and belittle Americans with disabilities—and she will continue to champion their rights as president.

12. EARLY CHILDHOOD EDUCATION

Expanding early childhood education has been close to Hillary Clinton's heart throughout her career. As first lady of Arkansas, she introduced the Home Instruction for Parents of Preschool Youngsters (HIPPY) program, which helps parents teach their children at home before they begin kindergarten. As a U.S. senator, she called for a national initiative to help establish high-quality pre-K programs, including providing pre-K at no cost to children from low-income homes and homes with limited English speaking. As president, Hillary will continue to fight to give every child access to a quality education, starting with our youngest learners.

As president, Hillary will:

- **Make preschool universal for every 4-year-old in America.** Despite research showing its benefits, only about half of the roughly 8.1 million 3- and 4-year-olds in the United States are enrolled in preschool, with only one in four enrolled in publicly funded preschool. Hillary believes that every child deserves the same strong start. That's why she will work to ensure that every 4-year-old in America has access to high-quality preschool in the next 10 years.

- **Significantly increase child care investments so that no family in America has to pay more than 10 percent of its income to afford high-quality child care.** The cost of child care has increased by nearly 25 percent during the past decade, while the wages of working families have stagnated. While families across America are stretched by skyrocketing costs, child care has become more important than ever before—both as a critical work support for the changing structure of American families and as an essential component of a child's early development. These high costs severely squeeze working families, prevent too many children from getting a healthy start, and act as a disincentive for parents to stay in the workforce. Hillary will fight for every family in America to have access to high quality, affordable child care by significantly increasing the federal government's investment in child care subsidies and providing tax relief for the cost of child care to working families.

- **Improve the quality of child care and early learning by giving a RAISE to America's child care workforce.** One of the key drivers of high-quality child care is a supported and effective child care workforce. Yet, despite the high cost of child care, too many workers are not receiving a living wage, which fuels turnover and undermines the quality of care— and also causes many of those caring for and educating our children to live in poverty themselves. To increase the quality of child care in America and pay child care workers for the true value of their work, Hillary will create the Respect and

Increased Salaries for Early Childhood Educators (RAISE) initiative. In line with Clinton's Care Workers Initiative, RAISE will fund and support states and local communities that work to increase the compensation of child care providers and early educators and provide equity with kindergarten teachers by investing in educational opportunities, career ladders, and professional salaries.

- **Double our investment in Early Head Start and the Early Head Start–Child Care Partnership program.** Early Head Start provides comprehensive services to our youngest learners and their families—including health, nutrition, and pre-literacy support with a strong focus on children's social and emotional development. The Early Head Start–Child Care Partnership program brings Early Head Start's evidence-based curriculum into the child care setting to provide comprehensive, full-day, high-quality services to low-income families. To ensure our children have a strong foundation to learn, Hillary will double the number of children served by Early Head Start and the Early Head Start–Child Care Partnership program.

- **Expand access to evidence-based home visiting programs.** There is increasing scientific evidence that brain development in the earliest years of childhood is crucial to economic success. That's why Hillary will double our investment in home visiting programs such as the Maternal, Infant, and Early Childhood Home Visiting (MIECHV) program. These programs—which provide home visits by a social worker or nurse during and directly after pregnancy—significantly improve maternal and child health, development, and learning.

- **Award scholarships of up to $1,500 per year to help as many as 1 million student parents afford high-quality**

child care. More than 25 percent of all college students are balancing school with raising a child. We should support them, not only because the economic benefit of a college degree lifts their own earning prospects, but also because it lifts the future earnings of their children too. To support America's student parents, Hillary will launch the Student Parents in America Raising Kids (SPARK) program. SPARK will award scholarships of up to $1,500 per year to as many as 1 million student parents. Recipients can use the awards for costs that create barriers to success—including child care and emergency financial aid.

- **Increase access to high-quality child care on college campuses by serving an additional 250,000 children.** Student parents face many challenges, with greater financial and time constraints than many of their peers. College students who are parents leave school with an average debt that is 25 percent higher than non-parents. The demands of parenting mean that student parents spend two hours less on average per day on educational activities. And while nearly half of student parents attend two-year colleges, less than half of all two-year college campuses in America offer on-campus child care services. Student parents need our support. Hillary will work to dramatically increase access to child care on campus by increasing funding for campus-based child care centers.

13. FIXING AMERICA'S INFRASTRUCTURE

In my first 100 days as president, I will work with both parties to pass a comprehensive plan to create the next generation of good jobs. Now the heart of my plan will be the biggest investment in American infrastructure in decades, including establishing an infrastructure bank that will bring private sector dollars off the sidelines and put them to work there.

In America, we build great things together—from the transcontinental railroad to the interstate highway system to the Hoover Dam. But today, our investments in infrastructure are roughly half what they were 35 years ago. That's why Hillary Clinton has announced a $275 billion, five-year plan to rebuild our infrastructure—and put Americans to work in the process. She'll work to pass her infrastructure plan in her first 100 days of office, as part of a comprehensive agenda to create the next generation of good-paying jobs.

As president, Hillary will:

- **Repair and expand our roads and bridges.** Hillary will make smart investments to improve our roads, reduce congestion, and slash the "pothole tax" that drivers silently pay each and every day.

- **Lower transportation costs and unlock economic opportunity by expanding public transit options.** Hillary will encourage local governments to work with low-income communities to ensure unemployed and underemployed Americans are connected to good jobs.

- **Connect all Americans to the internet.** Hillary will work to ensure that by 2020, 100 percent of households in America will have access to affordable broadband. She will also invest new resources in bringing free Wi-Fi to public buildings and public transportation.

- **Invest in building world-class American airports and modernize our national airspace system.** These invest-ments will reduce carbon emissions and save travelers and airlines an estimated $100 billion in avoided delays over the next 15 years.

- **Build energy infrastructure for the 21st century.** We can unlock America's clean energy potential by modernizing infrastructure like dams, levees, and wastewater systems—saving billions of gallons in clean drinking water and generating clean energy.

14. GUN VIOLENCE PREVENTION

Too many families in America have suffered—and continue to suffer—from gun violence. It's the leading cause of death among young African American men—more than the following nine causes combined. America cannot go on like this.

As president, Hillary will:

- **Expand background checks** to more gun sales—including by closing the gun show and internet sales loopholes—and strengthen the background check system by getting rid of the so-called "Charleston Loophole."

- **Take on the gun lobby** by removing the industry's sweeping legal protection for illegal and irresponsible actions (which makes it almost impossible for people to hold them accountable), and revoking licenses from dealers who break the law.

- **Keep guns out of the hands of domestic abusers, other violent criminals, and the severely mentally ill** by supporting laws that stop domestic abusers from buying and owning guns, making it a federal crime for someone to intentionally buy a gun for a person prohibited from owning one, and closing the loopholes that allow people suffering from severe mental illness to purchase and own guns. She will also support work to keep military-style weapons off our streets.

Hillary has a record of advocating for commonsense approaches to reduce gun violence:

- As first lady, she co-convened a White House Summit on School Violence after the Columbine tragedy, and strongly defended the Brady Bill, which instituted federal background checks on some gun sales.

- As senator, she co-sponsored and voted for legislation that would close the gun show loophole, voted against the dangerous immunity protections for gun dealers and manufacturers, and co-sponsored legislation to extend and reinstate the assault weapons ban.

- As a candidate, she is honored to have the endorsement of many groups working to take on the epidemic of violence, including the Brady Campaign to Prevent Gun Violence, the Newtown Action Alliance, and Everytown for Gun Safety— including Moms Demand Action for Gun Sense in America.

15. HEALTH CARE

Hillary Clinton has led and will continue to lead the fight to expand health care access for every American—even when it means standing up to special interests. When insurance companies spent millions to stop her efforts to reform health care in the '90s, she refused to give up. Instead, she worked across the aisle to help pass the Children's Health Insurance Program. Today, it covers 8 million kids. She has never given up on the fight for universal coverage.

As president, Hillary will:

- **Defend and expand the Affordable Care Act, which covers 20 million people.** Hillary will stand up to Republican-led attacks on this landmark law—and build on its success to bring the promise of affordable health care to more people and make a "public option" possible. She will also support letting people over 55 years old buy into Medicare.

- **Bring down out-of-pocket costs like copays and deductibles.** American families are being squeezed by rising out-of-pocket health care costs. Hillary believes that workers should share in slower growth of national health care spending through lower costs.

- **Reduce the cost of prescription drugs.** Prescription drug spending accelerated from 2.5 percent in 2013 to 12.6 percent in 2014. It's no wonder that almost three-quarters of Americans believe prescription drug costs are unreasonable. Hillary believes we need to demand lower drug costs for hardworking families and seniors.

- **Protect consumers from unjustified prescription drug price increases from companies that market long-standing, life-saving treatments and face little or no competition.** Hillary's plan includes new enforcement tools that make drug alternatives available and increase competition, broaden emergency access to high-quality treatments from developed countries with strong safety standards, and hold drug companies accountable for unjustified price increases with new penalties.

- **Fight for health insurance for the lowest-income Americans in every state by incentivizing states to expand Medicaid**—and make enrollment through Medicaid and the Affordable Care Act easier.

- **Expand access to affordable health care to families regardless of immigration status.** Hillary will expand access to affordable health care to families regardless of immigration status by allowing families to buy health insurance on the health exchanges regardless of their immigration status.

- **Expand access to rural Americans, who often have difficulty finding quality, affordable health care.** Hillary will explore cost-effective ways to make more health care providers eligible for telehealth reimbursement under Medicare and other programs, including federally qualified health centers and rural health clinics.

- **Defend access to reproductive health care.** Hillary will work to ensure that all women have access to preventive care, affordable contraception, and safe and legal abortion.

- **Double funding for community health centers, and support the healthcare workforce:** As part of her comprehensive health care agenda, Hillary is committed to doubling the funding for primary-care services at community health centers over the next decade. Hillary also supports President Obama's call for a near tripling of the size of the National Health Service Corps.

16. HIV AND AIDS

We do have the tools to end this epidemic once and for all, but we need to rededicate ourselves to fighting HIV and AIDS and leaving no one behind. That means continuing to increase research and expanding the use of medications like PrEP. It means capping out-of-pocket expenses and drug costs and building on President Obama's national HIV and AIDS strategy. ... And let's reform outdated, stigmatizing HIV criminalization laws.

The AIDS crisis in America began as a quiet, deadly epidemic— and because of discrimination and disregard, it remained that way for far too long. When many in positions of power turned a blind eye, activists, advocates, scientists, and ordinary, heroic people fought with courage and compassion for a national commitment to address the disease. Due to their efforts, the United States has made great progress in the prevention and treatment of HIV and AIDS.

But we still have work to do. HIV and AIDS continue to disproportionately impact communities of color, transgender people, young people and gay and bisexual men. There are still 1.2 million people living with HIV in the United States today, with about 50,000 people newly diagnosed each year. We have reached a critical moment in this fight.

Hillary will continue to fight towards the goal of an AIDS-free generation. As president, she will:

- **Work to fully implement the National HIV/AIDS Strategy.** The National HIV/AIDS Strategy provides an important roadmap in our march towards an AIDS-free generation. As president, Hillary will continue to implement this strategy and ensure a wide range of advocates and stakeholders are advising the Office of National HIV/AIDS Policy on execution.

- **Invest in research to end HIV and AIDS.** The AIDS crisis looks very different now than it did 20 years ago. Our nation's commitment to scientific research means that most people diagnosed with HIV today can live long lives with consistent treatment. Researchers at NIH and elsewhere are poised to make even more progress towards developing long-acting treatments and a cure for HIV. Hillary will support robust investments to ensure this progress continues, and she will protect funding for this vital scientific research.

- **Cap out-of-pocket expenses for people living with HIV and AIDS.** It is unacceptable that a pharmaceutical company can raise the price of medicine for HIV and AIDS patients by more than 5,000 percent. Hillary has a plan to hold the pharmaceutical industry accountable and lower the cost of prescription drugs for Americans, including medications that help to prevent and treat HIV. She'll cap monthly and annual out-of-pocket costs for prescription drugs at $250 and empower Medicare to negotiate lower drug prices. She will also end subsidies drug companies get for direct-to-consumer advertising and instead invest that money in research.

- **Expand utilization of HIV prevention medications, including pre-exposure prophylaxis (PrEP).** PrEP and other medications have proved effective in preventing HIV infections and should be accessible to everyone. Hillary will increase CDC investment to increase knowledge about and uptake of PrEP to ensure populations at greatest risk of infection have access to the drug—particularly transgender individuals and black men who have sex with men (MSM).

- **Fight to extend Medicaid coverage to provide life-saving health care to people living with HIV.** Of the 70,000 people living with HIV who were uninsured before the Affordable Care Act, roughly 47,000 should have been newly eligible for Medicaid. However, the refusal of some states to expand Medicaid coverage has left many ineligible. Hillary will fight until every state expands Medicaid coverage.

- **Reform outdated, stigmatizing HIV criminalization laws.** Hillary will work with advocates, HIV and AIDS organizations, Congress, and others to review and reform outdated and stigmatizing federal HIV criminalization laws— and will call on states to do the same. She will continue to aggressively enforce the Americans with Disabilities Act and other civil rights laws to fight HIV-related discrimination.

- **Increase the number of people on HIV treatment worldwide.** Programs like PEPFAR have made a significant impact on our fight against HIV and AIDS. These efforts have created the framework for progress and enjoyed bipartisan support here at home and broad support around the world. As president, Hillary will increase global funding for HIV and AIDS treatment and prevention.

Hillary has fought for decades to combat HIV and AIDS—and the stigma and pain that accompany it:

- As first lady, Hillary brought together global leaders to strategize and coordinate efforts to take on HIV and AIDS. She advocated for increased funding for U.S. prevention and research efforts—especially for pediatric AIDS—and honored scientists committed to AIDS research.

- In the U.S. Senate, Hillary put forward legislation to expand global AIDS research and assistance and to increase prevention and education. She voted for the creation of PEPFAR and to defend and protect the Ryan White Act. Hillary also voted to increase funding to combat HIV and AIDS. She co-sponsored legislation to extend Medicaid coverage to low-income people with HIV and expand resources for HIV testing and education.

- As secretary of state, Hillary launched a campaign to usher in an AIDS-free generation through prevention and treatment—targeting the populations at greatest risk of contracting HIV. Under her leadership, American aid directly supporting people on antiretroviral treatment increased over 200 percent to reach over 6.7 million men, women, and children around the world. She oversaw the repeal of the HIV travel ban, which prevented people with HIV and AIDS from entering the United States, and led efforts to end mother-to-child transmission.

17. IMMIGRATION REFORM

Hillary has been committed to the immigrant rights community throughout her career. As president, she will work to fix our broken immigration system and stay true to our fundamental American values: that we are a nation of immigrants, and we treat those who come to our country with dignity and respect—and that we embrace immigrants, not denigrate them.

As president, Hillary will:

- **Introduce comprehensive immigration reform.** Hillary will introduce comprehensive immigration reform with a pathway to full and equal citizenship within her first 100 days in office. It will treat every person with dignity, fix the family visa backlog, uphold the rule of law, protect our borders and national security, and bring millions of hardworking people into the formal economy.

- **End the three- and 10-year bars.** The three- and 10-year bars force families—especially those whose members have different citizenship or immigration statuses—into a heartbreaking dilemma: remain in the shadows, or pursue a green card by leaving the country and loved ones behind.

- **Defend President Obama's executive actions—known as DACA and DAPA—against partisan attacks.** The Supreme Court's deadlocked decision on DAPA was a heartbreaking reminder of how high the stakes are in this election. Hillary believes DAPA is squarely within the president's authority and won't stop fighting until we see it through. The estimated 5 million people eligible for DAPA—including DREAMers and parents of Americans and lawful residents—should be protected under the executive actions.

- **Do everything possible under the law to protect families.** If Congress keeps failing to act on comprehensive immigration reform, Hillary will enact a simple system for those with sympathetic cases—such as parents of DREAMers, those with a history of service and contribution to their communities, or those who experience extreme labor violations—to make their case and be eligible for deferred action.

- **Enforce immigration laws humanely.** Immigration enforcement must be humane, targeted, and effective. Hillary will focus resources on detaining and deporting those individuals who pose a violent threat to public safety, and ensure refugees who seek asylum in the U.S. have a fair chance to tell their stories.

- **End family detention and close private immigration detention centers.** Hillary will end family detention for parents and children who arrive at our border in desperate situations and close private immigrant detention centers.

- **Expand access to affordable health care to all families.** We should let families—regardless of immigration status—buy into the Affordable Care Act exchanges. Families who want to purchase health insurance should be able to do so.

- **Promote naturalization.** Hillary will work to expand fee waivers to alleviate naturalization costs, increase access to language programs to encourage English proficiency, and increase outreach and education to help more people navigate the process.

- **Support immigrant integration.** Hillary will create a national Office of Immigrant Affairs, support affordable integration services through $15 million in new grant funding for community navigators and similar organizations, and significantly increase federal resources for adult English language education and citizenship education.

18. JOBS AND WAGES

From the interstate highway system to the Apollo program, our country has a strong tradition of bipartisan investments in our future. Hillary Clinton will break through the gridlock in Washington to make these investments possible again—with a plan she will work to pass in her first 100 days in office.

Hillary will make it a central priority to make sure every American can find a good-paying job, with rising incomes across the board. In order to create jobs today and help businesses create them in the future, she'll make the largest investment in good-paying jobs since World War II.

As president, Hillary will:

- Launch our country's boldest investments in infrastructure since the construction of our interstate highway system in the 1950s.

- Advance our commitment to research and technology in order to create the industries and jobs of the future.

- Establish the U.S. as the clean energy superpower of the world—with half a billion solar panels installed by the end of her first term and enough clean, renewable energy to power every home in America within 10 years of her taking office.

- Strengthen American manufacturing with a $10 billion "Make It In America" plan.

- Cut red tape, provide tax relief and expand access to capital so small businesses can grow, hire, and thrive.

- Ensure that the jobs of the future in caregiving and services are good-paying jobs, recognizing their fundamental contributions to families and to America.

- Pursue smarter, fairer, tougher trade policies that put U.S. job creation first and get tough on nations like China that seek to prosper at the expense of our workers. This includes opposing trade deals like the Trans-Pacific Partnership that do not meet a high bar of creating good-paying jobs and raising pay.

- Commit to a full-employment, full-potential economy and break down barriers so that growth, jobs, and prosperity are shared in every community in America.

19. K-12 EDUCATION

Hillary Clinton believes that every child, no matter his or her background, should be guaranteed a high-quality education. That's why she has been working to improve and support our public schools for decades, but our work isn't done. Hillary will ensure that every child can fulfill his or her God-given potential.

As president, Hillary will:

- **Launch a national campaign to modernize and elevate the profession of teaching.** America is asking more of our educators than ever before. They are preparing our kids for a competitive economy, staying on top of new pedagogies, and filling gaps that we as a country have neglected—like giving low-income kids, English-language learners, and kids with disabilities the support they need to thrive. We ask so much of our educators, but we aren't setting them up for success. That's why Hillary will launch a national campaign to elevate and modernize the teaching profession, by preparing, supporting, and paying every child's teacher as if the future of our country is in their hands—because it is.

- **Provide every student in America an opportunity to learn computer science.** There are more than half a million open jobs that require computing skills—across the country and in every major industry. But the majority of schools in the United States don't offer computer science. Hillary will provide states and school districts funding to help scale computer science instruction and lesson programs that improve student achievement or increase college enrollment and completion in CS Ed fields.

- **Rebuild America's schools.** In cities and rural communities across America, there are public schools that are falling apart—schools where students are learning in classrooms with rodents and mold. That's unacceptable, and it has to change. That's why Hillary will build on the highly successful Build America Bonds program to provide cities and towns the capital they need to rebuild their schools. These "Modernize Every School Bonds" will double the Build America Bonds subsidy for efforts to fix and modernize America's classrooms— from increasing energy efficiency and tackling asbestos to upgrading science labs and high-speed broadband.

- **Dismantle the school-to-prison pipeline.** Schools should be safe places for students to learn and grow. But in too many communities, student discipline is overly harsh—and these harsh measures disproportionately affect African American students and those with the greatest economic, social, and academic needs. Hillary will work to dismantle the school-to-prison pipeline by providing $2 billion in support to schools to reform overly punitive disciplinary policies, calling on states to reform school disturbance laws, and encouraging states to use federal education funding to implement social and emotional support interventions.

Hillary has been working to improve and support our public schools for decades:

- As a young law student working for Marian Wright Edelman, Hillary went undercover to investigate "segregation academies" in Alabama.

- As first lady of Arkansas, she chaired the Arkansas Educational Standards Commission, fighting to raise academic standards, increase teacher salaries, and reduce class sizes.

- As first lady of the United States, she chaired the first-ever convening on Hispanic children and youth, which focused on improving access to educational opportunities.

- As a U.S. senator, she served on the Senate Health, Education and Labor Committee, as a key member shaping the No Child Left Behind Act, with the hope that it would bring needed resources and real accountability to improve educational opportunities for our most disadvantaged students.

20. LABOR AND WORKERS' RIGHTS

Labor unions helped build America's middle class, and organized labor remains critical to fulfilling America's basic bargain: If you work hard and do your part, you should be able to get ahead and stay ahead. We need to strengthen and protect America's workforce.

As president, Hillary will:

- **Invest in good-paying jobs.** In her first 100 days as president, Hillary will work with both parties to make bold investments in infrastructure, manufacturing, research and technology, clean energy, and small businesses. This will create millions of good-paying jobs, including for labor and other hard-working Americans across the country.

- **Restore collective bargaining rights for unions and defend against partisan attacks on workers' rights.** Hillary was an original co-sponsor of the Employee Free Choice Act. Hillary will fight to strengthen the labor movement and to protect worker bargaining power. She will continue to stand up against attacks on collective bargaining and work to strengthen workers' voices.

- **Prevent countries like China from abusing global trade rules, and reject trade agreements, like the TPP, that don't meet high standards.** Hillary will strengthen American trade enforcement so we stand up to foreign countries that aren't playing by the rules—like China is doing right now with steel, and fight for American workers. She will say no to trade deals, like the Trans-Pacific Partnership, that do not meet her high standard of raising wages, creating good-paying jobs, and enhancing our national security.

- **Raise the minimum wage and strengthen overtime rules.** Hillary will work to raise the federal minimum wage to $12, and support state and local efforts to go even higher—including the "Fight for $15." She also supports the Obama administration's expansion of overtime rules to millions more workers.

- **Invest in high-quality training, apprenticeships, and skill-building for workers.**

- **Encourage companies to invest in workers.** Hillary will reward companies that share profits and invest in their workers. She will crack down on companies that move profits overseas to avoid paying U.S. taxes and she will make companies that export jobs give back the tax breaks they've received in America.

- **Protect workers from exploitation,** including employer misclassification, wage theft, and other forms of exploitation.

- **Ensure policies meet the challenges families face in the 21st century economy.** Hillary will fight for equal pay for women and guarantee paid leave, two changes that are long overdue. And she will provide relief from the rising costs of necessities like child care and housing.

- **Protect retirement security.** After working hard for decades, Americans deserve a secure and comfortable retirement. Hillary will fight to protect retirement security, enhance – not privatize – Social Security, and push back against any efforts to undermine retirement benefits.

21. LGBT RIGHTS AND EQUALITY

Thanks to the hard work of generations of LGBT advocates and activists who fought to make it possible, our country won a landmark victory last June when the Supreme Court recognized that in America, LGBT couples—like everyone else—have the right to marry the person they love.

We've come so far, but we still have work to do.

As president, Hillary will:

- **Fight for full federal equality for LGBT Americans.** Hillary will work with Congress to pass the Equality Act, continue

President Obama's LGBT equality executive actions, and support efforts underway in the courts to protect people from discrimination on the basis of gender identity and sexual orientation in every aspect of public life.

- **Support LGBT youth, parents, and elders.** Hillary will end so-called "conversion therapy" for minors, combat youth homelessness by ensuring adequate funding for safe and welcoming shelters, and take on bullying and harassment in schools. She'll end discriminatory treatment of LGBT families in adoptions, and protect LGBT elders against discrimination.

- **Honor the military service of LGBT people.** Hillary applauds the Pentagon's decision to allow transgender personnel to serve openly, and as Commander-in-Chief, she will upgrade service records of LGBT veterans dismissed due to their sexual orientation.

- **Fight for an AIDS-free generation.**

- **Protect transgender rights.** Hillary will work to protect transgender individuals from violence, make it easier for transgender Americans to change their gender marker on identification documents, and invest in law enforcement training focused on fair and impartial policing, including in interactions with LGBT people.

- **Promote human rights of LGBT people around the world.** Hillary will promote LGBT human rights and ensure America's foreign policy is inclusive of LGBT people, including increasing our investment in the Global Equality Fund to advance human rights.

- Hillary has been a vocal advocate for LGBT rights throughout her career.

- In the U.S. Senate, Hillary championed legislation to address hate crimes, fought for federal non-discrimination legislation to protect LGBT Americans in the workplace, and advocated for an end to restrictions that blocked LGBT Americans from adopting children.

- As secretary of state, Hillary advanced LGBT rights abroad and enforced stronger anti-discrimination regulations within the State Department, declaring on the global stage that "gay rights are human rights, and human rights are gay rights." She led the effort to pass the first-ever U.N. Resolution on LGBT Human Rights, launched the Global Equality Fund, ended State Department regulations that denied same-sex couples and their families equal rights, helped implement LGBT-friendly workplace policies, and updated the State Department's policy so that transgender individuals' passports reflect their true gender.

22. MAKING COLLEGE DEBT-FREE AND TAKING ON STUDENT DEBT

Hillary has a comprehensive plan to put higher education within reach for all Americans, and take on the crisis of student debt.

Here's what every student and family should expect under Hillary's plan:

Costs won't be a barrier

- **Every student should have the option to graduate from a public college or university in their state without taking on any student debt.** By 2021, families with income up to $125,000 will pay no tuition at in-state four-year public colleges and universities. And from the beginning, every student from a family making $85,000 a year or less will be able to go to an in-state four-year public college or university without paying tuition.

- **All community colleges will offer free tuition.**

- **Everyone will do their part.** States will have to step up and invest in higher education, and colleges and universities will be held accountable for the success of their students and for controlling tuition costs.

- **A $25 billion fund will support historically black colleges and universities, Hispanic-serving institutions, and other minority-serving institutions** in building new ladders of opportunity for students.

- **The one-quarter of all college students who are also parents will get the support they need and the resources they deserve.**

23. MANUFACTURING

Manufacturing is a vital source of good-paying jobs in our economy, and making things in America is critical to innovation and our prosperity. We have to support manufacturers and workers so we can compete and win in the global economy.

As president, Hillary will:

- **Strengthen American manufacturing** through a $10 billion investment in "Make it in America" partnerships that bring together workers and labor, business, universities, community colleges, and government at every level to harness the strength of manufacturing communities across America. Businesses that take part will pledge not to shift jobs or profits from these partnerships overseas. And we will support strong "Buy American" standards so we make things here.

- **Prevent countries like China from abusing global trade rules and reject trade agreements that don't meet high standards.** Hillary will strengthen American trade enforcement so we stand up to foreign countries that aren't playing by the rules–like China is doing right now with steel—and fight for American workers. She will say no to trade deals, like the Trans-Pacific Partnership, that do not meet her high standard of raising wages, creating good-paying jobs, and enhancing our national security.

- **Revitalize the hardest-hit manufacturing communities** by creating tax incentives to encourage investment in communities that have faced or are about to face significant manufacturing job losses.

- **Crack down on companies that ship jobs and earnings overseas** and create incentives for companies to bring back jobs to the U.S.

- **Invest in America's manufacturing workforce to ensure that it will always be the best in the world.** Hillary will expand apprenticeships and training so our manufacturing workforce is always the best in the world.

As a U.S. senator, Hillary co-founded the bipartisan Senate Manufacturing Caucus, fought Bush administration efforts to cut support for manufacturing, and called for a "New Manhattan Project" to rebuild American manufacturing.

Her plan builds on her career-long commitment to manufacturing, as well as on her previous proposals to invest in renewable energy and rebuild America's infrastructure—two major investments that will drive demand for manufacturing across the country and strengthen our long-run competitiveness.

24. MENTAL HEALTH

I believe that together we can make sure that the next generation gets quality mental health care—without shame, without stigma, without barriers. And that we can do so much more to help people right here and now.

More than 40 million adults in America—nearly 1 in 5—and 17 million children are coping with a mental health problem. Too many individuals are being left to deal with these issues on their own, and many face complicating life circumstances like drug and alcohol addiction, homelessness, incarceration, or chronic health conditions.

These Americans and their families need our support. Hillary Clinton strongly believes we have to bring mental and behavioral health care on par with physical health care—and end the shame and stigma associated with treatment. To that end, she has announced a comprehensive mental health agenda that will:

- **Promote early diagnosis and intervention.** The majority of Americans living with lifelong mental health illnesses show signs of distress at an early age, and yet few are treated. As president, Hillary will increase public awareness and action to address maternal depression, infant mental health, and trauma and stress in the lives of young children. She will scale up funding for programs through which pediatricians and schools seek to identify and support children facing behavioral problems. And she will encourage colleges and universities to provide comprehensive mental health services.

- **Launch a national initiative for suicide prevention.** America is facing the highest suicide rate in 30 years—and it's becoming increasingly prevalent among adolescents, college students, veterans, and older adults. As president, Hillary will create a national, cross-governmental suicide prevention initiative to be led by the surgeon general and involve all relevant agencies, from HHS to the VA to USDA. She'll provide federal support for suicide prevention programs in high schools and on college campuses, and she'll work to ensure schools are meeting the mental health needs of all students—particularly LGBT students and students of color.

- **Integrate our nation's mental and physical health care systems so that health care delivery focuses on the "whole person" and expand community-based treatment.** Hillary will work to foster better integration of our health care systems so that high-quality behavioral care—for mental health problems and as well as addiction—is available in general health care settings. She'll launch a national strategy to increase the number of mental health providers. And she will support the creation of top grade, comprehensive community health centers in every state where behavioral care is available.

- **Prioritize treatment over jail for low-level, nonviolent offenders and help train law enforcement officers in responding to conflicts involving persons with mental illness.** Hillary will increase investments in local programs, such as specialized courts, drug courts, and veterans' treatment courts, which emphasize treatment and rehabilitation over incarceration. She will also direct the attorney general to issue guidance to federal prosecutors, instructing them to prioritize treatment over incarceration for low-level, nonviolent offenders. And she will ensure adequate training for law enforcement on crisis intervention so that officers can properly and safely respond to individuals with mental illness.

- **Enforce mental health parity to the full extent of the law.** The Mental Health Parity and Addiction Equity Act of 2008, which Hillary proudly co-sponsored, requires group health plans to provide the same level of benefits for mental health as other medical conditions. Despite the law, too many Americans seeking mental health treatment still get turned away. Hillary will strengthen federal monitoring to make sure insurers are complying with the mental health parity law—and she'll make it easier for patients to file a complaint when their rights are violated.

- **Improve access to housing and job opportunities.** Hillary will launch a joint initiative among HUD, HHS, and USDA to expand community-based housing opportunities for individuals with mental illness and other disabilities. She'll work with private employers and state and local mental health authorities to expand job opportunities for Americans with mental health issues. And she'll increase support for the Protection and Advocacy for Individuals with Mental Illness (PAIMI) program.

- **Invest in brain behavioral science research.** As part of a broad new investment in scientific research, Hillary will provide new federal funding for research into brain development and human behavior, promote research partnerships across sectors, and ensure data is widely shared.

25. MILITARY AND DEFENSE

We need a smart and sustainable defense budget driven by strategy—not by bluster and loose talk.

Hillary Clinton will be a president who doesn't just support our military rhetorically. As a former member of the Senate Armed Services Committee, she understands the issues facing our military and veterans and has a long record working to deliver real results for them.

As president, Hillary will:

- **Provide budgetary certainty to facilitate reforms and enable long-term planning.** The recent budget deal reached between the Congress and the White House is a promising first step in providing government agencies with much needed fiscal stability. But we must go further by ending the sequester for both defense and non-defense spending in a balanced way.

- **Invest in innovation and capabilities that will allow us to prepare for and fight 21st-century threats.** That includes leveraging our information advantage through what's called "net-centric warfare" capabilities and preparing for asymmetric threats.

- **Create a defense budget that reflects good stewardship of taxpayer dollars.** As president, Hillary will prioritize defense reform initiatives, curbing runaway cost growth in areas like health care and acquisition and stretching every dollar.

- **Take care of our veterans and their families—it's part of our solemn duty.** Hillary has proposed a comprehensive plan to ensure timely access to quality care; eliminate the claims and appeals backlog; make sure our vets continue to have access to education and economic opportunity; fight substance abuse, mental health disorders, and homelessness; and support our military families.

26. NATIONAL SECURITY

As secretary of state, Hillary Clinton worked to restore America's leadership in the world after it was badly eroded by eight years of the Bush administration's go-it-alone foreign policy. She oversaw significant accomplishments, from building a global coalition to impose crippling sanctions against Iran, to brokering a ceasefire in Gaza and protecting Israel to supporting President Obama's decision to bring Osama bin Laden to justice, and much more. Defending America and our core values is one of the cornerstones of Hillary's campaign.

As president, Hillary will:

- **Ensure we are stronger at home.** We are strongest overseas when we are strongest at home. That means investing in our infrastructure, education, and innovation—the fundamentals of a strong economy. She will also work to reduce income inequality, because our country can't lead effectively when so many are struggling to provide the basics for their families.

- **Stick with our allies.** From the Middle East and Asia to Europe and our own hemisphere, Hillary will strengthen the essential partnership that is a unique source of America's strength. Hillary knows that NATO is one of the best investments that America has ever made. And she'll continue to support Israel's ability to defend itself, including by ensuring its Qualitative Military Edge, and oppose efforts to marginalize Israel on the world stage while supporting efforts to bring about a two-state solution. Hillary also will invest in partnerships in Latin America, Africa, and Asia with people and nations who share our values and vision for the future.

- **Embrace all the tools of American power,** especially diplomacy and development, to be on the front lines solving problems before they threaten us at home. Diplomacy is often the only way to avoid a conflict that could end up exacting a much greater cost. It takes patience, persistence, and an eye on the long game—but it's worth it. This includes:

◊ **Preventing Iran from acquiring a nuclear weapon.** Hillary will vigorously enforce the nuclear agreement with Iran and implement a broader strategy to confront Iran's bad behavior in the region, particularly the threat it poses to Israel.

• **Building stronger ties between Cubans and Americans.** Hillary supports President Obama's initiative to re-establish diplomatic relations with Cuba and calls on Congress to lift the embargo, while continuing to press for reforms.

• **Be firm but wise with our rivals**. Countries like Russia and China often work against us. Hillary has gone toe-to-toe with Russia and China and many other different leaders around the world. She knows we have to be able to both stand our ground when we must, and find common ground when we can.

◊ **Stand up to Vladimir Putin.** Hillary has gone toe-to-toe with Putin before, and she'll do it again. She'll stand shoulder to shoulder with our European allies and push back on and deter Russian aggression in Europe and beyond, and increase the costs to Putin for his actions.

◊ **Hold China accountable.** Hillary will work with allies to promote strong rules of the road and institutions in Asia, and press China to play by the rules—including in cyberspace, on currency, human rights, trade, territorial disputes, and climate change—and hold it accountable if it does not, while working with China where it is in our interest.

- **Have a real plan for confronting terrorists.** The threat we face from terrorism is real, urgent, and knows no boundaries. Hillary has laid out a comprehensive plan to defeat ISIS by: taking out ISIS's stronghold in Iraq and Syria, working with our allies to dismantle global terror networks, and hardening our defenses at home.

Hillary has a record of defending America and our core values:

- She built the toughest sanctions regime in history on Iran—twisting arms in China, Russia, and dozens of other countries—to force Iran to the negotiating table. And when pressure started working, she sent her closest aides to explore a deal that would cut off Iran's path to a nuclear weapon.

- She personally negotiated an end to Hamas rockets raining down on Israel in 2012 and worked to build stronger defense programs for Israel, including upgrading the Iron Dome rocket defense system, which has saved the lives of so many Israelis.

- She fought to make women's rights a priority in international relations. She stood up against sex trafficking of women and children, intervened in Saudi Arabia to stop child marriage, and led the fight for a U.N. Security Council resolution to combat sexual violence against women and children around the world that passed unanimously.

- She worked to ensure ratification of the New START treaty, which will make the world safer by reducing U.S. and Russian nuclear arsenals to their smallest size in 50 years.

27. PAID FAMILY AND MEDICAL LEAVE

The United States is the only developed nation in the world with no guaranteed paid leave of any kind. Supporting families isn't a luxury—it's an economic necessity. It's past time for our policies to catch up to the way families live and work today.

As president, Hillary will:

- **Guarantee up to 12 weeks of paid family and medical leave** to care for a new child or a seriously ill family member, and up to 12 weeks of medical leave to recover from a serious illness or injury of their own.

- **Ensure hardworking Americans get at least two-thirds of their current wages**, up to a ceiling, while on leave.

- **Impose no additional costs on businesses, including small businesses.**

- **Fund paid leave by making the wealthy pay their fair share—not by increasing taxes on working families.** Hillary will pay for her paid leave plan with tax reforms that will ensure the wealthiest Americans pay their fair share.

Hillary has a lifelong record of fighting for families:

- After graduating from Yale Law School, she went to work at the Children's Defense Fund, where she helped expand access to education for children with disabilities.

- As first lady of Arkansas, she helped start Arkansas Advocates for Children and Families.

- As first lady of the United States, she helped win the fight for Family Medical Leave Act. When Bill Clinton became president, Hillary was on the front lines working to ensure the Family and Medical Leave Act (FMLA) was the first bill he signed into law.

- As U.S. senator from New York, she fought for paid leave. Hillary helped expand FMLA to wounded soldiers and their families. And in her campaign for president in 2007, she proposed a national paid leave program and called for guaranteeing paid parental leave for all federal employees.

28. PROTECTING ANIMALS AND WILDLIFE

Hillary Clinton is committed to promoting animal welfare and protecting animals from cruelty and abuse.

As president, Hillary will:

- **Protect wildlife in the United States by keeping public lands public**—not auctioning them off to the highest bidder— and making more resources available to farmers, ranchers, and forest landowners who are taking steps to conserve our wildlife, lands, and waters.

- **Combat international wildlife trafficking** by shutting down the U.S. market for illegal wildlife products and combating international animal trafficking and poaching, which harms the environment and fuels terrorist activity.

- **Protect pets and domesticated animals** by making sure facilities like animal breeders, zoos, and research institutions create plans to protect the animals in their care during disasters; strengthening regulations of "puppy mills" and other harmful commercial breeding facilities; and supporting the Preventing Animal Cruelty and Torture (PACT) Act.

- **Protect farm animals from inhumane treatment** by encouraging farms to raise animals humanely and working to eliminate the use of antibiotics in farm animals for non-therapeutic reasons.

- **Protect horses** by ending the slaughter of horses for human consumption and cracking down on the practice of horse soaring, in which chemicals or other inhumane methods are applied to horses' limbs to exaggerate their gait.

Hillary has a strong record of standing up for animal rights:

- As U.S. senator from New York, Hillary spearheaded efforts to prohibit the U.S. Department of Agriculture from buying chickens for the federal school lunch program that have been injected with therapeutic antibiotics. She pushed for stricter FDA review of animal drugs, co-sponsored legislation to protect animal rights and prohibit animal fighting, and earned a perfect score from The Humane Society Legislative Fund.

- As secretary of state, Hillary elevated U.S. efforts to combat poaching and wildlife trafficking and promote conservation.

29. RACIAL JUSTICE

As president, Hillary Clinton will fight to break down all the barriers that hold Americans back and build ladders of opportunity for all people—so that every child in America can live up to his or her God-given potential.

As president, Hillary will:

- **Reform our broken criminal justice system** by reforming sentencing laws and policies, ending racial profiling by law enforcement, strengthening the bonds of trust between communities and police, and more.

- **Protect the right to vote** by fighting to repair the Voting Rights Act and implementing universal, automatic voter registration so that every American will be registered to vote when they turn 18, unless they opt out.

- **Protect immigrants' rights and keep families together** by fighting for comprehensive immigration reform, including a full and equal pathway to citizenship and an end to family detention and private immigrant detention centers.

- **End the epidemic of gun violence in our communities.** Gun violence is the leading cause of death for young African American men—more than the next nine leading causes combined. We must do more to crack down on gun stores that flood our communities with illegal guns and deprive our children of their futures.

- **Fight against environmental injustice.** Clean air and clean water are basic human rights. But too many children in low-income housing are exposed to lead. African American children are twice as likely to suffer from asthma as white children. Half of our nation's Latino population lives in areas where the air quality does not meet the EPA's health standards—and climate change will put vulnerable populations at even greater risk. As president, Hillary will work to reduce air pollution, invest in the removal of toxins like lead, develop greener and more resilient infrastructure, tackle energy poverty, and boost efforts to clean up highly polluted toxic sites.

- **Close the education achievement gap** by making sure every child has a world-class education from birth through college. Hillary will double America's investment in Early Head Start, ensure that every 4-year-old in America has access to high-quality preschool, drive student achievement in K-12 schools, make college affordable, and relieve the crushing burden of student debt.

- **End violence against the transgender community— particularly women of color.**

- **Revitalize the economy in communities that have been left out and left behind through a "Breaking Every Barrier Agenda"** that includes $125 billion in targeted investments to create good-paying jobs, rebuild crumbling infrastructure, and connect housing to opportunity.

- **Ensure equal treatment for citizens in Puerto Rico.** Hillary is committed to making sure Puerto Ricans have a voice and are treated equally. She believes that Puerto Ricans must be treated equally by Medicare, Medicaid, and other programs that benefit families. She will also work with the people of Puerto Rico and with advocates from all sides to answer the fundamental question of their political status.

Hillary has been fighting for racial justice her entire career:

- As a young lawyer working for the Children's Defense Fund, Hillary went to South Carolina to work to stop the incarceration of teenagers in adult prisons, and she investigated school segregation in Alabama at so-called "private academies."

- In Arkansas, she started a legal aid clinic to ensure that low-income people had access to real legal representation; she helped start a program to help low-income parents prepare their kids for school success, which is now in more than 20 states; and she helped to found the Arkansas Single Parent Scholarship Fund, which helped nearly 40,000 single parents with their education.

- As first lady, she continued her advocacy for children and families, helping to pass the Children's Health Insurance Program (CHIP), which now covers more than 8 million kids, helping reform the foster care and adoption system, and advocating for the expansion of Medicaid to cover foster kids until they are 21. She pushed for the expansion of Head Start and advocated for quality child care and equal pay for women to help break down barriers for working parents.

- As a U.S. senator, she worked to improve pre-K programs and provide parenting help for at-risk families and pushed to expand CHIP to cover more kids. She co-sponsored legislation to end racial profiling and implement sentencing reforms to address crack-cocaine disparities, and she fought to restore voting rights and expand programs that help people re-enter society after they have served time. She introduced legislation to protect voting rights; supported increased funding for HIV and AIDS programs, spotlighting the disproportionate impact on African American women; and worked with then-Senator Obama to fight against lead poisoning.

30. RURAL COMMUNITIES

Too many rural communities aren't reaping the rewards of our nation's economic success—despite their critical role in our economy. Unemployment and poverty rates present a real challenge to these communities while accessible health care and education are too often out of reach.

As president, Hillary will:

- **Spur investment.** Hillary will create a national infrastructure bank to improve rural transportation and broadband access and grow the rural economy by expanding access to capital. She'll also expand the New Markets Tax Credit that will encourage investments to prevent communities from spiraling downward after a major economic shift or plant closing.

- **Support family farms.** Hillary will increase funding to support the next generation of farmers and ranchers in local food markets and regional food systems. And she'll create a focused safety net to help family farms get through challenging times.

- **Promote clean energy.** Hillary will encourage our nation's commitment to clean energy by assisting farms that conserve and improve natural resources. She'll also strengthen the Renewable Fuel Standard and double loans that help support the bio-based economy.

- **Expand opportunity.** Hillary will increase funding for Early Head Start, universal pre-K, free community college, and support for telemedicine and Medicaid expansion.

31. SMALL BUSINESS

Small businesses all over the country are ready to grow and hire, and entrepreneurs are ready to venture out on their own—if they can just get that next loan, enter a new market, or have one fewer form to fill out.

As president, Hillary will make it easier to start and grow a small business in America by:

- **Unlocking access to capital.** We need to give small businesses—including women- and minority-owned small businesses—access to the financing they need to build, grow, and hire. Hillary will work to boost small-business lending by easing burdens for community banks and credit unions. Her plan will also allow entrepreneurs to defer student-loan payments with no interest while they get their ventures off the ground.

- **Cutting red tape to streamline the process of starting a small business.** It shouldn't take longer to start a small business in the United States than it does in Canada or Denmark. Hillary will offer state and local governments new federal incentives to cut red tape and streamline unnecessary licensing to make it less costly to start a small business.

- **Providing tax relief and simplification for small businesses.** America's smallest businesses—those with one to five employees—spend 150 hours and $1,100 per employee making sure they comply with federal tax laws. That's more than 20 times higher than the average for larger firms. Hillary will create a new standard deduction for small businesses— like the one available to individual filers. She will simplify the rules so small businesses can track and file their taxes as easily as filling out a checkbook or printing a bank statement. And her plan would quadruple the start-up tax deduction to significantly lower the cost of starting a business.

- **Incentivize health care benefits for small businesses and their employees.** Hillary will expand the health care tax credit for small employers with up to 50 employees through the Affordable Care Act. And she will simplify complex phase-out and eligibility rules so that it's easier for many more small businesses to get the credit and cover their workers.

- **Opening new markets.** Every small business across America should be able to enter new markets—whether those markets are across town or across the world. We should invest in the roads, bridges, ports, and airports that make it easier for small businesses to reach new customers, and encourage innovations that unlock new markers for small businesses.

- **Making sure small businesses get paid—not stiffed.** Hillary believes it is outrageous when big businesses like Donald Trump's build their fortunes by repeatedly stiffing the small businesses that do work for them. She will stop large companies from using expensive litigation hurdles to deny small businesses payment for services, and she'll give small businesses recourse to take on predatory behavior.

- **Supporting small-business owners and entrepreneurs.** Hillary will work to provide incubators, mentoring, and training to 50,000 entrepreneurs and small-business owners in underserved communities across the country.

- **Make the federal government more responsive to small business.** Hillary will push the federal agencies to make government more user-friendly, guaranteeing a 24-hour response time to small businesses with questions about federal regulations and access to capital programs.

32. SOCIAL SECURITY AND MEDICARE

Throughout her career, Hillary has stood up for Medicare and Social Security. She is committed to preserving, protecting, and strengthening these lifelines for today's seniors and for future generations.

Social Security

For 80 years, Social Security has been America at its best. Social Security reflects our shared belief that every American should be able to retire with dignity after decades of hard work. That no American should face poverty because he or she is disabled, or when a loved one dies. That we all have an obligation to each other.

Social Security isn't just a program—it's a promise. As president, Hillary will:

- **Defend Social Security against Republican attacks.** Republicans are using scare tactics about the future and effectiveness of Social Security to push through policies that would jeopardize it. The real threat is Republican attempts to undermine the bedrock of the system. Hillary believes that Social Security must remain what it has always been: a rock-solid benefit that seniors can always count on—not subject to the budget whims of Congress or to the fluctuations of the stock market. She fought Republican efforts to undermine Social Security when she was a senator and throughout her career, and she will fight them as president. As president, she would:

◊ Fight any attempts to gamble seniors' retirement security on the stock market through privatization.

◊ Oppose reducing annual cost-of-living adjustments.

◊ Oppose Republican efforts to raise the retirement age—an unfair idea that will particularly hurt the seniors who have worked the hardest throughout their lives.

◊ Oppose closing the long-term shortfall on the backs of the middle class, whether through benefit cuts or tax increases.

• **Expand Social Security for those who need it most and who are treated unfairly by the current system**—including women who are widows and those who took significant time out of the paid workforce to take care of their children, aging parents, or ailing family members. Social Security works well, but it should work better. Hillary will fight to expand Social Security for those who need it most and who are treated unfairly today. For instance:

◊ The poverty rate for widowed women 65 or older is nearly 90 percent higher than for other seniors—in part because when a spouse dies, families can face a steep benefit cut. For a two-earner couple, those benefit cuts can be as much as 50 percent. Hillary believes that we have to change that by reducing how much Social Security benefits drop when a spouse dies, so that the loss of a spouse doesn't mean financial hardship or falling into poverty.

◊ Millions of women—and men—take time out of the paid workforce to raise a child, take care of an aging parent or look after an ailing family member. Caregiving is hard work that benefits our entire economy. However, when Americans take time off to take care of a relative, that can reduce their Social Security benefits at retirement, since those benefits are calculated based on their top 35 years of earnings. No one should face meager Social Security checks because they took on the vital role of caregiver for part of their career. Americans should receive credit toward their Social Security benefits when they are out of the paid workforce because they are acting as caregivers.

• **Preserve Social Security for decades to come by asking the wealthiest to contribute more.** Social Security must continue to guarantee dignity in retirement for future generations. Hillary understands that there is no way to accomplish that goal without asking the highest-income Americans to pay more, including options to tax some of their income above the current Social Security cap and taxing some of their income not currently taken into account by the Social Security system.

Medicare

Medicare is the bedrock of health care coverage for more than 50 million American seniors and people with disabilities. As senator, Hillary co-sponsored and sponsored bills to reduce the impact of the Medicare prescription drug gap by reducing the price of pharmaceuticals for seniors.

As president, Hillary will:

- **Fight Republican attempts to repeal the Affordable Care Act.** The Affordable Care Act made preventive care available and affordable for an estimated 39 million people with Medicare and saved more than 9 million people with Medicare thousands of dollars in prescription drug expenses.

- **Fight back against Republican plans to privatize or "phase out" Medicare as we know it.** Republicans have called for privatizing or even "phasing out" Medicare and shifting millions more seniors into private plans that would dramatically raise costs. Hillary will stand against these attempts to weaken the program.

- **Drive down drug costs for seniors and other Americans.** Hillary will ensure Medicare can negotiate lower drug prices with pharmaceutical companies, so we lower costs for seniors.

- **Reform Medicare delivery systems to deliver value and quality to our seniors and people with disabilities.**

33. TECHNOLOGY AND INNOVATION

America has always been a global technology leader. Today, technology and the internet are transforming nearly every sector of our economy, from manufacturing and transportation to energy, content creation, and health care. We can harness this power in a way that works for all Americans: creating good-paying jobs and boosting economic growth, making our communities safer and smarter, and making educational opportunities more accessible.

As president, Hillary will:

Build the tech economy on Main Street by:

- Investing in computer science and STEM education

- Creating a lifelong learning system that is better tailored to 21st-century jobs

- Increasing access to young entrepreneurs—including letting young entrepreneurs defer student loan payments.

- Attracting and retaining top talent from around the world

- Investing in science and technology research and development, as well as in technology transfer

- Ensuring benefits are flexible, portable, and comprehensive, as the economy changes and as Americans join the labor force in new capacities

Invest in world-class digital infrastructure by:

- Committing that 100 percent of households in America will have access to high-speed, affordable broadband by 2020

- Deploying 5G wireless and other next-generation systems that can deliver faster wireless connections and enable the Internet of Things

- Connecting public spaces like airports, mass transit systems, recreation centers, and career centers to high-speed internet so they can offer free wifi to the public

- Launching a model digital communities program that encourages communities to foster greater access to high-speed internet for their residents at affordable prices

- Hillary has been a champion of internet freedom—and she understands we must position American innovators to lead the world in the next generation of technology revolutions while defending universal access to the global, digital marketplace of ideas and protecting individual privacy and security.

As president, Hillary will:

Advance America's global leadership in technology and innovation by:

- Fighting for an open internet abroad

- Working to leave internet governance to the global community of engineers, companies, civil society groups, and internet users—not to governments

- Growing American technology exports, while fighting to protect U.S. IP against piracy

- Promoting cyber security at home and abroad

- Safeguarding the free flow of information across borders

- Updating procedures concerning cross-border requests for data by law enforcement

Set rules of the road to promote innovation while protecting privacy by:

- Reducing barriers to entry to promote healthy competition

- Defending net neutrality

- Improving the patent system to reward innovators

- Ensuring an effective copyright system that protects creative content, while unlocking access to orphan works and promoting open-licensing arrangements for materials supported by federal grant funding

- Affirming strong consumer protection values without stifling innovation

- Protecting online privacy and security

Beyond enabling innovation and economic growth, Hillary believes we should look to technology and data to provide better services to the American people, and make government simpler, smarter, and more effective.

34. VETERANS AND THEIR FAMILIES

Hillary Clinton's father, Hugh Rodham, was a chief petty officer at Naval Station Great Lakes during World War II. He instilled in Hillary at an early age the importance of supporting our men and women in uniform, as well as military families and veterans—and empathy for the challenges that many servicemembers and veterans face.

Hillary believes that by supporting our veterans, we strengthen our military, our economy, and our country. She knows that we cannot separate supporting our veterans from our broader commitment to take care of our troops—soldiers, sailors, airmen, Marines, Coast Guardsmen—and their families.

To support our veterans and ensure they have the opportunities and tools they need to succeed upon returning home, Hillary will:

- **Fundamentally reform veterans' health care to ensure access to timely and high quality care and block efforts to privatize the VA**—including improving health care for women at the VHA, ending the veteran suicide epidemic, and continuing efforts to identify and treat invisible, latent, and toxic wounds of war that affect veterans, family members, and caregivers after their service.

- **Build a 21st-century Department of Veterans Affairs to deliver world-class care.** Hillary was outraged by the recent scandals at the VA, and as president, she will demand accountability and performance from VA leadership. Many veterans have to wait an unacceptably long time to see a doctor or to process disability claims and appeals. Hillary will make the Veterans Health Administration (VHA) a seamless partner in health care. She does not believe that privatization will solve the problems that the VHA is facing—this department must deliver high-quality care while acting as an integrated payer-purchaser and facilitating a full range of services for all veterans, regardless of where they live.

- **Empower veterans and strengthen our economy and communities by connecting their unique skills to the jobs of the future.** Hillary will make the Post-9/11 G.I. Bill a lasting part of our social contract with those who serve, expand tax credits for veterans' employment, improve certification and credentialing programs, strengthen veteran entrepreneurship programs, and create pathways for servicemembers to enter growing career fields. She will also protect veterans from discrimination and predatory companies and work to end veteran homelessness.

- **Overhaul VA governance to create a new veteran-centric model of excellence** by creating a culture of accountability, service, and excellence at the VA; providing budgetary certainty; and ensuring our veterans are buried with the honor, distinction, and integrity they deserve.

Our military families serve alongside our men and women in uniform. To strengthen services and support for military families, Hillary will:

- **Realign the demands of a military career to accommodate 21st-century family realities while maintaining a strong force** by enabling more flexibility in military careers and giving servicemembers and their families a greater say in their lives. That includes increasing access to child care both on and off the base, maintaining a commitment to extended leave policies, and more.

- **Back military spouses as they pursue education, seek jobs, build careers and secure their finances** by expanding spousal employment support and training initiatives while in service and during transition.

- **Ensure military children receive a high-quality education and the resources to succeed** by improving military schools, enhancing the experience of military children in public schools, and ensuring key benefits are available for all military families.

And to keep our military strong and resilient, Hillary will:

- **Sustain and strengthen the all-volunteer force,** including the reserve and National Guard. Hillary will support smart compensation and benefits reform; adopt inclusive personnel policies, including aggressively combating military sexual assault and harassment; welcome women to compete for all military positions; and allow transgender Americans to serve openly in the military.

35. VOTING RIGHTS

Ever since the Supreme Court eviscerated key provisions of the Voting Rights Act in 2013, Republican governors and legislatures across the country have proposed and passed laws making it harder to vote, systemically disempowering millions of voters— particularly people of color, poor people, and young people. At a time when so many Americans are disenfranchised, that's the opposite of what we should be doing. Hillary Clinton believes we must take action to restore the Voting Rights Act and do everything we can to make it easier—not harder—for Americans to vote. And she believes that all American citizens, no matter where they reside, should have the right to vote for the president of the United States.

As president, Hillary will:

- **Automatically register voters.** Hillary will work so that every citizen is automatically registered to vote when they turn 18, unless they opt out, and make sure that voter registration rolls are accurate and secure.

- **Repair the Voting Rights Act.** Hillary will fight to restore the portions of the Voting Rights Act that were struck down by the Supreme Court to make sure that all citizens enjoy the full protections they deserve—especially in states where they have been disproportionately targeted by laws that restrict voting access to the polls. She will fight back against harmful restrictions on voting across the country, so that minority voters, young people, low-income voters, seniors, and women are equally capable as others at expressing their voices and their votes in our democracy.

- **Set a national standard for early voting.** In an effort to reduce long lines and give more people with family or work obligations an opportunity to vote, Hillary will set a national standard for early voting, giving voters at least 20 days to vote in the evenings or on weekends before election day.

- **Restore voting rights.** Americans who have paid their debts to society and have served their sentences should have the right to vote, and Hillary will support legislation to make sure their voting rights are restored.

- **Take action.** Hillary will implement the recommendations of the president's bipartisan commission to improve voting.

36. WALL STREET REFORM

The financial crisis showed how irresponsible behavior in the financial sector can devastate the lives of everyday Americans— costing 9 million workers their jobs, driving 5 million families out of their homes, and wiping out more than $13 trillion in household wealth. Hillary Clinton has a plan to reduce the risk of future crises and make our financial system fairer and more accountable.

Hillary's plan will tackle dangerous risks in the financial system:

- **Impose a risk fee on the largest financial institutions.** Big banks and financial companies would be required to pay a fee based on their size and their risk of contributing to another crisis.

- **Close loopholes that let banks make risky investments with taxpayer money.** The Volcker Rule prohibits banks from making risky trading bets with taxpayer-backed money—one of the core protections of the post-financial crisis Wall Street reforms. However, under current law these banks can still invest billions through hedge funds, which are exempt from this rule. Hillary would close that loophole and strengthen the law.

- **Hold senior bankers accountable when a large bank suffers major losses.** When a large bank suffers major losses with sweeping consequences, senior managers should lose some or all of their bonus compensation.

- **Make sure no financial firm is ever too big or too risky to be managed effectively.** Hillary's plan would give regulators more authority to force overly complex or risky firms— including banks, hedge funds and other non-bank financial institutions—to reorganize, downsize, or break apart.

- **Tackle financial dangers of the "shadow banking" system.** Hillary's plan will enhance transparency and reduce volatility in the "shadow banking system," which includes certain activities of hedge funds, investment banks, and other non-bank financial companies.

- **Impose a tax on high-frequency trading.** The growth of high-frequency trading has unnecessarily placed stress on our markets, created instability, and enabled unfair and abusive trading strategies. Hillary would impose a tax on harmful high-frequency trading and reform rules to make our stock markets fairer, more open, and transparent.

Hillary would also hold both corporations and individuals on Wall Street accountable by:

- **Prosecuting individuals when they break the law.** Hillary would extend the statute of limitations for prosecuting major financial frauds, enhance whistleblower rewards, and provide the Department of Justice and the Securities and Exchange Commission with more resources to prosecute wrongdoing.

- **Holding executives accountable when they are responsible for their subordinates' misconduct.** Hillary believes that when corporations pay large fines to the government for violating the law, those fines should cut into the bonuses of the executives who were responsible for or should have caught the problem. And when egregious misconduct happens on an executive's watch, that executive should lose his or her job.

- **Holding corporations accountable when they break the law.** Hillary will make sure that corporations can't treat penalties for breaking the law as merely a cost of doing business, so we can put an end to the patterns of corporate wrongdoing that we see too often today.

37. WOMEN'S RIGHTS AND OPPORTUNITY

America has taken tremendous strides when it comes to expanding opportunity for women—but many women still face barriers to entering and advancing in the workforce, and the ability of women to make their own health decisions is under assault. Hillary believes that issues that affect women's lives are family issues, economic issues, and crucial to our future competitiveness. She has been fighting for women and girls her entire career, and she's just getting started.

As president, Hillary will:

- **Work to close the pay gap.** Women earn less than men across our economy—and women of color often lose out the most. We should promote pay transparency across the economy and work to pass the Paycheck Fairness Act—a bill Hillary introduced as senator—to give women the tools they need to fight discrimination in the workforce.

- **Fight for paid leave.** No one should have to choose between keeping their job and taking care of a sick family member, and no parent should have to go back to work right after they welcome a newborn baby.

- **Make quality, affordable child care a reality for families.**

- **Increase the minimum wage.** Women represent nearly two-thirds of all minimum-wage workers in America. A higher minimum wage will help close the gender pay gap, lift millions of women out of poverty, and have a ripple effect across our economy. Hillary will also work to end the so-called "tipped minimum wage."

- **Defend and enhance Social Security.** We need to defend Social Security from Republican attacks and enhance it to meet new realities—especially for women.

- **Protect and expand on the Affordable Care Act,** which has helped address discrimination in our health care system and brought health coverage to millions more women.

- **Confront violence against women.** One in five women in America is sexually assaulted while in college. Twenty-two percent of women experience severe physical violence by an intimate partner at some point in their lifetime. American women are 11 times more likely to be murdered with guns than women in other high-income countries. It's time to address violence against women—and Hillary will put forward bold plans to do that.

- **Proudly stand with Planned Parenthood.** Hillary is proud to have earned the endorsement of the Planned Parenthood Action Fund. She will always defend the essential health and reproductive care that Planned Parenthood provides for women.

- **Protect women's health and reproductive rights.** Women's personal health decisions should be made by a woman, her family, and her faith, with the counsel of her doctor. Hillary will fight back against Republican attempts to restrict access to quality, affordable reproductive health care. She will defend access to affordable contraception, preventive care, and safe and legal abortion—not just in principle, but in practice.

- **Promote women's rights around the globe.** In far too many parts of the world, women are still held back by social, economic, and legal barriers. Hillary will promote gender equality around the world.

Hillary has a record of fighting for women and girls:

- After graduating from Yale Law School, Hillary became an advocate for kids and families at the Children's Defense Fund.

- As first lady of Arkansas, she helped start Arkansas Advocates for Children and Families.

- As first lady of the United States, Hillary led the U.S. delegation to the U.N. Fourth World Conference on Women in Beijing, where she proclaimed that "women's rights are human rights." She also advocated for the Family and Medical Leave Act, worked to increase funding for child care, and helped start the National Campaign to End Teen and Unplanned Pregnancy.

- As senator from New York, Hillary championed access to emergency contraception and voted in favor of strengthening a woman's right to make her own health decisions. She also championed the Paycheck Fairness Act and co-sponsored the Lilly Ledbetter Fair Pay Act. She fought for legislation to guarantee paid sick leave and paid parental leave for all federal employees.

- As secretary of state, Hillary made women's rights a cornerstone of U.S. foreign policy.

38. WORKFORCE SKILLS AND JOB TRAINING

Americans need to be able to get ahead and stay ahead—that means putting the next generation of well-paying jobs within reach for everyone who is willing to work hard. Hillary Clinton believes that every American—especially young people—should be able to learn the skills they need to get hired, seize new opportunities at work, get promoted, and contribute in a 21st-century workforce.

Hillary's workforce and skills agenda will help people get good jobs with good wages throughout their careers:

- For workers and job-seekers, this means providing more robust, coherent, and accessible training programs and resources that are up to date for 21st-century technology and that lead to good jobs and lifelong skills and credentials.

- For training providers, Hillary will ensure that good programs that provide high-quality training, including at community colleges, are given the support they need to scale up and respond to the needs of the local workforce and employers— while insisting on accountability, transparency, and results.

- For government, Hillary will make sure federal, state, and local workforce development resources are used to bring together workers, unions, employers, and training providers at every level, in order to prepare workers for good jobs.

- For employers, this plan encourages businesses to invest in their workers for the long term through training, apprenticeships, and creating good jobs.

As part of this agenda, Hillary is calling for a tax credit for businesses that hire apprentices, providing much needed on-the-job training—especially for young Americans.

Her plan would put forward a tax credit for businesses of $1,500 per apprentice and would insist on accountability for employment and earnings outcomes for programs receiving the credit. Hillary's plan will also grant a bonus on that tax credit to businesses for providing opportunities specifically for young people.

B. DONALD TRUMP

(Source: Donald Trump's Official Website)

1. ECONOMIC VISION

Economic Vision: Winning the Global Competition

Last week's GDP report showed that the economy grew a mere 1.2% in the second quarter and 1.2% over the last year. It's the weakest recovery since the Great Depression – the predictable consequence of massive taxation, regulation, one-side trade deals and onerous energy restrictions.

This slow-growth low-jobs future doesn't have to be. While Hillary Clinton promises more of the same failed economy agenda that have pushed another 14 million out of the workforce in the last 7 years – and that has placed forty percent of Detroit in poverty – Donald Trump is outlining a new economic vision based on a simple premise: all economic policy must be geared towards making it easier to hire, invest, build, grow and produce in America – creating a level playing field for our workers and businesses in global competition, and creating jobs here, not overseas.

High taxes and excessive regulation push jobs overseas, reduce wages, and create a smaller economy for everyone. Obama-Clinton have created a built-in advantage for our foreign competitors.

Reducing the burdens on the American economy, and creating fair trade deals, will lead to an explosion of new jobs, wealth and opportunity. That's what America First economics is all about – making America the best place in the world to do business, and the best place in the world to get a job, raise and rising standard of living.

Here is how we can accomplish that goal, and win the global competition for America:

1. Tax reform—

- Simplify taxes for everyone and streamline deductions. Biggest tax reform since Reagan.

- Lower taxes for everyone, making raising a family more affordable for working families.

- Reduce dramatically the income tax.

- We will simplify the income tax from 7 brackets to 3 brackets.

- Exclude childcare expenses from taxation.

- Limit taxation of business income to 15% for every business.

- Make our corporate tax globally competitive and the United States the most attractive place to invest in the world.

- End the death tax.

For every one percentage point of slower growth in a given year, that's one million fewer jobs for American workers. Reducing taxes on our workers and businesses, means that our workers can sell their products more cheaply here and around the world – meaning more factories, more hiring, and higher wages. It's time to stop punishing people for doing business in America.

President Obama has already increased taxes by $1.7 trillion during his administration. Hillary Clinton would raise taxes by an additional $1.3 trillion over the next 10 years. According to the Tax Policy Center's analysis of Hillary Clinton's tax plan: "Marginal tax rates would increase, reducing incentives to work, save, and invest, and the tax code would become more complex." In addition, Hillary would tax some small businesses by as much as nearly fifty percent; the Trump plan would limit taxes on all businesses to 15 percent of business income.

The child care exclusion will be an above-the-line deduction. Capped at the amount of average care costs in state of residence for age of child. Low-income taxpayers able to take deduction against payroll tax. The plan is structured to benefit working and middle class families, and more detail will be rolled out soon after the plans other elements.

2. *Regulatory reform—*

- A temporary pause on new regulations and a review of previous regulations to see which need to be scrapped.

- Require each federal agency to prepare a list of all of the regulations they impose on American business, and rank them from most critical to health and safety to least critical. Least critical regulations will receive priority consideration for repeal.

- Remove bureaucrats who only know how to kill jobs; replace them with experts who know how to create jobs.

- Targeted review for regulations that inhibit hiring. These include:

- The Environmental Protection Agency's Clean Power Plan, which forces investment in renewable energy at the expense of coal and natural gas, raising electricity rates;

- The EPA's Waters of the United States rule, which gives the EPA the ability to regulate the smallest streams on private land, limiting land use; and

- The Department of Interior's moratorium on coal mining permits, which put tens of thousands of coal miners out of work.

- Excessive regulation is costing our country as much as 2 trillion dollars a year, and we will end it.

Regulations may have cost us 600,000 small businesses since the start of the recent recession—largely because of new regulations on financing—and some 6 million fewer jobs. The Heritage Foundation has found that the Obama administration has imposed 229 major regulations (those with a cost of $100 million or more) at a cost of $108 billion annually.

3. Trade reform—

- Appoint trade negotiators whose goal will be to win for America: narrowing our trade deficit, increasing domestic production, and getting a fair deal for our workers.

- Renegotiate NAFTA.

- Withdraw from the TPP.

- Bring trade relief cases to the world trade organization.

- Label China a currency manipulator.

- Apply tariffs and duties to countries that cheat.

- Direct the Commerce Department to use all legal tools to respond to trade violations.

Our trade deficit in goods is almost $800 billion on an annual basis. The trade deficit subtracts from growth and costs the US jobs. This has hurt working Americans because good-paying manufacturing jobs are hard to find. Less than half of the population 25 and older without a high school diploma is in the workforce; the unemployment rate of those who are in the almost 30 percent higher than the overall unemployment rate. This leads to poverty and an increase in demands on the nation's social service network. Better trade policies can reverse this outcome dramatically.

Hillary Clinton has supported every major trade deal responsible for job losses in the United States, and will enact the TPP if given the chance.

TPP will hammer the car industry because it does not resolve, among other things, the substantial non-tariff barriers to U.S. cars being sold in Japan and other countries — including currency manipulation, excess supply and closed dealerships. According to the Peterson Institute, TPP would increase the automobile trading deficit by $23 billion by 2025.

4. Energy reform—

- Rescind all the job-destroying Obama executive actions including the Climate Action Plan and the Waters of the U.S. rule.

- Save the coal industry and other industries threatened by Hillary Clinton's extremist agenda.

- Ask Trans Canada to renew its permit application for the Keystone Pipeline.

- Make land in the Outer Continental Shelf available to produce oil and natural gas.

- Cancel the Paris Climate Agreement (limit global warming to 2 degrees Celsius) and stop all payments of U.S. tax dollars to U.N. global warming programs.

- Lift restrictions on American energy to increase:

- Economic output by $700 billion annually over the next 30 years,

- Wages by $30 billion annually over the next 7 years,

- GDP by more than $20 trillion over the next four decades, and

- Tax revenues by an additional $6 trillion over 40 years.

Energy costs the average American households $5,000 per year. As a percentage of income, the cost is greater for lower-income families. An America First Energy Plan will bring down residential and transportation energy costs, leaving more money in for American families as they pay less each month on power bills and gasoline for cars. This will also make electricity more affordable for U.S. manufacturers, which will help our companies create jobs and compete on the world stage.

President Obama sought to raise the price of energy for America's families and businesses. He's put much of Alaska's reserves off limits, decreased production on federal lands by 10 percent, put 87 percent of Outer Continental Shelf reserves out of service, and shut down Atlantic lease sales costing nearly 300,00 jobs. Hillary Clinton has pledged to protect and expand these job-killing policies.

Donald Trump is committed to clean air and water, without increasing the cost of electricity. Hillary Clinton will continue President Obama's goals of reducing methane emissions by 40-45 percent through standards for both new and existing sources, which will drastically increase the cost of natural gas; Donald Trump is committed to an "all of the above" energy plan that would encourage, not discourage, the use of natural gas and other American energy resources that will both reduce emissions but also reduce the price of energy and increase our economic output.

5. Other reforms, to be rolled out in the near future —

- Obamacare repeal and replacement—Obamacare will cost the economy 2 million full time jobs over the next decade. Hillary Clinton would expand Obamacare and create fully government-run socialized medicine.

- Infrastructure—28 percent of our roads are in substandard condition and 24 percent of bridges are structurally deficient or worse. Trump's plan will provide the growth to boost our infrastructure, Hillary Clinton's will not.

- Childcare— Childcare is now the single greatest expense for most American families — even exceeding the cost of housing in much of the country. Trump will allow families to exclude childcare costs from income, benefitting every family. Hillary will not.

- Crime— Homicides last year increased by 17 percent in America's fifty largest cities. That's the largest increase in 25 years. More than 2,000 have been shot in Chicago since January of this year alone. Donald Trump is the law and order candidate in this Presidential race.

Contrast with Hillary Clinton:

- Hillary Clinton accepts the CBO and Fed projections that the U.S. will grow only 2 percent per year. She doesn't believe in a better future for America – only Venezuela-style redistribution of a stagnant economy.

- Hillary Clinton will raise taxes by $1.3 trillion, leading to 300,000 lost jobs and lower wages.

- Hillary Clinton will increase spending by a minimum of $3.5 trillion.

- Hillary Clinton wants to increase regulations.

- Hillary Clinton is a globalist, supporting almost every major job-killing trade deal.

- Hillary Clinton wants to shut down American energy production, a tax on the poor.

2. HEALTHCARE REFORM

Healthcare Reform to Make America Great Again

Since March of 2010, the American people have had to suffer under the incredible economic burden of the Affordable Care Act—Obamacare. This legislation, passed by totally partisan votes in the House and Senate and signed into law by the most divisive and partisan President in American history, has tragically but predictably resulted in runaway costs, websites that don't work, greater rationing of care, higher premiums, less competition and fewer choices. Obamacare has raised the economic uncertainty of every single person residing in this country. As it appears Obamacare is certain to collapse of its own weight, the damage done by the Democrats and President Obama, and abetted by the Supreme Court, will be difficult to repair unless the next President and a Republican congress lead the effort to bring much-needed free market reforms to the healthcare industry.

But none of these positive reforms can be accomplished without Obamacare repeal. On day one of the Trump Administration, we will ask Congress to immediately deliver a full repeal of Obamacare.

However, it is not enough to simply repeal this terrible legislation. We will work with Congress to make sure we have a series of reforms ready for implementation that follow free market principles and that will restore economic freedom and certainty to everyone in this country. By following free market principles and working together to create sound public policy that *will broaden healthcare access, make healthcare more affordable and improve the quality of the care available to all Americans*.

Any reform effort must begin with Congress. Since Obamacare became law, conservative Republicans have been offering reforms that can be delivered individually or as part of more comprehensive reform efforts. In the remaining sections of this policy paper, several reforms will be offered that should be considered by Congress so that on the first day of the Trump Administration, we can start the process of restoring faith in government and economic liberty to the people.

Congress must act. Our elected representatives in the House and Senate must:

1. Completely repeal Obamacare. Our elected representatives must eliminate the individual mandate. No person should be required to buy insurance unless he or she wants to.

2. Modify existing law that inhibits the sale of health insurance across state lines. As long as the plan purchased complies with state requirements, any vendor ought to be able to offer insurance in any state. By allowing full competition in this market, insurance costs will go down and consumer satisfaction will go up.

3. Allow individuals to fully deduct health insurance premium payments from their tax returns under the current tax system. Businesses are allowed to take these deductions so why wouldn't Congress allow individuals the same exemptions? As we allow the free market to provide insurance coverage opportunities to companies and individuals, we must also make sure that no one slips through the cracks simply because they cannot afford insurance. We must review basic options for Medicaid and work with states to ensure that those who want healthcare coverage can have it.

4. Allow individuals to use Health Savings Accounts (HSAs). Contributions into HSAs should be tax-free and should be allowed to accumulate. These accounts would become part of the estate of the individual and could be passed on to heirs without fear of any death penalty. These plans should be particularly attractive to young people who are healthy and can afford high-deductible insurance plans. These funds can be used by any member of a family without penalty. The flexibility and security provided by HSAs will be of great benefit to all who participate.

5. Require price transparency from all healthcare providers, especially doctors and healthcare organizations like clinics

and hospitals. Individuals should be able to shop to find the best prices for procedures, exams or any other medical-related procedure.

6. Block-grant Medicaid to the states. Nearly every state already offers benefits beyond what is required in the current Medicaid structure. The state governments know their people best and can manage the administration of Medicaid far better without federal overhead. States will have the incentives to seek out and eliminate fraud, waste and abuse to preserve our precious resources.

7. Remove barriers to entry into free markets for drug providers that offer safe, reliable and cheaper products. Congress will need the courage to step away from the special interests and do what is right for America. Though the pharmaceutical industry is in the private sector, drug companies provide a public service. Allowing consumers access to imported, safe and dependable drugs from overseas will bring more options to consumers.

The reforms outlined above will lower healthcare costs for all Americans. They are simply a place to start. There are other reforms that might be considered if they serve to lower costs, remove uncertainty and provide financial security for all Americans. And we must also take actions in other policy areas to lower healthcare costs and burdens. Enforcing immigration laws, eliminating fraud and waste and energizing our economy will relieve the economic pressures felt by every American. It is the moral responsibility of a nation's government to do what is best for the people and what is in the interest of securing the future of the nation.

Providing healthcare to illegal immigrants costs us some $11 billion annually. If we were to simply enforce the current immigration laws and restrict the unbridled granting of visas to this country, we could relieve healthcare cost pressures on state and local governments.

To reduce the number of individuals needing access to programs like Medicaid and Children's Health Insurance Program we will need to install programs that grow the economy and bring capital and jobs back to America. The best social program has always been a job – and taking care of our economy will go a long way towards reducing our dependence on public health programs.

Finally, we need to reform our mental health programs and institutions in this country. Families, without the ability to get the information needed to help those who are ailing, are too often not given the tools to help their loved ones. There are promising reforms being developed in Congress that should receive bi-partisan support.

To reform healthcare in America, we need a President who has the leadership skills, will and courage to engage the American people and convince Congress to do what is best for the country. These straightforward reforms, along with many others I have proposed throughout my campaign, will ensure that together we will Make America Great Again.

3. VETERANS ADMINISTRATION REFORMS

Veterans Administration Reforms That Will Make America Great Again

The Goals of Donald J. Trump's Veterans Plan

The current state of the Department of Veterans Affairs (VA) is absolutely unacceptable. Over 300,000 veterans died waiting for care. Corruption and incompetence were excused. Politicians in Washington have done too little too slowly to fix it. This situation can never happen again, and when Donald J. Trump is president, it will be fixed – fast.

The guiding principle of the Trump plan is ensuring veterans have convenient access to the best quality care. To further this principle, the Trump plan will decrease wait times, improve healthcare outcomes, and facilitate a seamless transition from service into civilian life.

The Trump Plan Will:

1. **Ensure our veterans get the care they need wherever and whenever they need it.** No more long drives. No more waiting for backlogs. No more excessive red tape. Just the care and support they earned with their service to our country.

2. **Support the whole veteran**, not just their physical health care, but also by addressing their invisible wounds, investing in our service members' post-active duty success, transforming the VA to meet the needs of 21st century service members, and better meeting the needs of our female veterans.

3. **Make the VA great again** by firing the corrupt and incompetent VA executives who let our veterans down, by modernizing the VA, and by empowering the doctors and nurses to ensure our veterans receive the best care available in a timely manner.

The Trump Plan Gives Veterans the Freedom to Choose and Forces the VA to Compete For Their Dollars

Politicians in Washington have tried to fix the VA by holding hearings and blindly throwing money at the problem. None of it has worked. In fact, wait times were 50% higher this summer than they were a year ago. That's because the VA lacks the right leadership and management. It's time we stop trusting Washington politicians to fix the problems and empower our veterans to vote with their feet.

Under a Trump Administration, <u>all</u> veterans eligible for VA health care can bring their veteran's ID card to <u>any</u> doctor or care facility that accepts Medicare to get the care they need <u>immediately</u>. Our veterans have earned the freedom to choose better or more convenient care from the doctor and facility of their choice. The power to choose will stop the wait time backlogs and force the VA to improve and compete if the department wants to keep receiving veterans' healthcare dollars. The VA will become more responsive to veterans, develop more efficient systems, and improve the quality of care because it will have no other choice.

The Trump Plan Treats the Whole Veteran

We must care for the whole veteran, not just their physical health. We must recognize that today's veterans have very different needs than those of the Greatest Generation.

The Trump Plan Will:

1. **Increase funding for post-traumatic stress disorder (PTSD), traumatic brain injury and suicide prevention services to address our veterans' invisible wounds.** Service members are five times more likely to develop depression than civilians. They are almost fifteen times more likely to develop PTSD than civilians. This funding will help provide more and better counseling and care. More funding will also support research on best practices and state of the art treatments to keep our veterans alive, healthy and whole. With these steps, the Trump plan will help the veteran community put the unnecessary stigma surrounding mental health behind them and instead encourage acceptance and treatment in our greater society.

2. **Increase funding for job training and placement services (including incentives for companies hiring veterans), educational support and business loans.** All Americans agree that we must do everything we can to help put our service men and women on a path to success as they leave active duty by collaborating with the many successful non-profit organizations that are already helping. Service members have learned valuable skills in the military but many need help understanding how to apply those skills in civilian life. Others know how to apply those skills but need help connecting with good jobs to support their families. Still others have an entrepreneurial spirit and are ready to start creating jobs and growing the economy. The Trump plan will strengthen existing programs or replace them with more effective ones to address these needs and to get our veterans working.

3. **Transform the VA to meet the needs of 21st century service members.** Today's veterans have very different needs than those of the generations that came before them. The VA must adapt to meet the needs of this generation of younger, more diverse veterans. The Trump plan will expand VA services for female veterans and ensure the VA is providing the right support for this new generation of veterans.

4. **Better support our women veterans.** The fact that many VA hospitals don't permanently staff OBGYN doctors shows an utter lack of respect for the growing number female veterans. Under the Trump plan, every VA hospital in the country will be fully equipped with OBGYN and other women's health services. In addition, women veterans can always choose a different OBGYN in their community using their veteran's ID card.

The Trump Plan Will Make the VA Great Again

The VA health care program is a disaster. Some candidates want to get rid of it, but our veterans need the VA to be there for them and their families. That's why the Trump plan will:

1. **Fire the corrupt and incompetent VA executives that let our veterans down.** Under a Trump Administration, there will be no job security for VA executives that enabled or overlooked corruption and incompetence. They're fired. New leadership will focus the VA staff on delivering timely, top quality care and other services to our nation's veterans. Under a Trump Administration, exposing and addressing the VA's inefficiencies and shortcomings will be rewarded, not punished.

2. **End waste, fraud and abuse at the VA.** The Trump plan will ensure the VA is spending its dollars wisely to provide the greatest impact for veterans and hold administrators accountable for irresponsible spending and abuse. The days of $6.3 million for statues and fountains at VA facilities and $300,000 for a manager to move 140 miles are over. The Trump plan will clean up the VA's finances so the current VA budget provides more and better care than it does now.

3. **Modernize the VA.** A VA with 20th century technology cannot serve 21st century service members and their needs. The VA has been promising to modernize for years without real results. The Trump plan will make it happen by accelerating and expanding investments in state of the art technology to deliver best-in-class care quickly and effectively. All veterans should be able to conveniently schedule appointments, communicate with their doctors, and view accurate wait times with the push of a button.

4. **Empower the caregivers to ensure our veterans receive quality care quickly.** Caregivers should be able to easily

streamline treatment plans across departments and utilize telehealth tools to better serve their patients. As we have seen from the private sector, the potential for new, innovative technology is endless. Abandoning the wasteful and archaic mindset of the public sector will give way to tremendously effective veteran healthcare.

5. **Hire more veterans to care for veterans.** The more veterans we have working at the VA, the better the VA will be. They understand the unique challenges facing their community. To increase the number of veterans hired by the VA, this plan will add an additional 5 points to the qualifying scores of veterans applying for VA jobs.

6. **Embed satellite VA clinics in rural and other underserved areas.** The Trump Administration will embed satellite VA clinics within hospitals and other care facilities in rural and other underserved areas. This step will ensure veterans have easy access to care and local hospitals and care facilities can handle the influx of patients without backlogs while tapping the specialized knowledge of VA health specialists.

5. IMMIGRATION REFORM

Immigration Reform That Will Make America Great Again

The three core principles of Donald J. Trump's immigration plan

When politicians talk about "immigration reform" they mean: amnesty, cheap labor and open borders. The Schumer-Rubio immigration bill was nothing more than a giveaway to the corporate patrons who run both parties.

Real immigration reform puts the needs of working people first – not wealthy globetrotting donors. We are the only country in the world whose immigration system puts the needs of other nations ahead of our own. That must change. Here are the three core principles of real immigration reform:

1. **A nation without borders is not a nation.** There must be a wall across the southern border.

2. **A nation without laws is not a nation.** Laws passed in accordance with our Constitutional system of government must be enforced.

3. **A nation that does not serve its own citizens is not a nation.** Any immigration plan must improve jobs, wages and security for all Americans.

Make Mexico Pay for the Wall

For many years, Mexico's leaders have been taking advantage of the United States by using illegal immigration to export the crime and poverty in their own country (as well as in other Latin American countries). They have even published pamphlets on how to illegally immigrate to the United States. The costs for the United States have been extraordinary: U.S. taxpayers have been asked to pick up hundreds of billions in healthcare costs, housing costs, education costs, welfare costs, etc. Indeed, the annual cost of free tax credits alone paid to illegal immigrants quadrupled to $4.2 billion in 2011. The effects on jobseekers have also been disastrous, and black Americans have been particularly harmed.

The impact in terms of crime has been tragic. In recent weeks, the headlines have been covered with cases of criminals who crossed our border illegally only to go on to commit horrific crimes against Americans. Most recently, an illegal immigrant from Mexico, with a long arrest record, is charged with breaking into a 64 year-old woman's home, crushing her skull and eye sockets with a hammer, raping her, and murdering her. The Police Chief in Santa Maria says the 'blood trail" leads straight to Washington.

In 2011, the Government Accountability Office found that there were a shocking 3 million arrests attached to the incarcerated alien population, including tens of thousands of violent beatings, rapes and murders.

Meanwhile, Mexico continues to make billions on not only our bad trade deals but also relies heavily on the billions of dollars in remittances sent from illegal immigrants in the United States back to Mexico ($22 billion in 2013 alone).

In short, the Mexican government has taken the United States to the cleaners. They are responsible for this problem, and they must help pay to clean it up.

The cost of building a permanent border wall pales mightily in comparison to what American taxpayers spend every single year on dealing with the fallout of illegal immigration on their communities, schools and unemployment offices.

Mexico must pay for the wall and, until they do, the United States will, among other things: impound all remittance payments derived from illegal wages; increase fees on all temporary visas issued to Mexican CEOs and diplomats (and if necessary cancel them); increase fees on all border crossing cards – of which we issue about 1 million to Mexican nationals each year (a major source of visa overstays); increase fees on all NAFTA worker visas from Mexico (another major source of overstays); and increase fees at ports of entry to the United States from Mexico [Tariffs and foreign aid cuts are also options]. We will not be taken advantage of anymore.

Defend the Laws and Constitution of the United States

America will only be great as long as America remains a nation of laws that lives according to the Constitution. No one is above the law. The following steps will return to the American people the safety of their laws, which politicians have stolen from them:

Triple the number of ICE officers. As the President of the ICE Officers' Council explained in Congressional testimony: "Only approximately 5,000 officers and agents within ICE perform the lion's share of ICE's immigration mission...Compare that to the Los Angeles Police Department at approximately 10,000 officers. Approximately 5,000 officers in ICE cover 50 states, Puerto Rico and Guam, and are attempting to enforce immigration law against 11 million illegal aliens already in the interior of the United States. Since 9-11, the U.S. Border Patrol has tripled in size, while ICE's immigration enforcement arm, Enforcement and Removal Operations (ERO), has remained at relatively the same size." This will be funded by accepting the recommendation of the Inspector General for Tax Administration and eliminating tax credit payments to illegal immigrants.

Nationwide e-verify. This simple measure will protect jobs for unemployed Americans.

Mandatory return of all criminal aliens. The Obama Administration has released 76,000 aliens from its custody with criminal convictions since 2013 alone. All criminal aliens must be returned to their home countries, a process which can be aided by canceling any visas to foreign countries which will not accept their own criminals, and making it a separate and additional crime to commit an offense while here illegally.

Detention—not catch-and-release. Illegal aliens apprehended crossing the border must be detained until they are sent home, no more catch-and-release.

Defund sanctuary cities. Cut-off federal grants to any city which refuses to cooperate with federal law enforcement.

Enhanced penalties for overstaying a visa. Millions of people come to the United States on temporary visas but refuse to leave, without consequence. This is a threat to national security. Individuals who refuse to leave at the time their visa expires should be subject to criminal penalties; this will also help give local jurisdictions the power to hold visa overstays until federal authorities arrive. Completion of a visa tracking system – required by law but blocked by lobbyists – will be necessary as well.

Cooperate with local gang task forces. ICE officers should accompany local police departments conducting raids of violent street gangs like MS-13 and the 18th Street Gang, which have terrorized the country. All illegal aliens in gangs should be apprehended and deported. Again, quoting Chris Crane: "ICE Officers and Agents are forced to apply the Deferred Action for Childhood Arrivals (DACA) Directive, not to children in schools, but to adult inmates in jails. If an illegal-alien inmate simply claims eligibility, ICE is forced to release the alien back into the community. This includes serious criminals who have committed felonies, who have assaulted officers, and who prey on children... ICE officers should be required to place detainers on every illegal alien they encounter in jails and prisons, since these aliens not only violated immigration laws, but then went on to engage in activities that led to their arrest by police; ICE officers should be required to issue Notices to Appear to all illegal aliens with criminal convictions, DUI convictions, or a gang affiliation; ICE should be working with any state or local drug or gang task force that asks for such assistance."

End birthright citizenship. This remains the biggest magnet for illegal immigration. By a 2-to-1 margin, voters say it's the wrong policy, including Harry Reid who said "no sane country" would give automatic citizenship to the children of illegal immigrants.

Put American Workers First

Decades of disastrous trade deals and immigration policies have destroyed our middle class. Today, nearly 40% of black teenagers are unemployed. Nearly 30% of Hispanic teenagers are unemployed. For black Americans without high school diplomas, the bottom has fallen out: more than 70% were employed in 1960, compared to less than 40% in 2000. Across the economy, the percentage of adults in the labor force has collapsed to a level not experienced in generations. As CBS news wrote in a piece entitled "America's incredible shrinking middle class": "If the middle-class is the economic backbone of America, then the country is developing osteoporosis."

The influx of foreign workers holds down salaries, keeps unemployment high, and makes it difficult for poor and working class Americans – including immigrants themselves and their children – to earn a middle class wage. Nearly half of all immigrants and their US-born children currently live in or near, including more than 60 percent of Hispanic immigrants. Every year, we voluntarily admit another 2 million new immigrants, guest workers, refugees, and dependents, growing our existing all-time historic record population of 42 million immigrants. We need to control the admission of new low-earning workers in order to: help wages grow, get teenagers back to work, aid minorities' rise into the middle class, help schools and communities falling behind, and to ensure our immigrant members of the national family become part of the American dream.

Additionally, we need to stop giving legal immigrant visas to people bent on causing us harm. From the 9/11 hijackers, to the Boston Bombers, and many others, our immigration system is being used to attack us. The President of the immigration caseworkers union declared in a statement on ISIS: "We've become the visa clearinghouse for the world."

Here are some additional specific policy proposals for long-term reform:

Increase prevailing wage for H-1Bs. We graduate twice as many Americans with STEM degrees each year as find STEM jobs, yet as much as two-thirds of entry-level hiring for IT jobs is accomplished through the H-1B program. More than half of H-1B visas are issued for the program's lowest allowable wage level, and more than eighty percent for its bottom two. Raising the prevailing wage paid to H-1Bs will force companies to give these coveted entry-level jobs to the existing domestic pool of unemployed native and immigrant workers in the U.S., instead of flying in cheaper workers from overseas. This will improve the number of black, Hispanic and female workers in Silicon Valley who have been passed over in favor of the H-1B program. Mark Zuckerberg's personal Senator, Marco Rubio, has a bill to triple H-1Bs that would decimate women and minorities.

Requirement to hire American workers first. Too many visas, like the H-1B, have no such requirement. In the year 2015, with 92 million Americans outside the workforce and incomes collapsing, we need companies to hire from the domestic pool of unemployed. Petitions for workers should be mailed to the unemployment office, not USCIS.

End welfare abuse. Applicants for entry to the United States should be required to certify that they can pay for their own housing, healthcare and other needs before coming to the U.S.

Jobs program for inner city youth. The J-1 visa jobs program for foreign youth will be terminated and replaced with a resume bank for inner city youth provided to all corporate subscribers to the J-1 visa program.

Refugee program for American children. Increase standards for the admission of refugees and asylum-seekers to crack down on abuses. Use the monies saved on expensive refugee programs to help place American children without parents in safer homes and communities, and to improve community safety in high crime neighborhoods in the United States.

Immigration moderation. Before any new green cards are issued to foreign workers abroad, there will be a pause where employers will have to hire from the domestic pool of unemployed immigrant and native workers. This will help reverse women's plummeting workplace participation rate, grow wages, and allow record immigration levels to subside to more moderate historical averages.

6. COMPELLING MEXICO TO PAY FOR THE WALL

Compelling Mexico to Pay for the Wall

Introduction: The provision of the Patriot Act, Section 326 - the "know your customer" provision, compelling financial institutions to demand identity documents before opening accounts or conducting financial transactions is a fundamental element of the outline below. That section authorized the executive branch to issue detailed regulations on the subject, found at 31 CFR 130.120-121. It's an easy decision for Mexico: make a one-time payment of $5-10 billion to ensure that $24 billion continues to flow into their country year after year. There are several ways to compel Mexico to pay for the wall including the following:

- On day 1 promulgate a "proposed rule" (regulation) amending 31 CFR 130.121 to redefine applicable financial institutions to include money transfer companies like Western Union, and redefine "account" to include wire transfers. Also include in the proposed rule a requirement that no alien may wire money outside of the United States unless the alien first provides a document establishing his lawful presence in the United States.

- On day 2 Mexico will immediately protest. They receive approximately $24 billion a year in remittances from Mexican nationals working in the United States. The majority of that amount comes from illegal aliens. It serves as *de facto* welfare for poor families in Mexico. There is no significant social safety net provided by the state in Mexico.

- On day 3 tell Mexico that if the Mexican government will contribute the funds needed to the United States to pay for the wall, the Trump Administration will not promulgate the final rule, and the regulation will not go into effect.

- Trade tariffs, or enforcement of existing trade rules: There is no doubt that Mexico is engaging in unfair subsidy behavior that has eliminated thousands of U.S. jobs, and which we are obligated to respond to; the impact of any tariffs on the price imports will be more than offset by the economic and income gains of increased production in the United States, in addition to revenue from any tariffs themselves. Mexico needs access to our markets much more than the reverse, so we have all the leverage and will win the negotiation. By definition, if you have a large trade deficit with a nation, it means they are selling far more to you than the reverse - thus they, not you, stand to lose from enforcing trade rules through tariffs (as has been done to save many U.S. industries in the past).

- Cancelling visas: Immigration is a privilege, not a right. Mexico is totally dependent on the United States as a release valve for its own poverty - our approvals of hundreds of thousands of visas to their nationals every year is one of our greatest leverage points. We also have leverage through business and tourist visas for important people in the Mexican economy. Keep in mind, the United States has already taken in 4X more migrants than any other country on planet earth, producing lower wages and higher unemployment for our own citizens and recent migrants.

- Visa fees: Even a small increase in visa fees would pay for the wall. This includes fees on border crossing cards, of which more than 1 million are issued a year. The border-crossing card is also one of the greatest sources of illegal immigration into the United States, via overstays. Mexico is also the single largest recipient of U.S. green cards, which confer a path to U.S. citizenship. Again, we have the leverage so Mexico will back down.

Conclusion: Mexico has taken advantage of us in another way as well: gangs, drug traffickers and cartels have freely exploited our open borders and committed vast numbers of crimes inside the United States. The United States has borne the extraordinary daily cost of this criminal activity, including the cost of trials and incarcerations. Not to mention the even greater human cost. We have the moral high ground here, and all the leverage. It is time we use it in order to Make America Great Again.

7. U.S. – CHINA TRADE RELATIONS REFORM

Reforming the U.S.-China Trade Relationship to Make America Great Again

How We Got Here: Washington Politicians Let China off the Hook

In January 2000, President Bill Clinton boldly promised China's inclusion in the World Trade Organization (WTO) "is a good deal for America. Our products will gain better access to China's market, and every sector from agriculture, to telecommunications, to automobiles. But China gains no new market access to the

United States." None of what President Clinton promised came true. Since China joined the WTO, Americans have witnessed the closure of more than 50,000 factories and the loss of tens of millions of jobs. It was not a good deal for America then and it's a bad deal now. It is a typical example of how politicians in Washington have failed our country.

The most important component of our China policy is leadership and strength at the negotiating table. We have been too afraid to protect and advance American interests and to challenge China to live up to its obligations. We need smart negotiators who will serve the interests of American workers – not Wall Street insiders that want to move U.S. manufacturing and investment offshore.

The Goal of the Trump Plan: Fighting For American Businesses and Workers

America has always been a trading nation. Under the Trump administration trade will flourish. However, for free trade to bring prosperity to America, it must also be fair trade. Our goal is not protectionism but accountability. America fully opened its markets to China but China has not reciprocated. Its Great Wall of Protectionism uses unlawful tariff and non-tariff barriers to keep American companies out of China and to tilt the playing field in their favor.

If you give American workers a level playing field, they will win. At its heart, this plan is a negotiating strategy to bring fairness to our trade with China. The results will be huge for American businesses and workers. Jobs and factories will stop moving offshore and instead stay here at home. The economy will boom. The steps outlined in this plan will make that a reality.

When Donald J. Trump is president, China will be on notice that America is back in the global leadership business and that their days of currency manipulation and cheating are over. We will cut a better deal with China that helps American businesses and workers compete.

The Trump Plan Will Achieve The Following Goals:

1. **Bring China to the bargaining table** by immediately declaring it a currency manipulator.

2. **Protect American ingenuity and investment** by forcing China to uphold intellectual property laws and stop their unfair and unlawful practice of forcing U.S. companies to share proprietary technology with Chinese competitors as a condition of entry to China's market.

3. **Reclaim millions of American jobs and reviving American manufacturing** by putting an end to China's illegal export subsidies and lax labor and environmental standards. No more sweatshops or pollution havens stealing jobs from American workers.

4. **Strengthen our negotiating position** by lowering our corporate tax rate to keep American companies and jobs here at home, attacking our debt and deficit so China cannot use financial blackmail against us, and bolstering the U.S. military presence in the East and South China Seas to discourage Chinese adventurism.

Details of Donald J. Trump's US China Trade Plan:

Declare China a Currency Manipulator

We need a president who will not succumb to the financial blackmail of a Communist dictatorship. President Obama's Treasury Department has repeatedly refused to brand China a currency manipulator – a move that would force China to stop these unfair practices or face tough countervailing duties that level the playing field.

Economists estimate the Chinese Yuan is undervalued by anywhere from 15% to 40%. This grossly undervalued Yuan gives Chinese exporters a huge advantage while imposing the equivalent of a heavy tariff on U.S. exports to China. Such currency manipulation, in concert with China's other unfair practices, has resulted in chronic U.S. trade deficits, a severe weakening of the U.S. manufacturing base and the loss of tens of millions of American jobs.

In a system of truly free trade and floating exchange rates like a Trump administration would support, America's massive trade deficit with China would not persist. On day one of the Trump administration the U.S. Treasury Department will designate China as a currency manipulator. This will begin a process that imposes appropriate countervailing duties on artificially cheap Chinese products, defends U.S. manufacturers and workers, and revitalizes job growth in America. We must stand up to China's blackmail and reject corporate America's manipulation of our politicians. The U.S. Treasury's designation of China as a currency manipulator will force China to the negotiating table and open the door to a fair – and far better – trading relationship.

End China's Intellectual Property Violations

China's ongoing theft of intellectual property may be the greatest transfer of wealth in history. This theft costs the U.S. over $300 billion and millions of jobs each year. China's government ignores this rampant cybercrime and, in other cases, actively encourages or even sponsors it –without any real consequences. China's cyber lawlessness threatens our prosperity, privacy and national security. We will enforce stronger protections against Chinese hackers and counterfeit goods and our responses to Chinese theft will be swift, robust, and unequivocal.

The Chinese government also forces American companies like Boeing, GE, and Intel to transfer proprietary technologies to Chinese competitors as a condition of entry into the Chinese market. Such de facto intellectual property theft represents a brazen violation of WTO and international rules. China's forced technology transfer policy is absolutely ridiculous. Going forward, we will adopt a zero tolerance policy on intellectual property theft and forced technology transfer. If China wants to trade with America, they must agree to stop stealing and to play by the rules.

Eliminate China's Illegal Export Subsidies and Other Unfair Advantages

Chinese manufacturers and other exporters receive numerous illegal export subsidies from the Chinese government. These include - in direct contradiction to WTO rules - free or nearly free rent, utilities, raw materials, and many other services. China's state-run banks routinely extend loans these enterprises at below market rates or without the expectation they will be repaid. China even offers them illegal tax breaks or rebates as well as cash bonuses to stimulate exports.

China's illegal export subsidies intentionally distorts international trade and damages other countries' exports by giving Chinese companies an unfair advantage. From textile and steel mills in the Carolinas to the Gulf Coast's shrimp and fish industries to the Midwest manufacturing belt and California's agribusiness, China's disregard for WTO rules hurt every corner of America.

The U.S. Trade Representative recently filed yet another complaint with the WTO accusing China of cheating on our trade agreements by subsidizing its exports. The Trump administration will not wait for an international body to tell us what we already know. To gain negotiating leverage, we will pursue the WTO case and aggressively highlight and expose these subsidies.

China's woeful lack of reasonable environmental and labor standards represent yet another form of unacceptable export subsidy. How can American manufacturers, who must meet very high standards, possibly compete with Chinese companies that care nothing about their workers or the environment? We will challenge China to join the 21st Century when it comes to such standards.

The Trump Plan Will Strengthen Our Negotiating Position

As the world's most important economy and consumer of goods, America must always negotiate trade agreements from strength. Branding China as a currency manipulator and exposing their unfair trade practices is not enough. In order to further strengthen our negotiating leverage, the Trump plan will:

1. **Lower the corporate tax rate to 15%** to unleash American ingenuity here at home and make us more globally competitive. This tax cut puts our rate 10 percentage points below China and 20 points below our current burdensome rate that pushes companies and jobs offshore.

2. **Attack our debt and deficit** by vigorously eliminating waste, fraud and abuse in the Federal government, ending redundant government programs, and growing the economy to increase tax revenues. Closing the deficit and reducing our debt will mean China cannot blackmail us with our own Treasury bonds.

3. **Strengthen the U.S. military and deploying it appropriately in the East and South China Seas.** These actions will discourage Chinese adventurism that imperils American interests in Asia and shows our strength as we begin renegotiating our trading relationship with China. A strong military presence will be a clear signal to China and other nations in Asia and around the world that America is back in the global leadership business.

8. SECOND AMENDMENT RIGHTS

PROTECTING OUR SECOND AMENDMENT RIGHTS WILL MAKE AMERICA GREAT AGAIN

Donald J. Trump on the Right to Keep and Bear Arms

The Second Amendment to our Constitution is clear. The right of the people to keep and bear Arms shall not be infringed upon. Period.

The Second Amendment guarantees a fundamental right that belongs to all law-abiding Americans. The Constitution doesn't create that right – it ensures that the government can't take it away. Our Founding Fathers knew, and our Supreme Court has upheld, that the Second Amendment's purpose is to guarantee our right to defend ourselves and our families. This is about self-defense, plain and simple.

It's been said that the Second Amendment is America's first freedom. That's because the Right to Keep and Bear Arms protects all our other rights. We are the only country in the world that has a Second Amendment. Protecting that freedom is imperative. Here's how we will do that:

Enforce the Laws on the Books

We need to get serious about prosecuting violent criminals. The Obama administration's record on that is abysmal. Violent crime in cities like Baltimore, Chicago and many others is out of control. Drug dealers and gang members are given a slap on the wrist and turned loose on the street. This needs to stop.

Several years ago there was a tremendous program in Richmond, Virginia called Project Exile. It said that if a violent felon uses a gun to commit a crime, you will be prosecuted in federal court and go to prison for five years – no parole or early release. Obama's former Attorney General, Eric Holder, called that a "cookie cutter" program. That's ridiculous. I call that program a success. Murders committed with guns in Richmond decreased by over 60% when Project Exile was in place – in the first two years of the program alone, 350 armed felons were taken off the street.

Why does that matter to law-abiding gun owners? Because they're the ones who anti-gun politicians and the media blame when criminals misuse guns. We need to bring back and expand programs like Project Exile and get gang members and drug dealers off the street. When we do, crime will go down and our cities and communities will be safer places to live.

Here's another important way to fight crime – empower law-abiding gun owners to defend themselves. Law enforcement is great, they do a tremendous job, but they can't be everywhere all of the time. Our personal protection is ultimately up to us. That's why I'm a gun owner, that's why I have a concealed carry permit, and that's why tens of millions of Americans have concealed carry permits as well. It's just common sense. To make America great again, we're going to go after criminals and put the law back on the side of the law-abiding.

Fix Our Broken Mental Health System

Let's be clear about this. Our mental health system is broken. It needs to be fixed. Too many politicians have ignored this problem for too long.

All of the tragic mass murders that occurred in the past several years have something in common – there were red flags that were ignored. We can't allow that to continue. We need to expand treatment programs, because most people with mental health problems aren't violent, they just need help. But for those who are violent, a danger to themselves or others, we need to get them off the street before they can terrorize our communities. This is just common sense.

And why does this matter to law-abiding gun owners? Once again, because they get blamed by anti-gun politicians, gun control groups and the media for the acts of deranged madmen. When one of these tragedies occurs, we can count on two things: one, that opponents of gun rights will immediately exploit it to push their political agenda; and two, that none of their so-called "solutions" would have prevented the tragedy in the first place. They've even admitted it.

We need real solutions to address real problems. Not grandstanding or political agendas.

Defend the Rights of Law-Abiding Gun Owners

GUN AND MAGAZINE BANS. Gun and magazine bans are a total failure. That's been proven every time it's been tried. Opponents of gun rights try to come up with scary sounding phrases like "assault weapons", "military-style weapons" and "high capacity magazines" to confuse people. What they're really talking about are popular semi-automatic rifles and standard magazines that are owned by tens of millions of Americans. Law-abiding people should be allowed to own the firearm of their choice. The government has no business dictating what types of firearms good, honest people are allowed to own.

BACKGROUND CHECKS. There has been a national background check system in place since 1998. Every time a person buys a gun from a federally licensed gun dealer – which is the overwhelming majority of all gun purchases – they go through a federal background check. Study after study has shown that very few criminals are stupid enough to try and pass a background check – they get their guns from friends/family members or by stealing them. So the overwhelming majority of people who go through background checks are law-abiding gun owners. When the system was created, gun owners were promised that it would be instant, accurate and fair. Unfortunately, that isn't the case today. Too many states are failing to put criminal and mental health records into the system – and it should go without saying that a system's only going to be as effective as the records that are put into it. What we need to do is fix the system we have and make it work as intended. What we don't need to do is expand a broken system.

NATIONAL RIGHT TO CARRY. The right of self-defense doesn't stop at the end of your driveway. That's why I have a concealed carry permit and why tens of millions of Americans do too. That permit should be valid in all 50 states. A driver's license works in every state, so it's common sense that a concealed carry permit should work in every state. If we can do that for driving – which is a privilege, not a right – then surely we can do that for concealed carry, which is a right, not a privilege.

MILITARY BASES AND RECRUITING CENTERS. Banning our military from carrying firearms on bases and at recruiting centers is ridiculous. We train our military how to safely and responsibly use firearms, but our current policies leave them defenseless. To make America great again, we need a strong military. To have a strong military, we need to allow them to defend themselves.

14

THE RACE GETS CLOSER – SEPTEMBER 2016

From the beginning of the general campaign pollsters all over the country commenced taking polls literally every day to predict who would succeed to the Presidency. There were numerous polls examining every aspect of the election. Rupert Murdoch's Fox News, the leading right-wing Republican organ and the most watched and followed cable "news" network which, to many people, is not a "news" channel at all but the millennial version of "shock radio" was among the top polling references. CNN, Cable News Network, which portrayed itself as "centrist" sampled potential voters in its polls, while liberal-leaning MSNBC did the same as its two unrelated "brethren." Not to be outdone, NBC, CBS, and ABC, the traditional networks, conducted their poll, as did major national newspapers, such as the New York *Times*, the Washington *Post*, and the Los Angeles *Times*.

But as the election came closer, two polls appeared to emerge as dominant: *Five Thirty Eight* and *Real Clear Politics*. Both of these forecasters relied not only on their own polls, but were more of a shopping bag full of other polls.

FiveThirtyEight, sometimes referred to as **538**, is a website that focuses on opinion poll analysis, politics, economics, and sports blogging. The website, which takes its name from the number of electors in the United States Electoral College, was founded on March 7, 2008 as a polling aggregation website with a blog created by analyst Nate Silver. In August 2010, the blog became a licensed feature of *The New York Times* online. In July 2013, ESPN announced that it would become the owner of the FiveThirtyEight brand and site, and Silver was appointed as editor-in-chief. The ESPN-owned FiveThirtyEight began publication on March 17, 2014. In the ESPN era, the FiveThirtyEight blog has covered a broad spectrum of subjects including politics, sports, science, economics, and popular culture.

During the U.S. presidential primaries and general election of 2008, the site compiled polling data through a unique methodology derived from Silver's experience in baseball sabermetrics to "balance out the polls with comparative demographic data." He weighted "each poll based on the pollster's historical track record, sample size, and recentness of the poll".

Since the 2008 election, the site published articles – typically creating or analyzing statistical information – on a wide variety of topics in current politics and political news. These included a monthly update on the prospects for turnover in the U.S. Senate; federal economic policies; Congressional support for legislation; public support for health care reform, global warming legislation, LGBT rights; elections around the world; marijuana legalization; and numerous other topics. The site and its creator are best known for election forecasts, including the 2012 presidential election in which FiveThirtyEight correctly predicted the vote winner of all 50 states.

FiveThirtyEight applied two separate models to forecast the 2016 Presidential Primary elections – *Polls-Only* and *Polls-Plus* models. The *polls-only* model relied only on polls from a particular state, while the *polls-plus* model was based on state polls, national polls and endorsements. For each contest, *FiveThirtyEight* produced probability distributions and average expected vote shares per both of these models.[84]

As early as June 2015, *FiveThirtyEight* argued that Donald Trump "isn't a real candidate" and maintained that Trump could not win the nomination until late in the election season. When Donald Trump became the presumptive Republican nominee in May 2016, *New York* Times media columnist Jim Rutenberg wrote that *"predictions can have consequences"* and criticized *FiveThirtyEight* for underestimating Trump's chances. He argued that by giving "Mr. Trump a 2 percent chance at the nomination despite strong polls in his favor, they also arguably sapped the journalistic will to scour his record as aggressively as those of his supposedly more serious rivals."

In a long retrospective "How I Acted like a Pundit and Screwed up on Donald Trump," published in May 2016 after Trump had become the likely nominee, Silver reviewed how he had erred in evaluating Trump's chances early in the primary campaign. Silver wrote, "The big mistake is a curious one for a website that focuses on statistics. Unlike virtually every other forecast we publish at FiveThirtyEight, including the primary and caucus projections I just mentioned, our early estimates of Trump's chances weren't based on a statistical model. Instead, they were what we call 'subjective odds,' which is to say, educated guesses. In other words, we were basically acting like pundits, but attaching numbers to our estimates. And we succumbed to some of the same biases that pundits often suffer, such as not changing our minds quickly enough in the face of new evidence. Without a model as a fortification, we found ourselves rambling around the countryside like all the other pundit-barbarians, randomly setting fire to things".

On the Democratic side, *FiveThirtyEight* argued that Sen. Bernie Sanders could *"lose everywhere else after Iowa and New Hampshire"* and that the *"Democratic establishment would rush in to squash"* him if he doesn't.

FiveThirtyEight's predictions for each state primary, both for the Republican and the Democratic Party nominations, were based on statistical analysis, not on the analyst's opinions. The core data employed were polls, which FiveThirtyEight aggregated for each state (while also considering national polls) using essentially the same method it had employed since 2008. In the 2016 primaries, the projections also took into account endorsements. The website also kept track of the accumulation of national party convention delegates. In a comparison of prediction success published by Bloomberg News after the primary season was completed, FiveThirtyEight's prediction success tied for the highest percentage of correct primary poll winners, at 92%; but it lagged behind PredictWise in predicting a larger set of primaries.

* * *

RealClearPolitics (RCP) is a Chicago-based political news and polling data aggregator formed in 2000 by former options trader John McIntyre and former advertising agency account executive Tom Bevan. The site's founders say their goal is to give readers "ideological diversity." RCP has expanded to include a number of sister sites. *Politico* executive editor Jim VandeHei has called the site "an essential stop for anyone interested in politics."

Patrick Stack of *Time* magazine has described the site's commentary section as "right-leaning." The site has been described as being run by conservatives, and containing "opinion pieces from

THE POLITICS OF INSANITY – HUGO N. GERSTL

multiple media sources." In 2009 RealClearPolitics was described as a weblog "in the conservative pantheon" by Richard Davis.

Updated continuously, RealClearPolitics' websites aggregate content from a wide range of sources, sources that run the gamut of locations and political persuasions. Stories from the *Washington Post* and other large-circulation media frequently run alongside articles from such lesser-known papers as the *Ottawa Citizen*, while analyses from the liberal *New Republic* may be paired with conservative publications such as the *Weekly Standard*. McIntyre's purported objective is "to give readers ideological diversity. We're trying to stay immersed in the nation's political bloodstream at all times. That way, we can show you every small, little twist and turn, and give multiple sides to every story." Forbes Media LLC bought a 51% equity interest in the site in 2007. On May 19, 2015, it was announced that RealClearInvestors and Crest Media bought out Forbes's stake for an undisclosed amount.

RealClearPolitics aggregates polls for presidential and congressional races into averages, known as the RealClearPolitics average, which are widely cited by media outlets. *New York Times* contributor Neil Degrasse Tyson, wrote in an op-ed that "in swing states, the median result of all the polls conducted in the weeks prior to an election is an especially effective predictor of which candidate will win that election—even in states where the polls consistently fall within the margin of error." However, some statisticians say that it is sometimes misleading to average results from multiple polls. When Nate Silver of rival site FiveThirtyEight.com claimed RealClearPolitics.com was rigging its averages to favor Senator John McCain and other Republicans, McIntyre denied having a conservative bent, stating, "We're running a business, We have no interest in screwing around with that for partisan purposes." Silver later backed away from the claim and said the two sites had a friendly rivalry and grudging respect for each other.

Politics is never a clean, fun sport. In every Presidential election there have been vicious, often virulent personal attacks by each candidate on the other. The 2016 Presidential race has been no different, and despite the claims of each side that this is the dirtiest campaign of smear tactics in history, in retrospect and taking the "long view," that is not necessarily so. Nevertheless, this book would be incomplete without pointing out the main thrusts of each candidate's personal attack on the other:

Hillary Clinton attacks on Trump	Donald Trump attacks on Clinton
He's racist, sexist, and xenophobic.	She hasn't got the stamina to be president.
He's the most divisive candidate in history.	She's been in politics 30 years and judgment, or the knowledge to be
He's the only candidate in generations who will not reveal his tax returns.	She lied under oath to the FBI.
It's all about "You can't make America great again unless _I_ lead it there."	She was the worst Secretary of State in history.
Despite his claim of great wealth and being a friend of the worker, he has and cheated workers and his companies have filed bankruptcy _six times_.	She's the great enabler, who's responsible for her husband's philandering.
He does have the temperament, He doesn't have the temperament, the judgment, or the knowledge to be President of the United States.	She was an important part of Obama's presidency - the worst in U.S. History.
He lies every time he opens his mouth.	She doesn't have the temperament or the jugdgment to by President of the U.S.

Hillary Clinton attacks on Trump	Donald Trump attacks on Clinton
Go to the fact checker if you want to check the truth of whatever he says.	She lies every time she opens her mouth.
He used Trump Foundation money for his own personal benefit.	She and her husband made hundreds of millions of dollars through their foundation.
The "Trump University" scammed 35,000 people out of their life savings.	She is singlehandedly responsible for the mess we're in in the Middle East.
He said he wished the real estate market would bottom out - and he made a killing when it did.	She is responsible for the worst trade agreements in the history of the U.S.
	ISIS would not be around except for her policies.
Would you trust someone with his temperament to have his finger on nuclear button?	America is in worse shape than its ever been because of political insiders like her.

* * *

At the close of the Republican Convention, Donald Trump had actually pulled slightly ahead lf Hillary Clinton. When the Democratic Convention ended a week later, Clinton had erased Trump's lead and, at her widest lead, held nearly a 10 point margin over Trump.

According to FiveThirtyEight on July 30, 2016, Trump's chance of being elected President was 50.1% and Clinton's chance 49.9%. By August 14, 2016, Clinton had soared. FiveThirtyEight predicted Hillary Clinton's chance of winning was 89.2% to 10.8% for Donald Trump, and the Democrats were complacent and gloating. But from August 15 to the date of the first Presidential debate on September 26, support for Clinton steadily eroded until, by the eve of the debate her lead had shriveled. There was now a 54.8% chance that Clinton would win the election to a 45.2% that Trump would win the election.

Just before the debate, FiveThirtyEight predicted that Clinton would get 46.4 of the popular vote to 44.8 for Trump – less than a 2% spread. Since all polls have a 4% margin of error, the race was a statistical dead heat as the candidates entered the hall at Hofstra University in New York for the first Presidential debate.

At least equally, if not more important, in United States elections, the race for control of the Senate has swung in both directions. On July 23, 2016, FiveThirtyEight projected there was a 63.1% to 36.9% chance that the Republicans would keep control of the Senate, and thus the all important power to vote to approve the appointment of U.S. Supreme Court Justices. A week later, the Republicans still held a razor-thin margin, 50.7% to 49.3%. That was the last time to date of publication of this book that the Republicans were favored to maintain control of the Senate.

By a week later, August 7, 2016, the world had turned upside down and chances were now 72.7% to 27.3% that the Democrats would take control of the Senate. But since that time, the erosion in the Democratic hegemony has followed Hillary Clinton's hegemony in a steady downward trend. By September 15, FiveThirtyEight still predicted that the Democrats would win back the Senate, but only by 53.7% to 46.3%. As of September 26, the Democrats' chances had risen, but only slightly, to 57.1% to 42.9%, still anyone's race.

Real Clear Politics has reflected the FiveThirtyEight model to some degree, but its daily printout showed results from selected individual polls. As of September 26, 2016, the polls, taken as a whole, showed a statistical tie.

As of the date of the first Presidential Debate on the evening of September, no one could predict with any degree of confidence which candidate would win the Presidential election and which party would control the United States Senate.

15

THE FIRST PRESIDENTIAL DEBATE

Because of the importance of the first of three Presidential debates, which reflected the difference between both the style and the substance of the two candidates, the complete transcript of the First Presidential Debate of the 2016 General Election is set forth immediately below. Lester Holt of NBC served as the sole moderator of the debate. The audience was admonished not to applaud, cheer, boo, or otherwise interfere with the serious demeanor of the campaign. The debate is reported here without any emphasis, without any comment, and without any changes in order that the reader may draw her or his own conclusions:

* * *

HOLT: Well, I don't expect us to cover all the issues of this campaign tonight, but I remind everyone, there are two more presidential debates scheduled. We are going to focus on many of the issues that voters tell us are most important, and we're going to press for specifics. I am honored to have this role, but this evening belongs to the candidates and, just as important, to the American people. Candidates, we look forward to hearing you articulate your policies and your positions, as well as your visions and your values. So, let's begin.

We're calling this opening segment "Achieving Prosperity." And central to that is jobs. There are two economic realities in America today. There's been a record six straight years of job growth, and new census numbers show incomes have increased at a record rate after years of stagnation. However, income inequality remains significant, and nearly half of Americans are living paycheck to paycheck.

Beginning with you, Secretary Clinton, why are you a better choice than your opponent to create the kinds of jobs that will put more money into the pockets of American works?

CLINTON: Well, thank you, Lester, and thanks to Hofstra for hosting us.

The central question in this election is really what kind of country we want to be and what kind of future we'll build together. Today is my granddaughter's second birthday, so I think about this a lot. First, we have to build an economy that works for everyone, not just those at the top. That means we need new jobs, good jobs, with rising incomes.

I want us to invest in you. I want us to invest in your future. That means jobs in infrastructure, in advanced manufacturing, innovation and technology, clean, renewable energy, and small business, because most of the new jobs will come from small business. We also have to make the economy fairer. That starts with raising the national minimum wage and also guarantee, finally, equal pay for women's work.

CLINTON: I also want to see more companies do profit-sharing. If you help create the profits, you should be able to share in them, not just the executives at the top.

And I want us to do more to support people who are struggling to balance family and work. I've heard from so many of you about the difficult choices you face and the stresses that you're under. So let's have paid family leave, earned sick days. Let's be sure we have affordable child care and debt-free college.

How are we going to do it? We're going to do it by having the wealthy pay their fair share and close the corporate loopholes.

Finally, we tonight are on the stage together, Donald Trump and I. Donald, it's good to be with you. We're going to have a debate where we are talking about the important issues facing our country. You have to judge us, who can shoulder the immense, awesome responsibilities of the presidency, who can put into action the plans that will make your life better. I hope that I will be able to earn your vote on November 8th.

HOLT: Secretary Clinton, thank you. Mr. Trump, the same question to you. It's about putting money -- more money into the pockets of American workers. You have up to two minutes.

TRUMP: Thank you, Lester. Our jobs are fleeing the country. They're going to Mexico. They're going to many other countries. You look at what China is doing to our country in terms of making our product. They're devaluing their currency, and there's nobody in our government to fight them. And we have a very good fight. And we have a winning fight. Because they're using our country as a piggy bank to rebuild China, and many other countries are doing the same thing.

So we're losing our good jobs, so many of them. When you look at what's happening in Mexico, a friend of mine who builds plants said it's the eighth wonder of the world. They're building some of the biggest plants anywhere in the world, some of the most sophisticated, some of the best plants. With the United States, as he said, not so much.

So Ford is leaving. You see that, their small car division leaving. Thousands of jobs leaving Michigan, leaving Ohio. They're all leaving. And we can't allow it to happen anymore. As far as child care is concerned and so many other things, I think Hillary and I agree on that. We probably disagree a little bit as to numbers and amounts and what we're going to do, but perhaps we'll be talking about that later.

But we have to stop our jobs from being stolen from us. We have to stop our companies from leaving the United States and, with it, firing all of their people. All you have to do is take a look at Carrier air conditioning in Indianapolis. They left -- fired 1,400 people. They're going to Mexico. So many hundreds and hundreds of companies are doing this.

TRUMP: We cannot let it happen. Under my plan, I'll be reducing taxes tremendously, from 35 percent to 15 percent for companies, small and big businesses. That's going to be a job creator like we haven't seen since Ronald Reagan. It's going to be a beautiful thing to watch.

Companies will come. They will build. They will expand. New companies will start. And I look very, very much forward to doing it. We have to renegotiate our trade deals, and we have to stop these countries from stealing our companies and our jobs.

HOLT: Secretary Clinton, would you like to respond?

CLINTON: Well, I think that trade is an important issue. Of course, we are 5 percent of the world's population; we have to trade with the other 95 percent. And we need to have smart, fair trade deals.

We also, though, need to have a tax system that rewards work and not just financial transactions. And the kind of plan that Donald has put forth would be trickle-down economics all over again. In fact, it would be the most extreme version, the biggest tax cuts for the top percent of the people in this country than we've ever had.

I call it trumped-up trickle-down, because that's exactly what it would be. That is not how we grow the economy.

We just have a different view about what's best for growing the economy, how we make investments that will actually produce jobs and rising incomes.

I think we come at it from somewhat different perspectives. I understand that. You know, Donald was very fortunate in his life, and that's all to his benefit. He started his business with $14 million, borrowed from his father, and he really believes that the more you help wealthy people, the better off we'll be and that everything will work out from there.

I don't buy that. I have a different experience. My father was a small-businessman. He worked really hard. He printed drapery fabrics on long tables, where he pulled out those fabrics and he went down with a silkscreen and dumped the paint in and took the squeegee and kept going.

And so what I believe is the more we can do for the middle class, the more we can invest in you, your education, your skills, your future, the better we will be off and the better we'll grow. That's the kind of economy I want us to see again.

HOLT: Let me follow up with Mr. Trump, if you can. You've talked about creating 25 million jobs, and you've promised to bring back millions of jobs for Americans. How are you going to bring back the industries that have left this country for cheaper labor overseas? How, specifically, are you going to tell American manufacturers that you have to come back?

TRUMP: Well, for one thing -- and before we start on that -- my father gave me a very small loan in 1975, and I built it into a company that's worth many, many billions of dollars, with some of the greatest assets in the world, and I say that only because that's the kind of thinking that our country needs.

Our country's in deep trouble. We don't know what we're doing when it comes to devaluations and all of these countries all over the world, especially China. They're the best, the best ever at it. What they're doing to us is a very, very sad thing.

So we have to do that. We have to renegotiate our trade deals. And, Lester, they're taking our jobs, they're giving incentives, they're doing things that, frankly, we don't do.

Let me give you the example of Mexico. They have a VAT tax. We're on a different system. When we sell into Mexico, there's a tax. When they sell in -- automatic, 16 percent, approximately. When they sell into us, there's no tax. It's a defective agreement. It's been defective for a long time, many years, but the politicians haven't done anything about it.

Now, in all fairness to Secretary Clinton -- yes, is that OK? Good. I want you to be very happy. It's very important to me.

But in all fairness to Secretary Clinton, when she started talking about this, it was really very recently. She's been doing this for 30 years. And why hasn't she made the agreements better? The NAFTA agreement is defective. Just because of the tax and many other reasons, but just because of the fact...

HOLT: Let me interrupt just a moment, but...

TRUMP: Secretary Clinton and others, politicians, should have been doing this for years, not right now, because of the fact that we've created a movement. They should have been doing this for years. What's happened to our jobs and our country and our economy generally is -- look, we owe $20 trillion. We cannot do it any longer, Lester. **HOLT:** Back to the question, though. How do you bring back -- specifically bring back jobs, American manufacturers? How do you make them bring the jobs back?

TRUMP: Well, the first thing you do is don't let the jobs leave. The companies are leaving. I could name, I mean, there are thousands of them. They're leaving, and they're leaving in bigger numbers than ever.

And what you do is you say, fine, you want to go to Mexico or some other country, good luck. We wish you a lot of luck. But if you think you're going to make your air conditioners or your cars or your cookies or whatever you make and bring them into our country without a tax, you're wrong.

And once you say you're going to have to tax them coming in, and our politicians never do this, because they have special interests and the special interests want those companies to leave, because in many cases, they own the companies. So what I'm saying is, we can stop them from leaving. We have to stop them from leaving. And that's a big, big factor.

HOLT: Let me let Secretary Clinton get in here.

CLINTON: Well, let's stop for a second and remember where we were eight years ago. We had the worst financial crisis, the Great Recession, the worst since the 1930s. That was in large part because of tax policies that slashed taxes on the wealthy, failed to invest in the middle class, took their eyes off of Wall Street, and created a perfect storm.

In fact, Donald was one of the people who rooted for the housing crisis. He said, back in 2006, "Gee, I hope it does collapse, because then I can go in and buy some and make some money." Well, it did collapse.

TRUMP: That's called business, by the way.

CLINTON: Nine million people -- nine million people lost their jobs. Five million people lost their homes. And $13 trillion in family wealth was wiped out.

Now, we have come back from that abyss. And it has not been easy. So we're now on the precipice of having a potentially much better economy, but the last thing we need to do is to go back to the policies that failed us in the first place.

Independent experts have looked at what I've proposed and looked at what Donald's proposed, and basically they've said this, that if his tax plan, which would blow up the debt by over $5 trillion and would in some instances disadvantage middle-class families compared to the wealthy, were to go into effect, we would lose 3.5 million jobs and maybe have another recession.

They've looked at my plans and they've said, OK, if we can do this, and I intend to get it done, we will have 10 million more new jobs, because we will be making investments where we can grow the economy. Take clean energy. Some country is going to be the clean- energy superpower of the 21st century. Donald thinks that climate change is a hoax perpetrated by the Chinese. I think it's real.

TRUMP: I did not. I did not. I did not say that.

CLINTON: I think science is real.

TRUMP: I do not say that.

CLINTON: And I think it's important that we grip this and deal with it, both at home and abroad. And here's what we can do. We can deploy a half a billion more solar panels. We can have enough clean energy to power every home. We can build a new modern electric grid. That's a lot of jobs; that's a lot of new economic activity.

So I've tried to be very specific about what we can and should do, and I am determined that we're going to get the economy really moving again, building on the progress we've made over the last eight years, but never going back to what got us in trouble in the first place.

HOLT: Mr. Trump?

TRUMP: She talks about solar panels. We invested in a solar company, our country. That was a disaster. They lost plenty of money on that one.

Now, look, I'm a great believer in all forms of energy, but we're putting a lot of people out of work. Our energy policies are a disaster. Our country is losing so much in terms of energy, in terms of paying off our debt. You can't do what you're looking to do with $20 trillion in debt.

The Obama administration, from the time they've come in, is over 230 years' worth of debt, and he's topped it. He's doubled it in a course of almost eight years, seven-and-a-half years, to be semi- exact.

So I will tell you this. We have to do a much better job at keeping our jobs. And we have to do a much better job at giving companies incentives to build new companies or to expand, because they're not doing it.

And all you have to do is look at Michigan and look at Ohio and look at all of these places where so many of their jobs and their companies are just leaving, they're gone.

And, Hillary, I'd just ask you this. You've been doing this for 30 years. Why are you just thinking about these solutions right now? For 30 years, you've been doing it, and now you're just starting to think of solutions.

CLINTON: Well, actually...

TRUMP: I will bring -- excuse me. I will bring back jobs. You can't bring back jobs.

CLINTON: Well, actually, I have thought about this quite a bit.

TRUMP: Yeah, for 30 years.

CLINTON: And I have -- well, not quite that long. I think my husband did a pretty good job in the 1990s. I think a lot about what worked and how we can make it work again...

TRUMP: Well, he approved NAFTA...

CLINTON: ... million new jobs, a balanced budget...

TRUMP: He approved NAFTA, which is the single worst trade deal ever approved in this country.

CLINTON: Incomes went up for everybody. Manufacturing jobs went up also in the 1990s, if we're actually going to look at the facts.

When I was in the Senate, I had a number of trade deals that came before me, and I held them all to the same test. Will they create jobs in America? Will they raise incomes in America? And are they good for our national security? Some of them I voted for. The biggest one, a multinational one known as CAFTA, I voted against. And because I hold the same standards as I look at all of these trade deals.

But let's not assume that trade is the only challenge we have in the economy. I think it is a part of it, and I've said what I'm going to do. I'm going to have a special prosecutor. We're going to enforce the trade deals we have, and we're going to hold people accountable.

When I was secretary of state, we actually increased American exports globally 30 percent. We increased them to China 50 percent. So I know how to really work to get new jobs and to get exports that helped to create more new jobs.

HOLT: Very quickly...

TRUMP: But you haven't done it in 30 years or 26 years or any number you want to...

CLINTON: Well, I've been a senator, Donald...

TRUMP: You haven't done it. You haven't done it.

CLINTON: And I have been a secretary of state...

TRUMP: Excuse me.

CLINTON: And I have done a lot...

TRUMP: Your husband signed NAFTA, which was one of the worst things that ever happened to the manufacturing industry.

CLINTON: Well, that's your opinion. That is your opinion.

TRUMP: You go to New England, you go to Ohio, Pennsylvania, you go anywhere you want, Secretary Clinton, and you will see devastation where manufacture is down 30, 40, sometimes 50 percent. NAFTA is the worst trade deal maybe ever signed anywhere, but certainly ever signed in this country.

And now you want to approve Trans-Pacific Partnership. You were totally in favor of it. Then you heard what I was saying, how bad it is, and you said, I can't win that debate. But you know that if you did win, you would approve that, and that will be almost as bad as NAFTA. Nothing will ever top NAFTA.

CLINTON: Well, that is just not accurate. I was against it once it was finally negotiated and the terms were laid out. I wrote about that in...

TRUMP: You called it the gold standard. You called it the gold standard of trade deals. You said it's the finest deal you've ever seen.

CLINTON: No.

TRUMP: And then you heard what I said about it, and all of a sudden you were against it.

CLINTON: Well, Donald, I know you live in your own reality, but that is not the facts. The facts are -- I did say I hoped it would be a good deal, but when it was negotiated...

TRUMP: Not.

CLINTON: ... which I was not responsible for, I concluded it wasn't. I wrote about that in my book...

TRUMP: So is it President Obama's fault?

CLINTON: ... before you even announced.

TRUMP: Is it President Obama's fault?

CLINTON: Look, there are differences...

TRUMP: Secretary, is it President Obama's fault?

CLINTON: There are...

TRUMP: Because he's pushing it.

CLINTON: There are different views about what's good for our country, our economy, and our leadership in the world. And I think it's important to look at what we need to do to get the economy going again. That's why I said new jobs with rising incomes, investments, not in more tax cuts that would add $5 trillion to the debt.

TRUMP: But you have no plan.

CLINTON: But in -- oh, but I do.

TRUMP: Secretary, you have no plan.

CLINTON: In fact, I have written a book about it. It's called "Stronger Together." You can pick it up tomorrow at a bookstore...

TRUMP: That's about all you've...

(CROSSTALK)

HOLT: Folks, we're going to...

CLINTON: ... or at an airport near you.

HOLT: We're going to move to...

CLINTON: But it's because I see this -- we need to have strong growth, fair growth, sustained growth. We also have to look at how we help families balance the responsibilities at home and the responsibilities at business.

So we have a very robust set of plans. And people have looked at both of our plans, have concluded that mine would create 10 million jobs and yours would lose us 3.5 million jobs, and explode the debt which would have a recession.

TRUMP: You are going to approve one of the biggest tax cuts in history. You are going to approve one of the biggest tax increases in history. You are going to drive business out. Your regulations are a disaster, and you're going to increase regulations all over the place.

And by the way, my tax cut is the biggest since Ronald Reagan. I'm very proud of it. It will create tremendous numbers of new jobs. But regulations, you are going to regulate these businesses out of existence.

When I go around -- Lester, I tell you this, I've been all over. And when I go around, despite the tax cut, the thing -- the things that business as in people like the most is the fact that I'm cutting regulation. You have regulations on top of regulations, and new companies cannot form and old companies are going out of business. And you want to increase the regulations and make them even worse.

I'm going to cut regulations. I'm going to cut taxes big league, and you're going to raise taxes big league, end of story.

HOLT: Let me get you to pause right there, because we're going to move into -- we're going to move into the next segment. We're going to talk taxes...

CLINTON: That can't -- that can't be left to stand.

HOLT: Please just take 30 seconds and then we're going to go on.

CLINTON: I kind of assumed that there would be a lot of these charges and claims, and so...

TRUMP: Facts.

CLINTON: So we have taken the home page of my website, HillaryClinton.com, and we've turned it into a fact-checker. So if you want to see in real-time what the facts are, please go and take a look. Because what I have proposed...

TRUMP: And take a look at mine, also, and you'll see.

CLINTON: ... would not add a penny to the debt, and your plans would add $5 trillion to the debt. What I have proposed would cut regulations and streamline them for small businesses. What I have proposed would be paid for by raising taxes on the wealthy, because they have made all the gains in the economy. And I think it's time that the wealthy and corporations paid their fair share to support this country.

HOLT: Well, you just opened the next segment.

TRUMP: Well, could I just finish -- I think I...

(CROSSTALK)

HOLT: I'm going to give you a chance right here...

TRUMP: I think I should -- you go to her website, and you take a look at her website.

HOLT: ... with a new 15-minute segment...

TRUMP: She's going to raise taxes $1.3 trillion.

HOLT: Mr. Trump, I'm going to...

TRUMP: And look at her website. You know what? It's no difference than this. She's telling us how to fight ISIS. Just go to her website. She tells you how to fight ISIS on her website. I don't think General Douglas MacArthur would like that too much.

HOLT: The next segment, we're continuing...

CLINTON: Well, at least I have a plan to fight ISIS.

HOLT: ... achieving prosperity...

TRUMP: No, no, you're telling the enemy everything you want to do.

CLINTON: No, we're not. No, we're not.

TRUMP: See, you're telling the enemy everything you want to do. No wonder you've been fighting -- no wonder you've been fighting ISIS your entire adult life.

CLINTON: That's a -- that's -- go to the -- please, fact checkers, get to work.

HOLT: OK, you are unpacking a lot here. And we're still on the issue of achieving prosperity. And I want to talk about taxes. The fundamental difference between the two of you concerns the wealthy.

Secretary Clinton, you're calling for a tax increase on the wealthiest Americans. I'd like you to further defend that. And, Mr. Trump, you're calling for tax cuts for the wealthy. I'd like you to defend that. And this next two-minute answer goes to you, Mr. Trump.

TRUMP: Well, I'm really calling for major jobs, because the wealthy are going create tremendous jobs. They're going to expand their companies. They're going to do a tremendous job.

I'm getting rid of the carried interest provision. And if you really look, it's not a tax -- it's really not a great thing for the wealthy. It's a great thing for the middle class. It's a great thing for companies to expand.

And when these people are going to put billions and billions of dollars into companies, and when they're going to bring $2.5 trillion back from overseas, where they can't bring the money back, because politicians like Secretary Clinton won't allow them to bring the money back, because the taxes are so onerous, and the bureaucratic red tape, so what -- is so bad.

So what they're doing is they're leaving our country, and they're, believe it or not, leaving because taxes are too high and because some of them have lots of money outside of our country. And instead of bringing it back and putting the money to work, because they can't work out a deal to -- and everybody agrees it should be brought back.

Instead of that, they're leaving our country to get their money, because they can't bring their money back into our country, because of bureaucratic red tape, because they can't get together. Because we have -- we have a president that can't sit them around a table and get them to approve something.

And here's the thing. Republicans and Democrats agree that this should be done, $2.5 trillion. I happen to think it's double that. It's probably $5 trillion that we can't bring into our country, Lester. And with a little leadership, you'd get it in here very quickly, and it could be put to use on the inner cities and lots of other things, and it would be beautiful.

But we have no leadership. And honestly, that starts with Secretary Clinton.

HOLT: All right. You have two minutes of the same question to defend tax increases on the wealthiest Americans, Secretary Clinton.

CLINTON: I have a feeling that by, the end of this evening, I'm going to be blamed for everything that's ever happened.

TRUMP: Why not?

CLINTON: Why not? Yeah, why not?

(LAUGHTER)

You know, just join the debate by saying more crazy things. Now, let me say this, it is absolutely the case...

TRUMP: There's nothing crazy about not letting our companies bring their money back into their country.

HOLT: This is -- this is Secretary Clinton's two minutes, please.

TRUMP: Yes.

CLINTON: Yeah, well, let's start the clock again, Lester. We've looked at your tax proposals. I don't see changes in the corporate tax rates or the kinds of proposals you're referring to that would cause the repatriation, bringing back of money that's stranded overseas. I happen to support that.

TRUMP: Then you didn't read it.

CLINTON: I happen to -- I happen to support that in a way that will actually work to our benefit. But when I look at what you have proposed, you have what is called now the Trump loophole, because it would so advantage you and the business you do. You've proposed an approach that has a...

TRUMP: Who gave it that name? The first I've -- who gave it that name?

HOLT: Mr. Trump, this is Secretary Clinton's two minutes.

CLINTON: ... $4 billion tax benefit for your family. And when you look at what you are proposing...

TRUMP: How much? How much for my family?

CLINTON: ... it is...

TRUMP: Lester, how much?

CLINTON: ... as I said, trumped-up trickle-down. Trickle-down did not work. It got us into the mess we were in, in 2008 and 2009. Slashing taxes on the wealthy hasn't worked.

And a lot of really smart, wealthy people know that. And they are saying, hey, we need to do more to make the contributions we should be making to rebuild the middle class.

CLINTON: I don't think top-down works in America. I think building the middle class, investing in the middle class, making college debt-free so more young people can get their education, helping people refinance their -- their debt from college at a lower rate. Those are the kinds of things that will really boost the economy. Broad-based, inclusive growth is what we need in America, not more advantages for people at the very top.

HOLT: Mr. Trump, we're...

TRUMP: Typical politician. All talk, no action. Sounds good, doesn't work. Never going to happen. Our country is suffering because people like Secretary Clinton have made such bad decisions in terms of our jobs and in terms of what's going on.

Now, look, we have the worst revival of an economy since the Great Depression. And believe me: We're in a bubble right now. And the only thing that looks good is the stock market, but if you raise interest rates even a little bit, that's going to come crashing down.

We are in a big, fat, ugly bubble. And we better be awfully careful. And we have a Fed that's doing political things. This Janet Yellen of the Fed. The Fed is doing political -- by keeping the interest rates at this level. And believe me: The day Obama goes off, and he leaves, and goes out to the golf course for the rest of his life to play golf, when they raise interest rates, you're going to see some very bad things happen, because the Fed is not doing their job. The Fed is being more political than Secretary Clinton.

HOLT: Mr. Trump, we're talking about the burden that Americans have to pay, yet you have not released your tax returns. And the reason nominees have released their returns for decades is so that voters will know if their potential president owes money to -- who he owes it to and any business conflicts. Don't Americans have a right to know if there are any conflicts of interest?

TRUMP: I don't mind releasing -- I'm under a routine audit. And it'll be released. And -- as soon as the audit's finished, it will be released.

But you will learn more about Donald Trump by going down to the federal elections, where I filed a 104-page essentially financial statement of sorts, the forms that they have. It shows income -- in fact, the income -- I just looked today -- the income is filed at $694 million for this past year, $694 million. If you would have told me I was going to make that 15 or 20 years ago, I would have been very surprised.

But that's the kind of thinking that our country needs. When we have a country that's doing so badly, that's being ripped off by every single country in the world, it's the kind of thinking that our country needs, because everybody -- Lester, we have a trade deficit with all of the countries that we do business with, of almost $800 billion a year. You know what that is? That means, who's negotiating these trade deals?

We have people that are political hacks negotiating our trade deals.

HOLT: The IRS says an audit...

TRUMP: Excuse me.

HOLT: ... of your taxes -- you're perfectly free to release your taxes during an audit. And so the question, does the public's right to know outweigh your personal...

TRUMP: Well, I told you, I will release them as soon as the audit. Look, I've been under audit almost for 15 years. I know a lot of wealthy people that have never been audited. I said, do you get audited? I get audited almost every year.

And in a way, I should be complaining. I'm not even complaining. I don't mind it. It's almost become a way of life. I get audited by the IRS. But other people don't.

I will say this. We have a situation in this country that has to be taken care of. I will release my tax returns -- against my lawyer's wishes -- when she releases her 33,000 e-mails that have been deleted. As soon as she releases them, I will release, I will release my tax returns. And that's against -- my lawyers, they say, "Don't do it." I will tell you this. No -- in fact, watching shows, they're reading the papers. Almost every lawyer says, you don't release your returns until the audit's complete. When the audit's complete, I'll do it. But I would go against them if she releases her e-mails.

HOLT: So it's negotiable?

TRUMP: It's not negotiable, no. Let her release the e-mails. Why did she delete 33,000...

HOLT: Well, I'll let her answer that. But let me just admonish the audience one more time. There was an agreement. We did ask you to be silent, so it would be helpful for us. Secretary Clinton?

CLINTON: Well, I think you've seen another example of bait-and- switch here. For 40 years, everyone running for president has released their tax returns. You can go and see nearly, I think, 39, 40 years of our tax returns, but everyone has done it. We know the IRS has made clear there is no prohibition on releasing it when you're under audit.

So you've got to ask yourself, why won't he release his tax returns? And I think there may be a couple of reasons. First, maybe he's not as rich as he says he is. Second, maybe he's not as charitable as he claims to be.

CLINTON: Third, we don't know all of his business dealings, but we have been told through investigative reporting that he owes about $650 million to Wall Street and foreign banks. Or maybe he doesn't want the American people, all of you watching tonight, to know that he's paid nothing in federal taxes, because the only years that anybody's ever seen were a couple of years when he had to turn them over to state authorities when he was trying to get a casino license, and they showed he didn't pay any federal income tax.

TRUMP: That makes me smart.

CLINTON: So if he's paid zero, that means zero for troops, zero for vets, zero for schools or health. And I think probably he's not all that enthusiastic about having the rest of our country see what the real reasons are, because it must be something really important, even terrible, that he's trying to hide.

And the financial disclosure statements, they don't give you the tax rate. They don't give you all the details that tax returns would. And it just seems to me that this is something that the American people deserve to see. And I have no reason to believe that he's ever going to release his tax returns, because there's something he's hiding.

And we'll guess. We'll keep guessing at what it might be that he's hiding. But I think the question is, were he ever to get near the

White House, what would be those conflicts? Who does he owe money to? Well, he owes you the answers to that, and he should provide them.

HOLT: He also -- he also raised the issue of your e-mails. Do you want to respond to that?

CLINTON: I do. You know, I made a mistake using a private e- mail.

TRUMP: That's for sure.

CLINTON: And if I had to do it over again, I would, obviously, do it differently. But I'm not going to make any excuses. It was a mistake, and I take responsibility for that.

HOLT: Mr. Trump?

TRUMP: That was more than a mistake. That was done purposely. OK? That was not a mistake. That was done purposely. When you have your staff taking the Fifth Amendment, taking the Fifth so they're not prosecuted, when you have the man that set up the illegal server taking the Fifth, I think it's disgraceful. And believe me, this country thinks it's -- really thinks it's disgraceful, also.

As far as my tax returns, you don't learn that much from tax returns. That I can tell you. You learn a lot from financial disclosure. And you should go down and take a look at that.

The other thing, I'm extremely underleveraged. The report that said $650 -- which, by the way, a lot of friends of mine that know my business say, boy, that's really not a lot of money. It's not a lot of money relative to what I had.

The buildings that were in question, they said in the same report, which was -- actually, it wasn't even a bad story, to be honest with you, but the buildings are worth $3.9 billion. And the $650 isn't even on that. But it's not $650. It's much less than that.

But I could give you a list of banks, I would -- if that would help you, I would give you a list of banks. These are very fine institutions, very fine banks. I could do that very quickly.

I am very underleveraged. I have a great company. I have a tremendous income. And the reason I say that is not in a braggadocios way. It's because it's about time that this country had somebody running it that has an idea about money.

When we have $20 trillion in debt, and our country's a mess, you know, it's one thing to have $20 trillion in debt and our roads are good and our bridges are good and everything's in great shape, our airports. Our airports are like from a third world country.

You land at LaGuardia, you land at Kennedy, you land at LAX, you land at Newark, and you come in from Dubai and Qatar and you see these incredible -- you come in from China, you see these incredible airports, and you land -- we've become a third world country.

So the worst of all things has happened. We owe $20 trillion, and we're a mess. We haven't even started. And we've spent $6 trillion in the Middle East, according to a report that I just saw. Whether it's 6 or 5, but it looks like it's 6, $6 trillion in the Middle East, we could have rebuilt our country twice.

And it's really a shame. And it's politicians like Secretary Clinton that have caused this problem. Our country has tremendous problems. We're a debtor nation. We're a serious debtor nation. And we have a country that needs new roads, new tunnels, new bridges, new airports, new schools, new hospitals. And we don't have the money, because it's been squandered on so many of your ideas.

HOLT: We'll let you respond and we'll move on to the next segment.

CLINTON: And maybe because you haven't paid any federal income tax for a lot of years. (APPLAUSE) And the other thing I think is important...

TRUMP: It would be squandered, too, believe me.

CLINTON: ... is if your -- if your main claim to be president of the United States is your business, then I think we should talk about that. You know, your campaign manager said that you built a lot of businesses on the backs of little guys.

And, indeed, I have met a lot of the people who were stiffed by you and your businesses, Donald. I've met dishwashers, painters, architects, glass installers, marble installers, drapery installers, like my dad was, who you refused to pay when they finished the work that you asked them to do.

We have an architect in the audience who designed one of your clubhouses at one of your golf courses. It's a beautiful facility. It immediately was put to use. And you wouldn't pay what the man needed to be paid, what he was charging you to do...

TRUMP: Maybe he didn't do a good job and I was unsatisfied with his work...

CLINTON: Well, to...

TRUMP: Which our country should do, too.

CLINTON: Do the thousands of people that you have stiffed over the course of your business not deserve some kind of apology from someone who has taken their labor, taken the goods that they produced, and then refused to pay them?

I can only say that I'm certainly relieved that my late father never did business with you. He provided a good middle-class life for us, but the people he worked for, he expected the bargain to be kept on both sides.

And when we talk about your business, you've taken business bankruptcy six times. There are a lot of great businesspeople that have never taken bankruptcy once. You call yourself the King of Debt. You talk about leverage. You even at one time suggested that you would try to negotiate down the national debt of the United States.

TRUMP: Wrong. Wrong.

CLINTON: Well, sometimes there's not a direct transfer of skills from business to government, but sometimes what happened in business would be really bad for government.

HOLT: Let's let Mr. Trump...

CLINTON: And we need to be very clear about that.

TRUMP: So, yeah, I think -- I do think it's time. Look, it's all words, it's all sound bites. I built an unbelievable company. Some of the greatest assets anywhere in the world, real estate assets anywhere in the world, beyond the United States, in Europe, lots of different places. It's an unbelievable company.

But on occasion, four times, we used certain laws that are there. And when Secretary Clinton talks about people that didn't get paid, first of all, they did get paid a lot, but taken advantage of the laws of the nation.

Now, if you want to change the laws, you've been there a long time, change the laws. But I take advantage of the laws of the nation because I'm running a company. My obligation right now is to do well for myself, my family, my employees, for my companies. And that's what I do.

But what she doesn't say is that tens of thousands of people that are unbelievably happy and that love me. I'll give you an example. We're just opening up on Pennsylvania Avenue right next to the

White House, so if I don't get there one way, I'm going to get to Pennsylvania Avenue another.

But we're opening the Old Post Office. Under budget, ahead of schedule, saved tremendous money. I'm a year ahead of schedule. And that's what this country should be doing.

We build roads and they cost two and three and four times what they're supposed to cost. We buy products for our military and they come in at costs that are so far above what they were supposed to be, because we don't have people that know what they're doing.

When we look at the budget, the budget is bad to a large extent because we have people that have no idea as to what to do and how to buy. The Trump International is way under budget and way ahead of schedule. And we should be able to do that for our country.

HOLT: Well, we're well behind schedule, so I want to move to our next segment. We move into our next segment talking about America's direction. And let's start by talking about race.

The share of Americans who say race relations are bad in this country is the highest it's been in decades, much of it amplified by shootings of African-Americans by police, as we've seen recently in Charlotte and Tulsa. Race has been a big issue in this campaign, and one of you is going to have to bridge a very wide and bitter gap.

So how do you heal the divide? Secretary Clinton, you get two minutes on this.

CLINTON: Well, you're right. Race remains a significant challenge in our country. Unfortunately, race still determines too much, often determines where people live, determines what kind of education in their public schools they can get, and, yes, it determines how they're treated in the criminal justice system.

We've just seen those two tragic examples in both Tulsa and Charlotte.

And we've got to do several things at the same time. We have to restore trust between communities and the police. We have to work to make sure that our police are using the best training, the best techniques, that they're well prepared to use force only when necessary. Everyone should be respected by the law, and everyone should respect the law.

CLINTON: Right now, that's not the case in a lot of our neighborhoods. So I have, ever since the first day of my campaign, called for criminal justice reform. I've laid out a platform that I think would begin to remedy some of the problems we have in the criminal justice system.

But we also have to recognize, in addition to the challenges that we face with policing, there are so many good, brave police officers who equally want reform. So we have to bring communities together in order to begin working on that as a mutual goal. And we've got to get guns out of the hands of people who should not have them.

The gun epidemic is the leading cause of death of young African-American men, more than the next nine causes put together. So we have to do two things, as I said. We have to restore trust. We have to work with the police. We have to make sure they respect the communities and the communities respect them. And we have to tackle the plague of gun violence, which is a big contributor to a lot of the problems that we're seeing today.

HOLT: All right, Mr. Trump, you have two minutes. How do you heal the divide?

TRUMP: Well, first of all, Secretary Clinton doesn't want to use a couple of words, and that's law and order. And we need law and order. If we don't have it, we're not going to have a country.

And when I look at what's going on in Charlotte, a city I love, a city where I have investments, when I look at what's going on throughout various parts of our country, whether it's -- I mean, I can just keep naming them all day long -- we need law and order in our country.

I just got today the, as you know, the endorsement of the Fraternal Order of Police, we just -- just came in. We have endorsements from, I think, almost every police group, very -- I mean, a large percentage of them in the United States.

We have a situation where we have our inner cities, African-Americans, Hispanics are living in he'll because it's so dangerous. You walk down the street, you get shot.

In Chicago, they've had thousands of shootings, thousands since January 1st. Thousands of shootings. And I'm saying, where is this? Is this a war-torn country? What are we doing? And we have to stop the violence. We have to bring back law and order. In a place like Chicago, where thousands of people have been killed, thousands over the last number of years, in fact, almost 4,000 have been killed since Barack Obama became president, over -- almost 4,000 people in Chicago have been killed. We have to bring back law and order.

Now, whether or not in a place like Chicago you do stop and frisk, which worked very well, Mayor Giuliani is here, worked very well in New York. It brought the crime rate way down. But you take the gun away from criminals that shouldn't be having it.

We have gangs roaming the street. And in many cases, they're illegally here, illegal immigrants. And they have guns. And they shoot people. And we have to be very strong. And we have to be very vigilant.

We have to be -- we have to know what we're doing. Right now, our police, in many cases, are afraid to do anything. We have to protect our inner cities, because African-American communities are being decimated by crime, decimated.

HOLT: Your two -- your two minutes expired, but I do want to follow up. Stop-and-frisk was ruled unconstitutional in New York, because it largely singled out black and Hispanic young men.

TRUMP: No, you're wrong. It went before a judge, who was a very against-police judge. It was taken away from her. And our mayor, our new mayor, refused to go forward with the case. They would have won an appeal. If you look at it, throughout the country, there are many places where it's allowed.

HOLT: The argument is that it's a form of racial profiling.

TRUMP: No, the argument is that we have to take the guns away from these people that have them and they are bad people that shouldn't have them.

These are felons. These are people that are bad people that shouldn't be -- when you have 3,000 shootings in Chicago from January 1st, when you have 4,000 people killed in Chicago by guns, from the beginning of the presidency of Barack Obama, his hometown, you have to have stop-and-frisk.

You need more police. You need a better community, you know, relation. You don't have good community relations in Chicago. It's terrible. I have property there. It's terrible what's going on in Chicago.

But when you look -- and Chicago's not the only -- you go to Ferguson, you go to so many different places. You need better relationships. I agree with Secretary Clinton on this.

TRUMP: You need better relationships between the communities and the police, because in some cases, it's not good.

But you look at Dallas, where the relationships were really studied, the relationships were really a beautiful thing, and then five police officers were killed one night very violently. So there's some bad things going on. Some really bad things.

HOLT: Secretary Clinton...

TRUMP: But we need -- Lester, we need law and order. And we need law and order in the inner cities, because the people that are most affected by what's happening are African-American and Hispanic people. And it's very unfair to them what our politicians are allowing to happen.

HOLT: Secretary Clinton?

CLINTON: Well, I've heard -- I've heard Donald say this at his rallies, and it's really unfortunate that he paints such a dire negative picture of black communities in our country.

TRUMP: Ugh.

CLINTON: You know, the vibrancy of the black church, the black businesses that employ so many people, the opportunities that so many families are working to provide for their kids. There's a lot that we should be proud of and we should be supporting and lifting up.

But we do always have to make sure we keep people safe. There are the right ways of doing it, and then there are ways that are ineffective. Stop-and-frisk was found to be unconstitutional and, in part, because it was ineffective. It did not do what it needed to do.

Now, I believe in community policing. And, in fact, violent crime is one-half of what it was in 1991. Property crime is down 40 percent. We just don't want to see it creep back up. We've had 25 years of very good cooperation.

But there were some problems, some unintended consequences. Too many young African-American and Latino men ended up in jail for nonviolent offenses. And it's just a fact that if you're a young African-American man and you do the same thing as a young white man, you are more likely to be arrested, charged, convicted, and incarcerated. So we've got to address the systemic racism in our criminal justice system. We cannot just say law and order. We have to say -- we have to come forward with a plan that is going to divert people from the criminal justice system, deal with mandatory minimum sentences, which have put too many people away for too long for doing too little.

We need to have more second chance programs. I'm glad that we're ending private prisons in the federal system; I want to see them ended in the state system. You shouldn't have a profit motivation to fill prison cells with young Americans. So there are some positive ways we can work on this.

And I believe strongly that commonsense gun safety measures would assist us. Right now -- and this is something Donald has supported, along with the gun lobby -- right now, we've got too many military- style weapons on the streets. In a lot of places, our police are outgunned. We need comprehensive background checks, and we need to keep guns out of the hands of those who will do harm.

And we finally need to pass a prohibition on anyone who's on the terrorist watch list from being able to buy a gun in our country. If you're too dangerous to fly, you are too dangerous to buy a gun. So there are things we can do, and we ought to do it in a bipartisan way.

HOLT: Secretary Clinton, last week, you said we've got to do everything possible to improve policing, to go right at implicit bias. Do you believe that police are implicitly biased against black people?

CLINTON: Lester, I think implicit bias is a problem for everyone, not just police. I think, unfortunately, too many of us in our great country jump to conclusions about each other. And therefore, I think we need all of us to be asking hard questions about, you know, why am I feeling this way?

But when it comes to policing, since it can have literally fatal consequences, I have said, in my first budget, we would put money into that budget to help us deal with implicit bias by retraining a lot of our police officers.

I've met with a group of very distinguished, experienced police chiefs a few weeks ago. They admit it's an issue. They've got a lot of concerns. Mental health is one of the biggest concerns, because now police are having to handle a lot of really difficult mental health problems on the street.

CLINTON: They want support, they want more training, they want more assistance. And I think the federal government could be in a position where we would offer and provide that.

HOLT: Mr. Trump...

TRUMP: I'd like to respond to that.

HOLT: Please.

TRUMP: First of all, I agree, and a lot of people even within my own party want to give certain rights to people on watch lists and no- fly lists. I agree with you. When a person is on a watch list or a no-fly list, and I have the endorsement of the NRA, which I'm very proud of. These are very, very good people, and they're protecting the Second Amendment.

But I think we have to look very strongly at no-fly lists and watch lists. And when people are on there, even if they shouldn't be on there, we'll help them, we'll help them legally, we'll help them get off. But I tend to agree with that quite strongly.

I do want to bring up the fact that you were the one that brought up the words super-predator about young black youth. And that's a term that I think was a -- it's -- it's been horribly met, as you know. I think you've apologized for it. But I think it was a terrible thing to say.

And when it comes to stop-and-frisk, you know, you're talking about takes guns away. Well, I'm talking about taking guns away from gangs and people that use them. And I don't think -- I really don't think you disagree with me on this, if you want to know the truth.

I think maybe there's a political reason why you can't say it, but I really don't believe -- in New York City, stop-and-frisk, we had 2,200 murders, and stop-and-frisk brought it down to 500 murders. Five hundred murders is a lot of murders. It's hard to believe, 500 is like supposed to be good?

But we went from 2,200 to 500. And it was continued on by Mayor Bloomberg. And it was terminated by current mayor. But stop-and- frisk had a tremendous impact on the safety of New York City. Tremendous beyond belief. So when you say it has no impact, it really did. It had a very, very big impact.

CLINTON: Well, it's also fair to say, if we're going to talk about mayors, that under the current mayor, crime has continued to drop, including murders. So there is...

TRUMP: No, you're wrong. You're wrong.

CLINTON: No, I'm not.

TRUMP: Murders are up. All right. You check it.

CLINTON: New York -- New York has done an excellent job. And I give credit -- I give credit across the board going back two mayors, two police chiefs, because it has worked. And other communities need to come together to do what will work, as well.

Look, one murder is too many. But it is important that we learn about what has been effective. And not go to things that sound good that really did not have the kind of impact that we would want. Who disagrees with keeping neighborhoods safe?

But let's also add, no one should disagree about respecting the rights of young men who live in those neighborhoods. And so we need to do a better job of working, again, with the communities, faith communities, business communities, as well as the police to try to deal with this problem.

HOLT: This conversation is about race. And so, Mr. Trump, I have to ask you for five...

TRUMP: I'd like to just respond, if I might.

HOLT: Please -- 20 seconds.

TRUMP: I'd just like to respond.

HOLT: Please respond, then I've got a quick follow-up for you.

TRUMP: I will. Look, the African-American community has been let down by our politicians. They talk good around election time, like right now, and after the election, they said, see ya later, I'll see you in four years.

The African-American community -- because -- look, the community within the inner cities has been so badly treated. They've been abused and used in order to get votes by Democrat politicians, because that's what it is. They've controlled these communities for up to 100 years.

HOLT: Mr. Trump, let me...

(CROSSTALK)

CLINTON: Well, I -- I do think...

TRUMP: And I will tell you, you look at the inner cities -- and I just left Detroit, and I just left Philadelphia, and I just -- you know, you've seen me, I've been all over the place. You decided to stay home, and that's OK. But I will tell you, I've been all over. And I've met some of the greatest people I'll ever meet within these communities. And they are very, very upset with what their politicians have told them and what their politicians have done.

HOLT: Mr. Trump, I...

CLINTON: I think -- I think -- I think Donald just criticized me for preparing for this debate. And, yes, I did. And you know what else I prepared for? I prepared to be president. And I think that's a good thing.

(APPLAUSE)

HOLT: Mr. Trump, for five years, you perpetuated a false claim that the nation's first black president was not a natural-born citizen. You questioned his legitimacy. In the last couple of weeks, you acknowledged what most Americans have accepted for years: The president was born in the United States. Can you tell us what took you so long?

TRUMP: I'll tell you very -- well, just very simple to say. Sidney Blumenthal works for the campaign and close -- very close friend of Secretary Clinton. And her campaign manager, Patti Doyle, went to -- during the campaign, her campaign against President Obama, fought very hard. And you can go look it up, and you can check it out.

TRUMP: And if you look at CNN this past week, Patti Solis Doyle was on Wolf Blitzer saying that this happened. Blumenthal sent McClatchy, highly respected reporter at McClatchy, to Kenya to find out about it. They were pressing it very hard. She failed to get the birth certificate.

When I got involved, I didn't fail. I got him to give the birth certificate. So I'm satisfied with it. And I'll tell you why I'm satisfied with it.

482 THE POLITICS OF INSANITY – HUGO N. GERSTL

HOLT: That was...

TRUMP: Because I want to get on to defeating ISIS, because I want to get on to creating jobs, because I want to get on to having a strong border, because I want to get on to things that are very important to me and that are very important to the country.

HOLT: I will let you respond. It's important. But I just want to get the answer here. The birth certificate was produced in 2011. You've continued to tell the story and question the president's legitimacy in 2012, '13, '14, '15...

TRUMP: Yeah.

HOLT: .... as recently as January. So the question is, what changed your mind?

TRUMP: Well, nobody was pressing it, nobody was caring much about it. I figured you'd ask the question tonight, of course. But nobody was caring much about it. But I was the one that got him to produce the birth certificate. And I think I did a good job.

Secretary Clinton also fought it. I mean, you know -- now, everybody in mainstream is going to say, oh, that's not true. Look, it's true. Sidney Blumenthal sent a reporter -- you just have to take a look at CNN, the last week, the interview with your former campaign manager. And she was involved. But just like she can't bring back jobs, she can't produce.

HOLT: I'm sorry. I'm just going to follow up -- and I will let you respond to that, because there's a lot there. But we're talking about racial healing in this segment. What do you say to Americans, people of color who...

TRUMP: Well, it was very -- I say nothing. I say nothing, because I was able to get him to produce it. He should have produced it a long time before. I say nothing.

But let me just tell you. When you talk about healing, I think that I've developed very, very good relationships over the last little while with the African-American community. I think you can see that.

And I feel that they really wanted me to come to that conclusion. And I think I did a great job and a great service not only for the country, but even for the president, in getting him to produce his birth certificate.

HOLT: Secretary Clinton?

CLINTON: Well, just listen to what you heard. (LAUGHTER)

And clearly, as Donald just admitted, he knew he was going to stand on this debate stage, and Lester Holt was going to be asking us questions, so he tried to put the whole racist birther lie to bed.

But it can't be dismissed that easily. He has really started his political activity based on this racist lie that our first black president was not an American citizen. There was absolutely no evidence for it, but he persisted, he persisted year after year, because some of his supporters, people that he was trying to bring into his fold, apparently believed it or wanted to believe it.

But, remember, Donald started his career back in 1973 being sued by the Justice Department for racial discrimination because he would not rent apartments in one of his developments to African-Americans, and he made sure that the people who worked for him understood that was the policy. He actually was sued twice by the Justice Department.

So he has a long record of engaging in racist behavior. And the birther lie was a very hurtful one. You know, Barack Obama is a man of great dignity. And I could tell how much it bothered him and annoyed him that this was being touted and used against him.

But I like to remember what Michelle Obama said in her amazing speech at our Democratic National Convention: When they go low, we go high. And Barack Obama went high, despite Donald Trump's best efforts to bring him down.

HOLT: Mr. Trump, you can respond and we're going to move on to the next segment.

TRUMP: I would love to respond. First of all, I got to watch in preparing for this some of your debates against Barack Obama. You treated him with terrible disrespect. And I watched the way you talk now about how lovely everything is and how wonderful you are. It doesn't work that way. You were after him, you were trying to -- you even sent out or your campaign sent out pictures of him in a certain garb, very famous pictures. I don't think you can deny that.

But just last week, your campaign manager said it was true. So when you tried to act holier than thou, it really doesn't work. It really doesn't.

Now, as far as the lawsuit, yes, when I was very young, I went into my father's company, had a real estate company in Brooklyn and Queens, and we, along with many, many other companies throughout the country -- it was a federal lawsuit -- were sued. We settled the suit with zero -- with no admission of guilt. It was very easy to do.

TRUMP: I notice you bring that up a lot. And, you know, I also notice the very nasty commercials that you do on me in so many different ways, which I don't do on you. Maybe I'm trying to save the money.

But, frankly, I look -- I look at that, and I say, isn't that amazing? Because I settled that lawsuit with no admission of guilt, but that was a lawsuit brought against many real estate firms, and it's just one of those things.

I'll go one step further. In Palm Beach, Florida, tough community, a brilliant community, a wealthy community, probably the wealthiest community there is in the world, I opened a club, and really got great credit for it. No discrimination against African-Americans, against Muslims, against anybody. And it's a tremendously successful club. And I'm so glad I did it. And I have been given great credit for what I did. And I'm very, very proud of it. And that's the way I feel. That is the true way I feel.

HOLT: Our next segment is called "Securing America." We want to start with a 21st century war happening every day in this country. Our institutions are under cyber attack, and our secrets are being stolen. So my question is, who's behind it? And how do we fight it?

Secretary Clinton, this answer goes to you.

CLINTON: Well, I think cyber security, cyber warfare will be one of the biggest challenges facing the next president, because clearly we're facing at this point two different kinds of adversaries. There are the independent hacking groups that do it mostly for commercial reasons to try to steal information that they can use to make money.

But increasingly, we are seeing cyber attacks coming from states, organs of states. The most recent and troubling of these has been Russia. There's no doubt now that Russia has used cyber attacks against all kinds of organizations in our country, and I am deeply concerned about this. I know Donald's very praiseworthy of Vladimir Putin, but Putin is playing a really...

CLINTON: ... tough, long game here. And one of the things he's done is to let loose cyber attackers to hack into government files, to hack into personal files, hack into the Democratic National Committee. And we recently have learned that, you know, that this is one of their preferred methods of trying to wreak havoc and collect information. We need to make it very clear -- whether it's Russia, China, Iran or anybody else -- the United States has much greater capacity. And we are not going to sit idly by and permit state actors to go after our information, our private-sector information or our public-sector information.

And we're going to have to make it clear that we don't want to use the kinds of tools that we have. We don't want to engage in a different kind of warfare. But we will defend the citizens of this country.

And the Russians need to understand that. I think they've been treating it as almost a probing, how far would we go, how much would we do. And that's why I was so -- I was so shocked when Donald publicly invited Putin to hack into Americans. That is just unacceptable. It's one of the reasons why 50 national security officials who served in Republican information -- in administrations...

HOLT: Your two minutes have expired.

CLINTON: ... have said that Donald is unfit to be the commander-in-chief. It's comments like that that really worry people who understand the threats that we face.

HOLT: Mr. Trump, you have two minutes and the same question. Who's behind it? And how do we fight it?

TRUMP: I do want to say that I was just endorsed -- and more are coming next week -- it will be over 200 admirals, many of them here -- admirals and generals endorsed me to lead this country. That just happened, and many more are coming. And I'm very proud of it.

In addition, I was just endorsed by ICE. They've never endorsed anybody before on immigration. I was just endorsed by ICE. I was just recently endorsed -- 16,500 Border Patrol agents.

So when Secretary Clinton talks about this, I mean, I'll take the admirals and I'll take the generals any day over the political hacks that I see that have led our country so brilliantly over the last 10 years with their knowledge. OK? Because look at the mess that we're in. Look at the mess that we're in.

As far as the cyber, I agree to parts of what Secretary Clinton said. We should be better than anybody else, and perhaps we're not. I don't think anybody knows it was Russia that broke into the DNC. She's saying Russia, Russia, Russia, but I don't -- maybe it was. I mean, it could be Russia, but it could also be China. It could also be lots of other people. It also could be somebody sitting on their bed that weighs 400 pounds, OK?

TRUMP: You don't know who broke in to DNC.

But what did we learn with DNC? We learned that Bernie Sanders was taken advantage of by your people, by Debbie Wasserman Schultz. Look what happened to her. But Bernie Sanders was taken advantage of. That's what we learned.

Now, whether that was Russia, whether that was China, whether it was another country, we don't know, because the truth is, under President Obama we've lost control of things that we used to have control over.

We came in with the Internet, we came up with the Internet, and I think Secretary Clinton and myself would agree very much, when you look at what ISIS is doing with the Internet, they're beating us at our own game. ISIS.

So we have to get very, very tough on cyber and cyber warfare. It is -- it is a huge problem. I have a son. He's 10 years old. He has computers. He is so good with these computers, it's unbelievable. The security aspect of cyber is very, very tough. And maybe it's hardly doable.

But I will say, we are not doing the job we should be doing. But that's true throughout our whole governmental society. We have so many things that we have to do better, Lester, and certainly cyber is one of them.

HOLT: Secretary Clinton?

CLINTON: Well, I think there are a number of issues that we should be addressing. I have put forth a plan to defeat ISIS. It does involve going after them online. I think we need to do much more with our tech companies to prevent ISIS and their operatives from being able to use the Internet to radicalize, even direct people in our country and Europe and elsewhere.

But we also have to intensify our air strikes against ISIS and eventually support our Arab and Kurdish partners to be able to actually take out ISIS in Raqqa, end their claim of being a Caliphate.

We're making progress. Our military is assisting in Iraq. And we're hoping that within the year we'll be able to push ISIS out of Iraq and then, you know, really squeeze them in Syria.

But we have to be cognizant of the fact that they've had foreign fighters coming to volunteer for them, foreign money, foreign weapons, so we have to make this the top priority.

And I would also do everything possible to take out their leadership. I was involved in a number of efforts to take out Al Qaida leadership when I was secretary of state, including, of course, taking out bin Laden. And I think we need to go after Baghdadi, as well, make that one of our organizing principles. Because we've got to defeat ISIS, and we've got to do everything we can to disrupt their propaganda efforts online.

HOLT: You mention ISIS, and we think of ISIS certainly as over there, but there are American citizens who have been inspired to commit acts of terror on American soil, the latest incident, of course, the bombings we just saw in New York and New Jersey, the knife attack at a mall in Minnesota, in the last year, deadly attacks in San Bernardino and Orlando. I'll ask this to both of you. Tell us specifically how you would prevent homegrown attacks by American citizens, Mr. Trump?

TRUMP: Well, first I have to say one thing, very important. Secretary Clinton is talking about taking out ISIS. "We will take out ISIS." Well, President Obama and Secretary Clinton created a vacuum the way they got out of Iraq, because they got out -- what, they shouldn't have been in, but once they got in, the way they got out was a disaster. And ISIS was formed.

So she talks about taking them out. She's been doing it a long time. She's been trying to take them out for a long time. But they wouldn't have even been formed if they left some troops behind, like 10,000 or maybe something more than that. And then you wouldn't have had them.

Or, as I've been saying for a long time, and I think you'll agree, because I said it to you once, had we taken the oil -- and we should have taken the oil -- ISIS would not have been able to form either, because the oil was their primary source of income. And now they have the oil all over the place, including the oil -- a lot of the oil in Libya, which was another one of her disasters.

HOLT: Secretary Clinton?

CLINTON: Well, I hope the fact-checkers are turning up the volume and really working hard. Donald supported the invasion of Iraq.

TRUMP: Wrong.

CLINTON: That is absolutely proved over and over again.

TRUMP: Wrong. Wrong.

CLINTON: He actually advocated for the actions we took in Libya and urged that Gaddafi be taken out, after actually doing some business with him one time.

CLINTON: But the larger point -- and he says this constantly -- is George W. Bush made the agreement about when American troops would leave Iraq, not Barack Obama.

And the only way that American troops could have stayed in Iraq is to get an agreement from the then-Iraqi government that would have protected our troops, and the Iraqi government would not give that.

But let's talk about the question you asked, Lester. The question you asked is, what do we do here in the United States? That's the most important part of this. How do we prevent attacks? How do we protect our people?

And I think we've got to have an intelligence surge, where we are looking for every scrap of information. I was so proud of law enforcement in New York, in Minnesota, in New Jersey. You know, they responded so quickly, so professionally to the attacks that occurred by Rahami. And they brought him down. And we may find out more information because he is still alive, which may prove to be an intelligence benefit.

So we've got to do everything we can to vacuum up intelligence from Europe, from the Middle East. That means we've got to work more closely with our allies, and that's something that Donald has been very dismissive of.

We're working with NATO, the longest military alliance in the history of the world, to really turn our attention to terrorism. We're working with our friends in the Middle East, many of which, as you know, are Muslim majority nations. Donald has consistently insulted Muslims abroad, Muslims at home, when we need to be cooperating with Muslim nations and with the American Muslim community.

They're on the front lines. They can provide information to us that we might not get anywhere else. They need to have close working cooperation with law enforcement in these communities, not be alienated and pushed away as some of Donald's rhetoric, unfortunately, has led to.

HOLT: Mr. Trump...

TRUMP: Well, I have to respond.

HOLT: Please respond.

TRUMP: The secretary said very strongly about working with -- we've been working with them for many years, and we have the greatest mess anyone's ever seen. You look at the Middle East, it's a total mess. Under your direction, to a large extent.

But you look at the Middle East, you started the Iran deal, that's another beauty where you have a country that was ready to fall, I mean, they were doing so badly. They were choking on the sanctions. And now they're going to be actually probably a major power at some point pretty soon, the way they're going.

But when you look at NATO, I was asked on a major show, what do you think of NATO? And you have to understand, I'm a businessperson. I did really well. But I have common sense. And I said, well, I'll tell you. I haven't given lots of thought to NATO. But two things.

Number one, the 28 countries of NATO, many of them aren't paying their fair share. Number two -- and that bothers me, because we should be asking -- we're defending them, and they should at least be paying us what they're supposed to be paying by treaty and contract.

And, number two, I said, and very strongly, NATO could be obsolete, because -- and I was very strong on this, and it was actually covered very accurately in the New York Times, which is unusual for the New York Times, to be honest -- but I said, they do not focus on terror. And I was very strong. And I said it numerous times.

And about four months ago, I read on the front page of the Wall Street Journal that NATO is opening up a major terror division. And I think that's great. And I think we should get -- because we pay approximately 73 percent of the cost of NATO. It's a lot of money to protect other people. But I'm all for NATO. But I said they have to focus on terror, also.

And they're going to do that. And that was -- believe me -- I'm sure I'm not going to get credit for it -- but that was largely because of what I was saying and my criticism of NATO.

I think we have to get NATO to go into the Middle East with us, in addition to surrounding nations, and we have to knock the hell out of ISIS, and we have to do it fast, when ISIS formed in this vacuum created by Barack Obama and Secretary Clinton. And believe me, you were the ones that took out the troops. Not only that, you named the day. They couldn't believe it. They sat back probably and said, I can't believe it. They said...

CLINTON: Lester, we've covered...

TRUMP: No, wait a minute.

CLINTON: We've covered this ground.

TRUMP: When they formed, when they formed, this is something that never should have happened. It should have never happened. Now, you're talking about taking out ISIS. But you were there, and you were secretary of state when it was a little infant. Now it's in over 30 countries. And you're going to stop them? I don't think so.

HOLT: Mr. Trump, a lot of these are judgment questions. You had supported the war in Iraq before the invasion. What makes your...

TRUMP: I did not support the war in Iraq.

HOLT: In 2002...

TRUMP: That is a mainstream media nonsense put out by her, because she -- frankly, I think the best person in her campaign is mainstream media.

HOLT: My question is, since you supported it...

TRUMP: Just -- would you like to hear...

HOLT: ... why is your -- why is your judgment...

TRUMP: Wait a minute. I was against the war in Iraq. Just so you put it out.

HOLT: The record shows otherwise, but why -- why was...

TRUMP: The record does not show that.

HOLT: Why was -- is your judgment any...

TRUMP: The record shows that I'm right. When I did an interview with Howard Stern, very lightly, first time anyone's asked me that, I said, very lightly, I don't know, maybe, who knows? Essentially. I then did an interview with Neil Cavuto. We talked about the economy is more important. I then spoke to Sean Hannity, which everybody refuses to call Sean Hannity. I had numerous conversations with Sean Hannity at Fox. And Sean Hannity said -- and he called me the other day -- and I spoke to him about it -- he said you were totally against the war, because he was for the war.

HOLT: Why is your judgment better than...?

TRUMP: And when he -- excuse me. And that was before the war started. Sean Hannity said very strongly to me and other people -- he's willing to say it, but nobody wants to call him. I was against the war. He said, you used to have fights with me, because Sean was in favor of the war.

And I understand that side, also, not very much, because we should have never been there. But nobody called Sean Hannity. And then they did an article in a major magazine, shortly after the war started. I think in '04. But they did an article which had me totally against the war in Iraq.

And one of your compatriots said, you know, whether it was before or right after, Trump was definitely -- because if you read this article, there's no doubt. But if somebody -- and I'll ask the press -- if somebody would call up Sean Hannity, this was before the war started. He and I used to have arguments about the war. I said, it's a terrible and a stupid thing. It's going to destabilize the Middle East. And that's exactly what it's done. It's been a disaster.

HOLT: My reference was to what you had said in 2002, and my question was...

TRUMP: No, no. You didn't hear what I said.

HOLT: Why is your judgment -- why is your judgment any different than Mrs. Clinton's judgment?

TRUMP: Well, I have much better judgment than she does. There's no question about that. I also have a much better temperament than she has, you know? (LAUGHTER)

I have a much better -- she spent -- let me tell you -- she spent hundreds of millions of dollars on an advertising -- you know, they get Madison Avenue into a room, they put names -- oh, temperament, let's go after -- I think my strongest asset, maybe by far, is my temperament. I have a winning temperament. I know how to win. She does not have a...

HOLT: Secretary Clinton?

TRUMP: Wait. The AFL-CIO the other day, behind the blue screen, I don't know who you were talking to, Secretary Clinton, but you were totally out of control. I said, there's a person with a temperament that's got a problem.

HOLT: Secretary Clinton?

CLINTON: Whew, OK. (LAUGHTER) Let's talk about two important issues that were briefly mentioned by Donald, first, NATO. You know, NATO as a military alliance has something called Article 5, and basically it says this: An attack on one is an attack on all. And you know the only time it's ever been invoked? After 9/11, when the 28 nations of NATO said that they would go to Afghanistan with us to fight terrorism, something that they still are doing by our side.

With respect to Iran, when I became secretary of state, Iran was weeks away from having enough nuclear material to form a bomb. They had mastered the nuclear fuel cycle under the Bush administration. They had built covert facilities. They had stocked them with centrifuges that were whirling away.

And we had sanctioned them. I voted for every sanction against Iran when I was in the Senate, but it wasn't enough. So I spent a year-and-a-half putting together a coalition that included Russia and China to impose the toughest sanctions on Iran.

And we did drive them to the negotiating table. And my successor, John Kerry, and President Obama got a deal that put a lid on Iran's nuclear program without firing a single shot. That's diplomacy. That's coalition-building. That's working with other nations.

The other day, I saw Donald saying that there were some Iranian sailors on a ship in the waters off of Iran, and they were taunting American sailors who were on a nearby ship. He said, you know, if they taunted our sailors, I'd blow them out of the water and start another war. That's not good judgment.

TRUMP: That would not start a war.

CLINTON: That is not the right temperament to be commander-in-chief, to be taunted. And the worst part...

TRUMP: No, they were taunting us.

CLINTON: ... of what we heard Donald say has been about nuclear weapons. He has said repeatedly that he didn't care if other nations got nuclear weapons, Japan, South Korea, even Saudi Arabia. It has been the policy of the United States, Democrats and Republicans, to do everything we could to reduce the proliferation of nuclear weapons. He even said, well, you know, if there were nuclear war in East Asia, well, you know, that's fine...

TRUMP: Wrong.

CLINTON: ... have a good time, folks.

TRUMP: It's lies.

CLINTON: And, in fact, his cavalier attitude about nuclear weapons is so deeply troubling. That is the number-one threat we face in the world. And it becomes particularly threatening if terrorists ever get their hands on any nuclear material. So a man who can be provoked by a tweet should not have his fingers anywhere near the nuclear codes, as far as I think anyone with any sense about this should be concerned.

TRUMP: That line's getting a little bit old, I must say. I would like to...

CLINTON: It's a good one, though. It well describes the problem.

(LAUGHTER)

TRUMP: It's not an accurate one at all. It's not an accurate one. So I just want to give a lot of things -- and just to respond. I agree with her on one thing. The single greatest problem the world has is nuclear armament, nuclear weapons, not global warming, like you think and your -- your president thinks.

Nuclear is the single greatest threat. Just to go down the list, we defend Japan, we defend Germany, we defend South Korea, we defend Saudi Arabia, we defend countries. They do not pay us. But they should be paying us, because we are providing tremendous service and we're losing a fortune. That's why we're losing -- we're losing -- we lose on everything. I say, who makes these -- we lose on everything. All I said, that it's very possible that if they don't pay a fair share, because this isn't 40 years ago where we could do what we're doing. We can't defend Japan, a behemoth, selling us cars by the million...

HOLT: We need to move on.

TRUMP: Well, wait, but it's very important. All I said was, they may have to defend themselves or they have to help us out. We're a country that owes $20 trillion. They have to help us out.

HOLT: Our last...

TRUMP: As far as the nuclear is concerned, I agree. It is the single greatest threat that this country has.

HOLT: Which leads to my next question, as we enter our last segment here, the subject of securing America. On nuclear weapons, President Obama reportedly considered changing the nation's longstanding policy on first use. Do you support the current policy? Mr. Trump, you have two minutes on that.

TRUMP: Well, I have to say that, you know, for what Secretary Clinton was saying about nuclear with Russia, she's very cavalier in the way she talks about various countries. But Russia has been expanding their -- they have a much newer capability than we do. We have not been updating from the new standpoint.

I looked the other night. I was seeing B-52s, they're old enough that your father, your grandfather could be flying them. We are not -- we are not keeping up with other countries. I would like everybody to end it, just get rid of it. But I would certainly not do first strike.

I think that once the nuclear alternative happens, it's over. At the same time, we have to be prepared. I can't take anything off the table. Because you look at some of these countries, you look at North Korea, we're doing nothing there. China should solve that problem for us. China should go into North Korea. China is totally powerful as it relates to North Korea.

And by the way, another one powerful is the worst deal I think I've ever seen negotiated that you started is the Iran deal. Iran is one of their biggest trading partners. Iran has power over North Korea.

And when they made that horrible deal with Iran, they should have included the fact that they do something with respect to North Korea. And they should have done something with respect to Yemen and all these other places.

And when asked to Secretary Kerry, why didn't you do that? Why didn't you add other things into the deal? One of the great giveaways of all time, of all time, including $400 million in cash. Nobody's ever seen that before. That turned out to be wrong. It was actually $1.7 billion in cash, obviously, I guess for the hostages. It certainly looks that way.

So you say to yourself, why didn't they make the right deal? This is one of the worst deals ever made by any country in history. The deal with Iran will lead to nuclear problems. All they have to do is sit back 10 years, and they don't have to do much.

HOLT: Your two minutes is expired.

TRUMP: And they're going to end up getting nuclear. I met with Bibi Netanyahu the other day. Believe me, he's not a happy camper.

HOLT: All right. Mrs. Clinton, Secretary Clinton, you have two minutes.

CLINTON: Well, let me -- let me start by saying, words matter. Words matter when you run for president. And they really matter when you are president. And I want to reassure our allies in Japan and South Korea and elsewhere that we have mutual defense treaties and we will honor them.

It is essential that America's word be good. And so I know that this campaign has caused some questioning and worries on the part of many leaders across the globe. I've talked with a number of them. But I want to -- on behalf of myself, and I think on behalf of a majority of the American people, say that, you know, our word is good.

It's also important that we look at the entire global situation. There's no doubt that we have other problems with Iran. But personally, I'd rather deal with the other problems having put that lid on their nuclear program than still to be facing that.

And Donald never tells you what he would do. Would he have started a war? Would he have bombed Iran? If he's going to criticize a deal that has been very successful in giving us access to Iranian facilities that we never had before, then he should tell us what his alternative would be. But it's like his plan to defeat ISIS. He says it's a secret plan, but the only secret is that he has no plan.

So we need to be more precise in how we talk about these issues. People around the word follow our presidential campaigns so closely, trying to get hints about what we will do. Can they rely on us? Are we going to lead the world with strength and in accordance with our values? That's what I intend to do. I intend to be a leader of our country that people can count on, both here at home and around the world, to make decisions that will further peace and prosperity, but also stand up to bullies, whether they're abroad or at home.

We cannot let those who would try to destabilize the world to interfere with American interests and security...

HOLT: Your two minutes is...

CLINTON: ... to be given any opportunities at all.

HOLT: ... is expired.

TRUMP: Lester, one thing I'd like to say.

HOLT: Very quickly. Twenty seconds.

TRUMP: I will go very quickly. But I will tell you that Hillary will tell you to go to her website and read all about how to defeat ISIS, which she could have defeated by never having it, you know, get going in the first place. Right now, it's getting tougher and tougher to defeat them, because they're in more and more places, more and more states, more and more nations.

HOLT: Mr. Trump...

TRUMP: And it's a big problem. And as far as Japan is concerned, I want to help all of our allies, but we are losing billions and billions of dollars. We cannot be the policemen of the world. We cannot protect countries all over the world...

HOLT: We have just...

TRUMP: ... where they're not paying us what we need.

HOLT: We have just a few final questions...

TRUMP: And she doesn't say that, because she's got no business ability. We need heart. We need a lot of things. But you have to have some basic ability. And sadly, she doesn't have that. All of the things that she's talking about could have been taken care of during the last 10 years, let's say, while she had great power. But they weren't taken care of. And if she ever wins this race, they won't be taken care of.

HOLT: Mr. Trump, this year Secretary Clinton became the first woman nominated for president by a major party. Earlier this month, you said she doesn't have, quote, "a presidential look." She's standing here right now. What did you mean by that?

TRUMP: She doesn't have the look. She doesn't have the stamina. I said she doesn't have the stamina. And I don't believe she does have the stamina. To be president of this country, you need tremendous stamina.

HOLT: The quote was, "I just don't think she has the presidential look."

TRUMP: You have -- wait a minute. Wait a minute, Lester. You asked me a question. Did you ask me a question?

You have to be able to negotiate our trade deals. You have to be able to negotiate, that's right, with Japan, with Saudi Arabia. I mean, can you imagine, we're defending Saudi Arabia? And with all of the money they have, we're defending them, and they're not paying? All you have to do is speak to them. Wait. You have so many different things you have to be able to do, and I don't believe that Hillary has the stamina.

HOLT: Let's let her respond.

CLINTON: Well, as soon as he travels to 112 countries and negotiates a peace deal, a cease-fire, a release of dissidents, an opening of new opportunities in nations around the world, or even spends 11 hours testifying in front of a congressional committee, he can talk to me about stamina. (APPLAUSE)

TRUMP: The world -- let me tell you. Let me tell you. Hillary has experience, but it's bad experience. We have made so many bad deals during the last -- so she's got experience, that I agree. (APPLAUSE) But it's bad, bad experience. Whether it's the Iran deal that you're so in love with, where we gave them $150 billion back, whether it's the Iran deal, whether it's anything you can -- name -- you almost can't name a good deal. I agree. She's got experience, but it's bad experience. And this country can't afford to have another four years of that kind of experience.

HOLT: We are at -- we are at the final question.

CLINTON: Well, one thing. One thing, Lester.

HOLT: Very quickly, because we're at the final question now.

CLINTON: You know, he tried to switch from looks to stamina. But this is a man who has called women pigs, slobs and dogs, and someone who has said pregnancy is an inconvenience to employers, who has said...

TRUMP: I never said that.

CLINTON: .... women don't deserve equal pay unless they do as good a job as men.

TRUMP: I didn't say that.

CLINTON: And one of the worst things he said was about a woman in a beauty contest. He loves beauty contests, supporting them and hanging around them. And he called this woman "Miss Piggy." Then he called her "Miss Housekeeping," because she was Latina. Donald, she has a name.

TRUMP: Where did you find this? Where did you find this?

CLINTON: Her name is Alicia Machado.

TRUMP: Where did you find this?

CLINTON: And she has become a U.S. citizen, and you can bet...

TRUMP: Oh, really?

CLINTON: ... she's going to vote this November.

TRUMP: OK, good. Let me just tell you...

HOLT: Mr. Trump, could we just take 10 seconds and then we ask the final question...

TRUMP: You know, Hillary is hitting me with tremendous commercials. Some of it's said in entertainment. Some of it's said -- somebody who's been very vicious to me, Rosie O'Donnell, I said very tough things to her, and I think everybody would agree that she deserves it and nobody feels sorry for her. But you want to know the truth? I was going to say something...

HOLT: Please very quickly.

TRUMP: ... extremely rough to Hillary, to her family, and I said to myself, "I can't do it. I just can't do it. It's inappropriate. It's not nice." But she spent hundreds of millions of dollars on negative ads on me, many of which are absolutely untrue. They're untrue. And they're misrepresentations.

And I will tell you this, Lester: It's not nice. And I don't deserve that.

But it's certainly not a nice thing that she's done. It's hundreds of millions of ads. And the only gratifying thing is, I saw the polls come in today, and with all of that money...

HOLT: We have to move on to the final question.

TRUMP: ... $200 million is spent, and I'm either winning or tied, and I've spent practically nothing.

HOLT: One of you will not win this election. So my final question to you tonight, are you willing to accept the outcome as the will of the voters? Secretary Clinton?

CLINTON: Well, I support our democracy. And sometimes you win, sometimes you lose. But I certainly will support the outcome of this election. And I know Donald's trying very hard to plant doubts about it, but I hope the people out there understand: This election's really up to you. It's not about us so much as it is about you and your families and the kind of country and future you want. So I sure hope you will get out and vote as though your future depended on it, because I think it does.

HOLT: Mr. Trump, very quickly, same question. Will you accept the outcome as the will of the voters?

TRUMP: I want to make America great again. We are a nation that is seriously troubled. We're losing our jobs. People are pouring into our country. The other day, we were deporting 800 people. And perhaps they passed the wrong button, they pressed the wrong button, or perhaps worse than that, it was corruption, but these people that we were going to deport for good reason ended up becoming citizens. Ended up becoming citizens. And it was 800. And now it turns out it might be 1,800, and they don't even know.

HOLT: Will you accept the outcome of the election?

TRUMP: Look, here's the story. I want to make America great again. I'm going to be able to do it. I don't believe Hillary will. The answer is, if she wins, I will absolutely support her. (APPLAUSE)

HOLT: All right. Well, that is going to do it for us. That concludes our debate for this evening, a spirit one. We covered a lot of ground, not everything as I suspected we would.

The next presidential debates are scheduled for October 9th at Washington University in St. Louis and October 19th at the University of Nevada Las Vegas. The conversation will continue. A reminder. The vice presidential debate is scheduled for October

4th at Longwood University in Farmville, Virginia. My thanks to Hillary Clinton and to Donald Trump and to Hofstra University for hosting us tonight. Good night, everyone.

16

TOWARD THE FINISH LINE

The general consensus was that Hillary Clinton had trounced Donald Trump in the first debate by a large margin, 62% to 35%. Of a focus group of twenty "independent" "undecided" voters, 90%, stated they had now made up their minds to vote for Hillary Clinton. But as of September 27, 2016, the morning after the debate, FiveThirtyEight predicted there was a 55.7% chance that Clinton would win and a 44.2% chance for Trump to prevail.

THE BOMBS START DROPPING

After the debate, Trump's attempt to become more aggressive than ever fell flat on its face. Clinton had brought up in the first debate that Trump, who had bought the Miss Universe beauty pageant in the early 1990s 1995, referred to the winner, as "Miss Piggy" and "Miss Housekeeping." The following day, an unrepentant Trump stated on *Fox & Friends*, "She was the worst we ever had. She was a winner, and she gained a massive amount of weight, and we had a real problem. We had a real problem with her." The former Miss Universe responded that Trump would yell at her and tease her with offensive names, and despite her ad successes which earned his company a lot of money, Trump refused to pay her.

A week later came the tax return debacle. Throughout the primary and general campaign, Trump had been pressed to make his tax returns public. Claiming that he would not produce his tax returns because was being audited (which is not a legal reason not to produce them), Mr. Trump has still not produced the any returns. Several days after the debate, the *New York Times* unearthed page of records from 1995 that demonstrated that Trump had claimed $916 million in losses for that year and had most likely not paid _any_ federal income taxes for eighteen years! Trump responded that he was only doing what the law allowed him to do, and he didn't feel he had to pay taxes because "the tax system and the government is so screwed up." This did not go down well with the American voting public, over 80% of whom feel it's a civic duty to pay taxes.

But the biggest bombshell in the campaign to date occurred on Friday, October 7, 2016 when the *Washington Post* uncovered a "hot microphone" interview which Trump gave to Billy Bush, oddly enough a cousin to former President George W. Bush, in 2005, three months after he had married Melania and while she was pregnant with their son Barron. He was 59 years old at the time. Among other things, he said:

Trump: "You know ... I moved on her actually. You know she was down on Palm Beach."

Unknown voice: "She used to be great. She's still very beautiful."

Trump: "I moved on her and I failed. I'll admit it. I did try and f**k her. She was married. ... I moved on her very heavily. In fact,

I took her out furniture shopping. She wanted to get some furniture. I said, 'I'll show you where they have some nice furniture. ... I moved on her like a bitch, but I couldn't get there. And she was married. Then all of a sudden I see her, she's now got the big phony tits and everything. She's totally changed her look. ...'"

Trump: "You know I'm automatically attracted to beautiful — I just start kissing them. It's like a magnet. Just kiss. I don't even wait. And when you're a star they let you do it. You can do anything."

Unknown, but apparently Bush: "Whatever you want?"

Trump: "Grab them by the pussy. You can do anything."

This disclosure was followed by a number of interviews between Trump and broadcast personality Howard Stern, which was even more graphic, including Trump's statement that, "I guess you could call Ivanka (his daughter) a 'piece of ass.'"

The fallout was immediate. More than thirty Republican Senators, Congressional Representatives, and well-known personalities withdrew their endorsement of or support for Trump. Many of those called for him to withdraw from the Presidential race altogether, something which he adamantly refused to do, saying, "There's a _zero_ chance of that." When Trump "apologized" for his statements, he immediately went on to attack Hillary Clinton's husband, former President Bill Clinton, for his philandering during his days as Arkansas' governor and his days in the White House and continued that Hillary Clinton had lied about her knowledge of her husband's activities and then tried to destroy the women who'd been victimized by President Clinton. He threatened to bring the whole tawdry mess up at the Second Presidential Debate scheduled for Sunday, October 9.

A little less that two hours before the second debate, Trump announced that he had been speaking with four women, three of whom claimed to have had affairs with Bill Clinton and one of whom had been raped when she was 12 years old and Hillary Clinton had defended her assailant in Court. (The last charge was true but what Trump conveniently failed to reveal was that Hillary Clinton had been appointed by the Court to represent this person while she was a young attorney working for what was essentially a public charity law firm). Trump then announced that these four women would be sitting in the front row in the debate hall. The majority of the media jumped on this as a "cheap shot sideshow to distract people from Trump's wrongdoing." Mostly, however, the public realized that Bill Clinton's misdeeds occurred over thirty years ago and that *Hillary*, not Bill Clinton, was the one running for office.

THE SECOND PRESIDENTIAL DEBATE

FiveThirtyEight's Nate Silver wrote about the second debate as follows:

"The second presidential debate on Sunday night was a strange one. ... Donald Trump appear[ed] to be on the brink of a meltdown in the first 20 to 30 minutes, then steadied himself the rest of the way. But here's the bottom line: Based on post-debate polls, Hillary Clinton probably ended the night in a better place than she started it. And almost without question, she ended the weekend, counting the debate, the revelation on Friday of a 2005 tape in which Trump was recorded appearing to condone unwanted sexual contact against women, and the Republican reaction to the tape, in an improved position. ...

"At roughly the 20-minute mark of Sunday's debate, about the point at which Trump said that he'd appoint a special prosecutor to investigate Clinton and that she'd 'be in jail' if someone like him had been president, it seemed prudent to wonder whether Trump's campaign was over ... in the sense that we knew the outcome of the election for all intents and purposes. ...

"After all, the past two weeks have gone about as badly as possible for Trump. After having drawn the race to a fairly close position, Trump took one of the most lopsided defeats ever at the first debate in New York on Sept. 26. Then he engaged in a weeklong battle with a former Miss Universe ... *Then* the story broke that Trump had claimed losses of more than $900 million in 1995 and perhaps had not paid federal income taxes for 18 years.

"But wait, there's more! After a relatively effective vice presidential debate for Mike Pence earlier in the week, although it didn't appear to have helped Trump in the polling, The *Washington Post* dropped its story about the tape Friday afternoon. By Saturday, Republican defections were getting bad enough that Trump was fending off rumors that Pence would quit the race. And then Trump began his Sunday evening at a makeshift press conference that featured three women who have accused Bill Clinton of sexual harassment or sexual assault and a fourth woman who was raped by a man Hillary Clinton represented at trial in 1975. The Bill Clinton sex story might be of interest to parts of Trump's base, but most Americans are tired of hearing about it, at least in an election in which Bill Clinton isn't running for office. And *then* in the first 20 minutes of the debate, Trump brought up the Bill Clinton accusations again and threatened to imprison Hillary Clinton, without showing any contrition Republican leaders called for.

"But Trump made it through the rest of the debate with a relatively good performance, or at least, so I thought. He was oftentimes meandering but fairly measured, and he was effective at pressing Clinton on Obamacare and her email server. ... The key term, however, is 'relatively.' I've covered enough debates to know that other than in the really obvious cases, it can be hard to judge how voters will perceive a performance. So you grasp on to what you can find: prediction markets, which began to show Trump rebounding about halfway through the debate; real-time reaction from focus groups; and the sentiment of other journalists. ... Once expectations were lowered to the point that we in the media were speculating about whether Trump's own running mate might drop out, any half-decent performance was bound to look good.

"A CNN poll of debate watchers found that even though most voters thought Trump 'exceeded expectations,' 57 percent of them nevertheless declared Clinton the winner, compared with 34 percent for Trump. A YouGov poll of debate watchers showed a much closer outcome, but with Clinton also winning, 47 percent to 42 percent. [But even if we] call the debate a draw [and even if] the tape the Post published didn't damage Trump... Instead, let's say the polls look about the same a week from now as they do today, with Clinton holding a 5-6 percentage point lead. Maybe Clinton's numbers were a little inflated after the first debate and Trump has even gained a point or two, somehow.

"That's *still* a fairly awful position for Trump with time running out, undecided voters getting off the sidelines, early voting already taking place in many states and little or no ground game to help provide a strong finishing kick. There's the third debate, but without an extremely strong performance in that one, Trump is probably left hoping for an 'October surprise.' ... Or, obviously, things could get worse for Trump. And some 'October surprises,' such as further leaks of tax returns or embarrassing comments caught on tape, could work against him. His attempt to make an issue of Bill Clinton's past, which his campaign seems determined to pursue, could also backfire.

"In the end, your assessment of Trump's chances comes down to the same consideration as with a falling stock: How sound are the fundamentals? Is Trump the equivalent of a beleaguered bluechip that still has lots of hard assets? In Trump's case, the most valuable asset is probably possession of the Republican Party ballot line, which theoretically ought to be worth something given the circumstances of the race. Or was the whole business a sort of confidence trick, which was bound to implode once people began to lose faith in it?"

* * *

This book was "put to bed" on October 13, 2016, twenty-four days before the election. On September 25, FiveThirtyEight projected a 54.8% chance that Clinton would win the Presidency and a 45.2% chance that Trump would prevail. On the afternoon of October 12, 2016 the spread was 86.8% Clinton vs. 13.2% Trump. The same poll showed a "dead heat," a 55.4% chance that the Democrats would regain control of the Senate and a 44.6% chance that the Republicans would retain control of the Senate.

CONCLUSION

WE'VE BEEN DOWN

THIS ROAD BEFORE

17

By 4,000 B.C., humankind had advanced from caves to tents, then from tents to more permanent buildings. Settlements of two or three families had grown to towns, then cities, then nations. Much of what we experience today goes back a lot farther than we think. American politicians didn't invent the lust for power, greed, corruption, graft, or name-calling. I'm certain that when the bids went out to put up the pyramids – "lowest responsible responsive bidder gets the job" – Ahmenotep/Halliburton had fixed the winning bid, the Parthenon was built by Georgopoulos/Lockheed, and a likely slogan was "something for everyone and a bit left over for me." Actually, the Athenian city-state tried to clean up its political mess in a novel way: if you had been in political office for ten years, you were banished from Athens for the next ten years. A little more effective than today's "term limits."

Angry rhetoric? Dirty tricks? The 21st Century is an absolute novice compared to ancient Rome. A common bit of political advice in the days before Christ and for four hundred-fifty years thereafter was "*Fortiter calumniare, aliquid adhaerebit*" ("Sling plenty of mud and some of it will stick."). And there was a *lot* of mud slung. "How to screw your neighbor's wife (or, for that matter, his daughter, his son, his ward, or his sheep) for fun, profit, and political power," was more than a scatological exercise. In the upper echelons of the Palatine Hill, it was "business as usual," unless, like Richard Nixon in much later times, you disobeyed the "Eleventh Commandment" – "Thou Shalt Not Get Caught."

But the focus of this book is not on ancient history. For our purposes, we'll start with the 1980 election, when Ronald Reagan, the Great Communicator, ran for President. I could have picked any election prior to 1980, but I believe this is when the *current* climate of organized hate politics began. The era when the media became a serious player in politics, when there were more people and less resources to go around, and the time when we really started to go astray. That's not to say American politics was always "squeaky clean." To the contrary, the Presidential Elections between 1789 and 1976 were often brutal, immoral, and filled with extraordinary vitriol. For those of you interested in such stuff, Appendix "A" to this book furnishes capsule shots of those elections. For now, we'll stick to the elections that took place within the last three decades.

"Reality is malleable. It can be made to bend to your will. ... Roger Ailes was a real power player. He played a key role in getting George H.W. Bush elected over Michael Dukakis in 1988, and his book*, You Are the Message: Secrets of the Master Communicator*s, is a 'must read,' along with Sun-T'u'*s The Art of Wa*r, Machiavelli'*s The Princ*e, and Carl von Clausewitz'*s On Wa*r. He was the guy who dreamed up the town hall forum for Richard Nixon. He was Lee Atwater's mentor. All I lacked was influence over other human beings. Now *the*re was something worth having!" - Allen Raymond, former GOP Political consultant, author of *How to Rig an Election* (Simon & Schuster).

Raymond, who went to prison for his role in a scheme to jam the Democratic Party's phone lines during New Hampshire's 2002 Senate elections, says that dirty tricks are commonplace in the political world and reforms are badly needed.

The first use of the English phrase "dirty tricks" can be traced to Arthur Capel, the Earl of Essex, who wrote in 1670, "To me he called it a dirty trick." Thirteen years later, the Earl was found with his throat cut in the Tower of London, more dirty deed than dirty trick. The phrase entered the political vocabulary with a vengeance during the Watergate scandal as a phrase that once was equated with "pranks," "hardball" and "borderline slander." In 1973, it gained a more sinister meaning of "surreptitious disruption of an opponent's campaign." Joe Cummins, author of *Anything for a Vote: Dirty tricks, Cheap Shots and October Surprises in U.S. Presidential Campaigns*, notes that it was George Washington, while commanding general of the American revolutionary forces, who wrote of a British peace proposal, "They are practicing such low and dirty tricks, that men of sentiment and honor must blush at their Villainy." In 1828, *The United States Telegraph*, a newspaper supporting President Andrew Jackson, despite vilification in his re-election campaign for having married Rachel Robards before her divorce was complete, denounced its rival's coverage with *"The Intelligencer* at its dirty tricks again!"

The phrase may have had its modern genesis in the U.S. Navy. In its Nov. 20, 1944 issue, *Time* magazine reported a surprise predawn raid on Japanese land-based air power on the island of Luzon, as "The Dirty Tricksters."

Covert action has been used since time immemorial in both politics and intelligence operations. In the Carter-Reagan campaign of 1980, Carter's briefing book for a television debate mysteriously found its way into the hands of the Reagan camp. James Baker and William Casey were suspected of pulling that dirty trick; both men adamantly denied it. Casey wound up as Reagan's director of Central Intelligence working with Baker as White House chief of staff. Thus ended the Dirty Trick That Never Was.

The 1988 Bush vs. Dukakis election had an endless barrage of lies and disinformation. The Bush campaign was run by Lee

Atwater of Georgia, the ultimate ninja warrior of bad-boy politics. Karl Rove had, in fact, discovered Atwater and introduced him to the Bush family. George W. Bush, who also worked on the campaign, was in awe of Atwater's political savvy and immensely impressed by his take-no-prisoners political sensibility.

After skillful leaks and lies out of the GOP National Committee had defeated Gary Hart, Bob Dole and Pat Robertson, the Bush camp went ballistic on the Democrats' candidate, Michael Dukakis, with skillfully planted stories that Dukakis in the past had consulted a psychiatrist for depression. While the stories were completely untrue, that didn't stop President Reagan from compassionately telling reporters, when asked about this rumor, that he was "not going to pick on an invalid." From there, Atwater was able to destroy Dukakis with an endless carpet-bombing of unprecedented attack ads, like the viciously racist "Willie Horton" commercials about a black man who'd been charged with murder while on work-release in Massachusetts. When the smoke cleared, George Bush the Elder had won the election.

* * *

The source of some of the most outrageous domestic intrigue and international revolutionary conspiracy of its era was 42 Wall Street, the mahogany-lined law offices of Sullivan & Cromwell. Until his death in 1948 at the ripe old age of 94, founding partner William Nelson Cromwell was part court solicitor and part buc-caneer-for-hire to the greatest Robber Barons of the day. In 1879, Cromwell incorporated the Edison General Electric Company as a virtual monopoly over the American electric power industry. He did the same thing for Andrew Carnegie's United States Steel Corporation in 1901. Cromwell also orchestrated the enormous land grabs, strike-breaking, and corporate consolidations that led to Edward H. Harriman's takeover of the Union Pacific Railroad in 1898. Cromwell worked hand in glove with the premier Wall Street moneymen of the day, including J.P. Morgan, the Rockefellers, Kuhn Loeb & Co., Otto Kahn and Felix Warburg. So ruthlessly were the tactics of these syndicates in eliminating competitors and rigging prices in American markets, that even a conservative, Big-Business dominated Congress under Republican Senate majority leader Mark "Dollar" Hana was forced to pass the Sherman Anti-trust Act of 1890.

In the realm of international finance and in engineering political revolutions abroad, Cromwell set the world standard. In 1896, Cromwell was retained by the chief engineer of the failed French Panama Canal construction company, to convince the U.S. Government to pay $40 million for a pile of rusting construction equipment and the soon-to-expire development rights from the Colombian government. In one of the most audacious feats of covert corporate political warfare in history, Cromwell paid Hana a record bribe of $60,000, then proceeded to put together a secret syndicate of middleman bankers to surreptitiously buy up a controlling interest in the outstanding shares of "worthless" Compagnie stock at pennies on the dollar.

Beginning in 1902, $3.5 million was quietly paid out by a second syndicate organized by Cromwell that included J.P. Morgan and some of the largest bankers in New York, to repurchase these shares, bought up at the lowest price possible. When the Colombian government learned of the scheme, and balked at the terms in 1903, the deal seemed imperiled as the Colombians threatened to march on Colon in November to throw the Americans out and a crush a Panamanian revolt. At the same time, the scheme met with increasing resistance in Washington and in the press, led by Senator John Tyler Morgan (who had a stake in competing canal plan through Nicaragua) and Joseph Pulitzer, whose New York World newspaper had sought to expose the Panama conspiracy.

Cromwell let loose a team of secret agents, lawyers, and bankers to spark a "nationalist" revolution in Panama. In the meantime, President McKinley, whose support had been lukewarm, was gunned down by an anarchist in Buffalo, New York. After Teddy Roosevelt assumed office, things soon got back on track. As American war ships patrolled the waters off the Panamanian capitol of Colon in November 1903, Cromwell's agents bribed the Colombian Army, sending officers and enlisted men on their way, pockets jangling with silver, all the way back to Bogota. Despite the ensuing scandal, most of the press hailed the revolution of the "Panama Patriots" as a triumph for American-style democracy. The U.S. Congress voted to pay out the $40 million, and authorized another million in public underwriting for the bonds of the Panamanian railroad company owned by Cromwell. The distribution of the U.S. Government payments to stockholders and the Panamanians was, strangely, put in Cromwell's hands, rather than administered by the U.S. Treasury. The conspiracy's principal investors saw as high as a 1,250% return. For his $1.333 million investment, Cromwell personally took at least $18 million, while his law firm billed the United States $832,449 in legal fees.

* * *

Black propaganda is false information and material that purports to be from a source on one side of a conflict, but is actually from the opposing side. It is typically used to vilify, embarrass or misrepresent the enemy. Black propaganda contrasts with grey propaganda, the source of which is not identified, and white propaganda, in which the real source is declared and usually more accurate information is given, if also slanted or distorted. Black propaganda purports to emanate from a source other than the true source. This type of propaganda is associated with covert psychological operations. Sometimes the source is concealed or credited to a false authority and spreads lies, fabrications, and deceptions. Black propaganda is the "big lie," including all types of creative deceit.

Ultimately, black propaganda relies on the willingness of the receiver to accept the credibility of the source. If the creators or senders of the black propaganda message do not adequately understand their intended audience, the message may be misunderstood, seem suspicious, or fail altogether. Governments generally conduct black propaganda operations for two different reasons. First, by utilizing black propaganda a government is more likely to succeed in convincing their target audience that the information that they are seeking to influence them with is disguised, and that its motivations are not apparent. Second, there are diplomatic reasons behind the use of black propaganda. Black propaganda is necessary in order to obfuscate a government's involvement in activities that may be detrimental to its foreign policies.

Disinformation is a useful form of black propaganda due to the fact that disinformation campaigns are covert in nature and use various forms of false information. Disinformation can be defined as false information that is deliberately, and often covertly spread in order to influence public opinion and obscure the truth. Prior to, and during the Cold War, the Soviet Union successfully utilized this form of black propaganda on multiple occasions to their benefit. Joseph Stalin's dictatorship firmly believed in black propaganda and disinformation campaigns targeted against Western nations and the United States. One of Stalin's early successes in these operations targeted the United States through the use of the Moscow Bureau Chief at the New York Times, Walter Duranty. Duranty would ultimately win the Pulitzer Prize for his sympathetic writings praising the Soviet dictator, while failing to accurately report on the Ukrainian famine of 1932.

The Soviet Union utilized black propaganda during the Iranian hostage crisis that took place from 1979 until 1981. For strictly political purposes, and to show support for the hostages, Soviet diplomats at the United Nations vocally criticized the taking of the hostages. At this same time however, Soviet "black" radio stations within Iran called the National Voice of Iran openly broadcast strong support for the crisis in an effort to increase anti-American sentiment. This represented a clear utilization of black propaganda by the Soviet Union in order to have anti-American broadcasts appear as if they were actually originating from Iranian sources.

Throughout the Cold War, the Soviet Union effectively utilized the KGB in order to conduct its covert black forms of active measures. The KGB was responsible for clandestine campaigns targeting foreign governments, as well as influencing individuals and specific groups that were hostile towards the Soviet government and its policies.

Following the 9-1-1 attacks against the United States, the Pentagon organized and implemented the Office of Strategic Influence in an effort to improve public support abroad, mainly in Islamic countries. The head of OSI maintained the mission of "circulating classified proposals calling for aggressive campaigns that used not only the foreign media and the Internet, but also covert operations." Defense Secretary Donald Rumsfeld planned for what they called "a broad mission ranging from 'black' campaigns that used disinformation and other covert activities to 'white' public affairs that rely on truthful news releases." Therefore, OSI's operations could include the blackest of activities.

OSI's operations included contacting and emailing media, journalist, and foreign community leaders with information that would counter foreign governments and organizations that are hostile to the United States. In doing so, the emails would be masked by utilizing addresses ending with .com as opposed to using the standard Pentagon address of ".mil," and hide any involvement of the U.S. government and the Pentagon. The Pentagon is forbidden to conduct black propaganda operations within the American media, but is not prohibited for conducting these operations against foreign media outlets. The thought of conducting black propaganda operations and utilizing disinformation resulted in harsh criticism for the program. It closed down in 2002.

In Britain, the Political Warfare Executive operated a number of black propaganda radio stations during World War II. Gustav Siegfried Eins (GS1), which purported to be a clandestine German station, was one of the first such stations. The speaker, "Der Chef," purported to be a Nazi extremist, accusing Hitler and his henchmen of going soft. The station focused on alleged corruption and sexual improprieties of Nazi Party members. Another example was the British radio station *Soldatensender Calais*, which purported to be a radio station for the German military. Under the direction of Sefton Delmer, a British journalist who spoke perfect Berliner German, Soldatensender Calais and its associated shortwave station, *Kurzwellensender Atlantik*, broadcast music, up-to-date sports scores, speeches of Adolf Hitler for "cover" and subtle propaganda.

Radio Deutschland was another radio station employed by the British during the war aimed and designed to undermine German morale and create tensions that would ultimately disrupt the German war effort. The station was broadcast from a signal in close proximity on the radio dial to an actual German station. During the war most Germans actually believed that this station was in fact a German radio station and even gained the recognition of Germany's propaganda chief Joseph Goebbels. There were British black propaganda radio stations in most of the languages of occupied Europe as well as German and Italian.

German black propaganda usually took advantage of European racism and anti-Communism. On the night of April 27, 1944 German aircraft under cover of darkness dropped propaganda leaflets over occupied Denmark. These leaflets used the title of *Frihedsposten*, a genuine Danish underground newspaper, and claimed that the "hour of liberation" was approaching. They instructed Danes to accept "occupation by Russian or specially trained American Negro soldiers" until the first disorders resulting from military operations were over. The German Büro Concordia organization operated several black propaganda radio stations, many of which pretended to broadcast illegally from within the countries they targeted.

The *Protocols of the Elders of Zion* claimed to be the secret protocols of a vast Jewish conspiracy, and was often used as "evidence" by conspiracy theorists and anti-Semitic groups. It was proven to be a forgery produced by the Okhrana, the Tsarist Russian secret police. The Black Panther Coloring Book was distributed in the United States in the late 1960s in an attempt to discredit the Black Panther Party, and the civil rights movement in general. In Dreux, France, in 1982 the National Front distributed anonymous fake letters, supposedly from an Algerian living in France to a brother living in Algeria. These fake letters, which described immigration as a method of conquering France without war, were instrumental in the National Front victory in the 1983 local council elections in Dreux. In the run-up to the 2007 federal election in Australia, flyers were circulated around Sydney under the name of a fake organization called the Islamic Australia Federation. The flyers thanked the Australian Labor Party for supporting terrorism, Islamic fundamentalists, and the Bali bombing suspects. A group of Sydney-based Liberal Party members were implicated in the incident.

* * *

During the 1972 U.S. presidential election, Donald H. Segretti, a political operative for President Richard Nixon's reelection campaign, released a faked letter, on Senator Edmund Muskie's letterhead, falsely alleging that Senator Henry "Scoop" Jackson, against whom Muskie was running for the Democratic Party's nomination, had had an illegitimate child with a seventeen-year-old. Muskie, who had been considered the frontrunner, lost the nomination to George McGovern, and Nixon was reelected. The letter was part of a campaign of so-called "dirty tricks", directed by Segretti, and uncovered as part of the Watergate Scandal. Segretti went to prison in 1974 after pleading guilty to three misdemeanor counts of distributing illegal campaign literature.

The Federal Bureau of Investigation's Counter-intelligence program "COINTELPRO," was intended to "expose, disrupt, misdirect, discredit, or otherwise neutralize the activities of black nationalists, hate-type organizations and groups, their leadership, membership, and supporters." Black propaganda–that is, propaganda that disguises its source–was used famously against Communists and the Black Panther Party. It was also used against domestic opponents of the invasion of Vietnam, labor leaders, and Native Americans . COINTELPRO's use of black propaganda led to their creation of coloring books and cartoons. The FBI's strategy was captured in a 1968 memo: "Consider the use of cartoons, photographs, and anonymous letters which will have the effect of ridiculing the New Left. Ridicule is one of the most potent weapons which we can use against it." The FBI employed a similar tactic in 1968 to disrupt activities of the Ku Klux Klan, as hundreds of 'racist' flyers with misleading information were fabricated and made to appear as if they originated from known Klan leaders.

"The Penkovsky Papers" are an example of a black propaganda effort conducted by the United States' Central Intelligence Agency during the 1960's. The "Penkovsky Papers" were alleged to have been written by a Soviet GRU defector, Colonel Oleg Penkovsky, but was in fact produced by the CIA in an effort to diminish the Soviet Union's credibility at a pivotal time during the Cold War.

18

NEWT GINGRICH vs. BILL CLINTON – THE CONTRACT WITH AMERICA OR THE CONTRACT ON AMERICA?

Starting in 1994, politics took on its present nasty turn. What had been the dirty tricks of election politics for single candidates of both parties moved into the arena of blocs – the crystallization of party line votes and the inevitable gridlock. In 1992, Bill Clinton won the Presidency of the United States. At the same time, the Democrats won control of both houses of Congress.

Although now portraying himself as "cheerful" in his doomed-to-defeat run for the Republican Presidential standard-bearer in the 2011-2012 run for the nation's highest office, Newton Leroy "Newt" Gingrich has conclusively demonstrated the incredibly short memory of the electorate, reinventing himself yet again. How short-mined we are! In 1994 Gingrich, then a 9-time re-elected Congressman from Georgia, altered the game by changing the stakes. "If you have the Executive branch, I'm going to make sure my side has the Legislative Branch," and vice versa. This was by no means the first time that one party controlled one branch and the other party controlled the other branch. This had often happened in American history during mid-term elections, largely because Americans are impatient and very much "want it *now.*" It happened in the November 2010 mid-term election as well. That's the same mentality that's fueled the growth of credit card debt since the 1950's. Why wait 'til you have the cash to buy the "toys" you want? Purchase them *now* and pay on what our English friends across the Pond refer to as "the never never" plan. Somehow the mentality was – and continues to be to this day – if a President can't change things in *one term*, vote him (or her) out of office, and if Congress can't change things in *one two-year session*, vote the representatives and senators out of office as well.

Case in point: In 2008, Barack Obama won the U.S. Presidency on the promise of "Change We Can Believe In." The economy had started its recession shortly after the 2004 election. By mid-2008, the economy had "tanked." Real estate prices had taken a 25% downturn (on its way to a paralyzing 50% loss of value in the single most important asset most Americans cherish), banks had run out of money and begged the Government to bail them out (this during a Republican administration which had always prided itself on a *laissez faire* – hands off – policy). Make no mistake, things were pretty grim in the good ol' U.S. of A.

The Democrats found easy pickings by blaming George W. Bush's policies for the economic collapse of the country – as if one man could possibly be responsible for the downturn of 300,000,000 of his fellow citizens. When Barack Obama was elected President, the American people danced in the streets with glee. The deep recession – which might well have been a Depression, whatever you want to call it – would be over! "Happy Days Are Here Again!" After all, Obama had promised "Change We Can Believe In."

Lost amid the tumult and the shouting of the exuberant victors was a warning that President Obama had given several times during the campaign: "It took us *years* to get into this mess, and it will take us *years* to get out of this mess. It may not happen during my first administration (4 years) – it may take longer." That was not what the people wanted to hear and they didn't bother to listen to that part of the speech.

By 2010 there were some changes. The American Relief & Recovery Act was supposed to get America working once again. But the American public somehow thought that meant that *everyone* would have a job again – *right now*. When it didn't happen, the American public got *mad*. And they blamed the President. And they blamed Congress because there was a 10+% unemployment rate, the banks weren't lending any money, and the value of real estate kept going down and down. The 2010 mid-term elections showed precisely how angry the impatient American populace was.

It would be very easy to blame the Republicans for blocking every measure that President Obama wanted to see passed and for being "obstructionist." Very easy, but not very true. Make no mistake, at one point during President Obama's first term, the Democrats boasted 60 out of 100 Senators. They had the power to steamroll over any attempt at filibuster. In the House, the Democratic majority was even larger. Thus, if every Senator and Congressperson voted along strict party lines, there would have been no way – *none at all* – in which the Republicans could have stopped the social bills demanded by the electorate. While the Republicans railed against a "socialist state," and made other noises which minority parties have always made, the real failure to pass any meaningful laws or programs came from the Democratic disease – shoot yourself in the foot.

Until the 2012 election, that malaise could be laid at the doorstep of the philosophical differences between the parties: The Republicans, who traditionally represent about 39% of the voters, and who are by nature *laissez faire* Conservatives, tended to hang together, whereas the Democrats, with their free-wheeling spirit, represented almost as many different opinions as there were Congresspersons.

Of course, blaming the Democrats for the gridlock would also be too simplistic. Republicans traditionally have money – and, make no mistake, in the United States "Money talks, Bull***t walks." Slowly, the Republicans ate away at the Democratic supermajority – one election, one Representative, one Senator at a time. Shortly after President Obama's first year in power, the Democrats no longer had a filibuster-proof majority. Once again, nothing got done, it was a do-nothing Congress (only this time with a truly scary economic Panic), and the American people were *pissed off.*

The current spirit of confrontation rather than cooperation on a large scale did not begin with either Bush I or II. It began in 1993 when the Clinton administration, which had come flying into the White House with a strong Democratic majority, failed to pass its much-heralded plan for Universal Healthcare. It began with two strong politicians, each of whom preached morality while practicing something else entirely. Let's take a moment to examine each of these protagonists, restricting their histories to the "Contract with America," which President Clinton derisively called the "Contract *on* America."

William Jefferson "Bill" Clinton, born August 19, 1946, President of the United States from 1993 to 2001, became the Chief at 46, at the end of the Cold War. He was the first baby boomer president. Both he and his wife Hillary Rodham Clinton earned their Juris Doctor (J.D.) degrees from Yale Law School. During his administration, Clinton presided over the continuation of an economic expansion that would later become the longest period of peacetime economic expansion in American history. There was a budget surplus in 2000, the last full year of Clinton's presidency.

After a failed attempt at health care reform, Republicans won control of the House of Representatives in 1994 for the first time in forty years. They promised, but never-quite-delivered, what they called the "Contract with America," authored in part by Newt Gingrich. Two years later, in 1996, Clinton was re-elected. Later, he was impeached for perjury and obstruction of justice in connection with a scandal involving a White House intern. He was subsequently acquitted by the U.S. Senate. Clinton left office with the highest end-of-office approval rating of any U.S. president since World War II. Pundits quipped that if he had had another sex scandal during his term, his adoring public would have voted to overturn the two-term Presidential limit and he would have been elected again by a landslide.

Clinton and Gingrich came from remarkably similar backgrounds. Bill Clinton was born in Hope, Arkansas. His father, a traveling salesman, died in an automobile accident three months before Bill was born. Following Bill's birth, his mother traveled to New Orleans, leaving Bill in Hope with grandparents, who owned and operated a small grocery store. At a time, when the Southern United States were racially segregated, Clinton's grandparents sold goods on credit to people of all races. When Bill's mother returned from nursing school and shortly thereafter married Roger Clinton, who co-owned an automobile dealership in Hot Springs, Arkansas, the family moved to Hot Springs in 1950. Clinton remembers his stepfather as a gambler and an alcoholic, who regularly abused his mother and half-brother Roger Clinton, Jr., to the point where he intervened multiple times with the threat of violence in order to protect them.

Clinton attended Hot Springs High School, where he was an active student leader, avid reader, and musician. In 1963, Clinton visited the White House as a Boys Nation senator, where he met President John F. Kennedy. That same year, he heard Martin Luther King's 1963 *I Have a Dream* speech, which so moved him that he committed the entire speech to memory. With the aid of scholarships, Clinton attended Georgetown University, where he received a B.S. in Foreign Service. He spent the summer before his senior year, working as an intern for Arkansas Senator J. William Fulbright. Upon graduation, he won a Rhodes Scholarship to University College, Oxford where he studied Philosophy, Politics and Economics. While at Oxford he participated in Vietnam War protests. In later life, he admitted to smoking marijuana at the university, but famously said that he "never inhaled."

After Oxford, Clinton received his J.D. degree from Yale Law School in 1973. During his time at Yale, Clinton took a job with the McGovern campaign and was assigned to lead McGovern's effort in Texas. After Yale, Clinton became a professor at the University of Arkansas. A year later, he unsuccessfully ran for the House of Representatives, but he was elected Arkansas Attorney General in 1976 and Governor of Arkansas in 1978, becoming the youngest governor in the country at thirty-two. Clinton's defeat in the general election of 1980, made him the youngest ex-governor in the nation's history. He spent the next two years working on his re-election campaign. He was again elected governor and this time he kept his job for ten years.

The Clintons' personal and business affairs during the 1980s included transactions which became the basis of the Whitewater investigation which dogged his later presidential administration, but no indictments were made against the Clintons related to the years in Arkansas.

In 1987, Clinton gave the opening night address at the 1988 Democratic National Convention. This set the stage for his dramatic run for the Presidency. In the first contest, the Iowa caucus, he finished a very distant third. During the campaign for the New Hampshire Primary, rumors circulated about an extramarital affair with Gennifer Flowers. Clinton and his wife Hillary went on *60 Minutes* to refute the charges. Their television appearance was a calculated risk, but Clinton regained several delegates. He finished second in the New Hampshire primary, but after trailing badly in the polls and coming within single digits of winning, the media viewed it as a victory. On election night, Clinton labeled himself "The Comeback Kid," earning a strong second-place finish.

Ultimately, Clinton won the 1992 presidential election against Republican incumbent George H. W. Bush and billionaire populist Ross Perot, who ran as an independent. A significant part of Clinton's success was Bush's steep decline in public approval. By election time, the economy was souring and Bush saw his approval rating plummet. Clinton was inaugurated as the 42nd President of the United States on January 20, 1993. In his inaugural address he declared, "Our democracy must be not only the envy of the world but the engine of our own renewal. There is nothing *wrong* with America that cannot be cured by what is *right* with America."

On February 17, 1993, in a nationally televised address to a joint session of Congress, Clinton unveiled his economic plan: deficit reduction rather than a middle-class tax cut, which had been high on his campaign agenda. Shortly after taking office, Clinton signed the Family and Medical Leave Act of 1993, which required large employers to allow employees to take unpaid leave for pregnancy or a serious medical condition. While this action was popular, Clinton's attempt to fulfill another campaign promise of allowing openly homosexual men and women to serve in the armed forces ended up with a strange compromise, "Don't ask, don't tell," which allowed for homosexuals to serve in the military as long as they kept their sexuality secret.

Also in 1993, Clinton supported ratification of the controversial North American Free Trade Agreement. Opposition came chiefly from anti-trade Republicans, protectionist Democrats and Ross Perot supporters. The Agreement was signed into law by President Clinton on January 1, 1994.

One of the most prominent items on Clinton's legislative agenda was a health care reform plan aimed at achieving universal coverage through a national health care plan. Though initially well-received in political circles, it was ultimately doomed by well-organized opposition from conservatives, the American Medical Association, and the health insurance industry. Despite Clinton's party's holding a majority in Congress, the effort to create a national health care system ultimately died. Does this sound familiar? It was the first major legislative defeat of Clinton's administration. Two months later, after two years of Democratic Party control, the Democrats lost control of Congress in the mid-term elections in 1994, for the first time in forty years, largely due to the Gingrich co-authored promise of a "Contract With America.".

The Contract with America was introduced six weeks before the 1994 Congressional election, the first mid-term election of President Clinton's Administration, and was signed by all but two of the Republican members of the House and all of the Party's non-incumbent Republican Congressional candidates. It marked the first time since 1918 that a Congressional election had been run broadly on a national level, *i.e.* the politics of an unrelenting bloc. Its provisions represented the view of many conservative

Republicans on the issues of shrinking the size of government, promoting lower taxes and greater entrepreneurial activity, tort reform, and welfare reform. When the Republicans gained a majority of seats in the 104th Congress, the Contract was seen as a triumph for Party leaders such as Gingrich.

The Contract's actual text included a list of eight reforms the Republicans promised to enact, and ten bills they promised to bring to floor debate and votes, if they were made the majority following the election. More than half of its text came from Ronald Reagan's 1985 State of the Union Address. On the first day of their majority in the House, the Republicans promised to pass eight major reforms:

- require all laws that apply to the rest of the country to also apply to Congress;
- select a major, independent auditing firm to conduct a comprehensive audit of Congress for waste, fraud or abuse;
- cut the number of House committees and cut committee staff by one-third;
- limit the terms of all committee chairs;
- ban the casting of proxy votes in committee;
- require committee meetings to be open to the public;
- require a three-fifths majority vote to pass a tax increase;
- guarantee an honest accounting of the Federal Budget by implementing zero base-line budgeting.

The Republicans pledged "to bring to the floor ten bills, each to be given a full and open debate, each to be given a clear and fair vote, and each to be immediately available for public inspection." These bills represented significant changes to policy:

- a balanced budget requirement
- tax cuts for small businesses, families and seniors
- term limits for legislators
- social security reform
- tort reform, and
- welfare reform.

The momentum of the Republican Revolution stalled in late 1995 during a budget standoff between Congressional Republicans and Democratic President Bill Clinton. Speaker Gingrich and the new Republican majority wanted to slow the rate of government spending. Gingrich allowed previously approved appropriations to expire on schedule, thus allowing parts of the Federal government to shut down for lack of funds. However, Gingrich inflicted a blow to his public image by suggesting that the Republican hard-line stance over the budget was in part due to his feeling "snubbed" by the President during a flight to and from Yitzhak Rabin's funeral in Israel. Gingrich was subsequently lampooned by the media, with one editorial cartoon depicted him as having thrown a temper tantrum. Democratic leaders took the opportunity to attack Gingrich's motives for the budget standoff, which may have contributed to Clinton's re-election in November 1996 and significant losses for the Republican Party in Congress.

After the firestorm of the Contract with America died down, both Clinton and Gingrich were seen in a "different" light, particularly when it came to morals and ethics.

On January 21, 1997, the House voted 395 to 28 to reprimand Gingrich for ethics violations dating back to September 1994. The House ordered Gingrich to pay a $300,000 penalty, the first time in the House's 208-year history it had disciplined a Speaker for ethical wrongdoing. By 1998, Gingrich had become a highly visible and polarizing figure in the public's eye, making him a target for Democratic congressional candidates across the nation. Republicans lost five seats in the House in the 1998 midterm elections — the worst performance in 64 years for a party that didn't hold the presidency. Polls showed that Gingrich and the Republican Party's attempt to remove President Clinton from office was widely unpopular among Americans.

Facing another rebellion in the Republican caucus, Gingrich announced on November 6, 1998 that he would stand down as Speaker and would leave the House as well. He had been handily reelected to an 11th term, but declined to take his seat. Gingrich said, "I'm willing to lead but I'm not willing to preside over people who are cannibals."

Gingrich's personal life, like Clinton's, has hardly been a model of fidelity and is somewhat less than beyond reproach. He has been married three times. He first married Jackie Battley, his former high school geometry teacher, when he was 19 and she was 26. Gingrich left his wife in the spring of 1980 after having an affair with Marianne Ginther. According to Battley, Gingrich visited her later that year while she was in the hospital recovering from cancer surgery to discuss the details of their divorce. Six months after it was final, Gingrich wed Ginther. But his second marriage did not result in the cessation of his extracurricular activities. Gingrich began an affair with Callista Bisek, 23 years his junior, in the mid nineties, which, oddly enough, continued during the Congressional investigation of Bill Clinton and the Monica Lewinsky scandal.

In 2000, Gingrich married Bisek shortly after his divorce with second wife Ginther was finalized. A Baptist since graduate school, Gingrich converted to Catholicism, his wife's faith, on March 29, 2009.

Newt Gingrich was an outspoken critic of Barack Obama, whom he described as "the most radical president in American history." Gingrich argued that it is necessary to "save America" and stop Obama's "secular socialist machine." He has characterized Obama's universal health care reform as leading America towards authoritarianism, totalitarianism, and the end of democracy.

Although Clinton's morals were certainly questionable, history has treated him kinder than it has Gingrich. In the 1996 presidential election, Clinton was re-elected by a larger margin than in the first election. The Republicans lost a few seats in the House and gained a few in the Senate, but retained control of both. Clinton received over 70% of the Electoral College votes.

In a lame duck session after the 1998 elections, the House voted to impeach Clinton, based on allegations that Clinton had lied about his relationship with Lewinsky in a sworn deposition in the Paula Jones lawsuit. The House began impeachment hearings before the mid-term elections. Although the mid-term elections held in November 1998 were at the 6-year point in an 8-year presidency, the Democratic Party actually gained several seats. The Republican leadership called a lame duck session in December 1998 so it could continue the impeachment proceedings..

The two charges passed in the House, largely on the basis of Republican support, were for perjury and obstruction of justice. The perjury charge arose from Clinton's testimony about his relationship to Monica Lewinsky during a sexual harassment lawsuit (later dismissed, appealed and settled for $850,000) brought by former Arkansas state employee Paula Jones. The obstruction charge was based on his actions during the subsequent investigation of that testimony. The Senate later voted to acquit Clinton on both charges. The final vote was generally along party lines, with no Democrats voting guilty. Some Republicans voted not guilty for both charges.

Clinton remained popular with the public throughout his two terms as President, ending his presidential career with a 65% approval rating, the highest end-of-term approval rating of any President since Dwight D. Eisenhower. Clinton also oversaw a boom of the U.S. economy. Under Clinton, the United States had a projected federal budget surplus for the first time since 1969.

19

PROTECTING AGAINST PROGRESS: NAME CALLING – SOCIALISM AND OTHER EPITHETS

Americans have always been inventors of labels – an easy shorthand for more detailed explanations. If you think I'm joking, here are some shorthand labels that are quite popular today. Take a mental image "quiz" and see what you think of or picture when you hear the following words:

McDonalds

Coca-cola

Budweiser

Hollywood

New York City

9-1-1

Starbucks

Socialism

Fooled you with the last one, didn't I? Answer truthfully: Did you equate the word "Socialism" with "Communism?" Unquestionably, those whom "Liberals" call "Conservatives" or "Tea Party" would overwhelmingly answer "Yes." Equally unquestionably, "Liberals" would call "Conservatives" such things as "reactionary," "bigoted," and "racist."

Labels have been used both historically and lately as "buzz-words" to negate ideas, some of which just might lead to a better, more equitable society.

Take the current bombast over healthcare. I don't believe there is anyone in the United States who truly believes that the way we deliver healthcare in this country is ideal. Most Americans believe that medical care in the United States is "better than average," even though we rate far below such countries as France and Denmark. It *should* be better than average – *we pay more for our healthcare services and prescription drugs than any other nation on earth.*

I believe every American is entitled to affordable health care. If that makes me a "Communist" or a "Socialist" (more labels) in the eyes of many, so be it. I can live with that. Because the "sin" of "Communism" or "Socialism" is a damned sight easier to swallow than 40 million Americans going without health care.

I can hear the naysayers now: "If you want *socialized medicine* (another label), take a look at Canada and see how bad things are." I am not saying that Canada's system is without its faults - but you can point to exceptions that raise the ire of people in *any* field. For example, despite the tumult and the shouting about how medical fees are so exorbitant because of "huge malpractice verdicts," *less than 1% of medical malpractice cases result in "huge" (or even moderate) verdicts.* In California, medical malpractice non-economic damages have been limited to $250,000 for years.

So-called "Socialized" medicine exists in both France and Denmark and the World Health Organization has proclaimed that these nations furnish their citizens with the best overall health care in the world.

Let's review the naysayers comment again: "If you want *socialized medicine* take a look at Canada and see how bad things are."

Back in 1968, my son Jeff was born while I was in the Air Force. The *total* I paid for prenatal care, obstetrician, hospital, delivery, and postpartum services came to $7.50. My daughter Tracy was born a few years later, after I had gotten out of the military, in a civilian hospital and it cost me *one hundred times as much. Conservatives, who invariably decry "socialized medicine" wave the American flag and salute our military might. Perhaps they conveniently "forget" that we have had "socialized medicine" in the United States for years.* Our military - Army, Navy, Air Force, Marines - have provided full medical coverage for all military personnel and their dependents. After they retire, career military personnel are guaranteed lifelong medical care through Government programs. That is "socialized medicine," and we've had it for more years than I've been alive. I have never suffered because of being subjected to such care.

The same thing applies to Medicare, which, political yammering notwithstanding, is also "socialized medicine." I recently underwent my second cancer scare and went through 7 weeks of radiation therapy. I shudder to think what I would have had to pay but for Medicare and supplemental insurance - and what that would have done to my family's financial picture.

Those opposed to a universal healthcare system can call it "socialized medicine" or anything else they want, but the truth of the matter is that we have too many people who need healthcare and not enough facilities to provide 100% of what 100% of those people *want, immediately when they want it*. So tales of "rationing" are not entirely untrue and there will always be inequality. Those who can afford more and are willing to pay more will get faster, more complete care. Unfair? Yes, but that's the way of the world. England has lived that way since the end of World War II - you can supplement what care the Government provides with private care - which you pay for out of your own pocket.

I spoke to a radiation oncologist the other day – a wise and humane man named Patrick Feehan. He told me he had just come back from a conference where the point was raised that a 6% value-added tax – essentially a tax on *consumption*, not income – would enable us to provide excellent medical care for every man, woman, and child in America. It would be administered by the Government, which Conservatives warn will "take all our rights away and have death committees." Talk about dirty trick scare tactics! What is so insanely silly is that *we already are paying through the nose for medical care.*

Is there no sense in this Alice-in-Wonderland world called America? Suppose the *exact* amount of income generated by health insurance premiums were, instead, deposited into a government-administered program. Only this time around, the health insurance companies would not be allowed to grab *billions* of dollars each year for their shareholders. Do you seriously believe we would have a lesser grade of healthcare?

Or suppose we went to a single payer system where the administrator of that system could negotiate with the pharmaceutical companies who make sure that the term "Golden Age" means its when the big pharmaceutical reaps the most gold from older America. The United States pays more for medication than any other country in the world. "But," say those who want to keep the system the way it is, "it is only by keeping those prices as they are that we can insure that Americans get *pure* medications that are *up to U.S. standards.*" Balderdash! Most, if not all, of our prescription drugs are made overseas – in Ireland, Switzerland, Israel, and Germany. And, of course, that means "outsourced jobs" – another dirty word in political parlance.

Here are the results of a recent study by retail giant Costco. I defy anyone to prove these figures wrong. Did you ever wonder how much it costs a drug company for the active ingredient in prescription medications? Some people think it must cost a lot, since many drugs sell for more than $2.00 per tablet. We did a search of offshore chemical synthesizers that supply the active ingredients found in drugs approved by the FDA. As we have revealed in past issues of Life Extension a significant percentage of drugs sold in the United States contain active ingredients made in other countries. In our independent investigation of how much profit drug companies really make, we obtained the actual price of active ingredients used in some of the most popular drugs sold in America.

- **Celebrex:100 mg**: Consumer price (100 tablets): $130.27; Cost of general active ingredients: $0.60; Percent markup: 21,712%

- **Claritin:10 mg**: Consumer Price (100 tablets): $215.17; Cost of general active ingredients: $0.71; Percent markup: 30,306%

- **Keflex:250 mg**: Consumer Price (100 tablets): $157.39; Cost of general active ingredients: $1.88; Percent markup: 8,372%

- **Lipitor:20 mg**: Consumer Price (100 tablets): $272.37; Cost of general active ingredients: $5.80; Percent markup: 4,696%

- **Norvasc:10 mg**: Consumer price (100 tablets): $188.29;

Cost of general active ingredients: $0.14; Percent markup: 134,493%

- **Paxil:20 mg**: Consumer price (100 tablets): $220.27; Cost of general active ingredients: $7.60; Percent markup: 2,898%

- **Prevacid:30 mg**: Consumer price (100 tablets): $44.77; Cost of general active ingredients: $1.01; Percent markup: 34,136%

- **Prilosec: 20 mg**: Consumer price (100 tablets): $360.97; Cost of general active ingredients $0.52; Percent markup: 69,417%

- **Prozac:20 mg**: Consumer price (100 tablets) : $247.47; Cost of general active ingredients: $0.11; Percent markup: 224,973%

- **Tenormin:50 mg**: Consumer price (100 tablets): $104.47; Cost of general active ingredients: $0.13; Percent markup: 80,362%

- **Vasotec:10 mg**: Consumer price (100 tablets): $102.37; Cost of general active ingredients: $0.20; Percent markup: 51,185%

- **Xanax:1 mg**: Consumer price (100 tablets) : $136.79; Cost of general active ingredients: $0.024; Percent markup: 569,958%

- **Zestril:20 mg**: Consumer price (100 tablets) $89.89; Cost of general active ingredients $3.20; Percent markup: 2,809%

- **Zithromax:600 mg**: Consumer price (100 tablets): $1,482.19; Cost of general active ingredients: $18.78; Percent markup: 7,892%

- **Zocor:40 mg**: Consumer price (100 tablets): $350.27; Cost of general active ingredients: $8.63; Percent markup: 4,059%

- **Zoloft:50 mg**: Consumer price: $206.87; Cost of general active ingredients: $1.75; Percent markup: 11,821%

Since the cost of prescription drugs is so outrageous, I thought everyone should know about this. It pays to shop around! This helps to solve the mystery as to why they can afford to put a Walgreen's on every corner.

An investigative reporter for Channel 7 News in Detroit, did a story on generic drug prices gouging by pharmacies. He found in his investigation that some of these generic drugs were marked up as much as 3,000% or more. So often we blame the drug companies for the high cost of drugs, and usually rightfully so. But in this case, the fault clearly lies with the pharmacies themselves. For example if you had to buy a prescription drug, and bought the name brand, you might pay $100 for 100 pills. The pharmacist might tell you that if you get the generic equivalent, they would only cost $80, making you think you are saving $20. What the pharmacist is not telling you is that those 100 generic pills may have only cost him $10! At the end of the report, one of the anchors asked Mr. Wilson whether or not there were any pharmacies that did not adhere to this practice, and he said that Costco consistently charged little over their cost for the generic drugs.

Recently, I went to the Costco site, where you can look up any drug, and get its online price. It says that the in-store prices are consistent with the online prices. I was appalled. Just to give you one example, I searched for the drug Compazine which helps prevent nausea in chemo patients. 60 generic pills cost $54.99. At Costco, I could have bought 100 pills for $19.89. For 145 of a certain prescription pain pill, CVS charged $72.57. I could have got 150 of the same pills at Costco for $28.08.

* * *

The malaise is not limited to healthcare. Take public educa-tion – or *don't* take public education if you have the money not to. When I attended Los Angeles' Alexander Hamilton High School in the late 1950's that school had a full athletic program, a dis-tinguished school newspaper, a symphony orchestra, a marching band, a choir, a drama department, music classes for everyone, special interest after-school clubs for anyone who wanted to join, a fully-stocked school library with the latest books, classes in Lat-in, French, Spanish, Chemistry, Physics, Biology, etc. We were renowned for the quality of the plays and shows we put on. Even though we usually struggled to a barely winning football season, 75% of the students attended every game and cheered wildly. Most important, they had the Iowa Tests back then, the precursor to the SAT tests. Hamilton's *average* overall score was in the 94th percentile. I was fortunate enough to score in the 99+ percentile and got not so much as a single scholarship offer because so many others had a *higher* 99+ score than I did. Hamilton was not unique. It was made up of middle-class, ordinary students.

Private school? The only ones we ever heard about were the Catholic Schools, and they cost next to nothing. There was more than enough to keep us academically and culturally surfeited at Hamilton.

Contrast that with education in the United States today. My wife teaches in a private school in Monterey, California – a school which offers most of what I enjoyed at Hamilton High in the 50s, plus, of course, the requisite computers without which 21st century kids cannot function; and that school teaches *manners*, a forgotten art in today's world. It costs $20,000 per year in grades 1-8, close to $30,000 per year in the upper school. My wife's third grade class has 21 students. She has a co-teacher for 2/3 of the day, so there is an 11-1 ratio of students to teachers. Lorraine interacts with teachers in both public and private schools and, as always, teachers compare notes.

How do the public schools stack up? The average public elementary school on the Monterey Peninsula in California, a relatively affluent community, has 28-30 students in a class. My granddaughter Abby attends a 6th grade of 34 students and 1 teacher. The teacher has no assistants and, alarmingly, hardly any enrichment classes where he or she can send the children – and get a break to recharge his or her batteries during the day. The average public school has a football program, *no* orchestra, *no* band, *no* choir, *occasionally* a drama department, *no* music classes for anyone, a school library with old books, classes in Spanish, and occasional AP enrichment classes, mostly in math. Because of those spectacular failures "No Child Left Behind" and "Race to the Top," teachers teach *to the test,* with no time for creativity or anything else. Because of budgetary constraints, our school district loses a couple of teachers each year – and not due to attrition or retirement.

Yet a recent Republican Congress came up with the idea of giving the parents of private school students *vouchers* or tax incentives so they could have a "choice" of whether they wanted to send their children to public or private school. Since the vast majority of children who attend private school go there because their parents can *afford* to place them there, guess who was meant to profit from this scatterbrained idea? This was simply a reverse Robin Hood ploy – take from the *poor* and give to the *rich*. And, of course, since the government would provide vouchers or tax incentives to help out the private schools, that would mean there was that much less money to spend on public schools.

How do we propose to compete in an ever more competitive world when this is the state of our public education and only the wealthy can afford private school? We'd *better* be able to compete, or the middle class will almost totally erode in a generation. And yet, day after day the few remaining newspapers (now that we have the internet), the conservative commentators and politicos, and the Tea Party advocates rail against raising taxes. Exactly how do we propose to save, let alone pay for, public education? By "teaching to the test?" By raising a generation of automatons who can calculate figures but who are soulless because they have never been exposed to fine art or great music? A generation who believes South America is a *country* in Brazil? A generation whose cultural exposure is sated by *America's Got Talent* or *American Idol*.

I could provide at least twenty more examples of how we attach negative labels to mask the cancer of doing *nothing* – and we Americans, like Pavlov's dog – become so attuned to the negative labels we hear each day, that our knee-jerk reaction is to reject the *meaning* of the idea simply because it *sounds* threatening. Our ship of state is becoming much like the *Titanic* – as the huge iceberg looms ever closer, the passengers are fighting over whether or not they should call that brown appetizer in the buffet line "Liver Pâté" or "Chopped liver."

20

PERPETUATING THE POLITICS OF FEAR

Negative campaigning is nothing new. Promising the electorate "something they can count on" is something that started before the ancient Egyptians built the pyramids. The rubric, "Promise them what you have to and pray their memories are short," has been fundamental to politics from time out of mind. "Give them bread and circuses," became entrenched in the political literature of the Roman Empire.

So what's so different about the present state of political affairs in 21st Century America? Simply this: We have unconsciously enshrined in our political consciousness the words attributed to Adolf Hitler (*Mein Kampf*, vol. I, ch. X) and allegedly adapted by his propaganda genius, Dr. Josef Goebbels: "*If you repeat a lie often enough, it becomes the truth. If you tell a lie big enough and keep repeating it, people will eventually come to believe it. If you repeat a lie long enough, it becomes truth.*"

Although he may have been one of the most evil geniuses that ever lived, there can be no question that Goebbels was indeed a genius when it came to propaganda. His program almost singlehandedly bound more than fifty million supposedly intelligent, highly cultured people to *Der Fuehrer* for twelve years. Among his more notable quotes:

♦ "We strive not for truth, but effect. The worst enemy of any propaganda is intellectualism. For the lie to be believable, it should be terrifying. A lie repeated thousands of times becomes a truth."

♦ "Success is the important thing. Propaganda is not a matter for average minds, but rather a matter for practitioners. It is not supposed to be lovely or theoretically correct. I do not care if I give wonderful, aesthetically elegant speeches, or speak so that women cry. The point of a political speech is to persuade people of what we think right. We do not want to be a movement of a few straw brains, but rather a movement that can conquer the broad masses. Propaganda should be popular, not intellectually pleasing. It is not the task of propaganda to discover intellectual truths."

- Speech by Joseph Goebbels on 9 January 1928 to an audience of party members at the *Hochschule für Politik*, a series of training talks for Nazi party members in Berlin.

♦ "One should not as a rule reveal one's secrets, since one does not know if and when one may need them again. The essential English leadership does not depend on intelligence. Rather, it depends on a remarkably stupid thick-headedness. The English follow the principle that when one lies, one should lie big, and stick to it. They keep up their lies, even at the risk of looking ridiculous."

- „*Aus Churchill's Lügenfabrik*" („Churchill's Lie Factory"), 12 January 1941, *Die Zeit ohne Beispiel* (Munich: Zentralverlag der NSDAP., 1941), pp. 364-369

* * *

9-1-1 was a truly tragic event. We watched with horrified eyes on CNN or one of the networks as that jet plane slammed into the World Trade Center. Thousands of people were killed. It was historically unique in that it was the first time the United States had been "invaded" by a "foreign force." (Never mind that it really *wasn't* the first time – the American Revolution was fought on our soil, the War of 1812 was fought on *our* seas, and the War Between the States (called the Civil War in most history books), pitted brother against brother within the borders of our country).

Yet 9-1-1 has taken on a "Remember the Alamo" (Does *anyone really* remember the Alamo today?) cadence which has propelled the politics of *fear* for the last decade. Every time someone raised the specter of the economy or universal healthcare or the deplorable state of civil rights during the period 2000-2008 (remember the so-called "Patriot Act?"), the Republicans trotted out the need for *Security* because we were sure as hell going to be "*invaded*" by foreigners – "ragheads" – if we didn't tow the party line. And they never let you forget 9-1-1! Never. The "reasoning" behind Trump's current xenophobia seems to be curiously similar to the Nazi propaganda of the 1930's: *Sometimes the security of the nation is more important than individual "civil rights"* (which is something preached by the Commie-dominated A.C.L.U., and you *know* those people go to court at the drop of a hat to protect the *whackos* who are lucky enough to live in the Land of the Free and the Home of the Brave). *And if you want proof that our security measures are succeeding, you have it right before your very eyes: we have not been invaded or attacked since we put these security measures in place!*

Well … yes … I suppose that's right. But does proof that it hasn't yet happened mean it never *will* happen? Has anyone stopped to consider, for example, that government inspectors, even under the most stringent George W. Bush days, inspected only *6%* of all shipments coming into the U.S. from abroad? It doesn't take a rocket scientist to figure out that *94 out of every 100* shipments did *not* get inspected at all?

Let's take our thinking one step further. Those responsible for the events of September 11, 2001 did not constitute a large, organized army backed by a numerically superior armed force. At the very most, there were a dozen or so active participants. Has the need for *security* that we boasted about during the Bush years stopped every illegal immigrant from pouring across our porous borders? I think not.

21

DRIVING THE TESLA OF POLITICS AND ECONOMICS

By the late 1950's, we had become used to big, snazzy-looking *American* behemoths – cars that were models of "planned obsolescence" that we traded in every two or three years, and which had exhausted their useful life by 100,000 miles at the most. Think the Cadillac Eldorado with its long-swept fins, the Buick, the Mercury Montclair, and the ads for Plymouth – "Suddenly it's 1960!" Oh, sure, there were some foreign cars that reached our shore – the Mercedes Benz, which was the ethereal dream – or the Jaguar, or the Rolls Royce. A lot of "hippie types" even bought a funny-looking little car originally designed under Hitler – the "People's Car" – the *Volkswagen*, which many called "the pregnant roller skate." There were small, cheap foreign cars that were of no better quality than what Americans were building back then: such "classics" as the Nash Metropolitan, the Renault Dauphine, the Opel Kadet, and the Fiat 850 sports car, but since they were "European" they had a certain panache.

In the 1960's Japan started exporting cars to the United States – specifically the Datsun (which became better known when it changed its marque to the company name, Nissan), the Toyota, the Honda, and the Mazda. Americans laughed derisively back then and referred to these small, economical upstart cars as "Rice burners – ha, ha, ha!" These were "different" cars indeed. For one thing, they got much higher than normal gas mileage. For another, they lasted much longer than American cars, were built to much higher quality standards, and were decidedly more dependable. *They didn't break down and you stopped at the gas pump much less frequently.*

General Motors and Chrysler laughed and laughed. By the mid-1990's, they didn't know what had hit them. The government had to bail out Chrysler and GM watched the steady erosion of its sales. Of the "big three" only Ford had the foresight to learn from the Germans and the Japanese. By the late 1990's, the American manufacturers were crying "Unfair!" If Americans continued buying these Japanese imports, Americans would lose their jobs.

In 2001 Toyota and Honda introduced the hybrid car to America. What?!?! How *dare* they? The American manufacturers derided the hybrids by saying, "It's not time to buy one of those newfangled cars. You'll see … they haven't gotten the bugs out yet. They're unsafe. They could catch on fire if they were hit from behind." Turns out, Toyota had been marketing its Prius and Honda had been selling its Insight in Japan since 1997. They'd had four years to work out the bugs.

It's now 2016. My wife and I own a 2005 Prius, our second, which generally gets between 42 and 46 miles per gallon and can keep up with anything on the road. Not a day of trouble and not a day of special maintenance requirements. The car now has over 155,000 miles on the odometer and runs as well as it did on the day we purchased it new.

And how did the American manufacturers deal with this new phenomenon? By introducing ever bigger, "safer," costlier, more muscular cars that used even more fuel than earlier American models. Think the *Hummer* as the penultimate example of overweening insanity and "keep ahead of the Joneses" mentality at a time when gasoline was going up to $4.00 a gallon in the United States – still less than *half* the price of gasoline in Europe. But that's OK – we were at war in Iraq and Afghanistan and we needed to look ever more *macho* by driving something that looked like it was designed to carry troops and got all of 10 miles per gallon.

Guess what eventually happened? For the past several years, the Toyota Prius has been the best-selling car in America, while the Hummer had all the staying power of the dinosaur. When GM couldn't unload that loser on some unsuspecting Chinese company, it simply phased it out. "Legacy" marques - Oldsmobile, Plymouth, Pontiac, and Mercury were killed off, and the Saturn died an unlamented death.

How does this translate into solving The Politics of Insanity? What does this discussion about cars have to do with re-creating America as a first world country again? Nothing. And everything.

At the time the Prius was designed and created, Japan was facing some very difficult economic problems. The flying-high Japanese economy of the 1980s had crashed and burned. Japan has very few natural resources. OPEC was forcing the price of oil up more and more each year. Japan imports 100% of its petroleum. But Japan – like Germany, India, and China – has one very specific natural resource that ensures its continuing vitality: the *human* resource of creativity and quality-orientation – *pride* in what their country manufactures.

In the early 1990's, the Japanese had not yet perfected the fuel cell car or the electric car. The Americans *could have* perfected such a vehicle, but the big three had long ago purchased all of the existing technology, *and then they had carefully put that technology in some back drawer, while announcing to the world that they were "working on" the new technology!* You see, it was simply much cheaper for the American companies to use the *existing* technology which had been around since the very early 1900's and simply adjust the *outside skin* of their "new" cars to popular tastes.

The Japanese manufacturers were not big enough or powerful enough to take on the Big Three at that time. All they had going for them was innovation and guts. So while the Japanese would have to work for a longer time to perfect their own home-grown fuel cell or electric car, they *could* produce a *combination car* – a *hybrid* car which would utilize a 4-cylinder, efficient gasoline engine *and* an electric motor, which, while not "the perfect answer" still allowed for a credible car which would get *three times the gas mileage of standard gasoline-powered cars.*

They took a chance – just like the early motorcars took a chance that the public would embrace the new technology and move away from the centuries-old horse and buggy. And look what happened!

Today, America has jumped back into the race for a viable *electric* car – but it is *not* a product brought to us by the "Big Three." As a matter of fact, there is no longer a "Big Three," since Chrysler has been owned by Italy's Fiat for the past few years and before that it was owned by Germany's Daimler Benz. South African-born Elon Musk, today the 68th wealthiest man in the United States, took a mammoth risk by conceiving and marketing the *Tesla*, an all-electric car that can travel a distance of more than 200 miles without a recharge (compare that to the 40-mile-range Chevy *Volt* or the 100-mile range (maybe) Nissan Leaf; *and* he has established a network of electric charging stations throughout the United States.

So it is with politics. Maybe we are not yet ready to wholeheartedly embrace 100% of what the "liberals" want or 100% of what the "conservatives" want, but instead of trying to kill off *every part* of new ideas, wouldn't it be much more constructive – and wouldn't it solve many more problems? – if we constructed a "hybrid" system like the Prius, that would allow Americans the greatest flexibility and freedom *while we were busy designing the Tesla of a more perfect society?*

That's the *real* way to make Donald Trump's campaign slogan of "Make America Great Again" true. Can the answer to that question really be in doubt? Particularly when we realize that the world's natural resources – whether they are Republican, Democratic, Libertarian, Tea Party, or Green Party – are being depleted at a faster rate than ever and that, whether the Tea Party denies it or not, *Global warming is very real and we cannot simply put a band aid on this cancer?*

Case in point: I have been writing books for over twenty-five years. Until 2012, those books all used paper – lots of paper – whether they were hard cover or soft cover books. I have been practicing law for over 50 years. I can think of no industry that has used more paper on a regular basis than law except, perhaps, the publishing industry. Have you ever looked through a stack of medical records? How many trees were regularly consumed by a hospital's daily output of paper records? By the mid-1990's, the price of paper was skyrocketing just as the supply of trees was rapidly dwindling. What has happened in the last twenty years? Without politicizing what happened, and without giving credit (or blame) to Republicans or Democrats, there has been a profound revolution.

Today, more than 90% of the paper which had been used in the law industry, the publishing industry, or the health care industry is no longer even relevant. The federal government (with the exception of the United States Supreme Court) uses mandatory electronic filing in every United States Court. Using heavy, beautiful books to perform legal research is passé. With the coming of legal research tools such as Westlaw and Lexis, books are best used as doorstops. Of course, this has the concomitant advantage that the excess room we needed for large law offices to house hundreds of volumes of law books is no longer necessary.

Mailing voluminous legal documents? E-mail does it better, cheaper, and faster. I recently had a case in Federal Court where there were nearly 10,000 pages of documents. The particular district where the case was filed required *either forty* copies of those documents *or* the documents could be copied into pdf format and filed electronically. Try a very simple calculation: multiply 10,000 sheets of paper by 40 at a cost of 10 cents per copied sheet, plus mail. Don't even count the number of trees felled to make these copies. Just consider the cost savings by electronically copying and filing.

During the past few years, I have been plagued with the illnesses attendant on growing older (no one ever said growing old was easy) – from cancer to high blood pressure to high cholesterol to ... you name it. At least 95% of the doctors and hospitals I have gone to are now "paperless." A friend of mine, an outstanding orthopedic surgeon, loves to golf and regularly goes to Hawaii or Ireland or Scotland to do so. He takes his entire office with him – it will fit on a "Smart Phone" in a small corner of his carry-on suitcase.

Previously, more paper had been used in the book industry than in any other enterprise on earth. Earlier this year, Amazon reported that for every 100 paper books sold, that company sold *153* electronic books on its Kindle apparatus. They could – and did – sell those books at less than half the price of conventional books, and, shock of shocks, the Kindle actually had the heft and *feel* of a "real" book. What's more, you could get *hundreds* – perhaps even *thousands* – of "books" on a single Kindle E-book reader. Amazon is certainly not the only entrepreneur to embrace the new technology. Barnes & Noble has the Nook; Sony has its own reading device; and the I-Pad proclaims its "reader" is the easiest of all to use. It certainly won't be long before we have the Wal-Martization of the reading devices. After all, when the first hand-held electronic calculator came out, it retailed for over $300. Today you can get a faster, more powerful, smaller, lighter unit that does much, much more for anywhere from $3 to $12 a unit.

I propose a novel, previously untried solution in the political arena: *Let's stop wasting time, energy, emotions, and money fighting and arguing about non-issues. Rather, let us work together and come up with acceptable "hybrid" solutions which will work best for the greatest number of people, regardless of their political, religious, or other persuasions, so we can best mover our society forward.*

Think it can't be successfully done?

On October 12, 2010, 33 miners, who had been trapped in a mine in Chile for 69 days (!) were rescued – *every one of them alive.* The world cheered and cried happy tears. For more than a day, the terrors of a useless war in Afghanistan, the acrimony of the political season in America, and the spewing of hatred was simply wiped off the front pages as a truly *meaningful, miraculous* event – with a large number of very *human heroes* – emerged to take the spotlight.

Why not spend time going through the suggestions I have made? *Challenge them – that's what freedom of expression is all about. Better them!* I certainly don't possess a monopoly on brain cells or good ideas. Then, when you have done all the thinking and discussing and brainstorming you want to do – write, phone, e-mail, and *communicate* with your elected representatives. *Let them know that you want them to use their brains and their good common sense to come up with* solutions *rather than simply doing more of the same fighting and going nowhere. .*

And in this way, we – all of us – will take back the America we've known – the America whose best days are ahead of us!

On January 20, 1993, in his inaugural address, Bill Clinton said it all:

"Today, a generation raised in the shadows of the cold war assumes new responsibilities in a world warmed by the sunshine of freedom but threatened still by ancient hatreds and new plagues. Raised in unrivaled prosperity, we inherit an economy that is still the world's strongest but is weakened by business failures, stagnant wages, increasing inequality, and deep divisions among our own people. … **There is nothing *wrong* with America that cannot be cured by what is *right* with America.**"

And so it will be, despite 2016's "bump in the road" which I call *The Politics of Insanity.*

THE END